The Top 10 Greatest Generals: Alexander the Great, Hannibal, Julius Caesar, Attila the Hun, William the Conqueror, Saladin, Genghis Khan, Napoleon Bonaparte, Robert E. Lee, and George Patton

By Charles River Editors

About Charles River Editors

Charles River Editors was founded by Harvard and MIT alumni to provide superior editing and original writing services, with the expertise to create digital content for publishers across a vast range of subject matter. In addition to providing original digital content for third party publishers, Charles River Editors republishes civilization's greatest literary works, bringing them to a new generation via ebooks.

Visit charlesrivereditors.com for more information.

Introduction

A bust of Alexander, at the Louvre

Alexander the Great (356-323 B.C.)

"There is nothing impossible to him that will but try" – Alexander

Over the last 2,000 years, ambitious men have dreamed of forging vast empires and attaining eternal glory in battle, but of all the conquerors who took steps toward such dreams, none were ever as successful as antiquity's first great conqueror. Leaders of the 20ᵗʰ century hoped to rival Napoleon's accomplishments, while Napoleon aimed to emulate the accomplishments of Julius Caesar. But Caesar himself found inspiration in Alexander the Great (356-323 B.C.), the Macedonian King who managed to stretch an empire from Greece to the Himalayas in Asia at just 30 years old. It took less than 15 years for Alexander to conquer much of the known world.

As fate would have it, Alexander died of still unknown causes at the height of his conquests, when he was still in his early 30s. Although his empire was quickly divided, his legacy only grew, and Alexander became the stuff of legends even in his own time. Alexander was responsible for establishing 20 cities in his name across the world, most notably Alexandria in Egypt, and he was directly responsible for spreading Ancient Greek culture as far east as modern day India and other parts of Asia. For the ancient world, Alexander became the emblem of military greatness and accomplishment; it was reported that many of Rome's greatest leaders, including Pompey the Great, Augustus, and Caesar himself all visited Alexander's tomb in Alexandria, a mecca of sorts for antiquity's other leaders.

The Top 10 Greatest Generals provides an entertaining look at the facts, myths, and legends of one of history's most famous men and conquerors, while exploring the lasting legacy he left on the ancient world and today's world. Along with pictures of important people, places, and events, you will learn about Alexander the Great like you never have before, in no time at all.

Depiction of Hannibal

Hannibal (247-182 B.C.)

"God has given to man no sharper spur to victory than contempt of death." – Hannibal

A lot of ink has been spilled covering the lives of history's most influential figures, but how much of the forest is lost for the trees? In Charles River Editors' Legends of the Ancient World series, readers can get caught up to speed on the lives of antiquity's most important men and women in the time it takes to finish a commute, while learning interesting facts long forgotten or never known.

In the history of war, only a select few men always make the list of greatest generals. Napoleon. Caesar. Alexander. They are always joined by Hannibal, who has the distinction of being the only man who nearly brought Rome to its knees before its decline almost 700 years later. Rome never suffered a more horrifying defeat in its history than at Cannae, and indeed, Hannibal nearly rewrote the course of Western history during the Second Punic War. Even today there remains great debate on just how he accomplished his masterful invasion of Italy across the Alps. Since his army included war elephants, historians still argue over exactly where and how he crossed over 2,000 years after he managed that incredible feat.

Hannibal will always be listed among history's greatest generals, and his military campaign in Italy during the Second Punic War will always be studied, but part of the aura and mystique surrounding the Carthaginian legend is that there is still a lot of mystery. Since Carthage was destroyed by Rome a generation after Hannibal, most of what is known about Hannibal came from the very people he tormented in the late 2nd century B.C., and thus much of his background and life story is unknown. Moreover, while military historians are still amazed that he was able to maintain his army in Italy near Rome for nearly 15 years, scholars are still puzzled over some of his decisions, including why he never attempted to march on Rome in the first place.

The Top 10 Greatest Generals looks at the life of the Carthaginian hero, explores some of the mysteries and myths surrounding his life and campaigns, and analyzes his legacy, which has remained strong over 2,000 years after his death and promises to last many more. Along with pictures of important people, places, and events, you will learn about Hannibal like you never have before, in no time at all.

Julius Caesar (100-44 B.C.)

"I would rather be the first man in a humble village, than the second man in Rome" – Caesar

Possibly the most important man of antiquity, and even all of history, was Julius Caesar. Alexander Hamilton, the famous American patriot, once remarked that "the greatest man who ever lived was Julius Caesar". Such a tribute, coming from one of the Founding Fathers of the quintessential modern democracy in reference to a man who destroyed the Roman Republic, is testament to the enduring mark that Caesar left upon the world. The ultimate conqueror, statesman, dictator, visionary, and opportunist, during his time in power Caesar expanded the borders of Rome to almost twice their previous size, revolutionized the infrastructure of the Roman state, and destroyed the Roman Republic for good, leaving a line of emperors in its place. His legacy is so strong that his name has become, in many languages, synonymous with power: the Emperors of Austria and Germany bore the title *Kaiser*, and the *Czars* of Russia also owe the etymology of their title to Caesar. His name also crept further eastward out of Europe, even cropping up in Hindi and Urdu, where the term for "Emperor" is *Kaisar.*

Even in his time, Caesar was in many ways larger than life, and because of his legacy as virtual founder of the Roman Empire, much of what was written about – and by – him during his life and immediately after his assassination was politically motivated. His successor, Octavian

Augustus, had a strong interest in ensuring that Caesar's life be painted in a favorable light, while Caesar's political enemies attempted to paint him as a corrupt, undemocratic dictator who was destroying the old order of the Republic. This makes it exceedingly difficult to separate historical fact from apocryphal interjection, as the writings of Cicero (a rival of Caesar's) and the later biographies of Suetonius and Plutarch can be misleading. Nonetheless, along with Caesar's *De Bello Gallico*, his famous notes on his campaign against the Gauls, they remain our chief sources for Caesar's life – a life everyone agreed was nothing short of remarkable and changed the course of history forever.

The Top 10 Greatest Generals details the life of Rome's most famous leader and explains his legacy, which has only grown larger over 2,000 years and promises to last many more. Along with pictures of important people, places, and events, you will learn about Caesar like you never have before, in no time at all.

Mór Than's painting The Feast of Attila,

Attila the Hun (??-453 A.D.)

"A luxurious meal, served on silver plate, had been made ready for us and the barbarian guests, but Attila ate nothing but meat on a wooden trencher. In everything else, too, he showed himself temperate; his cup was of wood, while to the guests were given goblets of gold and silver. His dress, too, was quite simple, affecting only to be clean. The sword he carried at his side, the latchets of his Scythian shoes, the bridle of his horse were not adorned, like those of the other Scythians, with gold or gems or anything costly." – Priscus, *History of Bizantium*

A lot of ink has been spilled covering the lives of history's most influential figures, but how much of the forest is lost for the trees? In Charles River Editors' Legends of the Ancient World series, readers can get caught up to speed on the lives of antiquity's most important men and women in the time it takes to finish a commute, while learning interesting facts long forgotten or never known.

Attila, Emperor of the Hunnic Empire and thus most commonly known as Attila the Hun, is an idiosyncratic figure who has become more myth than man, not least because much of his life is shrouded in mystery. Perhaps the most famous "barbarian" in history, Attila was the lord of a vast empire spanning two continents, but he is best remembered for what he did not conquer. Though he seemingly had Rome at his mercy in 452, he ultimately decided not to sack the Eternal City, and a year later he had suffered a mysterious death.

What is known about Attila came mostly from Priscus, a guest of his court who wrote several books about Attila's life in Greek. Unfortunately, much of that work was lost to history, but not before the ancient writer Jordanes relied on it to write his own overexaggerated account of Attila's life. And like their leader, the Huns themselves are an instantly recognizable name with mysterious origins; most of what is known about the Huns came from Chinese sources thousands of miles and an entire continent away from Italy.

Naturally, the dearth of information and the passage of time have allowed myths and legends to fill in the most important details of Attila's life. Why did a man at war with the Roman Empire for so long decide not to sack Rome in 452? Did a meeting with Pope Leo the Great convince him to spare the capital of the Western half of the empire? Did a vision from St. Peter induce Attila to convert to Christianity? Was Attila murdered by his new bride? Many authors and chroniclers have provided many answers to the many questions, but the lack of answers has allowed Atilla to become the face of ancient barbarity and the embodiment of the furious nomadic conqueror.

The Top 10 Greatest Generals discusses the facts, myths, and legends surrounding the life of Attila, examining the historical record and the way in which his legacy has been shaped, all in an attempt to separate fact from fiction. Along with pictures and a bibliography, you will learn about Attila the Hun like you never have before.

English coin depicting William the Conqueror

William the Conqueror (circa 1028-1087)

"Stranger and conqueror, his deeds won him a right to a place on the roll of English statesmen, and no man that came after him has won a right to a higher place." – E.A. Freeman

A lot of ink has been spilled covering the lives of history's most influential figures, but how much of the forest is lost for the trees? In Charles River Editors' Legends of the Middle Ages series, readers can get caught up to speed on the lives of the most important medieval men and women in the time it takes to finish a commute, while learning interesting facts long forgotten or never known.

"We, conquered by William, have liberated the Conqueror's land". So reads the memorial to the British war dead at Bayeaux, Normandy. Commemorating those who gave their lives to free France in 1944, it also serves to remind us of an earlier conflict. For the English, the Norman conquest remains deeply embedded in the national psyche. As the last contested military invasion to have succeeded in conquering this proud island nation, the date of 1066 is the one every citizen can remember. For them, William will forever be the "Conqueror", the last invader to beat them in an open fight. For others, notably the French, he is the "Bastard", a reference not only to his lineage.

William's conquest of the island arguably made him the most important figure in shaping the course of English history, but modern caricatures of this vitally important medieval figure are largely based on ignorance. William is a fascinating and complex figure, in many ways the quintessential warrior king of this period. Inheriting the Duchy of Normandy while still an infant and forced to fight for his domain almost ceaselessly during his early years, William went on to conquer and rule England, five times larger and three times wealthier. In doing so, he demonstrated sophisticated political and diplomatic skill, military prowess and administrative acumen. Although he lived by the sword, he was a devout man who had only one wife, to whom he remained faithful.

However, peering back nearly 1,000 years to understand William does not just require a suspension of 21st century values and prejudices, because the evidence itself is far from complete. The historical record includes chronicles and documents, most notably the Anglo-Saxon Chronicle, the famous Domesday Book and the Bayeux tapestry, leaving scholars to attempt the meticulous and painstaking process of piecing together the narrative of his life and determining what William and the Normans might actually have been like. At the same time, those scholars are the first to admit the limitations of these abilities, since the few people who could write in medieval England and Normandy often had important agendas and prejudices of their own, or they were recording events decades after they occurred.

The Top 10 Greatest Generals chronicles the historic life and conquests of the medieval king and analyzes his monumental legacy. Along with pictures of important people, places, and events, you will learn about William the Conqueror like you never have before.

Sculpture of Saladin in Cairo, Egypt

Saladin (1137/8-1193)

"It is equally true that his generosity, his piety, devoid of fanaticism, that flower of liberality and courtesy which had been the model of our old chroniclers, won him no less popularity in Frankish Syria than in the lands of Islam." - René Grousset

A lot of ink has been spilled covering the lives of history's most influential figures, but how much of the forest is lost for the trees? In Charles River Editors' Legends of the Middle Ages series, readers can get caught up to speed on the lives of important medieval men and women in the time it takes to finish a commute, while learning interesting facts long forgotten or never known.

During a trip to Damascus, Syria in 1958, Egyptian President Gamal Abdel Nasser visited the tomb of Saladin. It was a symbolic visit for the pan-Arab leader, who sought to unite the Arab world and restore it to its past glory. For nationalists like Nasser and devout Muslims across the Middle East, Saladin's life and reign represent the pinnacle of that glory, more than 8 centuries after his death.

Saladin is widely considered one of the greatest generals in history and one of the most famous leaders of the Middle Ages, but he remains a paradox, both in personal and in historical terms. A military genius, he first served other generals and was overshadowed, late in life, by his greatest rival, Richard I of England. He was far more admired by his Christian enemies, who extolled his chivalry, than some of his Muslim rivals, who fought him for control of Egypt and Syria in the 12th century. His Christian enemies continued his name long after it was forgotten in the Middle East, only to spark a revival of his reputation in Arab culture in the 20th century.

Revered as the flower of Arab culture, he was really a Kurd who nearly destroyed it. Taught to Egyptian children as a native born Egyptian hero, he was, in fact, Egypt's conqueror, the man who destroyed its native dynasty and suppressed the local Shi'ite sect. Praised for his mild temper and mercy, he made it his mission in the last decade of his life to destroy the Frankish states created by the First Crusade in 1099. The most powerful man in the Levant for the last ten years of his life, he died a virtual pauper after giving away his personal fortune to the poor. Having united almost all of the Levant under one rule, he left it as divided as before. He founded a dynasty that was eventually destroyed by slaves.

Nevertheless, Saladin remains both a poignant and important symbol in the Middle East over 800 years after his death, making him as relevant as ever today. *The Top 10 Greatest Generals* chronicles the historic life and reign of the famous leader, and it analyzes his influential and enduring legacy. Along with pictures of important people, places, and events, you will learn about Saladin like you never have before.

Genghis Khan portrayed in a 14th century Yuan era album.

Genghis Khan (circa 1162-1227)

"Conquering the world from horseback is easy. It is dismounting and governing that is hard." – Genghis Khan

A lot of ink has been spilled covering the lives of history's most influential figures, but how much of the forest is lost for the trees? In Charles River Editors' Legends of the Middle Ages series, readers can get caught up to speed on the lives of the most important medieval men and women in the time it takes to finish a commute, while learning interesting facts long forgotten or never known.

In a world fascinated by men like Alexander the Great and Julius Caesar, Genghis Khan is one of history's greatest and most famous conquerors. No man, before or since, has ever started with so little and gone on to achieve so much. From a noble family but raised in poverty that drove him to the brink of starvation, Genghis Khan rose to control the second-largest empire the world has ever known (the largest being, arguably, the British Empire of the 18th and 19th centuries), and easily the largest empire conquered by a single man. And while many empires disintegrate upon the death of an emperor, like Alexander the Great's, Genghis Khan's empire endured and was actually enlarged by his successors, who went on to establish dynasties that in some cases lasted for centuries.

Though history is usually written by the victors, the lack of a particularly strong writing tradition from the Mongols ensured that history was largely written by those who Genghis Khan vanquished. Because of this, Genghis Khan's portrayal in the West and the Middle East has been extraordinarily (and in many ways unfairly) negative for centuries, at least until recent revisions to the historical record. Certainly Genghis Khan was not a peaceful man, or a particularly merciful one, and he famously boasted to the Khwaremzids that he was "the flail of God, come to punish you for your sins". However, the image of him as a bloodthirsty barbarian is largely the result of hostile propaganda. He was far more complex than the mere brute that his negative portrayals indicate, and though there is a slew of graves and depopulated regions to testify to the fact that he was not a gentle man, it would be simplistic and wrong to describe him merely as a madman bent on destruction for destruction's sake. In truth he was an extremely intelligent and extraordinarily ambitious man with a gift for warfare, empire-building and administration, and he was a political visionary who dreamed of a united Asia under Mongol control. He was neither the vile mass-murderer he is seen as in much of the Middle East, nor the shining, flawless hero he is often remembered as in Mongolia and western China.

Nor should this fractured tribal background confirm one of the longest-lasting impressions that people have held about Genghis Khan and his Mongols, that of wild horse-archers galloping out of the dawn to rape, pillage, murder and enslave. The Mongol army was a highly sophisticated, minutely organized and incredibly adaptive and innovative institution, as witnessed by the fact that it was successful in conquering enemies who employed completely different weaponry and different styles of fighting, from Chinese armored infantry to Middle-Eastern camel cavalry all the way to Western medieval knights and men-at-arms. Likewise, the infrastructure and administrative corps which governed Genghis Khan's empire, though largely borrowed from the Chinese, was inventive, practical, and extraordinarily modern and efficient. This was no fly-by-night enterprise but a sophisticated, complex and extremely well-oiled machine.

One thing all can agree on is that Genghis Khan's story is a fascinating tale of glory, strife, backstabbing, and, above all, ruthless willpower. *The Top 10 Greatest Generals* chronicles the amazing life of the conqueror, examines his accomplishments, and analyzes his legacy. Along with pictures of important people, places, and events, you will learn about Genghis Khan like you never have before, in no time at all.

Napoleon as King of Italy, by Andrea Appiani (1805)

Napoleon Bonaparte (1769–1821)

"Courage cannot be counterfeited. It is the one virtue that escapes hypocrisy." – Napoleon

When historians are asked to list the most influential people of the last 200 years, a handful of names might vary, but there is no question that the list will include Napoleon Bonaparte (1769-1821), the most successful French leader since Charlemagne and widely acknowledged as one of the greatest generals ever. Indeed, Napoleon was likely the most influential man of the 19th century, leaving an indelible mark on everything from the strategy and tactics of warfare to the Napoleonic Code that drafted laws across the continent. To defeat Napoleon, the Europeans had to form large coalitions multiple times, which helped bring about the entangling alliances that sparked World War I after Europe was rebuilt following Waterloo and the Congress of Vienna. Napoleon's influence on the United States was also palpable. To finance his endeavors, he struck a deal with President Thomas Jefferson that became the Louisiana Purchase, and it was Napoleonic warfare that was used throughout the Civil War, leading to massive casualties because the weaponry of the 1860s was now more advanced than the tactics of 1815.

When Napoleon died at St. Helena, he still engendered fear and distaste among the Europeans, but the man and his legacy continued to be held in awe across the world. In Napoleon's time, emperors and leaders still hoped to become the next Julius Caesar. After the Napoleonic Era, emperors and generals hoped to become the next Napoleon. For the next century, military leaders and even civilians struck Napoleonic poses when having their pictures taken, and phrases like "Napoleonic complex" and "meeting one's Waterloo" are now common phrases in the English lexicon. It would be truly impossible to envision or understand geopolitics in the West over the last two centuries without Napoleon.

With the passage of time, Napoleon's legacy has had time to crystallize, but the legends, myths, and controversies about the man and his empire continue to swirl. Was he really short? Did his men shoot the nose off the Sphinx? Was he a good chess player? Was he poisoned by the British? In the rush to analyze his stunningly successful military record or question whether he was very short or a great chess player, people often overlook his political reign and personality. This title addresses the controversies, myths, legends and battles, but it also humanizes a man who famously dominated most of the European continent while loving an indomitable woman whose political calculations matched if not surpassed his. Along with pictures of Napoleon and other important people, places and events in his life, you will learn about the French emperor like you never have before, in no time at all.

Robert E. Lee (1807-1870)

"It is well that war is so terrible, otherwise we should grow too fond of it." –Robert E. Lee

With the exception of George Washington, perhaps the most famous general in American history is **Robert E. Lee** (January 19, 1807 – October 12, 1870), despite the fact he led the Confederate Army of Northern Virginia against the Union in the Civil War. As the son of U.S. Revolutionary War hero Henry "Light Horse Harry" Lee III, and a relative of Martha Custis Washington, Lee was imbued with a strong sense of honor and duty from the beginning. And as a top graduate of West Point, Lee had distinguished himself so well before the Civil War that President Lincoln asked him to command the entire Union Army. Lee famously declined, serving his home state of Virginia instead after it seceded.

Lee is remembered today for constantly defeating the Union's Army of the Potomac in the Eastern theater from 1862-1865, considerably frustrating Lincoln and his generals. His leadership of his army led to him being deified after the war by some of his former subordinates, especially Virginians, and he came to personify the Lost Cause's ideal Southern soldier. His reputation was secured in the decades after the war as a general who brilliantly led his men to amazing victories against all odds.

Despite his successes and his legacy, Lee wasn't perfect. And of all the battles Lee fought in, he was most criticized for Gettysburg, particularly his order of Pickett's Charge on the third and final day of the war. Despite the fact his principle subordinate and corps leader, General James Longstreet, advised against the charge, Lee went ahead with it, ending the army's defeat at Gettysburg with a violent climax that left half of the men who charged killed or wounded.

Although the Civil War came to define Lee's legacy, he was involved in some of American history's other turning points, including the Mexican-American War and the capture of John Brown. *The Top 10 Greatest Generals* closely examines Lee's war records, but it also humanizes the cheerful husband who was raised and strove to be dignified and dutiful. Along with pictures of Lee and other important people and events in his life, you will learn about the great general like you never have before.

George Patton (1885-1945)

"Americans love to fight, traditionally. All real Americans love the sting and clash of battle. You are here today for three reasons. First, because you are here to defend your homes and your loved ones. Second, you are here for your own self respect, because you would not want to be

anywhere else. Third, you are here because you are real men and all real men like to fight." –
George Patton, Speech to the Third Army

A lot of ink has been spilled covering the lives of history's most influential figures, but how much of the forest is lost for the trees? In Charles River Editors' American Legends series, readers can get caught up to speed on the lives of America's most important men and women in the time it takes to finish a commute, while learning interesting facts long forgotten or never known.

Rommel, Guderian, Liddell-Hart and JFC Fuller: early exponents and practitioners of armored warfare. These tactics were to break the stalemate that had characterized World War I. Advocates of the tank and above all speed, it was their ideas which decimated Saddam Hussein's forces in the 1990 Gulf War. But among the proponents and practitioners of armored warfare, the brash, bold, arrogant and eccentric George S. Patton remains the world's greatest armored commander by the one yardstick that really counts: the battlefield. In 1944-45, Patton's Third Army raced across northern Europe, covering more ground and destroying more enemy resources than any other equivalent force in history.

Patton is one of America's most celebrated generals and one of the most famous generals of the 20th century, but his story has its origins in the form of a shy, dyslexic boy who could cry uncontrollably and who viewed his own emotional intelligence as unmanly. Patton was a fascinating, complicated and controversial man whose life story ranges between genius, folly and tragedy, with absolute determination the one constant theme.

He was also a man constantly on the move, whether it was as an Olympic athlete or as one of the first American soldiers to work with tanks in World War I, but his life's work truly went toward revolutionizing warfare on and off the battlefield. Between the two World Wars, he wrote at length about mechanized warfare and tactics, and during the Second World War he worked his way up colorfully, controversially, and capably, all of which made him more conspicuous during the war. Patton's shocking death just a few months after the war ended ensured that the general died at the height of his fame and would always be remembered for his legendary attitude and exploits.

The Top 10 Greatest Generals profiles the amazing life and career of the American war hero, while also examining his personality and analyzing his lasting legacy. Along with pictures of important people, places, and events, you will learn about Patton like you never have before.

Alexander the Great

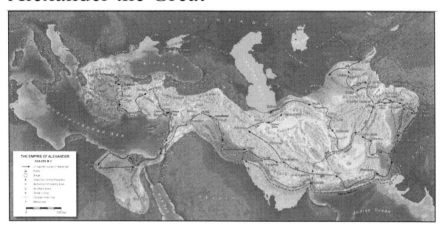

Alexander's empire at the time of his death in 323 BC.

Chapter 1: The Brightest Flame, 356-336 B.C.

Of the handful of rulers who, by right of conquest, have gone down in the annals of history as being worthy of the epithet "the Great", Alexander III of Macedonia is, perhaps, the greatest. In just over two decades he succeeded in creating the third largest Empire in recorded history (the second largest, if we consider only empires created by a single ruler) and established a legacy as a strategist, conqueror, and warrior philosopher that endures to this day. From his ascent to the throne of Macedon onwards he always appeared larger than life, endowed with superhuman abilities, a fact that Alexander himself took care to encourage, fomenting rumours of his divine parentage. As a result, he was a legendary figure in his own time, and he continues to be mentioned routinely in contemporary literature, music and film.

As a cautionary tale of the evils that *hubris* can bring about or as an example to look back upon – his attempts to pacify the unruly province of Bactria (modern Afghanistan) being especially relevant – Alexander remains a major source of inspiration for many contemporary politicians and thinkers. In a classic example of the light that is twice as bright burning only half as long, Alexander died under mysterious circumstances at the age of 32. Just what he could have achieved had he not died will never be known, but what is known is that Alexander was not even close to being finished when he died. It is believed he planned to invade the Arabian Peninsula, and he often talked of an invasion of Europe, a monumental task which, had he actually lived to carry it out, would have had unfathomable consequences for the entire course of Western history.

Alexander was born on 6 Hekatombeion (July) of 356 BC, in Pella, Macedonia. Pella was the ancient royal capital of the kingdom of Macedonia, a hardscrabble warrior state that had always existed, perched on the border between the Greek city states and the Balkans, on the brink between "civilised" Greek living and barbarianism. Alexander's mother was Olympias, a strong-willed and manipulative daughter of the King of Epirus, another Balkan state, and Philip II of Macedon, king of Macedonia.

That Alexander was even born is an amazing story in its own right, beginning with Philip II's incredibly unlikely rise to power. Though he was the son of a Macedonian King, Philip spent some of his early years in captivity, held prisoner in Thebes. Philip was something of a military genius in his own right, and after being freed from captivity, he succeeded in conquering much of northern Greece and repelling several enemy pretenders. His military victories were largely achieved as a result of his revolutionary Macedonian Phalanx, a tool which Alexander himself would later use to great effect. At the time, the chief strength of the Greek armies was their hoplite heavy infantry, strictly drilled soldiers who wore heavy bronze armour and fought with large round wood-and-bronze shields that covered over half their bodies. Hoplites traditionally fought with 9-foot spears, but Philip armed his own phalanx with 18-foot pikes, significantly outreaching the hoplites or, indeed, any other heavy infantry in the world at the time. Philip also developed another instrument of warfare that Alexander would later perfect, the Companion Cavalry, an elite mounted unit which would attack enemies on the flanks while the infantry pinned them in place.

Bust of Philip II of Macedon

Alexander came into the world dogged by rumor. According to popular belief, he was not the son of Philip, but of Zeus himself (a notion which mother Olympias doubtless encouraged). According to the chief sources for his life, the historians Plutarch, Arrian and Quintus Curtius Rufus, his birth was accompanied by great portents, but little is known of the earliest decade of his life – most likely because there is not much to tell. His father Philip was occupied expanding the kingdom of Macedon south and east, and Alexander was raised by a string of tutors. Because the Macedonian aristocracy, despite being looked down upon as boors by the more sophisticated Greeks, had pretensions of gentility, Alexander was tutored extensively in philosophy, oratory, history, music, riding, athletics and wrestling, as any young Greek nobleman would have been.

At the age of 10, Alexander started people talking for the first time since his birth when he accompanied his father to a horse fair. There, Philip was presented with a great Thessalian charger, but the horse was so aggressive it refused to be mounted, much to Philip's disgust. Alexander, however, realised that the horse was literally starting at shadows – chiefly its own. He quieted the horse and succeeded in mounting it, at which Philip is said to have told him, "find yourself a bigger kingdom than Macedonia, my son, for it is too small for your ambition". Obviously pleased with his son's impressive performance, Philip consented to buy the horse for Alexander, who named the beast Bucephalus, or "hard-head". Bucephalus was to be one of Alexander's most faithful companions, accompanying him on his conquest all the way to India.

19th century depiction of Alexander taming the wild horse.

Some years later, when Alexander was in his 13th year of age, Philip, still wishing to "Hellenise" (turn Greek) his son as much as possible, decided he needed a tutor. To coach the young Alexander he hired none other than the renowned philosopher Aristotle, a legend among Greek thinkers whose services he only managed to obtain after he promised to rebuild Aristotle's hometown of Stageira, repopulating it with freed slaves and pardoned exiles. Aristotle tutored Alexander in an academy, alongside his boyhood friends Ptolemy, Haephaestion and Kassander, who would later be his generals and play crucial roles in his conquests. It was during Aristotle's tutelage that Alexander became familiar with the Iliad, identifying himself especially with the mythical figure of Achilles, the mightiest of the Greek warriors, who was once offered a famous choice: long life and obscurity, or a premature death and fame that would last to the ends of history.

Ancient Bust of Aristotle

Portrait depicting Aristotle tutoring Alexander

After three years under the auspices of Aristotle, Alexander received his first chance to forge his own undying legacy when his father left Macedonia to wage war on Byzantion, leaving Alexander – aged 16 – as regent of Macedon. Philip's absence, and the presence of an untested ruler on the Macedonian throne, inspired several of Philip's subject and satellite states to revolt: the Thracians rose up in arms, but Alexander proved up to the task and crushed their forces, erecting the first of many "Alexandrias", the city of Alexandropolis in Thrace. Philip was extremely pleased with his son's performance and, in order to test his mettle further, when he returned from his campaign he dispatched Alexander, at the head of a small army, to pacify the remainder of Thrace. During this time, in 338 BC, Alexander also defeated a force sent from Illyria to attack Macedonia, as well as succeeding in his task of quelling the revolt in Thrace. He was summoned from the field with his army by Philip, who had used a flimsy pretext to involve himself in the affairs of the Greek city-states and was marching southwards at the head of the Macedonian army. Together, they marched through the pass at Thermopylae (where, years before, a Spartan army under King Leonidas and their Thespian allies had fought one of history's most famous and legendary battles against the Persian Empire, Greece's historic enemy), defeating the Theban garrison dispatched to stop them, and advanced into Greece proper.

Once in Greece, Philip and Alexander's main concerns were the powerful cities of Thebes and Athens, which had united their armies and resources against them. They marched on the city of Amphissa, whose citizens had begun tilling fields sacred to the oracle at Delphi, prompting Philip's invasion on the pretext he had been invited by concerned followers of the oracle. After forcing Amphissa to surrender, Philip sent Thebes and Athens a last offer of peace, but upon having it rejected, marched southwards. The Macedonian army marched quickly, but it found its path blocked by the Thebans and Athenians near Chaeronea. The Thebans were confident, having recently developed an outstanding martial tradition which had led to their vanquishing none other than the renowned Spartans, and battle was rapidly joined. Philip took command of the right wing of his army and gave the left to Alexander – cannily ensuring that his most seasoned generals were there to make sure the young boy did not blunder – and Alexander did not disappoint his father's trust. As Philip lured the enemy with a false retreat, Alexander personally led a cavalry charge that smashed through the Theban forces, instigating a general rout among the Athenian troops and forcing the Thebans, alone and surrounded, to surrender. The victorious Macedonians marched southwards, where they met no further resistance and were greeted with offers of alliance by all the major cities (save Sparta, which traditionally stood aloof from such matters). Philip united these cities in what became known as the League of Corinth, an all-Greek coalition formed with the express purpose of waging war on Persia, with Philip himself as *Hegemon*, or supreme commander.

It should have been Alexander's finest hour: he had proven himself in the field, he was the hero of Chaeronea, and he enjoyed the esteem of both his father and many of the leading Macedonian nobles. However, his triumph quickly turned sour. Shortly after returning to Pella, Philip set his wife Olympias aside in favour of the young Cleopatra, the niece of one of his generals. Alexander was furious at this, particularly as it jeopardised his position as Philip's heir, and he had a violent falling-out with his father during the wedding celebrations, to the point that the ever-volatile Philip actually drew his sword on his son. Philip was well and truly drunk by then, and succeeded only in sprawling on the floor, prompting Alexander to remark: "here is the man who you would have lead you against the Persians; he stumbles jumping from one seat to the next".

Following his quarrel with his father, Alexander was forced to flee Macedonia with Olympias, but he was recalled to court some six months after, Philip's anger having mellowed in his absence. Shortly thereafter Cleopatra gave birth to a son, also named Philip, which must have given Alexander cause for concern, and then the following year to a daughter. Yet Philip seems to have genuinely wanted to have Alexander succeed him, so much so that he wanted him by his side at a royal wedding celebration in 338 B.C. It was during these festivities that Pausanias, the captain of Philip's royal bodyguard, stabbed the king in the heart, killing him. Pausanias's motives were never established, though it his highly likely he was in Persian pay, as he was killed trying to escape. Whatever the reasons for his actions, Philip was dead. With Philip's other son only being a year old, there was no question who would succeed Philip. Alexander was proclaimed King by Philip's generals and the leading men in Macedonia. At age 20, he was ruler of Macedon and *Hegemon* of the League of Corinth.

Chapter 2: The Conqueror of Greece and Persia, 336-330 B.C.

"How great are the dangers I face to win a good name in Athens." – attributed to Alexander

Alexander's ascent to the throne of Macedon was not unopposed, however. Fearful of political rivals challenging the claim of a young and relatively untested monarch whose father had died so suddenly and mysteriously, Alexander had many of his political rivals, chief among them those who had a tenable claim to the throne, executed. Olympias, who had returned from exile, also took advantage of the turmoil to have Cleopatra, Philip's widow, and her daughter by him, burned alive. It is also likely that she tried to poison Philip's son by Cleopatra, but a botched attempt (or perhaps natural causes) made him mentally disabled, and thus no longer a threat. For his part, Alexander was furious at this barbarity, which prompted an estrangement which lasted for years.

Alexander also had to contend with problems outside of Macedonia. News of the *Hegemon's* death had not gone unnoticed, and virtually all of Philip's conquests rose up in arms: the Thracians, Thessalians, Athenians and Thebans all discarded their alliances with Macedon, rushing to occupy the passes in the north of Greece against Alexander's forces. Ignoring suggestions of a political solution to the uprising, Alexander led his cavalry on an encircling march around the Thessalian forces sent to bar his way, surrounding them and forcing them into surrender before marching southwards. The Greek city-states, terrified by the speed of his advantage, promptly sued for peace, recognising him as *Hegemon*. Alexander was formally invested with the title in the city of Corinth, where he also famously encountered the renowned philosopher Diogenes the Cynic. Alexander, who through his tutelage by Aristotle had developed an admiration for wise men, asked Diogenes if the King of Macedon might do anything for him. Diogenes, who was sitting in the public square at the time, sourly looked up at him and told Alexander that he could; he could get out of his sun. This remark prompted Alexander to later say, "If I could not be Alexander, I would be Diogenes". Plutarch would later write that Alexander and Diogenes died on the same day in 323 B.C.

A 16ᵗʰ century depiction of the famous encounter between Alexander and Diogenes

His position in Greece now secure, Alexander turned northwards, and in 335 B.C. he succeeded in securing his northern frontiers for good in a lightning campaign which crushed the armies of the Thracians and Illyrians utterly in a series of vicious battles. It was a remarkable display of soldiering, but one that the Greek cities seemed content to ignore: while Alexander was occupied in the Balkans, Thebes and Athens rose in revolt once more, despite their promises of friendship. Furious, Alexander marched his army southwards. This time, despite the entreaties of many of his advisors, he would show no mercy. When Thebes, abandoned by Athens, continued to resist him, he razed the city to the ground. This effectively ended all further resistance in Greece, and with his position as *Hegemon* firmly established, Alexander decided it was time to pursue his father's dream; it was time to invade Persia.

Ever since the famous Persian invasions that had been repelled by the Athenians at Marathon and then by the Spartans at Thermopylae and Plataea, Greece and Persia had been at odds. For the past few years they had enjoyed an uneasy peace, but that peace was shattered when, in 334 B.C., Alexander crossed the Hellespont into Persia. He brought with him an army of 50,000 infantry, 6,000 cavalry and a navy of over 100 ships, a mixed force of Macedonians, Greeks, Thracians and Illyrians, all chosen for their specific strengths (the Thessalians, for example, were famous cavalrymen). This mongrel force would become Alexander's *modus operandi* for the remainder of his campaigns.

Alexander's invasion was immediately challenged. At the Granicus, in modern Turkey, Alexander crushed a force of 30,000 Persian troops sent to oppose him, and during the battle he led the cavalry himself, as he was accustomed to doing. The destruction of this Persian field army granted him control of virtually all the neighbouring territory, and he captured the city of Sardis before marching on the fortress of Halicarnassus, which fell after a vicious siege. From there, he proceeded into Lycia and Pamphylia, systematically conquering all the coastal territory of Asia Minor. He then marched inland, where he famously visited the city of Gordium, seat of a renowned temple. The temple housed a cart whose parts were held together by a supposedly unsolvable knot, and legend had it that any man who could untie it would be made King of Asia. Alexander, disdaining any attempt at trying to fumble at the knot with his fingers, simply drew his sword and hacked it in two.

After wintering in Asia Minor, Alexander crossed into the Persian heartland in 333 B.C. Finally moved to action by what he at least perceived as a serious threat, the Persian emperor Darius III mustered an army that most sources suggest numbered almost 100,000 men, and marched against Alexander. Battle was joined at Issus, in November of 333 B.C. The battle was vicious, and Alexander lost more than 7,000 men, but he annihilated the Persian army, inflicting more than 20,000 casualties upon them and forcing them to flee the field. Darius escaped in the rout, but Alexander's men captured his royal treasury, his wife, daughters and mother. Alexander disdainfully refused an offer from Darius of a peace treaty and land concessions, claiming that as he was now King of Asia, it fell to him to decide how to dispose of his possessions. Alexander then marched into Syria, which he conquered with relative ease, but his attempts at pacifying the region in short order were frustrated first by the city of Tyre and then again by the stronghold of Gaza. Both cities had colossal fortifications that required the construction of siege works and engines of war on a scale hitherto unseen to reduce, and the resistance from both garrisons was exceedingly fierce, prompting Alexander to kill all men of fighting age and sell survivors into slavery when they were finally taken. At Gaza, as Alexander personally led an attack against the walls, he was struck by a missile from above and seriously injured in the shoulder, one of the many serious wounds he was to accrue in his time as a fighting King.

Mosaic depicting the Battle of Issus

Having witnessed the fate of Tyre and Gaza, the garrison of Jerusalem capitulated to Alexander without a fight, allowing him to push southwards into Egypt. The ancient kingdom of the Pharaohs had been reduced to a vassal state of Persia, and its inhabitants greeted Alexander like a liberator, the entire country falling to him without a fight. In 332 BC Alexander made a pilgrimage to the shrine of Siwa, in the Egyptian desert, where the Oracle proclaimed him ruler of the world and son of Ammon, the Egyptian patriarchal deity, leading Alexander to adopt the title "Son of Zeus Ammon". Coins minted by him, from there on out, showed him with ram's horns as a mark of his divine parentage. It is unclear whether Alexander truly believed the rumors of his own divinity, but it is undeniable that the Oracle's verdict severely inflated his pride, prompting the first accusations of *hubris* from his supporters, some of whom also grumbled that Alexander was getting dangerously close to going native. Alexander, unphased by these murmurings, journeyed to northern Egypt, where he founded Alexandria in Egypt, his most famous city. After letting his soldiers recuperate and receiving reinforcements, in 331 B.C. he struck eastwards and marched into Mesopotamia, the Persian heartland.

Darius once again marched to oppose him, but Alexander met his forces at Gaugamela and battle was once again joined. Darius had at his disposal anywhere between 100,000 and 250,000 men, while Alexander's force numbered less than 50,000, but once again the relentless machine of the Macedonian phalanx proved its worth by pinning down all of the superior Persian force and resisting all attempts to break through its lines, including attacks by war elephants and scythe-wheeled chariots. Meanwhile, Alexander led his Companion Cavalry and the Macedonian right wing in a flanking movement which outran its enemy pursuit and then struck straight for the center of the Persian formation, against Darius himself. The attack smashed through the Persian lines, causing the Persian center to crumble, and the entire Persian army was routed. Darius fled the field, but Alexander was unable to immediately pursue because his left flank, under general Parmenion, had been pushed back and was in danger of being overrun. This delay allowed Darius to escape, but his defeat was absolute: about 50,000 Persian dead, unknown numbers captured, and the entirety of their baggage train in Alexander's hands. Darius eluded Alexander's pursuit and vanished into the mountainous region of Ectebana (modern Iran). Abandoning his chase to consolidate his territorial gains, Alexander marched into Babylon, where he was acclaimed as a conquering hero. He then marched on Susa, where he captured the Imperial Persian treasury, thus endowing himself and his army with unimaginable wealth. Finally, Alexander advanced towards the royal capital, Persepolis. His way was contested by an enemy army at the Persian gate, but he smashed the enemy force and continued onwards, entering Persepolis in 330 B.C.

While he had entered Babylon peacefully, Alexander decided to make a statement in Persepolis. He allowed his troops to pillage the city for days on end, permitting them to finally take their revenge upon the hated Persian adversaries, and the palace of Xerxes, the famous Persian Emperor who had been defeated at Salamis and Plataea, was put to the torch. It is unclear whether this gesture was a deliberate insult, revenge for Xerxes ordering the burning the Acropolis of Athens, or whether it was the result of one of Alexander's famous drunken binges, but the end result was that the palace and much of the city were reduced to ash.

Alexander was now effectively the ruler of the whole Persian Empire, as well as king of Macedon and *Hegemon* of the League of Corinth besides. All of Asia Minor, the Middle-Eastern seaboard, and Egypt now owed him allegiance, but he wanted more. Prophecies in Jerusalem, Siwa, and Gordium had declared him the future King of Asia, and Alexander wanted to be ruler in name as well as in practice. This could never happen as long as Darius was still alive and still capable of rallying men to his banner, so after letting his army plunder their fill and rest in Persepolis, Alexander marched once more. He chased Darius farther eastwards, from Ectebana into Media, then into Parthia (Western Afghanistan). As Darius's supporters tallied his defeats, they began to slip away.

Eventually, the inevitable happened and Darius, alone and friendless, was deserted by his last troops and taken prisoner by Bessus, one of his generals and governor of Bactria (Central Afghanistan). Bessus kept Darius prisoner for a time as he continued to retreat from Alexander, but when the Macedonian troops threatened to overtake him Bessus had Darius murdered, and his body cast into a ditch. It is likely that Alexander, advancing with the Macedonian vanguard, found Darius dead, but he later claimed that Darius had been alive when he reached him, and had named him his successor. With Darius gone, Alexander could proclaim himself Great King of Persia, but his claim was threatened by a rival: Bessus, having murdered Darius, proclaimed himself Great King in turn and retreated into the heartland of Bactria, defying Alexander to challenge him. Such overt defiance could not be left unpunished: in 330 B.C., Alexander marched into Bactria at the head of his army, to crush Bessus and make himself King.

Alexander at Issus, as depicted in a Roman mosaic.

Chapter 3: Central Asia and the Indian Campaign, 330-324 B.C.

Many conquerors have entered Afghanistan with force, but few have been successful, and none would ever describe the region's pacification as easy. Alexander's incursion also came at considerable cost. With his veteran army, he pursued the pretender Bessus into Bactria, but even he was unprepared for the difficulties he was to face: the natives were hostile to a man, the terrain was either mountainous (and virtually impassable to all troops but light infantry) or a barren desert with no water or forage. Alexander reconfigured his army for the hostile terrain, shortening the pikes of his phalanx and lightening the armour of his heavy infantry and cavalry, but even that was not enough. For the first time, Alexander faced an enemy who stubbornly refused to be brought to battle. Bessus, who had been at Gaugamela, must have realised that he could never hope to face the relentless meat-grinder of the Macedonian war machine in open battle, so he decided to play to the strengths of his native Bactrian, Sogdianan and Scythian troops: he employed hit-and-run guerrilla tactics, dispersing his forces across the whole of the theater of war. Bessus never concentrated them in numbers sufficient for Alexander to pin them down and destroy them, instead striking out at isolated garrisons, baggage and supply convoys, and vulnerable detachments. Flying columns sent out to rescue beleaboured outposts were often ambushed, and with virtually every local, it seemed, either feeding Bessus's troops information or actively fighting alongside them, Alexander began to lose his temper. It was time for the Bactrians to reap the whirlwind.

Alexander scarcely needed to worry about public opinion with regards to his treatment of the hostile natives, especially where his Macedonian soldiers and generals, who considered them barely human, were concerned. He began to employ pacification by force: entire cities were razed to the ground and their inhabitants sold into slavery, to be rebuilt anew and colonised by veterans of the Macedonian army who were now disabled or too old for service for the most part. These former soldiers were offered large financial incentives to settle in the troubled province. Furthermore, whole regions were depopulated, with their inhabitants either driven out, sold into slavery or killed, and the regions were re-colonized with Persian subjects imported from the more tractable lands to the west. This virtual genocide was accompanied by the foundation of half a dozen cities to help pacify the surrounding lands, including Alexandria on the Jaxartes, and Alexandria Eschate ("The Furthermost") in what is now Tajikistan. At least one of them still stands today, and is one of the most important cities in the region – Kandahar.

The prolonged campaign, the miserable weather conditions, the hostile population and the constant grind of being forced to fight a seemingly invisible enemy while constantly worrying about receiving a knife in the back from supposedly pacified locals began to wear on Alexander's men. The progress of Alexander's conquests, which barring his great sieges had been lightning-fast, slowed to a crawl, and there was no guaranteeing that what had been conquered would actually *stay* conquered.

Dissension and disillusionment, not least with Alexander himself, were rife. Many of Alexander's generals openly advocated turning back to Mesopotamia, if not Macedonia itself, and there was growing concern, openly voiced – the Macedonian King famously being a first among equals, and thus open to criticism – about Alexander's "going native". He had begun to adopt certain elements of local dress and took the Persian title of *Shahanshah* ("King of Kings"), but what truly soured his generals against him was the adoption of the Persian custom of *proskynesis*. Quite what *proskynesis* was is unclear, but it is certain that it was some form of obeisance, a courtesy that the many Persian generals and courtiers now accompanying Alexander felt obliged to render him as befitted his title of King of Kings.

The Macedonian generals, however, were having none of it: obeisances were traditionally left to Gods alone, and this, coupled with Alexander's previous declaration that he was the son of Zeus Ammon, was seen as *hubris* of the highest degree. Tempers frayed, then finally snapped: at a banquet that year, Alexander infamously took a spear to Cleitus the Black, one of his generals, in a drunken brawl. Cleitus, who had saved Alexander's life at Gaugamela, had insulted Alexander's Persian courtiers, prompting Alexander to rise in fury and run him through. Tortured with remorse, he took to his rooms and did not emerge for days: it was Alexander's darkest hour.

THE MURDER OF CLITUS.

Portrait depicting the death of Cleitus, by Andre Castaigne

For Alexander, there was no respite. There were at least two plots to assassinate him during this period, one of which implicated Alexander's general and boyhood friend Philotas, who was also the son of Parmenion, another general of Alexander's who had served with his father and had held the left at Gaugamela. Philotas was executed for his part in the plot and Parmenion, who had been left behind by Alexander at Ectebana, was assassinated to prevent reprisals. A further plot was uncovered later that year, this time involving Alexander's pages and his personal historian, Callisthenes. Increasingly beset by difficulties, it seemed as though Alexander's entire invasion of Bactria and the adjoining territories might unravel completely, with not even Bessus's betrayal and assassination in 329 BC serving as respite. When Bessus's own people captured him and turned him over, Alexander reportedly had his nose and ears cut off, which was an Ancient Persian custom for punished rebels. Ancient accounts conflict on how Bessus ultimately died, but they all agree that he was tortured in some fashion or another.

THE PUNISHMENT OF BESSUS.

Portrait of Bessus being crucified, by Andre Castaigne

If anything the man who took his place, the Bactrian Spitamenes, was even more resourceful and cunning than his predecessor, and it took an absolutely titanic amount of gold, men and vicious fighting (including the storming of scores of hill forts in terrain inaccessible to siege engines, during which Alexander received a serious wound) to finally defeat him. After the Battle of Gabai, where Alexander crossed a river on a huge craft in the face of a colossal arrow-storm and annihilated Spitamenes's levies, the Bactrian general was murdered by his own troops. There was peace at last.

It was an uneasy peace, however. Alexander knew this, and because he intended to press on still further eastwards, he knew he could not leave Bactria in his rear in a state of unrest, as it would compromise his lines of supply and communication, which were already stretched dangerously thin. Accordingly, in 328 B.C. he took as a wife the daughter of a powerful local chieftain, Roxana. This union angered many of Alexander's generals, Persian and Macedonian alike: the Macedonians felt that Alexander should marry a girl of noble Macedonian or Greek birth, and saw this as further proof of Alexander's going native; the Persians, who looked down upon the Afghans as second-class subjects, would have had him marry a girl of Persian royal blood. Alexander ignored them, however, knowing the importance of keeping Bactria compliant, and when he finally marched south and east he was accompanied by thousands of Bactrian and Sogdianan cavalry, implacable foes turned willing allies.

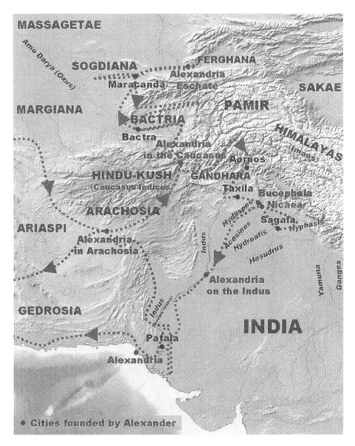

Alexander must have been glad to leave Bactria and its adjoining provinces at his back, but his troubles were far from over. Alexander was planning to march onwards, into India, and had made overtures to the wild tribesmen that inhabited the region that is now Pakistan, but he had been abruptly refused. The chieftains of the hill clans who guarded the passes of the mighty Hindu Kush mountains were determined to make a fight of it, secure in the knowledge that the high passes of their domains were virtually unconquerable. Alexander, never one to accept defiance, made his preparations and, in midwinter, a season traditionally reserved for rearmament and regrouping, he began his campaign. The Aspasioi, the Guraeans and the Assakenoi, inhabitants of the rocky valleys of north-western Pakistan, all opposed him, so Alexander destroyed their fortresses one by one, determined to extinguish them. The hill clans were fierce fighters, and each fortress, small though they generally were, was only carried by storm after days of vicious fighting which resulted in grievous losses among the Macedonian ranks. To give an idea of the brutality of this conflict, Alexander himself was seriously wounded twice during two separate sieges, taking a javelin through the shoulder fighting the Aspasioi and then a spear-thrust to the ankle in the assault against the Assakenoi fortress of Massaga. His reprisal was fierce: every fortress of the hill clans that did not surrender him was razed to the ground, and its inhabitants put to the sword, to the last man.

Despite the war-weariness of his veterans and many of his generals, after having vanquished the hill tribes Alexander pressed south and east into the Punjab. There he clashed with the most powerful enemy he had encountered since he had vanquished Darius at Gaugamela, the great Indian ruler Rajah Porus, whose domains included virtually the whole Punjab and who commanded an army tens of thousands strong. Alexander's force came face to face with Porus's army at the Hydaspes River, in 326 B.C. Despite Porus's strong defensive position, Alexander succeeded in forcing a crossing. When Porus threw forward his war elephants, the shock element of his force, Alexander's indomitable phalanx proved equal to the task: his men had faced war elephants before, and instead of bracing to resist their charge they opened their ranks, letting the beasts charge through, then encircled them and brought them and their riders down with their pikes. The phalanx then made short work of the lightly armoured Indian infantry, while Alexander's Companion Cavalry and allied horsemen drove the enemy skirmishers and horsemen from the field. Porus was captured still trying to fight, and Alexander was so impressed with his bravery that he made him governor of his previous kingdom, even going so far as to grant him additional lands.

It was also around this time that one of Alexander's oldest and closest companions, the mighty stallion Bucephalus, finally succumbed to the rigours of campaign and died, though it is unclear whether as a result of illness or a wound. Alexander was distraught at his loss as only a true cavalryman who has lived at his mount's side and shared his last morsel of food with him can be, and he ordered a great monument erected to Bucephalus, on the site of which he founded the city of – appropriately – Bucephala. Given the close association between Alexander and his horse, generals from around the world followed Alexander's lead and ensured that they used a favorite horse as well, from Julius Caesar to Robert E. Lee.

A coin from the Seleucid Empire depicting Bucephalus

Some viewed the death of Bucephalus as a sign from the gods that it was time for Alexander to go home, but he persisted on marching ever onwards, despite the fact that his army was exhausted. Many of his veterans had not seen their homes and their loved ones in over a decade, and the lines of supply and communication back to Macedon were stretched so perilously thin that it was unlikely that any reinforcements would be forthcoming. Moreover, Alexander's continual attempts to blend the Hellenistic and Persian cultures together, including the induction of Persian youths into the Companion Cavalry and his personal bodyguards, were souring his Greek and Macedonian soldiers against him. Finally, upon reaching the Hyphasis River, they could take it no more. They laid down their arms and refused to march another step eastwards.

Alexander raged, begged, entreated, and even threatened, but his soldiers had had enough. Further east lay still more powerful Indian kingdoms who, rumor had it, would await them on the eastern bank of the mighty river Ganges with hundreds of thousands of cavalry and infantry, and thousands of war elephants and charioteers besides. Alexander flew into a black rage, refusing all visitors for days, but eventually he relented, realizing that no matter how great their love for him might be, he could not persuade his veterans to march further south. After erecting a monument on the Hyphasis River to mark the easternmost edge, he at last turned his army westwards for the first time in almost 10 years.

The way back to Persia was fraught with peril, and Alexander's army suffered grievously. They encountered fierce resistance from local tribes along the Indus, and upon reaching the Persian Gulf Alexander dispatched the majority of his army into Iran, while he himself led a contingent through the desolate wasteland of the Gedrosian Desert, a barren and inhospitable region that virtually decimated his force. In 324 B.C. Alexander finally reached the Persian city of Susa, but the grim tally of his men told the tale of the price of glory all too clearly.

Chapter 4: "To the Strongest", 323 B.C.

Macedonian Tetradrachm depicting Alexander with Heracles's headgear, 336-325 B.C.

Factionalism, sloth, and greed had run rampant among many of the governors and other officials of the middle and high levels of Persian infrastructure whom Alexander had wisely chosen to largely leave in their place (rather than substitute them with men who had no idea what their job entailed). Doubtless many of them, when he had marched into Bactria, believed that he would never return, and accusations of bribery and corruption were rife. Thus, Alexander's progress to Susa was marked by a string of executions, as he rapidly made examples of the officials who displeased him. Once he reached the city, Alexander took good care of his beloved veterans: their back pay – which sometimes amounted to several years' worth of salary – was paid in full, with decorations and bonuses for all, and Alexander also promised he would ship injured and old veterans home under General Craterus, one of his ablest commanders. However, this last gesture seems to have been misconstrued by his men: perhaps they thought he wanted to replace the Macedonian units in his army entirely with Persian ones, since Persian youngsters were being taught to fight in the Macedonian phalanx formation. Certainly it cannot be that they did not wish to go home at last, not when they were finally so close.

Whatever their reasons, Alexander's men mutinied once again. For three days they refused to listen to reason, but this time Alexander seems to have greeted their balking with heartbreak rather than rage. It was only after Alexander threatened to appoint some of his Persian subjects to the rank of general and rename Persian regiments with titles properly belonging to old and sacred Macedonian units that his men relented. To show goodwill, Alexander feasted several thousand of his veterans, dining at their tables and making the rounds among them until late into the night. He also attempted to harmonize relationships between Macedonians and Persians by conducting a mass marriage between many of his officers and Persian noblewomen, though to little success. It is around this time that Alexander's closest boyhood friend, Hephaestion, died suddenly under mysterious circumstances, a blow from which Alexander never truly recovered. He grieved Hephaestion for days on end, refusing to leave his quarters.

Busts of Alexander (left) and Hephaestion

It was in action that Alexander found solace. Never a man to sit on his hands or rest upon his laurels, Alexander began planning his future campaigns, which may have included attempts to subdue the Arabian Peninsula or make another incursion into India. But fate had other plans for the young Macedonian king. One night, while feasting his admiral Nearchus, he drank too much and took to bed with a fever. At first, it seemed like the fever was merely a consequence of his excess, and there was not much concern for his health, but when a week had elapsed and there was still no sign of his getting better, his friends and generals began to grow concerned. The fever grew, consuming him to the point that he could barely speak. After two weeks, on June 11th, 323 B.C., Alexander the Great, King of Macedon, *Hegemon* of the League of Corinth, King of Kings, died.

The circumstances of Alexander's death are unclear. Certainly there were plenty of ambitious men, even among his inner circle, who might have wanted him dead, yet all of the main historians for Alexander's life discount the possibility of foul play, claiming no poison was used, and slow-acting venom capable of prolonging a man's agony for two weeks seems technologically unviable for the period in question. Perhaps Alexander was simply exhausted: he was a famous binge drinker, like his father, which did little for his health, and he had been on campaign for more than a decade, having sustained at least three serious wounds in the process. Even today scientists and doctors still try to diagnose Alexander based on accounts of his death, naming potential natural causes like malaria, typhoid fever, or meningitis.

On his deathbed, some historians claim that when he was pressed to name a successor, Alexander muttered that his empire should go "to the strongest". Other sources tell us that he passed his signet ring to his general Perdiccas, thereby naming him successor, but whatever his choices were or may have been, they were ignored. Alexander's generals, all of them with the loyalty of their own corps at their backs, would tear each other apart in a vicious internal struggle that lasted almost half a century before four factions emerged victorious: Macedonia, the Seleukid Empire in the east, the Kingdom of Pergamon in Asia Minor, and the Ptolemaic dynasty in Egypt. During the course of these wars, Alexander's only heir, the posthumously born Alexander IV, was murdered, extinguishing his bloodline for ever. And though it was unclear what killed Alexander, his subordinates were fully aware of the value of his body. According to ancient accounts, Ptolemy eventually took control of Alexander's body, and Alexander's sarcophagus eventually made its way to Alexandria, where it remained for at least the next 500 years.

Bust of Alexander's friend and general, Ptolemy

As the most famous man of history, Alexander's tomb was a must-see for the leaders of antiquity, and apparently his original gold sarcophagus was replaced with a glass casing, allowing his body to ve viewed. Ancient historians wrote some entertaining anecdotes of unknown veracity about certain leaders' visits to Alexander's tomb. Pompey the Great (who took the name Magnus and cut his hair based on Alexander) and Julius Caesar were said to have viewed Alexander's body without causing a stir, but historians claim that when Augustus visited Alexander's tomb, he accidentally knocked Alexander's nose off. And perhaps as a way to emphasize Caligula's insanity, historians claim the young Roman emperor took Alexander's breastplate for his own use. The last known date in which a Roman emperor visited Alexander's tomb was in 200 A.D, but it's unclear what happened to Alexander's body and tomb after that. The location of Alexander's body remains lost to history.

Despite the infighting among them, one thing Alexander's generals did agree upon was their Hellenistic culture. Most famously, Ptolemy's line firmly established the Hellenistic culture of the Greeks while ruling over Egypt. By marrying within their family line, the Ptolemaic pharaohs kept their Hellenistic heritage until the very end of Ptolemy's line, which died with Cleopatra in 30 B.C.

Alexander and his successors also succeeded in "Hellenizing" Persia and parts of Asia Minor, and their influence is still readily visible. Anthropologists have found that some of the earliest Buddha statues constructed in India bear an uncanny resemblance to Ancient Greek depictions of Apollo

This Buddha, with a combined Greco-Buddhist style, dates from the 1ˢᵗ-2ⁿᵈ century A.D.

Further west, much of Alexander's old empire was eventually conquered in the following centuries by Rome, including Cleopatra's Egypt. But instead of ending the Hellenistic culture, the Roman Empire further reinforced it. Having conquered Greece itself around 100 B.C., the Roman Empire heavily assimilated the Greeks' culture into its own. Latin was an offshoot of the Greeks' language, the Romans' mythology was nearly identical, and Roman poetry, literature and art all closely resembled what was produced to their east in the preceding centuries.

When Alexander died at the age of 32, he had made himself the most powerful man in the world. His dominions stretched from the Punjab to modern Albania, making him one of the most successful conquerors in recorded history. That he was brave to the point of recklessness is undoubted: he was on the front lines of every major battle his army ever fought. That he was a brilliant strategist who never lost a single battle is also out of the question, but much of his personal life remains fraught with mystery and speculation: some of our sources tell us he was handsome, tall, blond-haired; others that he was short, stocky, and with one dark eye and one blue. His relationship with his childhood companion Hephaestion has never been fully established, with some modern historians claiming that they were lovers and others discounting the theory. Was he a man given to excessive appetites, an arrogant hedonist who ruined himself with drink, food, and sex, as some claim, or the spartan, austere "first among equals" that others describe? Most likely we will never know the whole truth.

What remains certain, however, is that he profoundly changed the course of history forever. Quite aside from his own personal conquests, his successors went on to found empires that lasted for centuries, and local legend has it that the wild olive trees that grow in some regions of Afghanistan sprang from the olive seeds that Macedonian soldiers spat out on the march – not to mention the presence of Balkan features such as red hair and blue eyes among a significant amount of the locals there to this day. Legends of Alexander crop up amid the popular mythology of half the world, and while some among the Persian Empire called him "the accursed", it is now widely believed that the story of the prophet Dhul-Qarnayn ("The Two-Horned One") in the Qur'an is a reference to Alexander. However he is remembered, it's clear that no land Alexander set foot upon has ever truly forgotten him.

On the eve of the Battle of Gaugamela, Alexander's general Parmenion urged a diplomatic solution, telling Alexander he should negotiate with Darius and accept the generous terms the King of Kings was willing to provide. Alexander, it is said, simply smiled and replied, "And so I would if I were Parmenion. But I am Alexander, so I cannot."

In the end, for better or for worse, he was simply that: Alexander.

Bibliography

Readers interested in learning more about Alexander should refer to the highly readable ancient sources on his life, available for free on the internet or in annotated edition in most local bookshops:

Arrian, *Anabasis Alexandri*

Quintus Curtius Rufus, *Historia Alexandrii Magni*

Plutarch, *Life of Alexander the Great*

Those looking for a more up-to-date, comprehensive history of Alexander and his empire should consult Robin Lane Fox's excellent *Alexander the Great.*

Hannibal

Depiction of Hannibal crossing the Alps

Chapter 1: Early Life and Military Distinction, 247-218 B.C.

The classical age has given us some of History's greatest generals. The battles, tactics and campaigns of the likes of Alcibiades, Alexander, Caesar and Lysander are still studied at staff colleges and military academies throughout the world today, long after military equipment and doctrine have far outstripped those of their period, and with good reason. For speed of march, efficiency of supply and logistics, and sheer battlefield acumen, they are in many ways unmatched today, and there is no doubt that even among such exalted company Hannibal of Carthage, son of Hamilcar, stood supreme. In a little over two decades of near-continuous warfare, the man who would become known as the Scourge of Rome would come within a hair's breadth of destroying the mightiest empire of his age, almost altering the course of history forever.

Most of what the histories have to say about Hannibal came to us from his greatest enemies, for shortly after his death Carthage was utterly annihilated by the Roman legions, and they left no annals behind to tell us what the Carthaginians may have thought of their greatest soldier. That said, it is known that Hannibal was disliked by many of the most prominent Carthaginian factions, who were always loath to support him even in the hour of his greatest success, but their dislike was nothing compared to the utter hatred – largely born of fear – that the Romans felt for him. They could not belittle his achievements, so they attacked the only thing that was open to question – his character. Roman historians named him arrogant, ruthless, vicious, hedonistic, and cruel, and though some of his actions do bear out these labels, others seem to contradict them entirely.

Thus, a fine controversy has raged over the years, with some historians arguing that Hannibal's character was beyond reproach, like his generalship, while others argue that he was everything his Roman detractors suggested, and more. The truth, as always, is likely to lie somewhere in the middle. Like many classical figures on whom much has been written, but almost always second-hand, Hannibal remains something of a mystery. He never left any personal documents behind, or if he did they did not survive antiquity, so today we are left to confine ourselves to examining his public persona and his achievements, and catching the occasional glimpse of the man behind the mask.

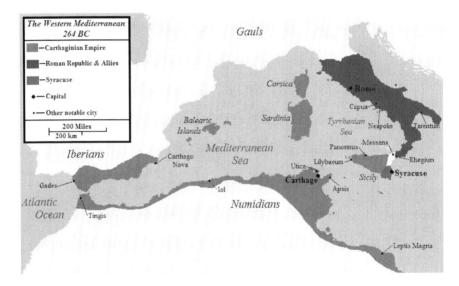

Hannibal was born in Carthage in 247 BC, the first-born son of Hamilcar "The Thunderbolt" Barca, a prominent Carthaginian nobleman and a successful general who had distinguished himself leading Carthage's forces during the First Punic War against Rome ("Punic" being the adjective the Romans reserved for all things Carthaginian). Though Hamilcar used the cognomen Barca (meaning "thunderbolt"), it's unclear whether that was passed down to his sons, though historians still generally refer to Hannibal as Hannibal Barca. Regardless, with such a fine martial tradition in his family, it naturally followed that Hannibal too would join the Carthaginian army, rather than engage in the other great pastime of the city's nobility, trade.

With the state of the Mediterranean basin being what it was in 247 BC, it followed that there would be plenty of employment for soldiers. Indeed, Hannibal was born into a world of strife. Carthage, the northern African superpower, had grown rich on trade and the intelligent use of force, but their position of supremacy was being challenged by the rising star of Rome, which by this time was also aggressive, expansionistic, and heavily slanted towards conquest and the military rather than peaceable trade. Given that, it was inevitable that Rome would come into conflict with Carthage, and had already done so during the first Punic War, a brutal and bitter conflict which had lasted for over two decades and resulted in a Roman victory and the loss of large swaths of Carthaginian land across the Mediterranean. While the two great powers were at war, other factions, such as Syracuse and the Seleukids, had also attempted to carve out a larger piece of the Mediterranean pie.

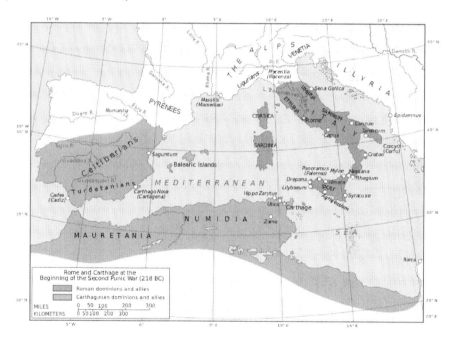

Rome and Carthage after the First Punic War

Carthage's struggles with Rome in the first Punic War, and their overreliance on mercenary forces, had left them so bankrupt they were unable to pay off their surviving veterans, leading to widespread uprisings by their mercenary contingents that turned into a war in their own right. This further impoverished Carthage and caused the loss of even more territories as they were forced to scrape the barrel of their manpower dry to crush the rebellions. Rome, however, was in no position to take full advantage of Carthage's weakness: 23 years of war had virtually annihilated her army and navy, and both factions needed time to draw breath, re-arm, and levy new armies and taxes. It was in this uncertain time, the breathless calm before the inevitable storm, that Hannibal grew to boyhood.

When Hannibal was 11, and proceeding with the typical education of a Carthaginian military nobleman's child (by all accounts he excelled at horsemanship, wrestling, and other martial pursuits), his father Hamilcar, who was desperate to find Carthage a new source of revenue to replace the lost territories of Sardinia and Corsica, managed to persuade the Carthaginian ruling elite of the desirability of the military conquest of the Iberian peninsula, the riches of which, he argued, could fund Carthage's re-armament for the next war. The Carthaginian rulers consented, and in 236 B.C. Hamilcar went about preparing the invasion of Spain, which at the time was a loose collection of tribes with no ambitions beyond their local territory. Furthermore, annexation of land on the Iberian Peninsula was unlikely to anger Rome unduly, even though the Republic's forces were also pursuing their own interests in the north of the Peninsula. In fact, containment of Roman expansion may also have been part of Hamilcar's strategy.

Hannibal, though barely 11 at the time, begged his father for leave to accompany the expedition. At first, it appears as though Hamilcar was reluctant to let someone so young join him on his campaign, but due to repeated pleas by Hannibal, he seems to have relented. Whatever his reasons, the young Hannibal was certainly with the Carthaginian army when it marched along the coast of North Africa to the strait of Gibraltar, where, under Hamilcar's supervision, the troops were ferried across the narrow strait and onto Spanish soil. The journey took Hamilcar's army some months, but at the time the Carthaginian navy was in such a parlous state that there were simply not enough ships available to transport the army by sea from Carthage itself, leading Hamilcar to take the longer coastal route.

Once there, however, Hamilcar's army was vastly successful in prosecuting war on the peninsula itself. The Iberian tribes, inferior in equipment and training, could not hope to resist the Carthaginian troops, and despite stiff fighting they were defeated piecemeal and annexed, a process which, though relatively rapid, nonetheless took several years. During this time, Hannibal grew to adolescence, tutored in warfare by Greek instructors who instructed him by detailing the conquests of Alexander, Alcibiades, and Pyrrhus of Epirus, all of whom he would come to greatly admire and hold in high esteem. Of course, Hannibal also witnessed his father Hamilcar's successes as a commander first-hand. It is likely that Hamilcar himself, when campaign matters permitted, would have taken time to instruct his son himself, for they appear to have been close. Indeed, Hamilcar was determined that Hannibal himself, when the time came, should take up his mantle and proceed with the crusade that had occupied most of his military life: the destruction of Rome. Hamilcar had never recovered from the humiliation of being defeated by the Republic's forces, and longed for the day when he might lead Carthage's troops against Rome once again, and to this end he spent much time instilling in his son an implacable hatred of Carthage's sworn enemy. Such was Hamilcar's zeal for his cause, and his desire to bind his son to it, that he had Hannibal accompany him to a shrine in the town of Peniscola (near modern Valencia) and bid him swear upon the altar that he would be Rome's enemy for evermore. Hannibal duly did so, adding, "As soon as I have come of age, I swear that I will bring Rome low by fire and the sword".

Hamilcar's campaigns continued successfully, and he even began to consolidate his gains by founding a string of cities, including, popular legend has it, the port city of Barcino (from Barca, his family name), on the site of modern-day Barcelona. However, Hamilcar's success came to an abrupt end in 228 B.C. when, leading his army across a river against an army of Iberian tribesmen, he fell from his horse and, dragged down by his armour, drowned. Hannibal was 19 at the time, and already a proven battlefield commander, having taken command of a detachment of Carthaginian troops at some point during Hamilcar's campaigns and already displaying a glimmer of the military genius that would characterise his later career in his handling of his soldiers.

Hannibal grieved deeply for his father's death, but his sorrow was somewhat lessened by the appointment of his older brother-in-law, general Hasdrubal, to overall command of the army. Having another family member commanding in Iberia, rather than an unknown quantity, meant more opportunity for advancement, and Hannibal was pleased to accept a position on Hasdrubal's staff, where he had ample opportunity to prove his mettle. Meanwhile, Hasdrubal, who was less bellicose than Hamilcar, set about consolidating his father-in-law's gains, pursuing a policy of appeasement and settlement in the territories that Hamilcar had already annexed. After all, the main purpose of the Iberian invasion had been to generate revenue, and there could be no tax collecting while there was a war raging. Accordingly, Hasdrubal, much to Hannibal's chagrin, signed a peace treaty with Rome and established a *de facto* frontier along the northern valley of the Ebro, with both factions promising they would refrain from straying across the river. Quite what Hannibal made of Hasdrubal's decision to sign a peace treaty with his and his father's sworn enemy is unclear, but he cannot have been pleased by the fact. Nevertheless, like a good soldier, he obeyed, and he was given cause to rejoice when, in 226 BC, an alliance was formed between the Carthaginians and the Gaulish tribes of the Po valley in Northern Italy, tribesmen hostile to Rome who had already once memorably sacked the great city itself. Rome responded, and in 225 B.C. they annexed the area known as Cisalpine Gaul, dashing Hannibal's hopes of a joint invasion of Italian soil.

It was around this time that Hannibal, then in his early twenties, took to wife the Iberian princess Imilce, the daughter of a powerful tribal leader. As part of his successful – and highly remunerative – policy of consolidation, Hasdrubal had insisted that many of his young, unmarried officers take local highborn ladies of marriageable age to wife, and Hannibal's marriage seems to have been born of that policy rather than any particular passion he might have felt for Imilce. Hannibal continued in Hasdrubal's employ for several years, firmly establishing himself as one of the most resourceful Carthaginian commanders in Iberia, until, in 221 BC, his brother-in-law was murdered. Hasdrubal was killed by a Celt assassin, but who paid the cut-throat's purse is likely to remain a mystery. Certainly there were plenty of people who wanted him dead: the Iberians he had pacified had cause to dislike him, the Romans might well have viewed him as a significant obstacle to their interests in Iberia, and they were doubtless feeling threatened by the possibility of a Gaulish-Carthaginian invasion of the Italian peninsula; moreover, the Carthaginian court itself was notorious for intrigue and political plotting, so there is a distinct possibility that it was someone in Carthage who wanted Hasdrubal dead, for their own ends.

Be it as it may, Hasdrubal's death was a golden opportunity for Hannibal. He had already proven himself to be a resourceful commander, and in addition to his undoubted merits he had the good fortune to be the child of the mighty Hamilcar Barca. By 221 B.C., Hannibal also had proven himself to be his father's son militarily. When the time came for the army of Iberia to choose its commander, he was named general to universal popular acclaim, and his appointment was promptly validated by Carthage.

At the age of 26, Hannibal was now commander of the entirety of the Carthaginian forces in Iberia, with but one objective: to bring fire and the sword to Rome.

Chapter 2: The Scourge of Rome, 218-216 B.C.

For two years, Hannibal bided his time, consolidating his position in the Iberian peninsula and massing his forces, abiding by one of the greatest military truths and one which doubtless his tutors and his father, with their tales of Alexander and Alcibiades, had contributed to instill in him: numbers do not matter so much as concentration of force, i.e. what troops are available to fight in one single critical location, at any given time. Meanwhile, even as Hannibal was preparing to strike out against their very heart, the Romans seem to have grown unusually complacent; after all, Hannibal was new to overall command, and with both Hamilcar and Hasdrubal dead, they must have felt themselves secure. When in 218 BC Hannibal resurrected his brother-in-law's plan for a joint Gaulish and Carthaginian invasion of the Italian peninsula, the Romans were caught napping, something which they would live to regret in the following years.

Hannibal needed a *casus belli*, and in 219 B.C. the Romans obliged him with one, forming an alliance with the powerful Iberian city of Saguntum, well south of the line drawn along the Ebro, and unilaterally declaring it a Roman protectorate. Hannibal took this for outright rebellion, and acted accordingly, investing the city and besieging it for eight months until it fell. He then protested to Carthage that Rome had broken the terms of their agreement with them, declaring that there could be only one feasible course of action: war. The Carthaginian rulers, having been burned once before, were wary of becoming embroiled in a new conflict with Rome, but such was Hannibal's popularity with the troops in the Iberian peninsula that, with the memory of the Mercenary Wars still fresh in their minds, they acceded to his demands rather than risk a full-blown mutiny.

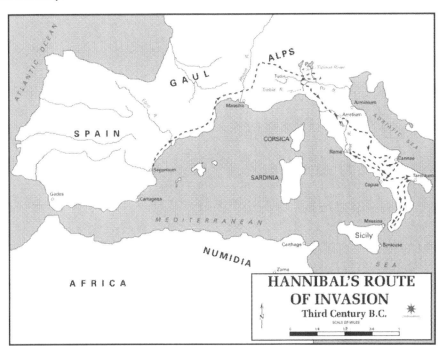

Estimated March of Hannibal's Invasion of Italy by the United States Military Academy

In the spring of 218 B.C., at the head of approximately 50,000 infantry, 15,000 cavalry, and 50 war elephants, Hannibal began marching northeast. His plan was breathtakingly ambitious: he would march through the Pyrenees, across southern Gaul, over the Alps and into Italy proper, thereby avoiding the heavily fortified border in the northwest of Italy. It was a route no general had ever taken before, let alone a general with so many animals (including elephants). His father Hamilcar had been defeated trying to invade southern Italy and attempting to outfight the Roman navy at sea; Hannibal would not make the same mistake.

Pushing aside with contemptuous ease the stiff resistance of the Pyrenean tribes, who contested every step of the way from their strongholds of the mountain passes, Hannibal pushed forwards with remarkable speed, leaving behind a detachment of some 10,000 Iberian soldiers to keep his lines of communication open and pacify the tumultuous region. He then marched on into southern Gaul, negotiating with the local chieftains and outfighting those who had a mind to contest his advance. His speed of maneuver, and his ability to move his army across rough terrain, proved unmatched in the ancient world since the time of Alexander the Great. By that point, his army, which now numbered some 40,000 infantry, 8,000 cavalry, and around 40 war elephants, danced up the valley of the Rhone to evade a Roman force sent to bar his passage southwards through the strategically vital gap in the mountains where the Alps meet the Mediterranean. With that route closed to him, Hannibal, undaunted, struck south and east across the Alps themselves.

Exactly what route he took is still the subject of hotly contested debate today, and even Roman scholars writing shortly after his prodigious feat seem to have no clear idea of where precisely he made his passage, but one thing is certain: it was one of the most remarkable maneuvers in military history. There were no roads greater than a goat-track across the Alps, none of them continuous, and the high passes were smothered by snow, often year-round, with drifts dozens of feet deep. Moreover, those passes included other hazards, such as potential rockfalls, and the barren terrain offered limited supplies. To top it all off, these passes were crawling with bellicose tribesmen who lived by banditry and hid in impregnable fortresses perched atop sheer crags. To Hannibal's army, most of them Iberians from the sun-baked plains of southern Spain or Carthaginians from the hot deserts of Northern Africa, the Alps must have looked like an icy Hell.

Hannibal's passage of the Alps remains the most famous event of his life and legend, and even though the location of his crossing matters little compared to the fact that he ultimately did get across, it has nonetheless been the most compelling mystery of his life for over 2,000 years. Even ancient historians were intrigued and tried to figure out the answer. The well known ancient Greek historian Polybius mentioned that Hannibal's men came into conflict with a Celtic tribe, the Allobroges, which was situated near the northern part of the range along the banks of the river Isère. The famous Roman historian Livy, writing over 150 years after Polybius, claimed Hannibal took a southerly route.

It is believed that both historians used the same source, a soldier in Hannibal's army, Sosylus of Lacedaemon, who wrote a history of the Second Punic War. Geographers and historians have pointed to the 6 most likely mountain passes that could have actually been used and then tried to narrow it down by finding one that seems to match the descriptions of both Livy and Polybius. A handful of historians used those accounts to theorize that Hannibal crossed the Alps at the **Col du Montgenèvre** pass, which would have been in the southern part of the range near northwest Italy. That also happened to be one of the better known road passes in the ancient world, and it was used often for diplomacy.

Wherever the crossing, and despite the innumerable difficulties, Hannibal got across. He reached the rolling foothills of Northern Italy several months later, at the head of 20,000 infantry, 4,000 cavalry, and a mere handful of war elephants (the great beasts having fared none too well, as was to be expected, in the mountain passes). If figures relating to his troop numbers before and after his celebrated crossing are to be believed, only half of the men Hannibal marched into the Alps marched back out again, and Hannibal must have known that no supply convoys could ever hope to cross where his army had passed. Nor, with the Roman navy's supremacy in the Mediterranean, could he have much hope of resupply or retreat by sea. Like Caesar would do nearly 170 years later crossing the Rubicon, Hannibal had cast the die. He and his men were left with no choice but victory or death.

Depiction of Hannibal's men crossing the Alps

Costly as it was, Hannibal's choice to cross the Alps was not done so for vainglorious reasons. By appearing suddenly in Northern Italy, crossing terrain that was reckoned to be impassable, Hannibal took the Romans completely by surprise, and the main Roman army that had been mobilised to fight Hannibal was caught completely wrong-footed. When news of Hannibal's appearance reached its commander, Publius Scipio (father of the redoubtable Scipio Africanus, who would cross swords with Hannibal himself in the years to come), he was in the process of pushing his men across the Pyrenees and into Iberia. He quickly loaded his rearguard onto ships, sailed across to Italy, and hurried to intercept Hannibal by forced march.

Scipio engaged Hannibal's forces at Ticinus, but he could only hope to fight a delaying action with the limited troops at his disposal. Hannibal's celebrated Numidian cavalry routed Scipio's forces, and would have killed Scipio himself had it not been for Scipio Africanus's timely rescue. Emboldened by this Roman defeat, the Gauls of the Po valley rose in revolt, sending a large force (around 20,000 men) to join Hannibal's army. Hannibal then marched his force south of Scipio's main base at Placentia, on the Trebia river, cutting him off from the support of Consul Sempronius Longus, who was marching up from southern Italy to come to his aid and bring Hannibal to battle. However, when the provisions promised to his army by the Cisalpine Gauls failed to materialize, Hannibal was forced to abandon his tactically superior position to capture the supply depots at Clastidium, allowing Longus and Scipio to join their forces near the Trebia.

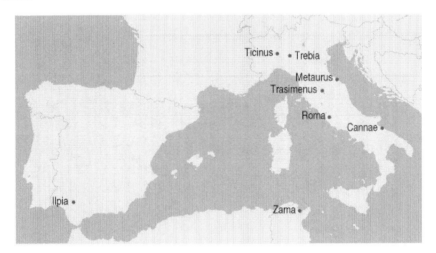

Although the Roman Senate was now hurriedly raising legions in Rome, and two powerful Roman armies had joined together, Hannibal apparently remained unfazed. He promptly marched on the Roman camp on the Trebia, making a show of force and inviting Scipio and Longus to attack him. The two Roman generals obliged, throwing their celebrated infantry across the Trebia in order to attack Hannibal's forces, arrayed on the bluffs above the river. Exhausted by their river crossing, the Roman troops became entangled in a bloody melee with Hannibal's infantry, fighting each other to a standstill until Hannibal unveiled his master stroke. Concealed from the Roman infantry by the terrain until the last moment, his light infantry and cavalry stormed into the Roman flanks, enveloped the entire force and, trapping the legions with their backs to the river, annihilated them. It was a crushing victory for Hannibal, and a disaster for Rome. It would be the first of many.

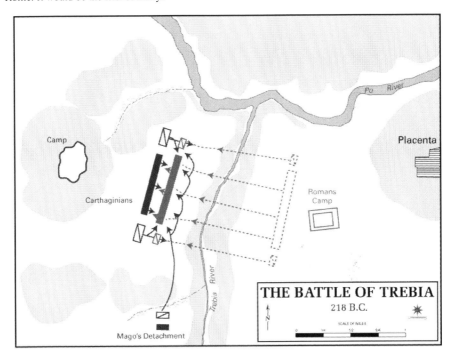

By this point, the campaigning season, which traditionally stopped during the winter months, was virtually over. Hannibal decided to winter his troops in Cisalpine Gaul, but he quickly wore out his welcome there. Possibly because the Gauls were displeased at how Hannibal had used their levies to grind down the Roman forces, the supplies they provided were stilted and ungenerous. In early spring, Hannibal decided to find himself a more secure base and made ready to carry the war into Italy proper. However, despite the winter lull, the Romans had not been idle. Two consular armies, under consuls Servilius and Flaminius, had marched at the beginning of the new year to block Hannibal's routes to the south and east, fortifying their positions there and effectively immuring him within northern Italy. A normal general would have thought himself trapped. Hannibal, however, had a plan. To the south lay the Apennines Mountains and the huge swampy delta of the Arno river, in modern Tuscany, an area reckoned impassable by any army.

Hannibal must have reckoned that after what he had faced in the Alps, he and his men were ready for any challenge. After a brief pause for consideration, he ordered his army to march for the Arno. The Apennines were less of a challenge than the Alps had been, and Hannibal's forces made decent enough time as they crossed through them, but Hannibal himself suffered a debilitating injury, losing an eye to a virulent infection (believed to be conjunctivitis) that kept him bedridden for a spell. His army then descended into the basin of the Arno, but the going was far harder than even Hannibal could have anticipated. The entire region was a festering swamp, with not a single scrap of dry, solid land for his men and horses to sleep on. Hannibal quickly realised he had marched his men into a death-trap. With no choice but to push on, he and his men marched uninterruptedly for four days and three nights, in water and mud that often came up to their waists, with no rest except what they could snatch on their feet. Hundreds, perhaps thousands of Hannibal's men perished on the march. Some were drowned, others were swallowed by quicksand, others contracted malaria or dysentery from drinking the swampy water, and still more simply died of exhaustion. By the end of the march, Hannibal had lost the last of his war elephants, as well as virtually all of his supplies and wheeled transport, but he was now in Etruria, Roman heartland, with both Flaminius and Servilius to the north of him.

As Polybius noted in his account, Hannibal had reached an important crossroad in his campaign. As Polybius wrote, "[Hannibal] calculated that, if he passed the camp and made a descent into the district beyond, Flaminius (partly for fear of popular reproach and partly of personal irritation) would be unable to endure watching passively the devastation of the country but would spontaneously follow him…and give him opportunities for attack." Hannibal needed to bring Flaminius to battle, to avoid the danger of having a large enemy force to his rear, but he found Flaminius too passive to give him the battle he sought.

In order to persuade the Consul – who had a healthy fear of his abilities – to take to the field against him, Hannibal set about ravaging the surrounding Etrurian countryside, sacking towns, burning markets and generally wreaking havoc in the hope that Flaminius would become so incensed that he would be forced to defend the Italian heartland, or that a direct order should arrive from Rome ordering him to do so. Hannibal, though his military strategy was sound, was not as strong in his political choices as he was in battle: by devastating Etruria, he lost support among the local people, whom he might otherwise have been able to lure away from their alliance to Rome. Moreover, despite Hannibal's best efforts, Flaminius stubbornly stayed put in his defensive position. Frustrated by the Roman general's supineness, Hannibal marched around Flaminius's flank and cut him off from Rome, the kind of turning movement in warfare that was rarely used in the ancient world but became standard fare (and often the ultimate strategic goal) over the next 2,000 years. Even with such a massive threat to his lines of supply and communication, Flaminius still refused to march, so Hannibal turned and marched southwards. This time, with the Senate demanding what exactly he was playing at, Flaminius had no choice but to chase him.

Flaminius marched his 30,000 men after Hannibal, but the Carthaginian forces outstripped him. Desperate to bring the enemy to battle, Flaminius pushed recklessly onwards without scouting his line of advance, a mistake which was to cost him dear. On the northern edge of Lake Trasimene, Flaminius marched his army through a narrow defile and onto a small plain that was ringed by wooded mountains, through which his trackers reported Hannibal had marched some time previously. It was only when the last of the Roman forces had marched through the defile that Hannibal swung the jaws of his trap shut: his cavalry rushed forward from concealed positions to close the only gap through which Flaminius's force could retreat, and then his entire army poured howling out of the woods and fell onto the Romans before they had the chance to take up battle positions. In the ensuing desperate melee, virtually the entire Roman army was wiped out: 15,000 or more, including Flaminius himself, were killed, cut down in the melee or drowned in the lake trying to swim to safety. Around 5,000 more Roman soldiers were captured, and the remainder scattered into the hills. In one masterful stroke, Hannibal had disposed of the last field army in Northern Italy, successfully executing antiquity's greatest ambush. Rome herself was now at his mercy.

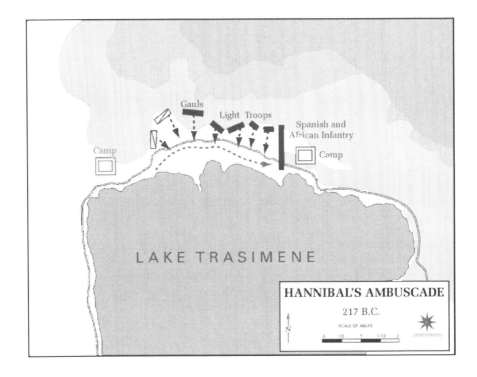

Gauls

Light Troops

Spanish and
African Infantry

Camp

Camp

LAKE TRASIMENE

HANNIBAL'S AMBUSCADE

217 B.C.

SCALE OF MILES

0   1/2   1   1-1/2   2

N

Chapter 3: Rome's Darkest Hour, 216 BC-203 B.C.

Hannibal was now in an ideal position to strike at Rome, but he chose not to do so. If he ever had any siege artillery in his baggage train (no mention is made of it in the original sources) then he lost it in the Alps or in the swamps of the Arno, because he had none available to invest Rome, nor, apparently, the engineering expertise either among his Carthaginian troops or his Gaulish levies to manufacture any. Without siege engines, he could still have chosen to ring the city with earthworks and lay siege to it, but instead he decided to march into Southern Italy, where he hoped to incite revolt among Rome's subject states.

Statue of Fabius Maximus

The Romans, desperate for something, anything, to rid themselves of this Carthaginian Nemesis, appointed General Fabius Maximus as Dictator, an extraordinary measure which was only undertaken in times of the greatest crisis. Maximus, who had a healthy respect for Hannibal's generalship and was painfully aware of what had befallen Roman armies in pitched battles against him, now developed the "Fabian Strategy", which focused on indirect, attritional warfare. This strategy called for relying on skirmishes, ambushes, and dilatory tactics to harass, undermine and frighten Hannibal's forces, avoiding pitched battle which would almost certainly have proven ruinous. Though Maximus's tactics were effective, this indirect mode of warfare was considered dishonourable, even cowardly, by many Romans, who derisively nicknamed him "Cunctator" ("The Delayer").

Frustrated by Maximus's tactics, Hannibal took out his spite by ravaging the country estates and cities of the Apulian region before making his way into Campania, one of the most important agrarian regions in Italy because of its vast fertile plains that produced harvests crucial to feeding the great masses of Rome. Even the threat to the Campanian exports failed to draw Maximus into open battle, but Hannibal was so overzealous in his harrowing of Campania that, he soon realised, come the winter his army would have nothing to live off. Accordingly, he decided to march back to Apulia, but found his path blocked by a number of different Roman contingents that Maximus had placed at crucial passes to bar his way back. Hannibal responded with customary brilliance, by feinting his entire army at a thickly wooded hill, suggesting he was going to march through the forest and ignore the pass, and when the Roman army repositioned to attempt to bar his way, promptly marched his men about and through the pass they had so obligingly left unguarded, a tactical master-stroke which so damaged Maximus's already tarnished reputation as a commander that he was forced to step down as Dictator. As British historian Adrian Goldsworthy noted, the maneuver was "a classic of ancient generalship, finding its way into nearly every historical narrative of the war and being used by later military manuals".

Hannibal spent the winter comfortably ensconced in Apulia, raiding the region to procure supplies for his army and making overtures to the Macedonians, the city-states of Syracuse, and many other erstwhile allies of Rome. He needed their help in the hopes they would provide him with men and supplies which were desperately needed since Carthage stubbornly refused to support him. Despite his successes, Hannibal was not particularly politically beloved at home, with many believing he was being too rash in provoking Rome. Frustrated, Hannibal resumed the campaigning season in the spring of 216 B.C. by capturing the city of Cannae, a crucial supply hub, and placing himself along the line that convoys from the ports and warehouses of the south needed to travel to reach Rome. This was something the Romans could not and did not take lying down. Rome raised the largest army in their city's history, a force of between 80,000 and 100,000 men, and marched south with Consuls Varro and Paullus at the head of the army. This military behemoth disregarded the delaying tactics that Maximus had favored, fully determined to destroy Hannibal once and for all as quickly as possible. Polybius described the unprecedented nature of this Roman army: "The Senate determined to bring eight legions into the field, which had never been done at Rome before, each legion consisting of five thousand men besides allies. ...Most of their wars are decided by one consul and two legions, with their quota of allies; and they rarely employ all four at one time and on one service. But on this occasion, so great was the alarm and terror of what would happen, they resolved to bring not only four but eight legions into the field."

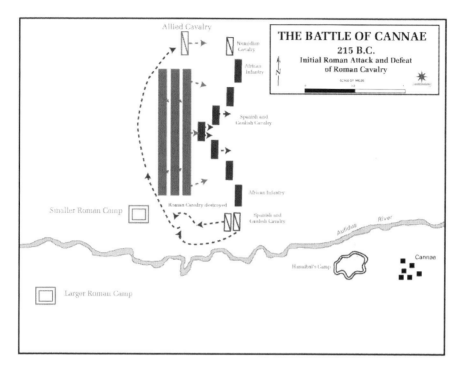

The lines at the beginning of the battle

Despite the massive horde headed his way, Hannibal was ready for them. He encamped his army near the Aufidus, a river not far from Cannae, and waited. His intelligence told him that Consul Varro, the more influential of the two Roman generals, was a firebrand, talented in attack but with a tendency to overreach himself, and Hannibal resolved to use this flaw to his advantage. Hannibal arrayed his army in the open, sure that Varro would be unable to resist the temptation to offer battle, and then deliberately placed his weakest infantry in the center of his battle-line. Varro led the Roman legions straight at the centre of Hannibal's formation, proceeding in characteristic bull-headed fashion and spearheading the assault himself. Hannibal's troops in the center yielded before the legions, as Hannibal had anticipated, sucking the bulk of the Roman force deep into the centre of Hannibal's formation. Meanwhile, the wings of Hannibal's infantry automatically swung against the flanks of the Roman force while Hannibal's cavalry, led by his celebrated general Maharbal, crushed the Roman cavalry and light infantry deployed to protect the formation's flanks and rear and, in so doing, succeeded in encircling it completely. The Roman force now found itself unable to run or maneuver, completely surrounded by Hannibal's forces. It was one of the earliest examples of the pincer movement in the history of warfare.

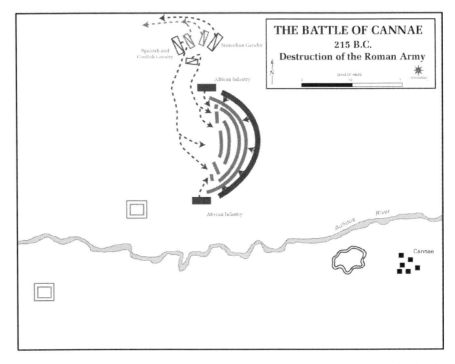

It was a massacre, one of the most vicious battles in the history of the world. Around 75% of the Roman army was cut down in the ensuing melee, which would be in the vicinity of between 50,000-80,000 soldiers depending on which initial estimates are considered to be accurate. Among the casualties was the luckless Consul Paullus, two-thirds of the city's Military Tribunes, a host of officials and noblemen from the most prominent Roman families, and almost a full third of the Senate. Hannibal's army killed so many prominent Romans that his men collected more than 200 gold signets from dead Romans, and he had the rings sent to Carthage to demonstrate his complete victory.

Livy described the scene, "So many thousands of Romans were dying ... Some, whom their wounds, pinched by the morning cold, had roused, as they were rising up, covered with blood, from the midst of the heaps of slain, were overpowered by the enemy. Some were found with their heads plunged into the earth, which they had excavated; having thus, as it appeared, made pits for themselves, and having suffocated themselves." If the casualty numbers are accurate, Hannibal's army slaughtered an average of 600 Roman soldiers every minute until nightfall ended the battle, and less than 15,000 Roman troops escaped, which required cutting their way through the center of Hannibal's army and fleeing to the nearby town of Canusium.

Cannae is still considered one of the greatest tactical victories in the history of warfare. As military historian Theodore Dodge described, "Few battles of ancient times are more marked by ability...than the battle of Cannae. The position was such as to place every advantage on Hannibal's side. The manner in which the far from perfect Hispanic and Gallic foot was advanced in a wedge in échelon... was first held there and then withdrawn step by step, until it had the reached the converse position... is a simple masterpiece of battle tactics. The advance at the proper moment of the African infantry, and its wheel right and left upon the flanks of the disordered and crowded Roman legionaries, is far beyond praise. The whole battle, from the Carthaginian standpoint, is a consummate piece of art, having no superior, few equal, examples in the history of war."

Furthermore, the fact Cannae was a complete victory with the wholesale annihilation of the enemy army made it the textbook example for military commanders to try to duplicate, usually, of course, without success. Cannae was the kind of annihilation that every commander from Caesar to Frederick the Great to Napoleon to Robert E. Lee sought, and that few save Caesar and Napoleon bagged whole armies is a testament as to the near impossibility of achieving a victory like Cannae.

The Battle of Cannae was an unqualified disaster for Rome, unprecedented in the annals of the city, and one with consequences which echoed around the Mediterranean. The Syracusans and Macedonians, now believing that Rome's star was on the wane, abandoned their alliances with the Republic and sided instead with Hannibal. With yet another Roman army decimated, Rome was again at Hannibal's mercy, as Livy noted: "Never before, while the City itself was still safe, had there been such excitement and panic within its walls. I shall not attempt to describe it, nor will I weaken the reality by going into details... it was not wound upon wound but multiplied disaster that was now announced. For according to the reports two consular armies and two consuls were lost; there was no longer any Roman camp, any general, any single soldier in existence; Apulia, Samnium, almost the whole of Italy lay at Hannibal's feet. Certainly there is no other nation that would not have succumbed beneath such a weight of calamity."

In just 20 months, Hannibal had destroyed 3 Roman armies, totaling about 16 legions and upwards of 150,000-200,000 men, and it is estimated that Rome had lost 20% of its adult men. Once again, however, Hannibal inexplicably wavered and opted not to attack Rome itself. Though he still lacked siege equipment, there would almost certainly have been someone among his allies with expertise in siege warfare, but Hannibal refused to march north, choosing instead to stay in southern Italy. Much of the blame for Hannibal's supineness, in this case, remains with the Carthaginian oligarchy, who once again refused to provide him with money, reinforcements, or the siege equipment he so vitally needed. According to legend, after Cannae the Numidian cavalry commander Maharbal suggested that Hannibal march on Rome. When Hannibal resisted, Maharbal was alleged to have said, "Truly the Gods have not bestowed all things upon the same person. Thou knowest indeed, Hannibal, how to conquer, but thou knowest not how to make use of your victory."

Whether Hannibal made the right decision or not, he could certainly have exerted himself a little more. In the event, he chose to capture several cities in southern Italy, and established his headquarters in Capua, one of the richest cities in Southern Italy, which had defected to his side after Cannae, as had much of the southern part of the Italian Peninsula. Hannibal's lassitude during this period, referred to by classical scholars as the "lazings of Capua", is uncharacteristic, but it allowed the Romans to rally. Hannibal contented himself to send a peace delegation to negotiate terms with Rome, but the Senate still refused to deal with Hannibal. Instead, Rome re-dedicated itself to raising more armies and fighting Hannibal.

In the wake of the catastrophe at Cannae, the Roman ruling elite re-evaluated Fabius Maximus's strategy, and began to use his tactics to harass, delay, and whittle down Hannibal's forces in the field, studiously avoiding open battle whenever they could. For years they harried Hannibal's armies, and while there were blunders that allowed Hannibal to lash out (three Roman armies were destroyed in the period between 215 and 212 B.C.) the victories were minor and ultimately meaningless. After almost half a decade of continuous warfare, Apulia was a scorched desert incapable of sustaining an army in the field, and Hannibal was getting no supplies either from his allies or from Carthage. Moreover, his allies were proving to be hopelessly ineffective in the field, meaning he either had to lead the force himself or risk losing one of his field armies. Whenever Hannibal did take command, the results were often devastating for Rome, but decisive victory eluded him. Rome could raise far more troops than Hannibal, unsupported, could ever hope to obtain, and a war of attrition was destined to favor them in the end. The tide was finally turning against Hannibal.

In 211, Hannibal received a massive blow as, while his army was in the field, the Romans besieged and captured, with great loss, his base at Capua. Still reeling from this news, his woes were compounded when he discovered that his Syracusan allies had also been crushed, with Sicily fallen to the Romans, and Philip, the king of Macedon, also defeated and driven out of the Roman dominions. Hannibal himself continued to prove himself a great general, inflicting several notable defeats upon all the armies sent against him, but they were, in the long term, meaningless. He fought on, but continued to lose territories throughout 210 and 209 B.C., and between 208 and 207 B.C. he was pushed ever southwards, finally being forced to retire to Apulia, where he anxiously awaited reinforcements under the command of his brother, Hasdrubal. At the eleventh hour, these reinforcements might have turned the tide, for once he had the troops at his command Hannibal planned to march upon Rome once and for all. However, Hasdrubal never reached Hannibal. He got himself entangled in a battle with the Romans on the Metaurus, and his army was defeated and he himself killed. Hannibal, knowing his situation in Apulia was untenable, was forced to retreat into Bruttium, the southernmost tip of the Italian peninsula, where he was also forced to endure the horror of having his brother's severed head tossed over the walls and into his camp.

For all intents and purposes, Hannibal's campaign in Italy was over. He succeeded in holding on in Bruttium for a further four years, but was never able to push northward and his army was fast dwindling to nothing, with his veterans being killed off and his mercenaries melting away. In 206 B.C., it was reported to him that Roman armies had occupied the entirety of Iberia, driving the Carthaginian forces from the peninsula, a victory obtained by his old enemy Scipio Africanus, who had utterly crushed the Carthaginians at Ilipa. Finally, in 203 B.C., he was peremptorily recalled to Carthage, 15 years and scores of victories after he had first entered Italy in arms. The reason for his recall was simple: Rome was on the march. A massive army, under the command of Scipio "Africanus", the General whose bravery had saved his eponymous father's life at the beginning of Hannibal's Italian campaign, was preparing to attack and destroy Carthage. Rome wanted revenge.

Hannibal, with the rings of the Roman Equestrians he had killed in the battle of Cannae, resting on a Roman standard.

Chapter 4: Rome's Revenge, 203–183 B.C.

While Hannibal had been in Italy, it had been relatively easy for the Carthaginian oligarchy, particularly the Hundred and Four, a federation of powerful traders, and Hannibal's chief political rival, Hanno the Great, to marginalize him. For years his political party, the Barcids, had struggled to obtain even a token amount of funds and troops for his enterprise, but Hannibal's arrival on the scene changed all that. Even his rivals could not deny the simple fact that, all else aside, the man could fight a battle like no other general alive. With Rome threatening invasion,

Hannibal was suddenly the necessary hero of the hour. Bolstering his Italian mercenaries with levies from Africa and Carthage, the Carthaginian ruling elite desperately invested the money that Hannibal had begged for throughout the last decade in order to assemble a scratch force capable of at least presenting an appearance of force against Scipio Africanus's army.

Hannibal can hardly have been thrilled to see the amount of trouble the Carthaginians went to in order to assemble an army that, had he had his way years before, might well have been completely unnecessary. Certainly it appears that he prepared to take the field with less than his customary ardor. At 45, he was still far from old, but ever since he had first left Carthage he had spent virtually all of his adult life fighting, and the strain was beginning to tell. By all accounts he was in poor health, and prone to sickness. Indeed, rather than seek to bring Scipio Africanus to battle, in 202 B.C. Hannibal met the Roman general and attempted to talk peace. The army the Carthaginians had succeeded in gathering, not to mention the presence of Hannibal himself, convinced Scipio that he might be well-advised to seek a diplomatic solution, and the two began negotiations, which were helped by the fact that both generals recognized a kindred spirit in the other. Through negotiations, Carthage was forced to give up much, especially considering Hannibal's roster of victories, but Rome's star was on the rise once again, and Hannibal knew he could not hope to win a protracted war.

Hannibal agreed to Scipio's terms: Carthage would lose possession of Iberia and the Mediterranean islands, renouncing all claims to overseas territories but maintaining its heartland and African possessions, with the exception of the Numidian kingdom of Masinissa, who had declared for Rome. Reparations would be made, Scipio demanded, to Rome itself and to the countless families which Carthage's wars had decimated, and the Carthaginian army and fleet must both be reduced in numbers, in order for them to never again threaten Rome's supremacy. Hannibal, who recognised these terms, though harsh, as probably the best deal Carthage was likely to achieve, acceded to them, but the proposed peace between he and Scipio never happened. While the negotiations were going on, a Roman fleet which had gotten itself stranded upon the coast of Tunisia was seized by the Carthaginian navy and ransacked of all its supplies and equipment. When Scipio heard of this, he furiously demanded reparations, but, unaccountably, the Carthaginian oligarchy high-handedly turned him down. Perhaps they felt secure enough with Hannibal at the head of an army on Carthaginian soil to defy Rome, or perhaps the terms of the treaty stung their pride. Whatever their reasons, they could not have committed a bigger diplomatic error if they had gone out of their way to do so. Scipio departed the negotiations in a rage. There would be no terms.

Engraving of the Battle of Zama

On October 19th, 202 BC, on the plain of Zama, in modern Tunisia, battle was joined. Scipio Africanus led 34,000 Roman legionary infantry, including veteran survivors of Cannae, who had a score to settle with Hannibal, and 9,000 crack Numidian cavalry (the same heavy horse which Hannibal's general Maharbal had used to such devastating effect against the Romans for two decades). Hannibal himself marched to stop him with 45,000 Italian, Iberian, Gaulish and North African infantry (both mercenary and levied), 4,000 cavalry, and around 80 war elephants. For the first time in one of the battles of the Second Punic War, Hannibal had the infantry advantage and Rome had the cavalry advantage.

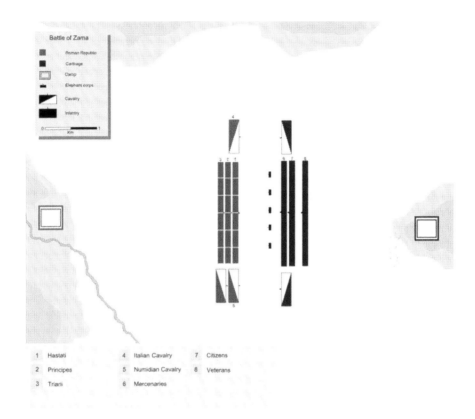

1	Hastati	4	Italian Cavalry	7	Citizens
2	Principes	5	Numidian Cavalry	8	Veterans
3	Triarii	6	Mercenaries		

Hannibal deployed his cavalry on the wings, then placed three lines of infantry, with his Italian veterans in reserve, behind his war elephants, which were to be his secret weapon. Scipio countered by placing his own infantry in three lines, with his veteran heavy infantry in reserve and his own cavalry, which outnumbered Hannibal's by more than two to one, on the flanks. Hannibal opened the battle by pushing forward his war elephants and light infantry, but Scipio checked their advance before they could smash into his battle-lines by unleashing a cloud of skirmishers who harried the elephants with storms of arrows and javelins, while the Roman cavalry blew trumpets to confuse and frighten the elephants, several of which turned the way they had come and charged into the Carthaginian left flank, creating chaos there. Scipio also intentionally opened gaps in his own line for the elephants to drive through harmlessly. Masinissa took advantage of this to charge home against the cavalry on that flank and drive it from the field, but he found himself embroiled in a chase orchestrated on the fly by Hannibal as the Carthaginian cavalry lured him away from the main battle.

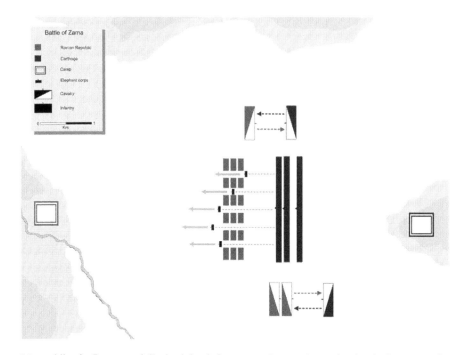

Meanwhile, the Roman and Carthaginian infantry were hammering each other in the center of the battle-line, with both sides momentarily gaining the advantage, only to be driven back in turn. The battle raged for hours, with neither side able to gain the upper hand, but eventually Masinissa, who had chased the Carthaginian cavalry clean off the field with his superior numbers, returned and charged the Carthaginian forces from behind, enveloping them. Scipio rallied his faltering and exhausted troops to one last great effort and they fell upon the Carthaginian troops, which were trapped and unable to maneuver.

Like Hannibal's masterpiece at Cannae, but this time with the roles inverted, the encircled force had nowhere to run. Thousands were cut down where they stood, with only around a tenth of Hannibal's original force, including Hannibal himself, succeeding in breaking free and escaping. For Carthage, the battle was an utter catastrophe, with over 20,000 dead and 20,000 taken prisoner, most of which were grievously wounded. Hannibal's first defeat was so dire that he lost all credibility in Carthage, and his enemies used it to blacken his reputation and forced him to surrender his generalship. With no army in the field, Carthage sued for peace, at far more costly terms than those which they could have accepted with no further loss of life.

Now that Carthage had surrendered virtually all military ambition, Hannibal himself devoted himself to politics. He secured his election to chief magistrate through the support of the Barcid party and introduced highly successful political and financial reforms, much to the chagrin of his rivals. Hannibal was so successful as a politician that Carthage, despite still being hampered by a heavy war indemnity, prospered to the point that the Romans demanded he step down as magistrate. Rather than do so, Hannibal voluntarily went into exile, worried he might expose Carthage to new Roman reprisals.

For the next eight years he was received as a mercenary commander at many middle-eastern courts, particularly at the court of Antiochus of Syria, in Ephesus, who was preparing for an invasion of Italy. Hannibal, ever conscious of his oath to his father, offered to take command of Antiochus's troops, but Antiochus declined the offer and was soundly beaten the following year. Antiochus, seeking a scapegoat, blamed Hannibal and proposed to sell him to the Romans, prompting him to move yet again. Strabo and Plutarch both wrote that Hannibal spent some time at the court of Artaxias I, and he eventually made his way back to Asia Minor and fought with Prusias I of Bithynia against King Eumenes II of Pergamon, a Roman ally. It was said that during one naval battle, Hannibal devised the idea of filling large pots with venomous snakes and throwing them onto the enemies' ships, wreaking havoc. After Hannibal defeated Eumenes in a couple of land battles, Rome demanded that Bythinia surrender Hannibal to them. The frightened Prusias complied, but Hannibal was determined not to let himself be taken alive and poisoned himself at Lybissa, in Asia Minor, in 183 B.C. Roman historians speculated he had long carried the poison in a ring in case he needed to use it in battle, but poison kept that long might very well no longer be effective. In any case, Hannibal left a letter behind which dryly remarked that his death should provide some comfort to the Romans by relieving them of the fear they had felt for so long, since they apparently could not abide waiting patiently for an old man to die. "Let us relieve the Romans from the anxiety they have so long experienced, since they think it tries their patience too much to wait for an old man's death."

Chapter 5: Hannibal's Legacy

What to make, then, of Hannibal? Certainly, despite the smattering of defeats he accumulated later on in his career, he was one of the most brilliant generals in ancient history, peerless save for, perhaps, Alexander and Caesar. Yet, as his general Maharbal famously remarked, Hannibal seemed to know how to win a battle, but not how to completely capitalize off of it. Half a dozen times during the course of his Italian campaign he could have marched on Rome and perhaps ended the war with a Carthaginian victory, but for various reasons he chose not to do so. Much of the blame for these decisions lies with the indecisiveness of the Carthaginian oligarchy, but Hannibal must bear his own portion of responsibility.

Nevertheless, despite these perceived failings, Hannibal was truly a figure which, even as he lived, was larger than life. His decades of relentless anti-Roman warfare transformed him into a monster in their eyes, with virtually no Roman family who could claim that they had not lost a family member to Hannibal's forces. It is telling that no matter how badly Hannibal defeated the Romans, they despised him so greatly that the Senate refused to negotiate with him, even from a position of great weakness. Hannibal was Rome's bogeyman, their nemesis, and long after his time, whenever Rome faced a disaster, Roman Senators would describe the disaster as *"Hannibal ante portas"* ("Hannibal before the Gates").

It is perhaps the greatest testament to his generalship and his character that the Romans themselves, his sworn enemies for most of his life, erected a statue of him in their Forum, making clear that they considered their victory in the Second Punic War Rome's greatest accomplishment to date. The greatest boast a Roman soldier could make, even in defeat, was "I fought against Hannibal".

Of course, Hannibal's legacy extended far beyond personality and psychology. There is a universal consensus that Hannibal was one of the greatest generals in history, and arguably the greatest. During the American Civil War, the Lincoln Administration was greatly concerned about General William Tecumseh Sherman cutting his supply lines and marching through enemy territory without any lines of communication for three months. Hannibal's armies stayed in Italy without Carthage's help for the better part of two decades. In the 1911 Encyclopoedia Britannica, Maximilian Otto Bismarck Caspari described Hannibal thusly:

"As to the transcendent military genius of Hannibal there cannot be two opinions. The man who for fifteen years could hold his ground in a hostile country against several powerful armies and a succession of able generals must have been a commander and a tactician of supreme capacity. In the use of strategies and ambuscades he certainly surpassed all other generals of antiquity. Wonderful as his achievements were, we must marvel the more when we take into account the grudging support he received from Carthage. As his veterans melted away, he had to organize fresh levies on the spot. We never hear of a mutiny in his army, composed though it was of North Africans, Iberians and Gauls. Again, all we know of him comes for the most part from hostile sources. The Romans feared and hated him so much that they could not do him justice. Livy speaks of his great qualities, but he adds that his vices were equally great, among which he singles out his more than Punic perfidy and an inhuman cruelty. For the first there would seem to be no further justification than that he was consummately skillful in the use of ambuscades. For the latter there is, we believe, no more ground than that at certain crises he acted in the general spirit of ancient warfare. Sometimes he contrasts most favorably with his enemy. No such brutality stains his name as that perpetrated by Claudius Nero on the vanquished Hasdrubal. Polybius merely says that he was accused of cruelty by the Romans and of avarice by the Carthaginians. He had indeed bitter enemies, and his life was one continuous struggle against destiny. For steadfastness of purpose, for organizing capacity and a mastery of military science he has perhaps never had an equal."

Whether Hannibal is the greatest general ever or merely one of the greatest makes for a good armchair debate, but regardless of his ranking, his influence on military tactics is undeniable. In particular, Hannibal demonstrated that warfare was about more than superior tactics in battle; Hannibal's success owed as much to his strategic outmaneuvering of his enemies. As historian Theodore Dodge notes, "Hannibal excelled as a tactician. No battle in history is a finer sample of tactics than Cannae. But he was yet greater in logistics and strategy. No captain ever marched to and fro among so many armies of troops superior to his own numbers and material as fearlessly and skillfully as he. No man ever held his own so long or so ably against such odds. Constantly overmatched by better soldiers, led by generals always respectable, often of great ability, he yet defied all their efforts to drive him from Italy, for half a generation. Excepting in the case of Alexander, and some few isolated instances, all wars up to the Second Punic War, had been decided largely, if not entirely, by battle-tactics. Strategic ability had been comprehended only on a minor scale. Armies had marched towards each other, had fought in parallel order, and the conqueror had imposed terms on his opponent. Any variation from this rule consisted in ambuscades or other stratagems. That war could be waged by avoiding in lieu of seeking battle; that the results of a victory could be earned by attacks upon the enemy's communications, by flank-maneuvers, by seizing positions from which safely to threaten him in case he moved, and by other devices of strategy, was not understood..."

Hannibal has always had his share of admirers in the centuries that followed, from Schlieffen to George Patton, but once again the greatest tribute to his ultimate military legacy was paid by Ancient Rome. Understanding Hannibal better than anyone, Rome completely adjusted the way it conducted war after the Battle of Cannae, At Cannae, the Roman infantry used the phalanx formation popularized by the Ancient Greeks, but that massed formation proved incapable of maneuvering once enveloped in Hannibal's pincer assault. Moreover, the Romans had their high command alternate between two consuls at the head of the army, which made for a poor and confusing line of chain of command. After Cannae, Rome reorganized their units to that they could mass together like a traditional phalanx but retain independent maneuverability by splitting into columns. Rome also did away with their binary leadership command structure and began relying on more professional forces instead of citizen armies.

The effect these changes had on Rome's destiny cannot be understated. Rome turned itself into the greatest military machine on the planet over the next several centuries, and having one consul at the head of legions instead of two created army loyalties to the consul in command, instead of Rome itself. This of course laid the groundwork for the civil wars that ultimately led to Caesar's destruction of the Roman Republic and the implementation of the Roman Empire. Thus, ironically, it was another of antiquity's greatest generals, Julius Caesar, who fulfilled Hannibal's goal of destroying the Roman Republic, as a result of Roman changes made in response to the carnage Hannibal inflicted upon them.

Certainly Hannibal would have relished that as his ultimate legacy.

Bibliography

Readers interested in learning more about Hannibal's remarkable life should refer to the ancient sources of Livy, Polybius, and Juvenal. Those looking for a more modern take on the Carthaginian general can consult the following excellent books:

A detailed discussion on where Hannibal crossed the Alps can be found at http://www.livius.org/ha-hd/hannibal/alps.html

Cotrell, Leonard: *Hannibal: Enemy of Rome*, (1992)

Bradford, Ernle: *Hannibal* (2000)

Peddie, John: *Hannibal's War* (2005)

Julius Caesar

Chapter 1: The Essence of Power – Caesar's Early Life

"If you must break the law, do it to seize power: in all other cases observe it." - Caesar

For a man destined to become the most famous man of history's most famous empire, the dearth of information surrounding Julius Caesar's early life and upbringing is somewhat surprising. Born Gaius Julius Caesar on July 12th, 100 BC, Caesar was the son of an ancient but minor patrician family, the Gens Iulia, who traced their ancestry back to one of the legendary founding figures of Rome, the Trojan hero Aeneas. Caesar's adopted heir, Augustus, would later commission Virgil to write the *Aeneid*. Ironically, the name Caesar would hold an imperial status across multiple continents, but the origin of the term "Caesar", technically his *cognomen* or "inherited nickname", is not precisely known, with ancient biographers ascribing it to the color of the first Caesar's eyes or the thickness of his hair (respectively *caesiis* or *caesaries* in Latin). For his own part, Caesar understandably favored a more martial interpretation, which had it that his ancestor had slain an elephant in battle.

One of the well-documented things about Caesar was that he was afflicted with what the Romans called the *Morbus Comitialis*, a form of epilepsy, which he managed to conceal from all but his closest associates throughout his life. While the diagnosis of epilepsy comes from what was written by Suetonius and Plutarch, some historians believe the ailment may have been a byproduct of malaria, and others have speculated that he suffered severe migraines. Still others believe he suffered a different form of seizure than epileptic seizures. Whatever it was, had Caesar's debilitating ailment been made common knowledge among the Republic during his life, there's no telling how history might have been changed.

What is also known about Caesar is that he grew up in a time of relative social and political turmoil, which is saying something considering Rome's burgeoning empire was constantly experiencing turbulent volatility. Around the turn of the century, war was being waged both on the Italian peninsula and abroad, with domestic politics pitting the conservative, aristocratic *optimates* against the populist, reformist *populares*. When Caesar was in his teens, this tension ultimately escalated into an all-out war that involved him on a deeply personal level. That is because one of the leading *populares* was his uncle Gaius Marius, a military visionary who had restructured the legions and extended the privileges of land ownership and citizenship to legionaries on condition of successful completion of a fixed term of service. In the years just before Caesar's birth, Marius had waged a successful campaign against several Germanic tribes. Having earned eternal fame in the Eternal City, Marius was appointed a consul several times, but in 88 B.C. he entered into conflict with his erstwhile protégé, the optimate Lucius Cornelius Sulla (whom Caesar must also have been acquainted with), over command of the army to be dispatched against Mithridates of Pontus, an enemy of Rome and its Greek allies.

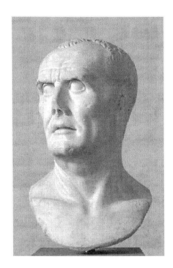

Bust of Gaius Marius, at Munich Glyptothek

Ironically, Marius's reforms had made the legions fiercely loyal to their individual generals, rather than the state, which allowed Sulla to march his army against Rome and force Marius into exile. With that, Rome's first civil war was officially under way.

Sulla's triumph proved short-lived, however. Just as Sulla departed for a campaign than Marius returned at the head of a scratch army of veterans and mercenaries, taking over the city and purging it of Sulla's optimate supporters. Though Marius died in 86 BC, his party remained in power, allowing Caesar to exploit his connection with his late uncle the following year when, at the age of 15, he was named High Priest of Jupiter, a state office of high honor. By that time, Caesar was also the patriarch of his family, with his father having passed away the previous year. It was a double responsibility which Caesar, despite his youthful age, proved more than capable of dealing with. Due to the social conventions that came with the post of High Priest, he was forced to break off a previous engagement to a relatively lowborn girl and instead take as a bride a young girl named Cornelia, the daughter of Sulla's ally Lucius Cornelius Cinna.

Bust of Sulla

Marius had reoccupied Rome while Sulla had been busy crushing Mithridates of Pontus, but with his death Cinna became the most powerful man in Rome itself. After Sulla finished mopping up the last scraps of resistance, he intended to take back Rome for himself at the head of his legions. He landed in the south of Italy and fought his way up the peninsula, defeating the armies dispatched from Rome to stop him. Some legions, including Cinna's, rose up in spontaneous revolt and went over to Sulla's side, and Cinna was murdered by his own men in the uprising. Sulla entered Rome in 82 B.C., becoming the first and only man to attack and conquer both Rome and Athens.

Upon his successful return to Rome, Sulla proclaimed himself *Dictator*, an all-powerful legislative authority which normally could be only vested in times of extraordinary crisis and never for more than a period of six months. Sulla's supporters went on a rampage across Rome, some of whom disinterred Marius's body and dismembered it before throwing the pieces into the Tiber River. Of course, the purge included the murder of Marius's most prominent supporters as well, all in an effort to allow Sulla to proclaim himself Dictator for Life.

As Marius's nephew, Caesar was a natural target of Sulla's purges, and he was stripped of lands, wealth and office. Caesar would have lost his wife too, but he refused to divorce her, earning himself a death sentence for his defiance that forced him to go into hiding. It was only the intervention of his mother's family, which included a number of pro-Sulla optimates, that managed to avert Sulla's wrath and got Caesar's death sentence commuted.

Caesar, wary of the fickle nature of dictators and no doubt sickened by what he had witnessed during the purges, decided to leave Rome and enlisted in the army, something which would have been impossible as High Priest of Jupiter; his office forbade him from touching horses, witnessing armies, or spending a night outside the city of Rome. Had Sulla not stripped Caesar of his title, the world might never have known his military genius.

Chapter 2: The Path to Consulship

"Fortune, which has a great deal of power in other matters but especially in war, can bring about great changes in a situation through very slight forces." - Caesar

Caesar may have excelled in his youth as a High Priest, but it was his military career that started him down the path to becoming an emperor, and at least before Napoleon, he was the general all subsequent generals hoped to emulate in the field.

Before he could become Napoleon's idol, however, Caesar started off his career as a common soldier. But Caesar was not a nameless face lost in the crowd. He soldiered with flair, serving with distinction in Asia and Cilicia, and after his valor during the siege of Mytilene he was ultimately awarded with the Civic Crown, Rome's second highest military decoration at the time. At the same time, Caesar appeared to grow very friendly with the King of Bithynia, Nicomedes, when he was sent on a diplomatic mission to negotiate the use of his fleet, so much so that rumours began of a supposed homosexual relationship between the two. Though Caesar always dismissed that as idle slander, political opponents continued to mock him as the Queen of Bithynia.

Meanwhile, things in Rome were beginning to change. In 80 B.C. Sulla ended his dictatorship – much to Caesar's disgust – and after having reestablished the consular offices he died two years later in 78 B.C. With Sulla gone, Caesar felt secure enough to return to the city, where he took up a highly successful career as an advocate and orator, displaying so much talent for rhetoric that it was said he might have been capable of eclipsing even the famous Cicero himself. Caesar was also noted for his body language, gesturing incredulously while pleading with a high-pitched voice.

Caesar had been a war hero, but he had not yet been a general. And he might never have been one if not for events outside his control. Having proven successful as a legal advocate, and dedicated to prove himself the best speaker the city of Rome could produce, Caesar boarded a ship headed to Greece in order to study with Cicero's former tutor. But Caesar never reached his destination; his ship was attacked by Cilician pirates and Caesar himself was captured and held prisoner on the small island of Pharmacusa.

Caesar reacted to his captivity with equanimity, displaying the cool arrogance that would become one of his defining character traits. Caesar cheerfully promised all the pirates that he would come back for them and crucify them all, a threat the pirates seem to have foolishly found humorous. Upon being informed that the pirates meant to ask for a ransom of twenty talents of silver, Caesar replied with aplomb: "Twenty? Caesar is worth twice as much, and more. Ask for fifty". The pirates accordingly did, and got them, too. What they also reaped, however, was Caesar's punishment. As soon as he was free, Caesar raised a fleet, hunted down the pirates, and personally had them crucified to the last man, as he had promised them he would do.

Following these exploits, and a daring campaign on the Roman border with Pontus which saw Caesar raise a scratch force of soldiers and repel a Pontine invasion, Caesar was elected military tribune upon his return to Rome in 73 B.C. It would be the beginning of a fairly rapid political ascent. Although several legions were employed during the following two years in crushing the revolt of the former gladiator Spartacus, Caesar appears to have played no part in the war, or at least none that was recorded. In 69 B.C. Cornelia died, possibly in childbirth, and Caesar once again departed Rome, this time bound for Hispania (Spain) where he was to serve as *quaestor*. This appointment was followed by his marriage to Pompeia (Sulla's grand-daughter, interestingly) and a string of relatively prominent political posts in Rome, where Caesar had the Appian Way rebuilt in his capacity as *aedile* and restored some of Marius' public works, in tribute to an uncle it appears Caesar cared deeply about.

In 63 B.C. Caesar allied himself with the powerful politician Titus Labienus to prosecute Gaius Rabirius, an optimate Senator, for murder. Caesar managed to defeat Cicero, who was responsible for Rabirius's defence, and this high-profile case gave him the necessary political ascendancy to run for the post of *Pontifex Maximus*, or High Priest of all of Rome. He secured his election despite accusations of bribery and demagogic oratory.

Caesar continued to be dogged by scandal when, shortly thereafter, he was accused of involvement in the Catiline conspiracy to seize power. Considered one of Rome's greatest scandals, the conspiracy included Catiline's attempt to strip the Senate of the power and eventually put an end to the Republic. The unraveling of the conspiracy, and Catiline's ultimate fate, were secured by Cicero in a famous series of speeches in the Senate, known as the Catiline Orations. In the first of the speeches, Cicero thunderously denounced Catiline while Catiline sat in the Senate, and all of the senators sitting next to Catiline slowly flocked away from him as Cicero spoke. Catiline would eventually die at the head of a small army of supporters against Roman legions, and everyone associated with his name and the conspiracy were political anathema in Rome.

Cicero Denouncing Catiline, **Cesare Maccari famous painting**

Despite attempts to impugn Caesar by accusing him of being associated with Catiline, the accusations did not stick. Caesar's lifelong rival, the optimate Marcus Porcius Cato, saw Caesar being passed a note during the trials of the Catiline conspirators and, smelling treason, demanded it be read out loud. Caesar coolly complied; it was a sentimental love-letter from Cato's half-sister, Servilia, to Caesar himself. Servilia also happened to be the mother of a young man named Marcus Brutus.

In 62 B.C., in his capacity as Pontifex Maximus, Caesar hosted the festival of *bona dea,* which was prohibited to men. However, a man named Publius Clodius Pulcher ("the handsome") was caught entering the festival dressed as a woman, supposedly in order to seduce Pompeia. Despite Pulcher being acquitted – he was from a very prominent family – Caesar later divorced Pompeia, famously explaining, "Caesar's wife must be above suspicion".

Although he had climbed several rungs up the political ladder, Caesar was at another crossroads in his life. Once again, external factors influenced his next major move. At this time, Caesar was heavily in debt, a result of much spending during his time as an *aedile* and his efforts to secure his election. He turned to Marcus Licinius Crassus, an extremely wealthy patrician who was fresh off his suppression of the famous slave rebellion led by Spartacus and eventually became a part of the First Triumvirate with Caesar and Pompey the Great. Crassus' patronage helped position Caesar to be appointed governor of Hispania Ulterior. In order to maintain political office, which made him immune from prosecution for his debts, he left for modern day Spain before his praetorship expired. Caesar made this move knowing that governors were immune from prosecution, but governors also had vitally important military responsibilities via command of whatever legions were garrisoned in their territory. It would be as governor that Caesar's military career truly took off, starting with his victories over a couple of local tribes. These military successes earned him the title Imperator, the Roman equivalent of the title of Commander.

Bust of Crassus

Having been designated Imperator, Caesar once again found himself having to make a crucial decision. The title of imperator entitled Caesar to one of Rome's most famous and prestigious public ceremonies, a triumph, which would ensure his popularity and practically make him a king for a day. At the same time, however, he badly wanted to run for Consul in 59 B.C., which would require being a private citizen. Since the triumph would not come before the election, Caesar had to choose between the two, and he ultimately decided to use his newly gained prominence to run for Consul, Rome's highest magisterial position at the time.

Despite rumours of corruption, vote-buying, and pandering by virtually all the candidates involved, chiefly Caesar himself, Caesar secured his election alongside the supine Marcus Bibulus, a long-standing optimate. Caesar himself had long since aligned himself with the *populares*, his uncle Marius's old faction. Caesar had been heavily sponsored in his run for Consul by Crassus, but now, in a brilliant stroke of diplomacy, he succeeded in reconciling

Crassus with Gnaeus Pompey Magnus, Rome's powerful and vastly successful general who had made a name for himself campaigning against Spartacus, Greek pirates, and Pontus. Alongside Pompey and Crassus, Caesar established the First Triumvirate, with Crassus supplying the funds, Pompey the muscle, and Caesar the political clout necessary for governing the city. Though later triumvirates officially wielded power, like the Second Triumvirate (which formed in the wake of Caesar's assassination and included his heir Augustus and longtime general Mark Antony), this First Triumvirate acted behind the scenes to run Rome unofficially. Thus, even though Bibulus was ostensibly Caesar's equal in power, in fact Caesar utterly ignored him, at one point passing a law for land redistribution to the poor in spite of his opposition. Roman satirists referred to his time in office as "the consulship of Julius and Caesar".

Bust of Pompey

Caesar knew that the vast amount of irregularities that had marked his consulship would almost certainly lead to prosecution by his many enemies as soon as his immunity expired with his term of office. Yet again, like he had to secure the governorship of Hispania, Caesar politically maneuvered to ensure his appointment to the governorship of Cisalpine Gaul (which was not in France, as the name might suggest, but in Northern Italy), Transalpine Gaul (Southern France), and Illyricum, an appointment which also came with the command of four legions. He departed for Gaul almost as soon as his term as Consul had ended, barely a step ahead of the law.

Chapter 3: Becoming a Military Legend - The Gallic Wars, 58-52 B.C.

Vercingetorix lays down his arms to Caesar, by Lyonel Royer (1899)

"I have fought sixty battles and I have learned nothing which I did not know at the beginning. Look at Caesar; he fought the first like the last." – Napoleon Bonaparte

In the first 40 years of his life, Caesar's political instincts had been matched only by his prodigious talent for spending money. Caesar's run as consul had left him vastly in debt, and he owed more money than even Crassus could rightly afford to part with. But as Caesar well knew, a Roman governorship was traditionally an extremely lucrative post, with the option of either taxing the province dry or leading military campaigns with the legions garrisoned there and then plundering opponents after successful battles.

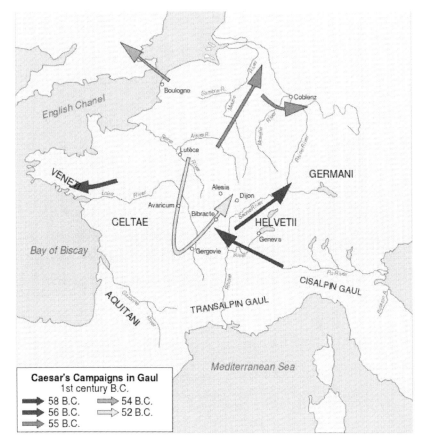

Caesar's Campaigns in Gaul
1st century B.C.

58 B.C.
56 B.C.
55 B.C.
54 B.C.
52 B.C.

Though he had proven himself a remarkably successful statesman, as governor Caesar opted for the latter choice. His previous military experience had proven he was an excellent soldier, and he had at his disposal four crack veteran legions, the 7th, 8th, 9th and 10th, the same men that had served under him in Spain. Using the pretext that several of Rome's Gaul allies had been defeated by the Suebi, a Germanic tribe which seemed intent upon migrating south and threatening Roman territories, Caesar advanced into Gaul and defeated them. Concerned by this sudden escalation in aggression, tribes in the north began to posture for a possible war. Caesar viewed that as an escalation of hostilities and, in turn, raised two new legions and marched upon the united tribes, who were marshalling their strength in the province inhabited by the wealthy and powerful Belgae (modern Belgium).

For the first time in his career, Caesar had blundered. Emboldened by his early successes against the warlike Suebi and perhaps thinking that the tribes were far too fragmented to unite against him, he marched straight into a trap at the Sabis River, where, in 57 B.C., the allied general Boduognatus caught his legions in the open while they were making the crossing. The light footmen and cavalry, mostly members of the Atrebates, Virumandui, and Belgae, succeeded in routing the Roman skirmishers and cavalry, then turning to savage the individual Roman legions and baggage train, most of whose soldiers had been unable to arm themselves properly and were rallying around any standard they could find. Meanwhile, the heavy infantry, comprised of Nervii, had come up and succeeded in driving a wedge between the four legions that made up the main force of Caesar's army. The situation was so desperate that Caesar himself was forced to take up sword and shield to rally his troops, and he was likely only saved from annihilation by the bitter fight his soldiers put up, which allowed the 8th and 9th Legions, which had been deployed a mile to the rear with the baggage train, to reach the battlefield by forced march and relieve him.

The arrival of fresh troops turned the tide, and the Gaulish light infantry and cavalry were driven from the field by the Roman missile troops, their light armour proving no match for the hail of javelins, sling bullets, and arrows that was being hurled their way. The Nervii, an extremely warlike people, refused to retreat or surrender even when they had been surrounded, and were cut down to the last man. Caesar's use of vast arrays of missile troops, and the fact that each individual legionary was a javelineer as well as a swordsman, was instrumental in securing this and later victories, as the Gauls were typically lightly armored and did not deploy many ranged weapons.

The victory at Sabis left Caesar in control of Belgica, the province inhabited by the Belgae, and he followed this success by conquering the vast majority of what was left of Gaul in the following year, advancing with a swiftness and economy of movement which would become a characteristic of his later military campaigns. In 55 B.C., following a Germanic invasion of Gaul by a tribe who had doubtless sensed weakness in the destabilised and newly conquered territory, Caesar built a bridge across the Rhine and pillaged the territory there as an indication that further incursions would not be tolerated. That same year he led the first Romans into Britain, accusing tribes there of aiding the Gauls against him. With winter fast approaching, Caesar's forces did not make their way far into the mainland that year, but the following year, 54 B.C., Caesar's men advanced into the island's interior and conquered a large swath of territory before a revolt in Gaul due to poor harvests once again drew him back across the Channel. The Romans eventually established enough of a presence to set up the outpost of Londinium, which ultimately morphed into one of the world's most famous cities today, London.

Despite Caesar's military successes, the political situation in Rome was deteriorating. Caesar had succeeded in securing a confirmation for his posting as governor for a further five years, not least thanks to his considerable military successes, but he was growing ever more estranged from Pompey the Great, who resented the younger man's ascendancy as a general and realized it threatened to eclipse him. When Caesar's daughter Julia, whom he had married to Pompey to cement their alliance before assuming the governorship, died in childbirth, the last link between the two men was severed. And when Crassus was killed campaigning in the East in 53 B.C., the Triumvirate came to an abrupt end.

Caesar wished to return to Rome to establish his political position there, but in 52 B.C. all of Gaul rose up in arms against him under the leadership of Vercingetorix of the Avernii, who was named High King. Vercingetorix turned out to be a canny fighter who avoided open battles against the superior Roman forces, and he even managed to defeat Caesar's men in several skirmishes. Eventually, however, Caesar lay siege to Vercingetorix and his men around Alesia and, despite being attacked front and rear by Vercingetorix's defenders and other Gauls who came to try to lift the siege, succeeded in defeating them both and taking the stronghold. This effectively marked the end of large-scale resistance in Gaul and brought it firmly under Roman control.

Caesar's successful campaigns in Gaul have become the stuff of military legend, in part because he had the foresight to document them himself. Caesar himself wrote a famous firsthand account of the Gallic Wars, apparently from notes he had kept during the campaigns, and he wrote *Commentarii de Bello Gallico* (Commentaries on the Gallic War) in the third person. Caesar's account described the campaigning and the battles, all as part of a propaganda campaign to win the popularity of the Roman people. As a result, he left out inconvenient facts, including how much of a fortune he made plundering, but the work still remains popular today, and it is still used to teach Latin.

Chapter 4: Becoming Dictator, 50-46 B.C.

"The die is cast." – Caesar upon crossing the Rubicon.

By the end of the Gallic wars, the alliance between Caesar and Pompey had devolved from alliance to rivalry, and when his governorship ended in 50 B.C., Pompey was ready to gain an upperhand in Rome. In 50 B.C., with his term as governor having ended, Caesar received a formal order by the Senate, largely the product of Pompey's machinations, to disband his army and return to Rome, but Caesar was certain that he was going to be held to account for his debts and other irregularities. Assuming that any trial he participated would likely be a witch-hunt specifically designed to permanently tarnish him, he would have none of it.

Refusing to obey the Senate, Pompey worked to have Caesar accused of treason. Things finally came to a head in 49 B.C. Leaving the majority of his forces in Gaul, Caesar headed south for Italy that January at the head of the 13th Legion, despite repeated remonstrations by the Senate and threats by Pompey. That month, Caesar and his men crossed the Rubicon River into Italy, thus entering Italy as invaders, and it's likely that similar exploits by his uncle Marius and Sulla were playing in his mind. According to Suetonius and Plutarch, as his troops filed by, he famously quoted the Greek playwright Menander, remarking: "The die is cast".

With Rome's most famous civil war now having started, Pompey was assigned by the Senate to defend Rome, but he apparently felt he did not have enough forces to confront Caesar. Pompey chose to abandon the city without giving battle, citing the inexperience of his troops when compared to Caesar's veterans as his reason for retreating, despite having vastly superior numbers. Caesar formally entered Rome shortly thereafter, taking control of the city and being recognised as Dictator by the senators who still remained.

Of course, with Pompey and his men still a threat, Caesar hadn't won yet. Leaving his principle subordinate Mark Antony to govern Rome for him, Caesar marched north and quickly defeated forces loyal to Pompey in Spain. He then turned south to pursue Pompey and several senators (mostly optimates) who were loyal to him, all of whom were still on the run. Pompey managed to slip away from Caesar's clutches and headed for nearby Greece, leading Caesar to cross the Mediterranean and disembark his men in Greece.

Pompey finally gave battle at Greece, quickly demonstrating why he had earned the title Magnus. The older general displayed a flash of his former self when he savaged Caesar's vastly outnumbered army at the Battle of Dyrrachium in July of 48 B.C., but one of the few who realized the extent of the victory was Pompey himself. Believing that he had not scored a major victory, Pompey refused to follow it up as Caesar retreated. Caesar himself realized it, noting, "Victory today would have been the enemy's, if only anyone among them had possessed the good sense to grasp it".

Pompey's chances of winning the civil war had been lost. Having joined up with seaborne reinforcements led by Mark Antony, Caesar brought Pompey to battle at Pharsalus and, despite being heavily outnumbered, succeeded in badly defeating Pompey's men. Pompey managed to flee in the ensuing rout, possibly by disguising himself as a common merchant. Caesar, satisfied with his victory, returned to Rome where he was hailed as a liberator and proclaimed Dictator once again, naming Mark Antony Master of the Horse, a position which effectively made the young general his second-in-command. In a token gesture, Caesar ran for Consul in what was a guaranteed victory and then resigned his dictatorship once he had secured his position – all this with his legions encamped outside the city serving a silent but persuasive threat.

Having heard a rumor that Pompey was attempting to raise men against him in Egypt, Caesar took ship for Alexandria, only to find upon his arrival that Pompey had been murdered on the orders of Egypt's young pharaoh, the boy-king Ptolemy XIII. According to legend, the pharaoh's treatment of Pompey enraged Caesar, as Pompey's callous demise was not befitting one of the greatest Romans of the age. Caesar's relationship with his rival had always been a complex one, and he is said to have wept when Ptolemy presented him with Pompey's head. Although Caesar was there chasing Pompey's men, he quickly became involved in Egypt's own civil war. As a consequence of Ptolemy's barbarity, Caesar impulsively decided to side with his sister Cleopatra in her bid for the throne of Egypt, escalating what was rapidly becoming an all-out civil war. Egypt at the time was a client state of Rome, though not a full-fledged province, and the main provider of grain for the ever-hungry city's depots. Again according to legend, Cleopatra famously seduced Caesar, who at 52 was over 30 years her senior, by being brought to him in a rolled-up carpet, and the ever ambitious Roman was also impressed by the lavish and exotic lifestyles Egypt's royalty enjoyed.

A bust of Cleopatra

While his romantic relationship with Cleopatra developed, Caesar resisted a siege by Ptolemy's forces in Alexandria throughout 48 B.C., then led his troops out of the city and defeated Ptolemy's army at the Battle of the Nile in January of 47 BC. Ptolemy's army was equipped as hoplites. The Ptolemy line was directly descended from one of Alexander the Great's Greek generals, had always considered themselves Greek and introduced military reforms to make their armies more similar to those of Macedonia and the Ancient Greeks. The hoplites fought with exceedingly long *sarissas* (pikes), but the cumbersome weapons made it impossible to defend themselves from the showers of javelins the Romans hurled before closing in. Making matters worse, the weapons were virtually useless once the Roman soldiers had gotten inside their reach, a fact that Macedonian and Greek hoplites had already painfully learned during Rome's conquest of Greece. Ptolemy's army was routed and he was killed in battle, officially ending Egypt's civil war.

Having ended the Egyptian civil war in Alexandria, Caesar was ready to return to Rome, which was about to be introduced to Egypt's young queen. At this point in his life, Caesar had been married to Calpurnia, who he had taken as a wife in 59 B.C., but having extramarital relationships was hardly abnormal for a powerful Roman at the time. Indeed he had enjoyed a similar one with Servilia, she of the incriminating note, some time previously, and that relationship was so public that Caesar had informally adopted Brutus, Servilia's son (named for, and descended from, the famous Brutus who had ejected the brutal Tarquins, the last kings of Rome, from the city). Thus, Caesar made no effort to hide Cleopatra from the world, installing her in his villa in the hills near Rome whenever she came to visit, something she did frequently. Their relationship was cemented by the birth of Caesarion, who Cleopatra claimed was Caesar's, and who bore Caesar's name and was said to bear a resemblance to him. Caesarion would be Caesar's only son.

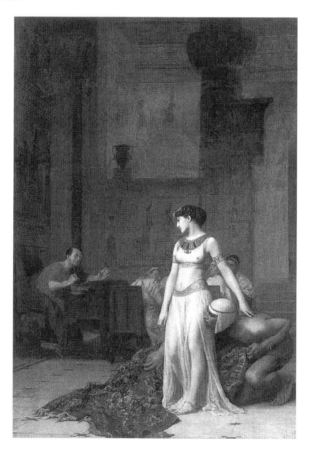

Cleopatra and Julius Caesar. Painting by Jean-Léon Gérôme

Never one for staying too long away from the action, shortly after his victory at the Nile Caesar embarked for a campaign in the Pontus, where he defeated Rome's old enemies so quickly and comprehensively that he remarked caustically that Pompey must have been an inferior general indeed to have required so long to subdue them. While he was in the Pontus, Caesar received intelligence that Cato the Younger had raised an army in Northern Africa and intended to march on Rome. Cato the Younger had a strong reputation among his contemporaries as a philosophical, moral and steadfast statesman who had long opposed Caesar and others' corruption. Having been part of the Senate group loyal to Pompey, Cato had been on the run since the civil war broke out.

Caesar quickly marshalled his forces and took ship for Thapsus, in Numydia, where he defeated Cato completely. A proud Stoic, Cato, according to the ancient patrician tradition, took his own life rather than endure the shame of defeat. According to Plutarch, Caesar's response upon hearing news of his suicide was, "Cato, I grudge you your death, as you would have grudged me the preservation of your life." A few years later, one of Cato's sons would participate in Caesar's assassination.

A statue of Cato the Younger reading Plato's dialogue *Phaedo* while preparing to kill himself.

Following his triumph over Cato, Caesar was feted in Rome and appointed Dictator for a period of 10 years and elected sole Consul, which left him secure enough in his position to leave once more, this time to deal with Pompey's sons, who had escaped to Spain and continued to prove troublesome. He succeeded in bringing them to battle at Munda in 45 B.C.. Despite being outnumbered almost two to one, Caesar took the offensive and attacked the enemy forces, which were commanded by Pompey's son Gnaeius Pompeius, and Titus Labenius, Caesar's onetime ally who had served under Caesar in Gaul and then later defected to Pompey's side when Caesar had crossed the Rubicon.

In its opening phases, the battle seemed to favor neither side in particular, obliging Caesar himself to join the ranks. His presence invigorated the men of the 10th Legion, which began to push back the Pompeian wing. At the same time, King Bogud of Mauritania, Caesar's ally, launched his cavalry against the enemy's rear. Labienus, the commander of the Pompeian cavalry, moved backwards to intercept them, but this led the embattled legions to think that Labienus was fleeing the field, so they broke formation and ran. In the ensuing rout, tens of thousands of them were slaughtered as they attempted to flee for safety, and all 13 of Pompeius's battle-standards, the famous Eagles, were captured by Caesar. Troops would ordinarily fight to the death to defend their Eagles, so the fact that all were taken is a clear indication of how complete the rout of Pompeius's forces was. Labienus himself was killed on the battlefield and buried with honor. With the last challengers to his utter dominion of Rome finally vanquished, Caesar returned to the city, where he was appointed Dictator for Life.

The Senate, which had been thickly staffed with Caesar's partisans and had grown increasingly servile, organised lavish games for Caesar's return to celebrate his triumph at Munda, something many Romans found to be in poor taste. After all, the battle at Munda has been against fellow Romans, led by scions of an ancient and noble house that Caesar had all but extinguished (though he had also granted clemency to a great number of his political rivals, who had since been welcomed back to Rome). It was the first sign of a growing popular disaffection with Caesar, which culminated in riots following the great triumphal games organised in honor of Caesar's other victories throughout the years. The presence of large amounts of veterans in the city, and the vast grants of land Caesar bequeathed to them, also served to irritate a significant number of the population. Although Caesar remained popular with the common people, he was beginning to lose some of their love, which did not go unnoticed among his rivals in the Senate, some of whom were already actively engaged in plotting his downfall after their hopes of a Pompeian victory in the field was dashed by Caesar's victory at Munda.

In 46 and 45 BC, Caesar occupied himself principally with political and social reform, rewarding his veterans with grants of land, passing laws that ensured his continuing popularity with the people (such as a restriction on the importation and purchase of luxury goods) and naming his successors. Having no male sons of his own except, perhaps, Caesarion, his bastard by Cleopatra, whom he never formally acknowledged, Caesar declared Gaius Octavius (Octavian), his nephew, to be his sole and rightful heir. This was done with the provision that, should Octavian die before him, his inheritance pass to Marcus Junius Brutus, Servilia's son. During this time, Caesar also introduced the Julian Calendar, derived from the Egyptian version, which did not follow the phases of the moon as the Roman calendar did and included the presence of an extra day in the month of February every four years. This calendar is virtually identical to the one that is still in use today and marked a fundamental shift in timekeeping, although doubtless at the time it must have been met with grumbling and confusion among the common people. To this day, the month of July is named after Caesar.

During these same years, however, dark shadows were gathering over Caesar, though he refused to acknowledge them or even to admit to noticing them. Hubris, it seemed, had finally taken Caesar in its grasp, and he remained intentionally or unintentionally oblivious to the enemies plotting behind his back. Despite warnings from Mark Antony, his wife Calpurnia, and many other members of his inner circle, he continued about his business while his enemies sharpened their knives.

Chapter 5: The Ides of March, 44 B.C.

"I have lived long enough both in years and in accomplishments." - Caesar

Caesar surely knew he had enemies; with a political career such as his, what man wouldn't have? However, he clearly underestimated just how much his ascendancy had begun to alienate some of the optimates and former Pompeians in the Senate and among the Roman aristocracy. Perhaps, having seen Sulla's relatively untroubled time as Dictator, he believed he could replicate the older man's feat. Perhaps he was simply pleased by the honors bestowed upon him by the panderers among the Senate and was unaware of their true feelings. Be that as it may, Caesar willingly or unwillingly made his presence at the head of the Roman Empire intolerable to many people.

Tensions began to rise in the wake of Caesar's triumph and victory games, which had already been marred by accusations of being in poor taste and overly lavish, when Roman mints began producing coins in honor of Caesar that featured his effigy upon them. This was a highly unusual practice, because effigies had generally been reserved for the dead. In many minds, such behavior smacked dangerously of monarchy, and the mutterings against Caesar increased.

Caesar also did himself no favors when he tolerated the behavior of some of his more overly enthusiastic supporters who, during a speech he gave in the *Rostrum* (the public orator's platform in the Forum), placed a laurel wreath on a statue depicting him, an honor properly reserved for Gods and Kings. When two tribunes had the wreath removed, Caesar had them both stripped of their office, a move which angered many of the conservative optimates who held Republican institutions to be sacred.

Despite these acts, Caesar still moved somewhat cautiously. Though he might have welcomed signs of adulation from the crowd, he took care to distance himself from any notion that he wished to be acclaimed as a king. When, on a different occasion, the crowd cheered him by shouting "*rex, rex, rex*" ("king, king, king") at him, he quieted them, and when Mark Antony tried to crown him in public with a laurel wreath Caesar demurred repeatedly, choosing instead to give the wreath in sacrifice. But however much he tried to distance himself from any notion of royalty or being a king, there was no denying the fact that Caesar, as Dictator for Life, was effectively wielding absolute power, a fact which did not escape many of his rivals or, for that matter, supporters attempting to advance themselves. One such man was Lucius Cotta, a rather servile individual who had the brilliant notion to actually petition the Senate to bestow the title of King upon Caesar, who was preparing plans for an invasion of Parthia, of which it had long been prophesied, "only a King will conquer her".

This may have been the last straw. What is known is that around this time, at some point in 45 B.C., complaints and grumbling gave way to conspiracy. The Roman Senate consisted of between 800-900 members, and a group of around 60 of them, who called themselves *Liberatores* (Liberators), began meeting in secret with the intent of plotting Caesar's assassination. These conspirators were led by Gaius Cassius Longinus and – most famously – by Marcus Junius Brutus. Brutus, who had been named second in line to Caesar's inheritance in Caesar's will and was the son of Caesar's onetime lover Servilia, is an enigmatic figure: his motives for heading a conspiracy against a man who at one time could almost have been considered his adoptive father have never been especially clear. Some suggest that he felt slighted that Octavian was named Caesar's heir in his stead, and others point to the deteriorating relationship between the two, because Brutus had aligned himself against Caesar and sided with Pompey during the civil war. There is even a suggestion that Servilia, who had grown estranged from Caesar, planted the notion in her son's head, and there's almost no doubt Brutus envisioned himself fulfilling a destiny similar to the famous ancestor who had expelled the last king from Rome.

Bust of Brutus

Whether it was one or a combination of these factors, Brutus seemed to consider Caesar's assassination necessary to defend the Republic against any form of monarchy that might arise. And Brutus was not interested in idle speculation: planning quickly became concrete and, after a number of secret meetings in various locations across the city, the *Liberatores* determined that Caesar would be killed on the floor of the Senate House, the most symbolic place for such an act.

According to Virgil, the dawning of the Ides of March of 44 B.C. (March 15th) was greeted by great portents across the breadth of the Roman dominions: the volcano of Etna is said to have erupted prodigiously, great flocks of crows were seen in the ominously dark skies above Rome, while the Alps were shaken by earthquakes, the "voices of the Gods" thundered above the German forests, and animals spoke in human tongues. No doubt Caesar, a level-headed man, would have dismissed all this talk as arrant nonsense, but what most Roman historians are adamant about is that his inner circle was replete with foreboding that morning. Rumors of an attempt on Caesar's life by the *Liberatores* had filtered through to Caesar's supporters, and Calpurnia begged him not to go to the Senate that day, virtually throwing herself at his feet in her worry. Caesar might have been swayed by his wife's misgivings, if nothing else in order to humor her, but for the intervention of Brutus himself. It is said that he took Caesar by the arm and, smiling, pointed out to him how absurd it would be if the Dictator of Rome were to not show himself in the Senate for fear of the ravings of a woman half-deranged with worry for her beloved husband. This swayed Caesar, who accordingly left for the Senate as he had originally planned.

Mark Antony had also gotten wind of the plot, having been approached by Servilius Casca, a

Liberator who was beginning to regret his involvement in the whole thing. He attempted to intercept Caesar on the Senate House steps, but was hustled off by other conspirators and was thus unable to reach him, a circumstance which doubtless had a bearing on Caesar's death. Antony, after all, had fought in Gaul, Greece, Egypt and Spain and was, above all, a fighting commander. Had Caesar's long time protégé reached him, who knows how things may have gone that day, but the two men were prevented from meeting.

Morte di Giulio Cesare **("Death of Julius Caesar"). By Vincenzo Camuccini, 1798**

When Caesar entered the Senate House, he was approached, as arranged, by a *Liberator* named Tillius Cimber, who presented him with a petition for the cancellation of the exile of his brother, who had been banished some time previously. Caesar ignored him and brushed roughly past, but Cimber seized hold of his robe, half-pulling his toga from him. Caesar snatched his toga away from Cimber, demanding "What is this violence?". It was at this point that Servilius Casca, who despite his confession to Antony had decided to go along with the plot after all – doubtless in fear of what the other *Liberatores* would do to him if he got cold feet – attacked. He also seized Caesar by his robe and, drawing his dagger, dealt the Dictator a glancing cut to the neck. Casca was no assassin, and the cut seems to have been trivial, so much so that Caesar, who had doubtless seen worse on campaign, turned and seized him by the neck, snarling "What are you doing, you wretch?". Casca panicked and, dropping his dagger, screamed "Help me, brothers!". His desperate entreaty broke the paralysis that had seized his fellow *Liberatores*, with upwards of 60 men descending upon Caesar. The Senators were not military men, which was made clear by the haphazard manner in which they stabbed Caesar with knives and daggers. Caesar, stabbed multiple times, tripped and fell to the ground, where the conspirators continued to savage him.

Despite the fact Caesar was stabbed nearly two dozen times, doctors concluded only one of them was a fatal wound.

As with all of history's decisive moments, the assassination of Caesar has taken on a legend of its own, and popular perception of the murder is often rooted more in colorful myth than reality. The most enduring myth about Caesar's death is that his last words were "Et tu, Brute? (Latin for "And you, Brutus?), but this is almost certainly apocryphal. Both Suetonius and Plutarch, which still remain the main sources for Caesar's life, report that he said nothing. Instead, they wrote that as Caesar lay dying on the Senate House floor, he caught sight of Brutus among his murderers and, rather than face this betrayal, he drew a part of his robe over his head.

Jean-Léon Gérôme's painting of Caesar's assassination

The majority of the *Liberatores*, terrified by the implications of what they had done, fled the scene, as did most of the Senators, who doubtless feared their presence would be taken for involvement. Caesar's body lay unattended for three hours before anyone came to attend to it, while Brutus and Cassius marched through the city center, proclaiming to all who would listen that Caesar's tyranny had come to an end and that Romans were free again. The conspirators quickly learned that their cries were mostly falling on deaf ears. Terrified of the threat to the peace that the vacuum of power caused by Caesar's demise would doubtless cause, most Roman citizens had locked themselves indoors as soon as they had gotten wind of what had happened.

Chapter 6: Caesar's Legacy

"I love the name of honor, more than I fear death." - Caesar

To the dismay of the conspirators and their supporters, which had included luminaries like Cicero, the assassination of Caesar failed to restore the Republic to its former glory. Instead, the vacuum of power created a struggle amongst those closest to Caesar. The conspirators were quickly exiled, and from the chaos of Caesar's death rose a new triumvirate, headed by Octavian, Caesar's nephew and heir, Mark Antony, his staunchest ally, and Lepidus, a powerful general. Together the men purged their enemies, combining to defeat Brutus and Cassius at the Battle of Phillipi in October of 42 B.C. Antony's most famous rival, Cicero, was hunted down attempting to flee, and after he was murdered, Antony had his hands and head nailed to the Rostra in the Forum.

Having defeated Caesar's conspirators, Octavian and Antony turned upon each other. With Antony controlling the eastern part of the Roman Empire, he began a famous relationship with Cleopatra. Octavian's decisive victory at the Battle of Actium in 30 B.C. ensured his victory, and after Antony and Cleopatra committed suicide, the politically calculating Octavian had Caesarion, Caesar's lone son, killed. Octavian, of course, would become the first of many Roman emperors over the next 500 years. Octavian would become Caesar Augustus, and the Republic of Rome never saw another dawn.

Love him or hate him, there is no doubt that Caesar was a remarkable man, and one who changed the course of world history for ever. In addition to the fact that his heir and his heir's descendants went on to rule over one of the greatest Empires the world has ever known, much of which was conquered and consolidated by Caesar himself, his influence is still felt in many aspects of our daily life. Caesar's name is still synonymous with power, and he continues to be one of history's most famous men, if not the most famous. The West also has Caesar to thank for the fact that the calendar consists of 365 days, with an extra day every four years.

Like Alexander in the centuries before Caesar's time, Caesar became the man every leader aspired to be, both politically and militarily. Over 2,000 years after his death, Caesar is still considered one of history's greatest generals, and it's easy to understand why. He was a brilliant strategist, and unmatched tactician who defeated virtually every enemy he ever encountered. He never lost a campaign, and his roll-call of triumphs, including in Spain, Gaul, Italy, Greece, Egypt, and Numydia, eclipses most if not all great generals. Moreover, Caesar was a soldier's soldier, never afraid to take up a sword himself when his men needed to see their general the most, as he did at the Sabis, at Pharsalus, and at Munda. It would take nearly 2,000 years before generals aimed to emulate anyone other than Caesar, and that man, Napoleon, had aimed to emulate Caesar.

Ironically, European royalty across the continent took his name as an imperial title, even though Caesar himself never was and never considered himself a royal. He had simple tastes in most things, and was never given to the excesses that plagued so many of his noble contemporaries or his successors – indeed, the only accusations of vice that were ever levied against him were the ones of having had a homosexual relationship with the King of Bythinia, when he was barely in his twenties. Ever the populist, he seems to have generally cared for the common people – both his veterans, who were richly rewarded for their services, and the "mob" of Rome itself which, usually so fickle, was so enamored with him that they were willing to cast their support behind Antony and Octavian purely because they promised justice for Caesar's murder.

No doubt he was proud, perhaps even arrogant, but then, given his achievements, he had reason to be. It is said that, while still in his teens, during a visit to Spain Caesar was shown a statue of that other great conqueror, Alexander the Great of Macedon. The story has it that Caesar was severely upset by this forcible reminder of Alexander's triumphs, for he had already reached an age at which the Macedonian King had already succeeded in subjugating all of Greece, and Caesar still had precious few achievements to his name. Though Alexander's empire was vaster at its pinnacle, it was divided upon his death. The empire Caesar forged would last over 500 more years.

Of course, the legacy of the most famous Roman has endured far longer.

Attila the Hun
Chapter 1: The Terror from the East

Attila's people, the Huns, are in many ways as enigmatic as he. Their exact roots are unclear, but they appear to have originated somewhere on the plains of central Asia, though some historians suggest they came from even further afield and that they once shared a border with China. Attila biographer William Herbert noted that ancient sources had two origins stories for the Huns (and gave a small but probably misplaced amount of credence to the stories):

"Two different accounts have been given by the old chroniclers of the origin of the Huns. The one, that they were descended from Magog the son of Japhet, brought forth by his wife Enech in Havilah, fifty-eight years after the deluge; the other, that the two branches of the Huns and Magyars were derived from Hunor and Magor, elder sons of Nimrod, who settled in the land of Havilah (meaning thereby Persia), and, having followed a deer to the banks of the Maeotis, obtained permission from Nimrod to settle there. By the agreement of all writers, the Huns were Scythians, and if the Scythian tribes were descended and named from Cush, son of Ham, the Huns could not have been of the blood of Japhet. A singular fabulous origin has been attributed to them.

Filimer king of the Goths, and son of Gundaric the great, having issued from Scandinavia and occupied the Scythian territory, found certain witches amongst his people, who were called in their language Aliorumnae or Alirunes, and he drove them far from his army into the desert, where they led a wandering life, and, uniting themselves with the unclean spirits of the wilderness, produced a most ferocious offspring, which lurked at first amongst the marshes, a swarthy and slender race, of small stature, and scarcely endowed with the articulate voice of a human being. It rarely, if ever, happens that a very old tradition is entirely without meaning or foundation, and it may perhaps be drawn from this absurd fable, that the Huns were of mixed descent between the Goths and Tartars."

The Chinese sources gave a pretty good contemporary description of the Huns, who they claimed originated to the northeast of China itself, as noted by Herbert:

"The Chinese make mention of the Huns 2207 BC dwelling to the NE, of China, feeding on the flesh of their flocks and dressed in skins. In their dealings with other people their affirmation held the place of an oath. They punished murder and theft, that is amongst themselves, with certain death. They accustomed their children to hunt and use arms. In their earliest years they shot birds and mice with arrows; growing bigger they pursued hares and foxes. No one amongst them could be deemed a man, till he had slain an enemy, or was bold and skilful enough to do so. It was their custom to attack their enemies unexpectedly, and to fly as rapidly when it was expedient. The great speed of their horses facilitated this mode of warfare, and the Chinese, who were accustomed to standing fight, could not pursue and vanquish them: and the Huns, if defeated, retired unto desert places, where the enemy would find it very grievous to follow them.

They were quite illiterate; their weapons were bows and arrows, and swords. They had more or fewer wives according to their means, and it was not unusual for a son to marry his stepmother, or a brother the widow of his brother. The Hun who could rescue the body of a slain comrade from the enemy became heir to all his property. They were anxious to make captives, whom they employed in tending their flocks. Thieves amongst other nations, they were faithful to each other.

They lived in tents placed upon wagons. The ancient Huns adorned their coffins with precious things, gold, silver, and jewels, according to the rank of the deceased, but they erected no tombs. Many servants and concubines followed the body at the funeral, and served it as if living; troops of righting men accompanied it, and at the full moon they began combats which lasted till the change. Then they cut off the heads of many prisoners, and each of the fighting men was rewarded with a measure of wine made from sour milk."

While Attila fatefully chose not to sack Rome and conquer the Western half of the empire, it is still likely that the Huns were indirectly responsible for the breakup of the Roman Empire a generation later, because their move westward in the 2nd, 3rd and 4th centuries AD has been identified by historians as one of the causes of the displacement of other "barbarian" tribes, including the Goths and the Vandals. Less than half a century before Attila's invasion of Italy, Alaric sacked Rome at the head of the Visigoths in 410, and various tribes flooded west, eventually destroying the Roman frontiers and overrunning many of their oldest provinces.

By all accounts the Huns were a fierce and warlike people, similar to the Mongols in that they were tribal horsemen from the steppes of Central Asia adept at fighting as archers on horseback. And like the Mongols their tactics proved devastating against slower-moving, heavily armored opponents who were unable to maneuver effectively against them. From the accounts of contemporaries who met them personally (chiefly Priscus, as quoted by Jordanes), they appear to have also resembled the Mongols. Attila in particular was described as being short, broad and bandy-legged, with tanned skin, a large head, slitted eyes, a sparse beard, and a flat nose.

Around 150 A.D. the Huns settled in the Caucasus, but later, around 350 AD, while maintaining their homebase on the Caucasus they pushed even further westward into Eastern Europe and subjugating much of the local population. This in turn forced the Goths, Franks and Vandals into France and Spain and helped set in motion the chain of events that would lead to the collapse of the Roman Empire in the late 5th century A.D. By the time Attila was born, probably sometime around 390-400 A.D., the borders of the Hunnic Empire would likely have stretched from the Caspian to Poland, not including the Balkans.

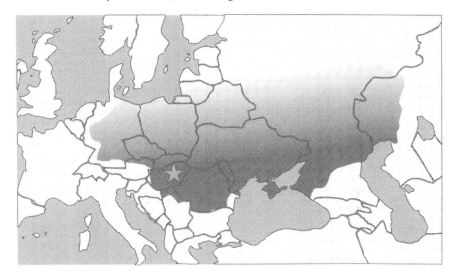

The extent of the Hunnic Empire under Attila.

As with so many other great conquerors of antiquity, like Alexander and Augustus, Attila had the fortune of being born into his nation's ruling family. He was the son of Prince Mundzuk, the younger brother of the Hunnic Kings Rugila and Octar, who jointly shared rule in what appears to have been traditional Hunnic fashion. However, there appears to have been no provision for another younger brother taking over the duties of kingship in the event of a King's death; when Octar perished in battle against the Burgundians in 432 A.D., Mundzuk did inherit his crown but Rugila continued to rule alone.

Rugila was in many ways the Philip of Macedon to Attila's Alexander. Though not much is known about him, several significant details can be gleaned from the chronicles. First, Rugila consolidated the Hunnic Empire and added significantly to Hunnic territorial posessions, particularly in the north and west of Europe, as the ill-fated campaign against the Burgundians (residents of Gaul) indicates. Many of Rugila's opponents were scattered "barbarian" tribes, which, though bellicose and formidable, were frequently defeated by the Huns and had been originally displaced by them in the east. At the same time, to the south Rugila's territories bordered those of far more formidable foes, whose holdings could promise far richer plunder and whose defeat would bring far more glory: the Western and Eastern Roman Empire.

For over a century, the Roman Empire had been in decline, with the loss of wealthy and vital provinces (particularly in the west) to marauding barbarians, causing loss of revenue and prestige. Increasingly, the once mighty Roman legions had begun to rely on the barbarians, particularly Goths, for use as auxiliaries, and even eventually handed over command to barbarian commanders, giving them unprecedented power. With the western provinces gone, Rome became increasingly strategically irrelevant, and this led to greater emphasis being placed upon the eastern provinces until, eventually and inevitably, the administrative capital of the Empire became the more secure and wealthy city of Constantinople.

Depiction of Theodosius

40 years before Rugila became sole ruler of the Huns, Theodosius, the last ruler of the unified Roman Empire, split his domains in half to leave each of his two sons an equal share. In 395, he willed his eldest, Arcadius, the eastern part of the Roman Empire, with Constantinople as its capital, while Honorius, his younger brother, was given the western portion of the Roman Empire, and Rome. The Eastern portion of the Roman Empire was by far the stronger, and it flourished even as the West declined, so that in the West the true rulers were the *magisteri militum,* the "Masters of Soldiers" (Commanders-in-Chief) who, because they held the loyalty of the army, were able to strongarm the Western Emperors into doing what they wished. One such man was Flavius Aetius, a ruthless and extremely competent soldier who in 433 fell into disfavor

with the Western Emperor and fled to Rugila's court. Aetius and Rugila were old friends because Aetius had been raised at Rugila's court and had spent a few years there as a young man in 409. Aetius's plight, or perhaps his suggestions, gave Rugila the opportunity to involve himself actively in the affairs of the Roman Empire for the first time. With his army at his back, he marched to the border of his domains and the Western Roman Empire in a deliberate show of force designed for one thing only, the reinstatement of Aetius as *magister militum*. The show of force worked, and the Emperor was forced to accede to Rugila's demands. Facing invasion, not to mention the possibility that a large part of Rugila's force would be led by the most able military commander the Roman Empire had seen in at least the past five decades, he reinstated Aetius as *magister militum* with full honors.

With a grateful Aetius now firmly in the saddle in the West, Rugila couldn't fulfill his dreams of expansion against the Western Roman Empire at the expense of a friend. Therefore, he decided to turn his attention to the East, and he was given a *casus belli* around 434, when some tribesmen that had previously sworn fealty to him decamped and retreated into territory held by the Eastern Roman Empire. Rugila immediately demanded that his traitorous followers be handed over to him, but apparently the Eastern Roman Emperor refused to comply with his requests, secure in his military might. Accordingly, Rugila gathered a large force of his warriors and in 435 marched into Thrace, then part of the Eastern Roman Empire, where he set about ravaging the area.

However, Rugila quickly discovered that the Thracians were a warlike people who fought in a manner not dissimilar to his own and were thus largely able to counter his tactics, and their troops were further bolstered by forces of Eastern Roman legionaries and auxiliaries. The campaign proved to be a disaster, and in the midst of it, Rugila died sometime in 435 AD. It is unclear what the manner of his death was, as the ecclesiastical chronicles from the area which form the bulk of our knowledge of this campaign record that Rugila was killed by a lightning bolt, presumably an avenging bolt from heaven for impious behavior. This seems an unlikely though not impossible fate, but the most logical explanation is that he was killed by an arrow, either in a skirmish or a battle. His army is said to have been completely wiped out by some infectious disease, possibly some form of cholera, though it seems unlikely that his whole force would be destroyed in such a fashion. If they did indeed all perish, then it can be assumed that neither Attila or Bleda were with him at the time, as following Rugila's death they were acclaimed as joint rulers of the Hunnic Empire.

Although no mention of Attila or Bleda participating in Rugila's campaigns is recorded, it is safe to assume that they would have done so at some point or another, or there would have been no cause for Rugila to nominate them as his successors or for the Hunnic noblemen to back their claims. As a Hunnic prince of the blood, Attila would have been raised to be a masterful horseman, an experienced archer, and an excellent swordsman, as well as being taught the intricacies of strategy and military tactics. It is perhaps not too much of a stretch to assume that

Aetius himself, in his brief time with the Huns in the early 430s, might have taught Attila some of what he knew. At the time of his and Bleda's ascent to the throne, Attila would probably have been in his 30s.

If the Eastern Roman Emperor had hoped to gain a reprieve with the death of Rugila, he was mistaken. Attila was ruthless, ambitious, and highly skilled in war, and his brother Bleda was by no means his inferior. They would take the expertly crafted war machine that Rugila had helped perfect and turn its might against the Romans, for the greater glory of the Hunnic Empire.

Chapter 2: The Barbarians Invade

Medieval depiction of Attila in the Nuremberg Chronicles

The first act of Bleda and Attila upon ascending to the throne of the Hunnic Empire was to threaten a resumption of the hostilities that had been interrupted by Rugila's death and the wiping out of his expeditionary force. They warned the Eastern Roman Emperor Theodosius II that unless the Hunnic fugitives that had sparked Rugila's war in the first place were returned, they would invade once again.

The two parties agreed to meet in north-eastern Serbia, pointedly on ground that had previously belonged to the Romans but had been occupied by the Huns under Rugila. There, the Roman envoys – who Attila and Bleda may or may not have known were under attack in Northern Africa from the Vandals and had other fish to fry – were forced into a humiliating treaty in order to remove the threat of the Huns from their northern border. The Romans meekly agreed to hand over the Hunnic refugees, who had appealed to them for protection, as well as agreeing to pay 8 *solidi* (36 grams of pure gold) for every Roman prisoner taken during Rugila's campaigns. In addition to this, the Romans were also forced to enter into a trade agreement with the Huns that required them, among other things, to pay over 100 kilograms of gold on a yearly basis, which Theodosius evidently judged a cheap price to keep the Huns away from his borders.

Satisfied with the terms of the treaty, Attila and Bleda headed back to the Hunnic heartland (modern Hungary), perhaps to ensure that there would be no dissent over their assumption of kingship among the Hunnic nobles and subordinate kings and clans of the Empire. Theodosius doubtlessly wanted to give himself some breathing space, as archaeological evidence and the period's chronicles indicate that during this time he undertook a massive series of reconstruction works focussing mainly on the fortification of the Danube, the border the Eastern Roman Empire shared with the Huns, and on increasing the size of the walls defending Constantinople, a mark of how much he was concerned about Hunnic aggression.

Around 436 A.D., Attila and Bleda launched their first campaign as rulers of the Hunnic Empire. Gathering a vast army of Hun warriors and vassal auxiliaries, including tribesmen from the Ostrogoths, Alamanni, Gepids and Heruli, all Germanic tribes that had been displaced and conquered by the Huns, Attila and Bleda marched against the Sassanid Empire. The Sassanids were the successors of the ancient Parthian Empire, the Romans' erstwhile enemies, and their domains extended south of the Hunnic Empire and east of the Eastern Roman Empire from the Arabian Peninsula to the Hindu Kush. The Sassanids, however, proved to be more than a match for Attila and Bleda; when the Huns' armies ravaged their way south and east into Armenia (then under Sassanid control), they were met and defeated by the Sassanid armies, which mobilized and struck back rapidly.

Deciding that the Sassanids were too bellicose, and with the lack of a decisive victory denying the Huns the credibility they needed in order to extort a viable (and profitable) peace settlement from them, Attila and Bleda decided to cut their losses and pull their army back to Hungary. It is possible that there might have been dissent and/or disaffection among the Hunnic princes and vassal states of the Empire in the wake of the Sassanid defeat, because the next known campaign of the Huns did not take place until 440 A.D. Unfortunately, since the Huns themselves put nothing in writing, there are no sources about what went on within the borders of their Empire when they were not in contact with other peoples who possess a tradition of written history. Thus it's unclear why there was an interval of relative peace for the countries bordering the Hunnic Empire between 436-440 A.D., but it may have been due to the fact that Attila and Bleda were occupied pacifying their own vassals.

In 440, Attila and Bleda decided to recommence their hostilities against the Eastern Roman Empire and gathered an army. Breaking their treaty with Theodosius II, they attacked the free trading post which, in accordance with the terms of their agreement, had been established by the Romans on the north bank of the Danube. The trading post had burgeoned into a bustling and wealthy center, its riches fueled by the new trade between Huns and Romans, and it proved to be an irresistible lure for Attila and Bleda. They fell upon it, and because it was protected by the terms of the treaty, it is unlikely to have possessed any serious fortifications or garrison. The Huns then crossed the Danube and marched southwards, burning as they went, until the had advanced into the Balkans. Halting before the walls of the city of Margus, Attila and Bleda demanded that the inhabitants hand over the town's Bishop, who they claimed owed Attila goods or tribute according to different chronicles. While the town elders gathered to discuss the Bishop's fate, the Bishop, presumably incensed that they would consider betraying him to the Huns, promptly decamped to the Hunnish lines and conspired with Attila and Bleda to have the gates opened for them.

The two brothers and their armies advanced south, where they encountered remarkably little opposition. It is unclear whether they were aware of this, as the events were occurring a good distance away with no clear line of communication in between, but at the same time as they began their invasion the Vandals under King Geiseric struck into Northern Africa and were overrunning the rich province of Carthage, Rome's breadbasket. The loss of Carthage was a catastrophe for the Romans, compounded by a Sassanid attack against the eastern borders of the Empire, and Theodosius was forced to pull troops from regions deemed strategically unimportant, such as the Balkans, in order to attempt to recover Carthage from the Vandals. At the same time, it is unclear whether Theodosius was overly naïve in trusting Attila and Bleda to keep their word, or whether he reckoned that it was better to risk losing the Balkans in order to preserve the more strategically viable province of Carthage. It is likely that he indeed hoped that the Huns would keep their word, as the Balkans were essentially the buffer between the Eastern Roman Empire and the Hunnic forces.

Due to the lack of garrisons or field armies in the Balkans, the Huns were able to take Viminacium, a sizable city of 40,000 inhabitants which would ordinarily have been home to a strong force of legionaries, then advanced to Singdinium (Belgrade), whose walls and fortress they razed to the ground before burning parts of the city and selling its inhabitants into slavery. Attila and Bleda then marched onwards, besieging the city of Sirmium, which fell to them shortly afterwards but was not wholly destroyed. The campaign then ended for the winter season, during which armies of the Classical and Dark Ages traditionally did not engage in warfare, and it appears likely that the Hunnic armies wintered in or near Sirmium. At some stage during their campaign, it appears as though Attila and Bleda either forced Roman military engineers into joining them or else suborned them with gold, because their future campaigns involved a modern siege train which they had not possessed prior to 441.

Theodosius, reacting at last to the threat on his northern border, emptied Sicily of troops in 442 in order to divert them towards the Balkans, where the Huns were still encamped. Attila and Bleda had made demands for an increase of the tribute to be sent to them from the Eastern Roman Empire, but Theodosius was apparently confident enough in the ability of his new levies to defeat the Huns and refused to accede to their demands. Attila and Bleda, infuriated by Theodosius's defiance and certain that their new modern military siege weapons, including battering rams, *ballistae* (giant crossbows capable of firing bolts taller than a man), and siege towers would provide the necessary advantage, prepared once again for war.

The renewed offensive against the Romans began in 443 with a string of Hunnic successes. The Huns made short work of the defensive outworks of Ratiara and Niassus, and then marched on Serdicca (Sofia) Arcadiopolis and Philippopolis (Plovdiv) before crossing the Dardanelles and attacking Constantinople itself. Theodosius made a last ditch attempt at protecting the city, launching an army against the Huns in a desperate attempt to stop them before they invested the walls, but the field force sent against Attila and Bleda was destroyed.

Despite the loss of that army, the fortifications that encircled Constantinople, including a triple wall and moat bristling with towers on which scores of siege weapons were emplaced, proved to be too massive even for the newly constituted Hunnic siege artillery to deal with. Frustrated by Constantinople's resistance, Attila and Bleda set about ravaging the Eastern Roman heartland and destroyed another Roman army sent against them near Gallipoli. Desperate and now devoid of field armies capable of opposing Attila and Bleda within marching distance, Theodosius was forced to sue for peace. He sent his *magister militum* Anatolius, who had already proven himself an able diplomat when he had managed to conclude a peace some years earlier with the Sassanids, to negotiate with Attila and Bleda.

This time, with Theodosius virtually at their mercy, the Huns were not inclined to be especially generous. They demanded a payment of over two tons of gold, ironically claiming that the Romans had violated the terms of their previous treaty (it is unclear how, since the campaign was a unilateral act of aggression by the Huns), and then went on to increase the yearly tribute from 115 kilograms of gold to almost 700. They further extorted even more money from Theodosius by insisting that he pay 54 grams of gold for each Roman prisoner held by the Huns, prisoners who almost certainly numbered in the thousands at that point following the defeats at Constantinople and Gallipoli. Satisfied, the Huns then pulled back across the Dardanelles and marched north to the Danube, returning to their homeland.

Despite once again forcing peace upon the Eastern Roman Empire, the Huns' campaigns were not yet over. There was one last chapter, a personal one, yet to be played out. At some point in 445, either during the march back to the Hunnic heartland or once the army was north of the Danube, Attila and Bleda departed together on a hunting trip. They outstripped their bodyguard and were alone for several hours, at the end of which only one man returned, wounded and alone: Attila. Exactly what happened on that day is shrouded in mystery, but what seems certain is that, despite his attempt to describe Bleda's death as an unfortunate hunting accident, Attila killed his own brother. Their relationship has never been chronicled in detail, but it has been suggested that there was no love lost between the two, presumably because both were too ambitious to be content with a divided throne, or possibly because each was displeased with the military and strategic decisions of the other. This animosity might have led either Attila or Bleda to plot murder, but if the attack were truly premeditated it seems more likely that the perpetrator would have ensured that he had a number of loyal men close at hand to even the odds rather than take his chances in a hand-to-hand duel. Instead, it appears as though the opportunity to strike a blow was snatched on the fly, possibly as a consequence of a quarrel which took place on the hunting trip itself and which acted as the proverbial straw which broke the camel's back.

Just as nobody can be sure of the motive, it is unclear which of the two brothers struck the first blow. According to a majority of the sources, it was Bleda who first drew his blade on Attila with murderous intent but Attila proved himself to be the better fighter and, having recovered from the surprise of Bleda's initial attack, was able to outfight and finally kill him. However, though this theory was widely accepted among ancient historians such as Priscus, it is worth noting that there exists the possibility that Attila himself initiated the attack and murdered Bleda outright.

When writing about Attila's physical appearance and his relationship with Bleda, Jordanes attributed Bleda's death to "treachery":

> "When Attila's brother Bleda who ruled over a great part of the Huns had been slain by Attila's treachery, the latter united all the people under his own rule. Gathering also a host of the other tribes which he then held under his sway he sought to subdue the foremost nations of the world---the Romans and Visigoths. His army is said to have numbered 500,000 men. He was a man born into the world to shake the nations, the scourge of all lands, who in some way terrified all mankind by the dreadful rumors noised abroad concerning him. He was haughty in his walk, rolling his eyes here and there, so that the power of his proud spirit appeared in the movement of his body. He was indeed a lover of war, yet restrained in action, mighty in counsel, gracious to suppliants and lenient to those who were once received into his protection. He was short of stature, with a broad chest and a large head: his eyes were small, his beard thin and sprinkled with gray: and he had a flat nose and a swarthy complexion showing the evidences of his origin."

It is also not known if any of the Hunnic or vassal noblemen expressed outrage at the death of Bleda or suggested that Attila had killed him through treachery, but it is interesting to note that there were no major campaigns launched by the Huns between 445 and 447 A.D., possibly because Attila felt the need to consolidate his position as sole ruler of the Hunnic Empire and ensure that no pretender attempted to use the rumor of his fratricide as leverage to back his own claim to the throne. Additionally, Attila needed to replenish his ranks, which had been depleted by the campaigns against the Eastern Roman Empire, though with the gold pouring into his coffers from Constantinople, he had no trouble doing this. He set about preparing himself for the greatest campaign yet.

Chapter 3: War in the West

Depiction of Attila in a Hungarian museum

In 447, having secured his position with his vassals at home and gathered a new army, Attila once again reneged on the terms of his treaty with the Eastern Roman Empire and launched a fresh attack against Theodosius's domains. This time, he advanced into Moesia (modern Bulgaria), where an army under Arnegliscus, the local *magister utriusque militiae* (Master of all Arms, i.e. infantry and cavalry), hastily marched against him.

Arnegliscus was a Goth fighting in Roman pay, and though the Goths (many of whom marched in Attila's ranks) had a reputation as extremely canny fighters, Arnegliscus was wary of Attila, having already been bloodied by him in his previous campaign alongside Bleda. Nonetheless, he knew that he must face Attila before he crossed the straits again and threatened Constantinople, so he marched from the military base at Marcianople with a combined force of Balkan garrisons, regulars from the legions of Constantinople, and contingents from Thrace.

The two armies met near Utus, and battle was rapidly joined and exceptionally hard fought, with both sides inflicting grievous losses upon each other. But eventually the Hunnic superiority in numbers and skill at arms began to tell, and the Roman forces were routed with Arnegliscus himself unhorsed and then killed while he fought in the front ranks of his force like a common infantryman.

Attila, furious at the losses Arnegliscus and his men had inflicted on his army, advanced on Marcianople, the garrison depot from which the Roman army had marched to defy him, and razed it to the ground. He destroyed the walls and fortress and set fire to the city, selling its inhabitants into slavery or slaughtering them, and then advanced towards Constantinople itself. Rumor had reached Attila of a calamity which had struck the city, a great earthquake that had toppled many of the town's most important buildings and vast stretches of the walls themselves. In the wake of the earthquake a plague had struck, killing thousands and seriously weakening the garrison. Constantinople, it seemed, was ready to fall.

Somehow, the Romans were remarkably able to rally. The city's prefect, aptly named Constantine, mobilized or conscripted great numbers of the city's population, including laborers and possibly even women, children and the elderly, and he was able to rebuild the city walls in record time. Meanwhile, Zeno, Theodosius's new *magister militum,* force-marched a contigent of crack Isaurian soldiers into the city to bolster its ailing garrison. Suddenly Attila was facing a city that, rather than being derelict and undermanned, was both encircled by continuous (albeit probably slightly shoddily built) walls and brimming with troops. Attila knew that his depleted force could never hope to invest Constantinople, so he turned away in disgust.

Denied his prize, Attila set about ravaging the Balkans, whose people most likely now lived in constant fear of him. Having destroyed the army of Anegliscus, who had been forced to scrape the barrel for troops by emptying most of the region's garrisons, Attila had free rein within the Balkans, as Theodosius seems to have decided to chalk the relatively unproductive and unwealthy region up as a loss rather than send new field armies against the Huns to be destroyed. In *Life of Saint Hypatius*, Callinicus described Attila's invasion: "The barbarian nation of the Huns, which was in Thrace, became so great that more than a hundred cities were captured and Constantinople almost came into danger and most men fled from it. ... And there were so many murders and blood-lettings that the dead could not be numbered. Ay, for they took captive the churches and monasteries and slew the monks and maidens in great numbers."

Attila next toyed with the idea of advancing into Greece itself, where he was certain there would be plenty more plunder and wealth to be had, but when he reached Thermopylae, the famous bottleneck invaders had to negotiate in order to enter Greece from the Balkans via land, he discovered that the way was blocked by a strong garrison. Possibly aware of the legendary defense that Leonidas and his Spartans and allied Greeks had put up against Xerxes's invading Persians, or simply having the tactical acumen to recognize that Thermopylae was a deathtrap, Attila dismissed the idea of attacking Greece.

Eventually, Theodosius realized that letting Attila continue to rampage throughout the Balkans was liable to lose him the region outright, so in 448 he agreed upon a new truce. A new lump sum was paid to the Huns, the tribute was once again increased, and a buffer zone was formally established between the two nations, with the Romans agreeing not to garrison or settle any territory within five days' ride of the Danube.

Attila returned home, but though he had repeatedly humbled the Eastern Roman Empire and made off with – quite literally – tons of their gold, he was not satisfied. He wanted more, which was why, for the first time, in 449 A.D., he turned his attention in a new direction – West. The reason Attila had been content to let the Western Roman Empire go about its business unmolested, aside from the fact that it was less wealthy than the Eastern Roman Empire, was that he was on good terms with Emperor Valentinian, and even better, even friendly ones, with the western *magister militum,* Aetius, who had been his father's guest. Aetius and Valentinian made sure that that cordial relationship remained so by frequent propitiatory gestures, but Attila was not exactly an easy man to be friends with. By 449 A.D, his relationship with Aetius and Valentinian had soured to the point that, when Geinseric, King of the Vandals and the Alans, approached him with a proposal of waging war against the Visigoths of the Kingdom of Toulouse in Gaul, he accepted.

Attila might have hesitated at carrying out an unprovoked and unilateral act of aggression against the Western Roman Empire, since he still considered Aetius something of a friend and mentor, but in 450 A.D. he was given the perfect casus belli. Valentinian had a sister named Honoria, who by all accounts was both foolish and headstrong. Honoria had been promised in marriage to Herculanus, a loyal supporter of Valentinian who had the misfortune of being both too old and too dull for Honoria's taste. Honoria fiercely disputed the match, but as a woman she had no real say in the matter. She was placed in seclusion, there to await her wedding day, but she contrived to smuggle a note out to Attila. Quite why she chose to do this is unclear, since the two had never met, unless she had conceived an uninformed opinion of him as a romantic and adventurous king. Whatever her reasons, she sent Attila a note begging him to rescue her from her plight, and enclosing a ring (presumably her engagement ring from Herculanus) with her letter. It is unclear whether she simply meant the ring as a token of good faith or a gift, or intended to show how little she thought of her engagement to Herculanus, or whether she fully intended to send Attila a proposal of marriage, but Attila chose to interpret her plea as the latter and gladly accepted her generous marriage proposal (ignoring the fact he was already married to a woman named Krezka). By taking Honoria as a bride, Attila promptly claimed half of Valentinian's empire as his due and proper dowry.

When news of this reached Valentinian, he reacted with predictable fury, declaring Honoria a crazed fool and Attila a pirate, and he naturally refused to even countenance the idea of ceding half of his empire to the Huns. Attila, gleefully seizing upon this excuse, gathered a host of unprecedented size, comprised of his own loyal Hunnic warriors and contingents from the farthest corners of his empire, including the Alamanni, the Bastarnae, the Gepids, the Heruli, the

Ostrogoths, the Rugians, the Scirii and the Thuringians. Once everyone flocked to his call, he had assembled a mighty host of almost 100,000 men.

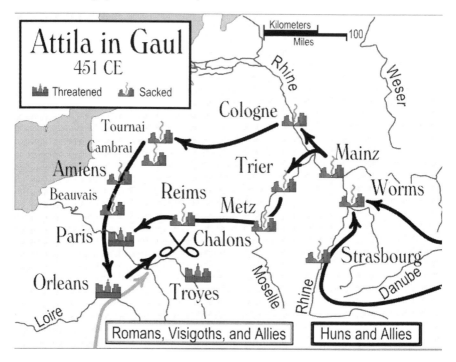

Once his army was ready, Attila marched towards Gaul, which was mostly occupied by Germanic tribes (including the Visigoths) but was notionally under Roman control. Attila crossed the Rhine in 451 A.D. and advanced from his own domains into Gaul proper, sacking the city of Divodurum (Metz) sometime in the spring of 451. Next he advanced on Rheims and sacked it, murdering Bishop Nicasius on his own altar in the process. The city of Tongeren and Paris were spared, presumably because their inhabitants wisely decided to avert the Huns' wrath by paying tribute, though the later chronicles attribute Attila's mercy to a miracle. The city of Troyes was also spared after its Bishop, Lupus, met with Attila outside the city walls and persuaded him to turn his horde aside (although it is possible he agreed to pay a tribute of gold or supplies).

As spring turned to early summer, Attila advanced against Aurelianum (Orleans), a vast and prosperous Gaulish city that notionally owed allegiance to the Romans. However, its ruler, Sangiban of the Alani, had evidently decided to cast in his lot with Attila and promised him that he could deliver the city without a single blow struck by having the gates opened to the Huns.

However, the inhabitants of Aurelianum were obviously more loyal than their leader and barred the gates against the Huns, refusing to let them into the city, forcing Attila to lay siege.

As Attila besieged the city, this delay allowed Aetius, then in Gaul, to mobilize. The *magister militum* had been appalled by the speed of Attila's advance and the size of his army, and since Aetius commanded only a few thousand second-tier auxiliary troops, he could not hope to oppose Attila alone. Desperate for troops, he turned to Eparchius Avitus, a local nobleman of vast wealth and influence (and future Western Roman Emperor) who had served under Aetius some 20 years before and still counted him as a friend. Avitus was able to provide Aetius with more troops, but more importantly he was able to persuade Theodoric, king of the Visigoths (not to be confused with Ostrogoth ruler Theodoric the Great), to pledge his army in Aetius's support. Avitus was also able to secure the help of Merovech, King of the Franks and founder of the Merovingian dynasty. This alliance with the Germanic tribes was a godsend for Aetius, swelling his numbers from around 10,000 to over 80,000 men. It was agreed he would be commander-in-chief, in deference to his military expertise and status as *magister militum,* but the individual warlords would retain command over their own armies.

Aetius then marched on Aurelianum with his newly constituted army at his back and reached the city in mid-June, arriving just in the nick of time. Attila had succeeded in breaching the city walls with his battering rams, and according to the chronicles his storming party was actually within the city itself when news of Aetius's advance reached him. By that point, Aurelianum was virtually in Attila's hands, its garrison shattered and its defenses broken open, but Attila was too canny to order his army into the city. Doing so would have put him in the unenviable position of being trapped in a hostile town with few supplies, a massive besieging force all around, and a breach already in the defenses made by his own siege.

Thus, Attila instead ordered his host to retreat east and marched away from Aetius for almost a week, until he found a defensive position he was confident his army could hold on June 20, 451, and stopped to give battle on the Catalaunian Plains. The night of June 20th, the advance party of Aetius's host, composed mainly of Merovech's Franks, fought a bitter and bloody skirmish against Attila's rearguard that would have been a notable battle in itself had it not been for the overall numbers of the armies that would face each other the following day. Thousands were slain on both sides, an event which did little to put Attila in a positive frame of mind. He had a healthy fear of Aetius's ability as a commander and was not certain of victory, and his mood was rendered even worse when the omens for the battle were taken by his soothsayers, who declared that disaster would befall the Huns but one of the enemy commanders would die. Hoping to cheat the omens, or at least strip the Western Roman Empire of its most able commander, Attila chose to give battle, though he deliberately delayed the confrontation until evening so he could be certain that the Hunnic army would be able to escape in the darkness if defeat struck. That was hardly the mark of a confident general.

"The Huns at the Battle of Chalons" by A. De Neuville

The chief feature of the Catalaunian Plains was a steep ridge which dominated the battlefield and both generals knew was a vital strategic feature, as the army that controlled the high ground would have a distinct advantage. The ridge became the scene of fierce fighting, with the Hunnic forces first seizing one end of the ridge while the Roman auxiliaries under Aetius held the left side of the hill. Aetius had placed the tribes of whose loyalty was still questionable in the center, so that they could not desert him without fighting his own men as well, and he placed Theodoric and his Visigoths on the right. Attila's men then attempted to seize the entirety of the high ground, but Theodoric and his Visigothic troops beat them to it and, fighting downhill, were able to rout the Huns from the tactically vital position.

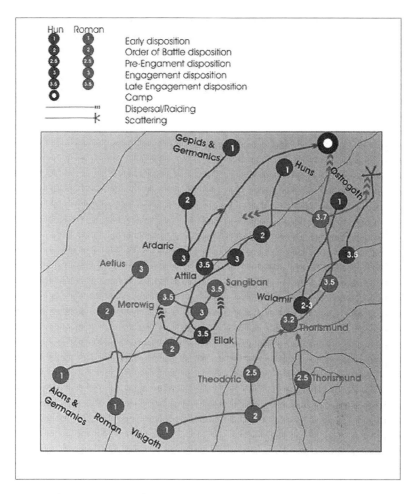

Gepids & Germanics

Huns

Ostrogoth

Ardaric

Aetius

Attila

Sangiban

Walamir

Merowig

Thorismund

Ellak

Theodoric

Thorismund

Alans & Germanics

Roman

Visigoth

The Huns, who were not noted for their discipline, fled in disarray, crashing into the ordered lines of the rest of Attila's force and throwing them into confusion. During the rout of the Hunnic forces sent to attack the ridge, Theodoric, leading the charge against the fleeing Huns, was killed when he fell from his horse and was trampled to death by his own charging men before he had time to rise. However, the Visigoths did not even notice their King's death, sweeping onwards and using the momentum of their headlong charge from the ridge to their advantage. The Visigoths smashed into Attila's center, where he himself stood in the battle line with his own household guard, and as it began to crack under the onslaught Attila fled the field to save his life. It is unlikely that the Visigoths, having caused and not even noticed their own sovereign's death, would have been inclined to take Attila prisoner, but he nevertheless escaped to the safety of his encampment, which as a precautionary measure he had ringed with the wagons of his supply train to act as a makeshift bulwark. A good number of Attila's soldiers, along with the remnants of his household guard, were able to find refuge inside the impromptu fortress, but the bulk of his army, panicked by the Visigothic charge and further sapped of their spirit when they saw their leader routed, fled in confusion. Those men were pursued by vengeful Romans, Visigoths and Franks who ignored the fortified camp and went for the easier pickings of fleeing men.

As Atilla had anticipated, the coming darkness saved the larger part of the Hunnic army, with the battlefield degenerating into the utter confusion common to night fighting: Aetius became separated from his own men and took refuge with a Visigothic unit, while the battlefield was so muddled that Theodoric's son Thorismund, having become thoroughly lost, actually rode into Attila's camp with a band of his household warriors and was wounded in the ensuing fight before his men managed to extricate him. The fighting petered off as the darkness became complete.

Jordanes described the fighting during this climactic battle:

"The armies met in the Catalaunian Plains. The battlefield was a plain rising by a sharp slope to a ridge which both armies sought to gain; for advantage of position is a great help. The Huns with their forces seized the right side, the Romans, the Visigoths and their allies the left, and then began a struggle for the yet untaken crest. Now Theodoric with his Visigoths held the right wing, and Aetius with the Romans the left. On the other side, the battle line of the Huns was so arranged that Attila and his bravest followers were stationed in the center. In arranging them thus the king had chiefly his own safety in view, since by his position in the very midst of his race, he would be kept out of the way of threatened danger. The innumerable peoples of diverse tribes, which he had subjected to his sway, formed the wings. Now the crowd of kings---if we may call them so---and the leaders of various nations hung upon Attila's nod like slaves, and when he gave a sign even by a glance, without a murmur each stood forth in fear and trembling, or at all events did as he was bid. Attila alone was king of kings over all and concerned for all.

So then the struggle began for the advantage of position we have mentioned. Attila sent his men to take the summit of the mountain, but was outstripped by Thorismud [crown prince of the Visigoths] and Aetius, who in their effort to gain the top of the hill reached higher ground, and through this advantage easily routed the Huns as they came up. When Attila saw his army was thrown into confusion by the event he [urged them on with a fiery harangue and . . .] inflamed by his words they all dashed into the battle.

And although the situation was itself fearful, yet the presence of the king dispelled anxiety and hesitation. Hand to hand they clashed in battle, and the fight grew fierce, confused, monstrous, unrelenting---a fight whose like no ancient time has ever recorded. There were such deeds done that a brave man who missed this marvelous spectacle could not hope to see anything so wonderful all his life long. For if we may believe our elders a brook flowing between low banks through the plain was greatly increased by blood from the wounds of the slain. Those whose wounds drove them to slake their parching thirst drank water mingled with gore. In their wretched plight they were forced to drink what they thought was the blood they had poured out from their own wounds.

Here King Theodoric [the Visigoth] while riding by to encourage his army, was thrown from his horse and trampled underfoot by his own men, thus ending his days at a ripe old age. But others say he was slain by the spear of Andag of the host of the Ostrogoths who were then under the sway of Attila. Then the Visigoths fell on the horde of the Huns and nearly slew Attila. But he prudently took flight and straightway shut himself and his companions within the barriers of the camp which he had fortified with wagons. [The battle now became confused: chieftains became separated from their forces: night fell with the Roman-Gothic army holding the field of combat.]

At dawn on the next day the Romans saw that the fields were piled high with corpses, and that the Huns did not venture forth; they thought that the victory was theirs, but knew that Attila would not flee from battle unless overwhelmed by a great disaster. Yet he did nothing cowardly, like one that is overcome, but with clash of arms sounded the trumpets and threatened an attack. [His enemies] determined to wear him out by a siege. It is said that the king remained supremely brave even in this extremity and had heaped up a funeral pyre of horse trappings, so that if the enemy should attack him he was determined to cast himself into the flames; that none might have the joy of wounding him, and that the lord of so many races might not fall into the hands of his foes. However, owing to dissensions between the Romans and Goths he was allowed to escape to his home land, and in this most famous war of the bravest tribes, 160,000 men are said to have been slain on both sides."

Jordanes's exaggerations aside, when dawn broke the weary Romans and Goths awoke to a field of slaughter and an enemy which, though outnumbered and surrounded, remained firmly defiant. Legend has it the Romans exclaimed, "Cadavera vero innumera" ("Truly countless bodies").

Nevertheless, Attila refused to countenance surrender, prepared to fight to the death. But Aetius, who was leery of the casualties he would sustain if he stormed the camp, hesitated, reckoning that it would be simpler to just starve Attila and his men out. His hand risked being forced, however, when the body of Theodoric was discovered, which prompted Thorismund to demand that a charge be led against the surrounded Huns.

Aetius, however, was as much a politician as he was a soldier, and he needed to be to have survived the intrigues of the imperial court for so long. If Attila were to die and the cream of the Hunnic army be destroyed, he reckoned, the Hunnic empire would disintegrate, in which case the Visigoths would lose the greatest threat to their own domains and their chief reason to stay restless allies of Rome, thereby costing Rome the Gaulish provinces. If, on the other hand, he allowed Attila to depart unmolested, he kept the Visigoths as his reluctant friends. Perhaps a lingering regard for the man he had once called his friend also stayed his hand. Whatever his reasons, Aetius took Thorismund aside and told him that he must immediately depart for the Visigothic kingdoms in order to make good his claim to the throne before his brothers seized it in his absence. Aetius then rid himself of the Franks by claiming that the Hunnic fugitives might intend to ravage their defenseless domains out of spite before returning home. He stayed on the field just long enough to plunder the dead and Attila's baggage train, and then departed himself.

Attila was understandably wary at first, thinking that the retreat was a ruse to draw him out into the open, but eventually he was persuaded that his enemies had truly gone. He and his battered army limped home, bloodied but not beaten.

Historians have since ranked the Battle of Châlons one of the most important of the late antiquity, and it was named one of history's 15 most important battles in Sir Edward Creasy's *The Fifteen Decisive Battles of the World*:

> "The discomfiture of the mighty attempt of Attila to found a new anti-Christian dynasty upon the wreck of the temporal power of Rome, at the end of the term of twelve hundred years, to which its duration had been limited by the forebodings of the heathen…Attila's attacks on the Western empire were soon renewed, but never with such peril to the civilized world as had menaced it before his defeat at Châlons; and on his death, two years after that battle, the vast empire which his genius had founded was soon dissevered by the successful revolts of the subject nations. The name of the Huns ceased for some centuries to inspire terror in Western Europe, and their ascendancy passed away with the life of the great king by whom it had been so fearfully augmented."

That sentiment was echoed by historian John Julius Norwich, who wrote, "It should never be forgotten that in the summer of 451 and again in 452, the whole fate of western civilization hung in the balance. Had the Hunnish army not been halted in these two successive campaigns, had its leader toppled Valentinian from his throne and set up his own capital at Ravenna or Rome, there is little doubt that both Gaul and Italy would have been reduced to spiritual and cultural deserts."

Conversely, ancient historian J.B. Bury argued that the battle was not truly decisive in the sense that the fate of Western civilization hung in the balance:

> "If Attila had been victorious, if he had defeated the Romans and the Goths at Orleans, if he had held Gaul at his mercy and had translated — and we have no

evidence that this was his design — the seat of his government and the abode of his people from the Theiss to the Seine or the Loire, there is no reason to suppose that the course of history would have been seriously altered. For the rule of the Huns in Gaul could only have been a matter of a year or two; it could not have survived here, any more than it survived in Hungary, the death of the great king, on whose brains and personal character it depended. Without depreciating the achievement of Aëtius and Theoderic we must recognise that at worst the danger they averted was of a totally different order from the issues which were at stake on the fields of Plataea and the Metaurus. If Attila had succeeded in his campaign, he would probably have been able to compel the surrender of Honoria, and if a son had been born of their marriage and proclaimed Augustus in Gaul, the Hun might have been able to exercise considerable influence on the fortunes of that country; but that influence would probably not have been anti-Roman."

Chapter 4: The Final Campaign

Attila's defeat on the Catalaunian plains at the hands of Aetius, Theodoric and Merovech seems not to have tarnished his reputation, despite the fact that his campaign was in many respects an abject failure. He had not significantly extended his borders or gained sufficient plunder to justify the vast loss of life that had occurred at the hands of the Romano-Gothic army, but there was no dissent at home and all his important vassals seem to have accepted his right to kingship as fairly set in stone.

This was made clear by the fact that Attila began making trouble for the Romans again in 452 A.D., just a year after the climactic battle in June 451. Despite his defeat, he clearly did not intend to let the Western Roman Empire frighten him, possibly because he construed Aetius's decision not to press the attack home on the Catalaunian Fields as weakness. Though he had a bone to pick with the Eastern Roman Empire (Marcian, Theodosius's successor, had stopped paying his predecessor's tribute), he renewed his demands for Honoria's hand, insisting that Valentinian honor the terms of the marriage agreement he had one-sidedly decided upon. When Valentinian once again indignantly refused, possibly confident that Aetius would see Attila off once again, Attila invaded.

Once again Attila gathered a vast force of tens of thousands of men, calling upon the soldiers of his subordinate nations, and marched into the Balkans. From there, rather than continue to skirt the Alps to the north and advance into Gaul that way, he struck into Italy proper through the northeastern corner in proximity of what would become Trieste. From there, he advanced into the area of the Venetian lagoon, whose inhabitants fled from his advance to the safety of the islets that dotted the vast marshy expanse of the estuary, a safety which many of them never left. These refugees would eventually go on to found the city of Venice, safe from the repeated Germanic invasions which ravaged the north of Italy.

Attila then advanced further south to the city of Aquileia, which seems to have given him particular offense. Perhaps the inhabitants were particularly defiant, or a delegation from the city was rude to him, but Attila decided to make an example of Aquileia for some reason. He besieged Aquileia and erected a castle on the scarp overlooking the city (modern-day Udine, which did not exist prior to the sack of Aquileia) in order to watch the city's destruction in comfort, and then had it utterly and completely razed to the ground, wiping it off the map for ever. Attila might have been concerned that his old rival Aetius would attack him as he engaged in the lengthy siege, but he need not have worried. Bereft of his Germanic allies, who would only have gotten involved in the war had Attila threatened their own domains directly, Aetius's army was vastly outnumbered by Attila's forces. He was forced to shadow Attila's march, containing the forays of his outriders and hoping to pick off a stray unit.

Attila's army was ravaged by an opponent of a far different nature. The mist-shrouded plains of the Po valley were an unhealthy place for any large body of men, and Attila's invasion ground to a dispiriting halt on the banks of the Po River, where disease began to run rampant through his camp. Hundreds died, seriously jeopardizing his invasion plans, and Attila's men had eaten the fertile breadbasket of the Po valley until nothing remained.

Realizing that Attila was facing difficulties, Valentinian decided it was an opportune time to talk. Three envoys were sent to talk with Attila: Gennadius Avienus and Trigetius, two important patrician politicians, and the Bishop of Rome himself, Pope (later Saint) Leo the Great. By the time the talks, which took place near the city of Mantua, were over, Attila had agreed to withdraw unconditionally from Italy and negotiate a truce with Valentinian, as well as giving up all claims to Honoria's hand. One of the seminal events of Attila's life had transpired, but what exactly happened?

Illustration of the meeting between Attila and Pope Leo from the Chronicon Pictum, circa 1360

The most popular account of the legendary meeting between Attila and Valentinian's delegation credits Pope Leo the Great with somehow talking the barbarian out of sacking Rome. Ecclesiastical chronicles that later recounted the event imbue Leo with quasi-miraculous powers of persuasion and depict him as being capable of harnessing the power of Heaven to persuade Attila of the sinfulness of sacking the foremost city in Christianity. Others credited a vision of St. Peter and St. Paul converting Attila on the spot, with the unrepentant pagan somehow undergoing a new religious fervor. Prosper, a Christian chronicler, wrote an account in 455 that credited Leo with convincing the king of the Huns to withdraw a few years earlier:

"Now Attila, having once more collected his forces which had been scattered in Gaul [at the battle of Chalons], took his way through Pannonia into Italy. . . To the emperor and the senate and Roman people none of all the proposed plans to oppose the enemy seemed so practicable as to send legates to the most savage king and beg for peace. Our most blessed Pope Leo - trusting in the help of God, who never fails the righteous in their trials - undertook the task, accompanied by Avienus, a man of consular rank, and the prefect Trygetius. And the outcome was what his faith had foreseen; for when the king had received the embassy, he was so impressed by the presence of the high priest that he ordered his army to give up warfare and, after he had promised peace, he departed beyond the Danube."

An anonymous account of the meeting likely relying in part on Prosper's account made the meeting even more miraculous:

"Attila, the leader of the Huns, who was called the scourge of God, came into Italy, inflamed with fury, after he had laid waste with most savage frenzy Thrace and Illyricum, Macedonia and Moesia, Achaia and Greece, Pannonia and Germany. He was utterly cruel in inflicting torture, greedy in plundering, insolent in abuse…He destroyed Aquileia from the foundations and razed to the ground those regal cities, Pavia and Milan; he laid waste many other towns, and was rushing down upon Rome.

Then Leo had compassion on the calamity of Italy and Rome, and with one of the consuls and a large part of the Roman senate he went to meet Attila. The old man of harmless simplicity, venerable in his gray hair and his majestic garb, ready of his own will to give himself entirely for the defense of his flock, went forth to meet the tyrant who was destroying all things. He met Attila, it is said, in the neighborhood of the river Mincio, and he spoke to the grim monarch, saying "The senate and the people of Rome, once conquerors of the world, now indeed vanquished, come before thee as suppliants. We pray for mercy and deliverance. O Attila, thou king of kings, thou couldst have no greater glory than to see suppliant at thy feet this people before whom once all peoples and kings lay suppliant. Thou hast subdued, O Attila, the whole circle of the lands which it was granted to the Romans, victors over all peoples, to conquer. Now we pray that thou, who hast conquered others, shouldst conquer thyself The people have felt thy scourge; now as suppliants they would feel thy mercy."

As Leo said these things Attila stood looking upon his venerable garb and aspect, silent, as if thinking deeply. And lo, suddenly there were seen the apostles Peter and Paul, clad like bishops, standing by Leo, the one on the right hand, the other on the left. They held swords stretched out over his head, and threatened Attila with death if he did not obey the pope's command. Wherefore Attila was appeased he who had raged as one mad. He by Leo's intercession, straightway promised a lasting peace and withdrew beyond the Danube."

These accounts led to the romanticization of the meeting and the role Leo the Great played in it.

Raphael's *The Meeting between Leo the Great and Attila* depicts Leo, escorted by Saint
Peter and Saint Paul, meeting with Attila outside of Rome

The Meeting of Leo I and Attila by Alessandro Algardi

In reality, religion likely had very little to do with Attila's decision to withdraw the Hunnic Army from Italy; Attila's advance had ground to a halt and he knew it. Not only had his forces exhausted their forward momentum, but disease had killed or weakened a great number of his men, and starvation threatened to overwhelm the rest. Not only had they devoured all of the available food in the Po Valley, which in turn supplied most of Italy with its produce, but 451 had brought a famine to Italy that left much of the peninsula on the verge of starvation. Even if Attila had managed to stir his men into marching southward, he would have been forced to supply his men long enough to besiege and take Rome and then would have been stuck with a city that was empty of food anyway. The 5th century Bishop Hydatius credited Attila's misfortune to divine intervention, writing, "The Huns, who had been plundering Italy and who had also stormed a number of cities, were victims of divine punishment, being visited with heaven-sent disasters: famine and some kind of disaster. In addition, they were slaughtered by auxiliaries sent by the Emperor Marcian and led by Aetius, at the same time, they were crushed in their [home] settlements....Thus crushed, they made peace with the Romans and all retired to their homes."

The ancient chroniclers also mention that Attila, who was fairly superstitious, had been warned that Alaric, the Goth who had sacked Rome in 410 A.D., had suffered a fairly grisly fate in the wake of his own assault. More prosaically, however, Attila had also received some distressing intelligence. Profiting from his absence, and the absence of the main Hunnic army, the Eastern Roman Empire had gone on the offensive and struck north through the Balkans and across the Danube, routing the skeleton garrisons of old men and untrained boys that Attila had left to protect the Hunnic heartland. The Eastern Roman general, confusingly also named Aetius, was rampaging at will across the plains of Hungary, and Attila had no choice but to march back north with his invasion ending in ignominious failure. Attila quickly force-marched the remnants of his army back through the northern Balkans and through Eastern Europe back into the Hunnic heartland. Aetius, hearing of his coming, wisely fell back towards the borders of the Eastern Roman Empire.

Attila, furious that Marcian had first dared stop the tribute and now even had the temerity to attack into his own domains, wasted no time in gathering an army with which he planned to strike south, in order to teach the impudent Marcian a lesson once and for all. However, his final ambition, which may have included the destruction of Constantinople itself, was not to be. In 453 A.D., Attila died.

Like many of the seminal events in Attila's life, the ending of it is shrouded in mystery. Several conflicting accounts and theories relating to Attila's death exist, but each of them is as feasible as the next. All accounts, however, agree that Attila's death took place in the spring of 453 A.D., during the wedding feast to celebrate his union with his latest wife (of whom he is reputed to have had dozens), a young Gothic girl named Ildico who was in all likelihood at least three decades his junior.

However, similarities between the accounts end there. According to Priscus, Attila was celebrating with vast amounts of wine when he was suddenly struck by a nosebleed. Normally this would not have been cause for concern, but the nosebleed was both unusually powerful and, despite efforts to staunch it, did not seem to abate. Eventually, it began flowing backwards into his throat and lungs, and Attila suffocated, choking to death on his own blood. Modern physicians have hazarded that Attila may have suffered from esophageal varices, a condition which can be aggravated by cirrhosis and which was triggered by Attila's excessive consumption of alcohol on the evening of his wedding feast, causing a rupture of the veins within his esophagus. His digestive tract then flooded with blood, which he began to retch out of his nose and mouth, confusing eyewitnesses who could have construed it as a nosebleed, and killing him either via suffocation or internal blood-loss.

Perhaps the best known account of Attila's death comes from Marcellinus Comes, an Eastern Roman ecclesiastical historian who wrote almost a century after the event in question. Marcellinus suggested that Attila was killed either by Ildico or one of his wives, by the former because she was terrified of him and was against the marriage, or by the latter because she was jealous of his newest bride. However, it is worth noting that Marcellinus, as an ecclesiastical historian who worked in Constantinople, had no reason to love Attila nor any desire to paint him in a favorable light, so the humiliating story of the great warrior Attila being murdered by a woman in his own bed would have made for a tale pleasing to his audience. Therefore, it is unlikely that this version of events is true.

A more modern theory put forth by several scholars with regards to Attila's death is that it was caused by premeditated foul play rather than a cold crime of passion. According to the historian Michael Babcock, the death of Attila was actually a plot orchestrated by Marcian himself, in which case he would either have been poisoned – hence the massive loss of blood during the banquet – or the woman who murdered him was an imperial agent (although the first possibility is by far more credible). Certainly Marcian, who was far more bellicose and hostile toward Attila than Theodosius, as his invasion of the Hunnic heartland had proved, had ample motive for wanting Attila dead, and as Eastern Roman Emperor he definitely possessed the means to make it happen. That said, it is likely the answer to what really caused Attila's death died with him.

After Attila was dead, his household warriors flew into a frenzy, lamenting the fact that he had died in such a fashion that made revenge against his perceived killers impossible. They celebrated his death with a great feast which lasted for days on end, at the end of which they placed Attila in a triple coffin, a smaller one of gold encasing his remains which was in turn placed within a silver coffin and, finally within an iron casket. His body was buried and a river diverted over his final resting place in order to destroy all evidence of where he lay, in case his enemies decided to desecrate his grave. Finally, his household warriors were either killed or took their own lives so that they could never disclose where Attila's body was entombed.

Upon Attila's death, the empire that he and his forefathers had painstakingly constructed quickly disintegrated. Although Attila had appointed his son Ellac as his successor, his brothers, of which there were literally dozens (chief among them Denzigich and Ernak) were not content to allow him to assume the kingship. The other brothers insisted that the various vassal kings of the Ostrogoths, Scirii, Rugians, Bastarnae, Thuringians, Alamanni, Gepids and Heruli (among others) swear fealty to specific brothers, rather than all of them giving their allegiance to Ellac. After a year of squabbling, matters came to a head. The vassal nations of the Gepids, Heruli, Ostrogoths, Rugii, Scirii, and Suebi united in a grand coalition whose one objective was to throw off the yoke of Hunnic rule. Their leader, Ardaric of the Gepids, was a doughty and resourceful general who had been one of Attila's most prized commanders, and he made short work of the Hunnic army that marched against them under Ellac and his brothers (who apparently put their differences aside temporarily to face the common enemy). Ellac's forces were routed, and he himself was cut down in single combat by Ardaric, who was old in war and had been fighting since before Ellac was born. With his death came the final disintegration of the Hunnic Empire, which would never again exist as a unified political entity. The age of the Huns was over.

Chapter 5: Attila's Legacy

Throughout history, Attila has enjoyed an unsurprisingly mixed reputation. To the citizens of the Roman Empire whom he waged a decades-long war against, he was "the Scourge of God", a terrifying epithet which another horse-borne conqueror – Genghis Khan – would later apply to himself when communicating with his enemies (though it does not appear likely that Genghis Khan would have been familiar with the life and achievements of Attila, who preceded him by almost a millennium).

Despite his reputation during antiquity, after his untimely death Attila seems to have enjoyed something of a public relations resurgence based on his legendary meeting with Pope Leo the Great. Attila, who was and likely remained an unrepentant pagan, was described in a subsequent medieval chronicle as having been persuaded by the apostles Saint Peter and Paul (who were obviously long in their graves by then) to spare the city of Rome his ravages. Some more fanciful chronicles also suggest that Attila converted on the spot, while others more practically insist that he asked for a holy crown in return, a myth later used by several royal dynasties in Eastern Europe who claimed descent from Attila to justify their kingship.

Legends aside, much of the reliable information about Attila came chiefly from the writings of Priscus, who knew him personally and was a guest at his court, but even then large portions of his work have been lost. The more fanciful Jordanes, who drew heavily on Priscus's work, is far less reliable and given to frequent flights of imagination; he described Attila carrying into battle the "Holy War Sword of the Scythians", which had been presented to him by Mars himself with the promise that he would be ruler of the whole world.

However, any goodwill Attila's sparing of Rome might have engendered seems to have vanished during the Middle Ages. Medieval writers savaged Attila and his reputation, and their influence still carries on to this day. Dante placed him in Hell in his *Inferno*, submerged in the Phlegeton, the boiling river of blood. Even in more modern times, Bram Stoker described him as a "fiend" in *Dracula* and had the notorious Count proudly claim ancestry from him. And though he is far more popular in Northern and Eastern Europe and Turkey than he ever was in the West, Attila was still a figure to be feared, and in many cases reviled, all the way to the beginning of the 20th century.

In the early 1900s Kaiser Wilhelm of Germany gave a speech which praised the military capabilities of Attila, most likely because he was under the impression Attila was of Germanic origin and wanted to liken Germany's war machine to the Huns. The British and American press gleefully seized upon the inevitable comparison with rampaging hordes of bloodthirsty barbarians tearing all that was civilized apart and labeled the Germans "the Huns", an epithet which they retained for all of World War I and up to World War II, when it was replaced with the less menacing "Krauts" and "Jerries".

Much of this misinformation about Attila stems from the fact that so little is known about his early life, with only the fragmentary Priscus and the imaginative Jordanes as authoritative sources (though he does appear, indirectly, in a number of ecclesiastical chronicles concerning the lives of clergymen he affected or ended). His invasion of Italy is well-documented, as are some of his campaigns against Byzantium, but much of what he did elsewhere is the subject only of informed speculation.

What is certain is that Attila's reputation was tarnished by a large amount of scorn, as his run-ins with Christians meant that the almost universally ecclesiastical scholars who wrote about him in the Dark and Middle Ages invariably characterized him as a villain. In fairness, Atilla was likely no more bloodthirsty than many conquerors, and even a good deal more tolerant and level-headed than most. Priscus describes Attila as a wise, clean-living man who abstained from worldly wealth and excess, a depiction wildly at odds with the popular perception of Attila as being a bloodthirsty barbarian. The veracity of Priscus's description is substantiated by the simple fact that no maniac bent solely on destruction would have been able to govern an empire as large and diverse as the Hunnic empire for two decades. Though he inherited a significant portion of his domains, Attila still presided over a territory which, at its height, stretched from Germany and Denmark in the west up to the Baltic in the north, down to the Balkans and the Black Sea in the south all the way to Kazakhstan.

Thus, Attila remains a fascinating, mysterious, and sometimes confusing figure. He was a successful general who based his strategy on lightning attacks, winning dozens of victories and filling his Empire's coffers with plunder and tribute. But he also approached the greatest battle of his lifetime, the Battle of the Catalaunian Fields against Aetius and his Germanic allies, with a remarkable amount of caution bordering on timidity. And his hesitation during his invasion of Italy, although justifiable, ultimately cost him his conquest of the Western Roman Empire, just as his retreat from Aurelianum meant that he was unable to expand the Hunnic Empire into Gaul. Though he had his reasons for such decisions, a more audacious conqueror might have seized the moment and pushed the boundaries of the Hunnic Empire further than Attila had or maybe even imagined. And though he could be utterly ruthless, as his destruction of Aquileia, the ransacking of other cities and the wholesale selling of entire populations into slavery proves, he could also be remarkably tolerant, as his sparing of other defenseless population centers shows. Additionally, the fact that he succeeded in keeping scores of diverse peoples faithful, by hook or by crook, shows a remarkable mastery of the intricacies of politics, since Ardaric's almost immediate defection in the wake of his death shows that only a strong arm was holding his followers in check.

Unfortunately, Attila's history will likely always remain exceedingly bare, particularly when it comes to the most interesting aspects of his life, since he only appears in detail in recorded history when interacting with the Eastern and Western Roman Empire. But like any historical legend, the fact that we must speculate about much of his life and death helps ensure Attila the Hun continues to fascinate future generations.

Priscus' Account of Attila and His Court

We set out with the barbarians, and arrived at Sardica, which is thirteen days for a fast traveller from Constantinople. Halting there we considered it advisable to invite Edecon and the barbarians with him to dinner. The inhabitants of the place sold us sheep and oxen, which we slaughtered, and we prepared a meal. In the course of the feast, as the barbarians lauded Attila and we lauded the Emperor, Bigilas remarked that it was not fair to compare a man and a god, meaning Attila by the man and Theodosius by the god. The Huns grew excited and hot at this remark. But we turned the conversation in another direction, and soothed their wounded feelings; and after dinner, when we separated, Maximin presented Edecon and Orestes with silk garments and Indian gems....

When we arrived at Naissus we found the city deserted, as though it had been sacked; only a few sick persons lay in the churches. We halted at a short distance from the river, in an open space, for all the ground adjacent to the bank was full of the bones of men slain in war. On the morrow we came to the station of Agintheus, the commander-in-chief of the Illyrian armies (magister militum per Illyricum), who was posted not far from Naissus, to announce to him the Imperial commands, and to receive five of those seventeen deserters, about whom Attila had written to the Emperor. We had an interview with him, and having treated the deserters with kindness, he committed them to us. The next day we proceeded from the district of Naissus towards the Danube; we entered a covered valley with many bends and windings and circuitous paths. We thought we were travelling due west, but when the day dawned the sun rose in front; and some of us unacquainted with the topography cried out that the sun was going the wrong way, and portending unusual events. The fact was that that part of the road faced the east, owing to the irregularity of the ground. Having passed these rough places we arrived at a plain which was also well wooded. At the river we were received by barbarian ferrymen, who rowed us across the river in boats made by themselves out of single trees hewn and hollowed. These preparations had not been made for our sake, but to convey across a company of Huns; for Attila pretended that he wished to hunt in Roman territory, but his intent was really hostile, because all the deserters had not been given up to him. Having crossed the Danube, and proceeded with the barbarians about seventy stadia, we were compelled to wait in a certain plain, that Edecon and his party might go on in front and inform Attila of our arrival. As we were dining in the evening we heard the sound of horses approaching, and two Scythians arrived with directions that we were to set out to Attila. We asked them first to partake of our meal, and they dismounted and made good cheer. On the next day, under their guidance, we arrived at the tents of Attila, which were numerous, about three o'clock, and when we wished to pitch our tent on a hill the barbarians who met us prevented us, because the tent of Attila was on low ground, so we halted where the Scythians desired....

(Then a message is received from Attila, who was aware of the nature of their embassy, saying that if they had nothing further to communicate to him he would not receive them, so they reluctantly prepared to return.)

When the baggage had been packed on the beasts of burden, and we were perforce preparing to start in the night time, messengers came from Attila bidding us wait on account of the late hour. Then men arrived with an ox and river fish, sent to us by Attila, and when we had dined we retired to sleep. When it was day we expected a gentle and courteous message from the barbarian, but he again bade us depart if we had no further mandates beyond what he already knew. We made no reply, and prepared to set out, though Bigilas insisted that we should feign to have some other communication to make. When I saw that Maximin was very dejected, I went to Scottas (one of the Hun nobles, brother of Onegesius), taking with me Rusticius, who understood the Hun language. He had come with us to Scythia, not as a member of the embassy, but on business with Constantius, an Italian whom Aetius had sent to Attila to be that monarch's private secretary. I informed Scottas, Rusticius acting as interpreter, that Maximin would give him many presents if he would procure him an interview with Attila; and, moreover, that the embassy would not only conduce to the public interests of the two powers, but to the private interest of Onegesius, for the Emperor desired that he should be sent as an ambassador to Byzantium, to arrange the disputes of the Huns and Romans, and that there he would receive splendid gifts. As Onegesius was not present it was for Scottas, I said, to help us, or rather help his brother, and at the same time prove that the report was true which ascribed to him an influence with Attila equal to that possessed by his brother. Scottas mounted his horse and rode to Attila's tent, while I returned to Maximin and found him in a state of perplexity and anxiety, lying on the grass with Bigilas. I described my interview with Scottas, and bade him make preparations for an audience of Attila. They both jumped up, approving of what I had done, and recalled the men who had started with the beasts of burden. As we were considering what to say to Attila, and how to present the Emperor's gifts, Scottas came to fetch us, and we entered Attila's tent, which was surrounded by a multitude of barbarians. We found Attila sitting on a wooden chair. We stood at a little distance and Maximin advanced and saluted the barbarian, to whom he gave the Emperor's letter, saying that the Emperor prayed for the safety of him and his. The king replied, "It shall be unto the Romans as they wish it to be unto me," and immediately addressed Bigilas, calling him a shameless beast, and asking him why he ventured to come when all the deserters had not been given up. . . .

After the departure of Bigilas, who returned to the Empire (nominally to find the deserters whose restoration Attila demanded, but really to get the money for his fellow-conspirator Edecon), we remained one day in that place, and then set out with Attila for the northern parts of the country. We accompanied the barbarian for a time, but when we reached a certain point took another route by the command of the Scythians who conducted us, as Attila was proceeding to a village where he intended to marry the daughter of Eskam, though he had many other wives, for the Scythians practise polygamy. We proceeded along a level road in a plain and met with navigable rivers--of which the greatest, next to the Danube, are the Drecon, Tigas, and Tiphesas--which we crossed in the Monoxyles, boats made of one piece, used by the dwellers on the banks: the smaller rivers we traversed on rafts which the barbarians carry about with them on carts, for the purpose of crossing morasses. In the villages we were supplied with food--millet instead of corn, and mead, as the natives call it, instead of wine. The attendants who followed us received millet, and a drink made of barley, which the barbarians call kam. Late in the evening, having travelled a long distance, we pitched our tents on the banks of a fresh-water lake, used for water by the inhabitants of the neighbouring village. But a wind and storm, accompanied by thunder and lightning and heavy rain, arose, and almost threw down our tents; all our utensils were rolled into the waters of the lake. Terrified by the mishap and the atmospherical disturbance, we left the place and lost one another in the dark and the rain, each following the road that seemed most easy. But we all reached the village by different ways, and raised an alarm to obtain what we lacked. The Scythians of the village sprang out of their huts at the noise, and, lighting the reeds which they use for kindling fires, asked what we wanted. Our conductors replied that the storm had alarmed us; so they invited us to their huts and provided warmth for us by lighting large fires of reeds. The lady who governed the village- -she had been one of Bleda's wives--sent us provisions and good-looking girls to console us (this is a Scythian compliment). We treated the young women to a share in the eatables. but declined to take any further advantage of their presence. We remained in the huts till day dawned and then went to look for our lost utensils, which we found partly in the place where we had pitched the tent, partly on the bank of the lake, and partly in the water. We spent that day in the village drying our things; for the storm had ceased and the sun was bright. Having looked after our horses and cattle, we directed our steps to the princess, to whom we paid our respects and presented gifts in return for her courtesy. The gifts consisted of things which are esteemed by the barbarians as not produced in the country--three silver phials, red skins, Indian pepper, palm fruit, and other delicacies.

Having advanced a distance of seven days farther, we halted at a village; for as the rest of the route was the same for us and Attila, it behoved us to wait, so that he might go in front. Here we met with some of the "western Romans," who had also come on an embassy to Attila--the count Romulus, Promotus governor of Noricum, and Romanus a military captain. With them was Constantius whom Aetius had sent to Attila to be his secretary, and Tatulus, the father of Orestes; these two were not connected with the embassy, but were friends of the ambassadors. Constantius had known them of old in the Italies, and Orestes had married the daughter of Romulus. The object of the embassy, was to soften the soul of Attila, who demanded the surrender of one Silvanus, a dealer in silver plate in Rome, because he had received golden vessels from a certain Constantius. This Constantius, a native of Gaul, had preceded his namesake in the office of secretary to Attila. When Sirmium in Pannonia was besieged by the Scythians, the bishop of the place consigned the vessels to his (Constantius') care, that if the city were taken and he survived they might be used to ransom him; and in case he were slain, to ransom the citizens who were led into captivity. But when the city was enslaved, Constantius violated his engagement, and, as he happened to be at Rome on business, pawned the vessels to Silvanus for a sum of money, on condition that if he gave back the money within a prescribed period the dishes should be returned, but otherwise should become the property of Silvanus. Constantius, suspected of treachery, was crucified by Attila and Bleda; and afterwards, when the affair of the vessels became known to Attila, he demanded the surrender of Silvanus on the ground that he had stolen his property. Accordingly Aetius and the Emperor of the Western Romans sent to explain that Silvanus was the creditor of Constantius, the vessels having been pawned and not stolen, and that he had sold them to priests and others for sacred purposes. If, however, Attila refused to desist from his demand, he, the Emperor, would send him the value of the vessels, but would not surrender the innocent Silvanus.

Having waited for some time until Attila advanced in front of us, we proceeded, and having crossed some rivers we arrived at a large village, where Attila's house was said to be more splendid than his residences in other places. It was made of polished boards, and surrounded with a wooden enclosure, designed, not for protection, but for appearance. The house of Onegesius was second to the king's in splendour, and was also encircled with a wooden enclosure, but it was not adorned with towers like that of the king. Not far from the enclosure was a large bath which Onegesius--who was the second in power among the Scythians-- built, having transported the stones from Pannonia; for the barbarians in this district had no stones or trees, but used imported material. The builder of the bath was a captive from Sirmium, who expected to win his freedom as payment for making the bath. But he was disappointed, and greater trouble befell him than mere captivity among the Scythians, for Onegesius appointed him bathman, and he used to minister to him and his family when they bathed.

When Attila entered the village he was met by girls advancing in rows, under thin white canopies of linen, which were held up by the outside women who stood under them, and were so large that seven or more girls walked beneath each. There were many lines of damsels thus canopied, and they sang Scythian songs. When he came near the house of Onegesius, which lay on his way, the wife of Onegesius issued from the door, with a number of servants, bearing meat and wine, and saluted him and begged him to partake of her hospitality. This is the highest honour that can be shown among the Scythians. To gratify the wife of his friend, he ate, just as he sat on his horse, his attendants raising the tray to his saddlebow; and having tasted the wine, he went on to the palace, which was higher than the other houses and built on an elevated site. But we remained in the house of Onegesius, at his invitation, for he had returned from his expedition with Attila's son. His wife and kinsfolk entertained us to dinner, for he had no leisure himself, as he had to relate to Attila the result of his expedition, and explain the accident which had happened to the young prince, who had slipped and broken his right arm. After dinner we left the house of Onegesius, and took up our quarters nearer the palace, so that Maximin might be at a convenient distance for visiting Attila or holding intercourse with his court. The next morning, at dawn of day, Maximin sent me to Onegesius, with presents offered by himself as well as those which the Emperor had sent, and I was to find out whether he would have an interview with Maximin and at what time. When I arrived at the house, along with the attendants who carried the gifts, I found the doors closed, and had to wait until some one should come out and announce our arrival. As I waited and walked up and down in front of the enclosure which surrounded the house, a man, whom from his Scythian dress I took for a barbarian, came up and addressed me in Greek, with the word Xaire, "Hail!" I was surprised at a Scythian speaking Greek. For the subjects of the Huns, swept together from various lands, speak, besides their own barbarous tongues, either Hunnic or Gothic, or--as many as have commercial dealings with the western Romans--Latin; but none of them easily speak Greek, except captives from the Thracian or Illyrian sea-coast; and these last are easily known to any stranger by their torn garments and the squalor of their heads, as men who have met with a reverse. This man, on the contrary, resembled a well-to-do Scythian, being well dressed, and having his hair cut in a circle after Scythian fashion. Having returned his salutation, I asked him who he was and whence he had come into a foreign land and adopted Scythian life. When he asked me why I wanted to know, I told him that his Hellenic speech had prompted my curiosity. Then he smiled and said that he was born a Greek and had gone as a merchant to Viminacium, on the Danube, where he had stayed a long time, and married a very rich wife. But the city fell a prey to the barbarians, and he was stript of his prosperity, and on account of his riches was allotted to Onegesius in the division of the spoil, as it was the custom among the Scythians for the chiefs to reserve for themselves the rich prisoners. Having fought bravely against the Romans and the Acatiri, he had paid the spoils he won to his master, and so obtained freedom. He then married a barbarian wife and had children, and had the privilege of eating at the table of Onegesius.

He considered his new life among the Scythians better than his old life among the Romans, and the reasons he gave were as follows: "After war the Scythians live in inactivity, enjoying what they have got, and not at all, or very little, harassed. The Romans, on the other hand, are in the first place very liable to perish in war, as they have to rest their hopes of safety on others, and are not allowed, on account of their tyrants to use arms. And those who use them are injured by the cowardice of their generals, who cannot support the conduct of war. But the condition of the subjects in time of peace is far more grievous than the evils of war, for the exaction of the taxes is very severe, and unprincipled men inflict injuries on others, because the laws are practically not valid against all classes. A transgressor who belongs to the wealthy classes is not punished for his injustice, while a poor man, who does not understand business, undergoes the legal penalty, that is if he does not depart this life before the trial, so long is the course of lawsuits protracted, and so much money is expended on them. The climax of the misery is to have to pay in order to obtain justice. For no one will give a court to the injured man unless he pay a sum of money to the judge and the judge's clerks."

In reply to this attack on the Empire, I asked him to be good enough to listen with patience to the other side of the question. "The creators of the Roman republic," I said, "who were wise and good men, in order to prevent things from being done at haphazard made one class of men guardians of the laws, and appointed another class to the profession of arms, who were to have no other object than to be always ready for battle, and to go forth to war without dread, as though to their ordinary exercise having by practice exhausted all their fear beforehand. Others again were assigned to attend to the cultivation of the ground, to support both themselves and those who fight in their defence, by contributing the military corn-supply.... To those who protect the interests of the litigants a sum of money is paid by the latter, just as a payment is made by the farmers to the soldiers. Is it not fair to support him who assists and requite him for his kindness? The support of the horse benefits the horseman.... Those who spend money on a suit and lose it in the end cannot fairly put it down to anything but the injustice of their case. And as to the long time spent on lawsuits, that is due to concern for justice, that judges may not fail in passing correct judgments, by having to give sentence offhand; it is better that they should reflect, and conclude the case more tardily, than that by judging in a hurry they should both injure man and transgress against the Deity, the institutor of justice....The Romans treat their servants better than the king of the Scythians treats his subjects. They deal with them as fathers or teachers, admonishing them to abstain from evil and follow the lines of conduct whey they have esteemed honourable; they reprove them for their errors like their own children. They are not allowed, like the Scythians, to inflict death on them. They have numerous ways of conferring freedom; they can manumit not only during life, but also by their wills, and the testamentary wishes of a Roman in regard to his property are law."

My interlocutor shed tears, and confessed that the laws and constitution of the Romans were fair, but deplored that the governors, not possessing the spirit of former generations, were ruining the State.

As we were engaged in this discussion a servant came out and opened the door of the enclosure. I hurried up, and inquired how Onegesius was engaged, for I desired to give him a message from the Roman ambassador. He replied that I should meet him if I waited a little, as he was about to go forth. And after a short time I saw him coming out, and addressed him, saying, "The Roman ambassador salutes you, and I have come with gifts from him, and with the gold which the Emperor sent you. The ambassador is anxious to meet you, and begs you to appoint a time and place." Onegesius bade his servants receive the gold and the gifts, and told me to announce to Maximin that he would go to him immediately. I delivered the message, and Onegesius appeared in the tent without delay. He expressed his thanks to Maximin and the Emperor for the presents, and asked why he sent for him. Maximin said that the time had come for Onegesius to have greater renown among men, if he would go to the Emperor, and by his wisdom arrange the objects of dispute between the Romans and Huns, and establish concord between them; thereby he will procure many advantages for his own family, as he all his children will always be friends of the Emperor and the Imperial family. Onegesius inquired what measures would gratify the Emperor and how he could arrange the disputes. Maximin replied: "If you cross into the lands of the Roman Empire you will lay the Emperor under an obligation, and you will arrange the matters at issue by investigating their causes and deciding them on the basis of the peace." Onegesius said he would inform the Emperor and his ministers of Attila's wishes, but the Romans need not think they could ever prevail with him to betray his master or neglect his Scythian training and his wives and children, or to prefer wealth among the Romans to bondage with Attila. He added that he would be of more service to the Romans by remaining in his own land and softening the anger of his master, if he were indignant for aught with the Romans, than by visiting them and subjecting himself to blame if he made arrangements that Attila did not approve of. He then retired, having consented that I should act as an intermediary in conveying messages from Maximin to himself, for it would not have been consistent with Maximin's dignity as ambassador to visit him constantly.

The next day I entered the enclosure of Attila's palace, bearing gifts to his wife, whose name was Kreka. She had three sons, of whom the eldest governed the Acatiri and the other nations who dwell in Pontic Scythia. Within the enclosure were numerous buildings, some of carved boards beautifully fitted together, others of straight, fastened on round wooden blocks which rose to a moderate height from the ground. Attila's wife lived here, and, having been admitted by the barbarians at the door, I found her reclining on a soft couch. The floor of the room was covered with woollen mats for walking on. A number of servants stood round her, and maids sitting on the floor in front of her embroidered with colours linen cloths intended to be placed over the Scythian dress for ornament. Having approached, saluted, and presented the gifts, I went out, and walked to another house, where Attila was, and waited for Onegesius, who, as I knew, was with Attila. I stood in the middle of a great crowd--the guards of Attila and his attendants knew me, and so no one hindered me. I saw a number of people advancing, and a great commotion and noise, Attila's egress being expected. And he came forth from the house with a dignified gait, looking round on this side and on that. He was accompanied by Onegesius, and stood in front of the house; and many persons who had lawsuits with one another came up and received his judgment. Then he returned into the house, and received ambassadors of barbarous peoples.

As I was waiting for Onegesius, I was accosted by Romulus and Promotus and Romanus, the ambassadors who had come from Italy about the golden vessels; they were accompanied by Rusticius and by Constantiolus, a man from the Pannonian territory, which was subject to Attila. They asked me whether we had been dismissed or are constrained to remain, and I replied that it was just to learn this from Onegesius that I was waiting outside the palace. When I inquired in my turn whether Attila had vouchsafed them a kind reply, they told me that his decision could not be moved, and that he threatened war unless either Silvanus or the drinking-vessels were given up....

As we were talking about the state of the world, Onegesius came out; we went up to him and asked him about our concerns. Having first spoken with some barbarians, he bade me inquire of Maximin what consular the Romans are sending as an ambassador to Attila. When I came to our tent I delivered the message to Maximin, and deliberated with him what answer we should make to the question of the barbarian. Returning to Onegesius, I said that the Romans desired him to come to them and adjust the matters of dispute, otherwise the Emperor will send whatever ambassador he chooses. He then bade me fetch Maximin, whom he conducted to the presence of Attila. Soon after Maximin came out, and told me that the barbarian wished Nomus or Anatolius or Senator to be the ambassador, and that he would not receive any other than one of these three; when he (Maximin) replied that it was not meet to mention men by name and so render them suspected in the eyes of the Emperor, Attila said that if they do not choose to comply with his wishes the differences will be adjusted by arms.

When we returned to our tent the father of Orestes came with an invitation from Attila for both of us to a banquet at three o'clock. When the hour arrived we went to the palace, along with the embassy from the western Romans, and stood on the threshold of the hall in the presence of Attila. The cup-bearers gave us a cup, according to the national custom, that we might pray before we sat down. Having tasted the cup, we proceeded to take our seats; all the chairs were ranged along the walls of the room on either side. Attila sat in the middle on a couch; a second couch was set behind him, and from it steps led up to his bed, which was covered with linen sheets and wrought coverlets for ornament, such as Greeks and Romans use to deck bridal beds. The places on the right of Attila were held chief in honour, those on the left, where we sat, were only second. Berichus, a noble among the Scythians, sat on our side, but had the precedence of us. Onegesius sat on a chair on the right of Attila's couch, and over against Onegesius on a chair sat two of Attila's sons; his eldest son sat on his couch, not near him, but at the extreme end, with his eyes fixed on the ground, in shy respect for his father. When all were arranged, a cup-bearer came and handed Attila a wooden cup of wine. He took it, and saluted the first in precedence, who, honoured by the salutation, stood up, and might not sit down until the king, having tasted or drained the wine, returned the cup to the attendant. All the guests then honoured Attila in the same way, saluting him, and then tasting the cups; but he did not stand up. Each of us had a special cupbearer, who would come forward in order to present the wine, when the cup-bearer of Attila retired. When the second in precedence and those next to him had been honoured in like manner, Attila toasted us in the same way according to the order of the seats. When this ceremony was over the cup-bearers retired, and tables, large enough for three or four, or even more, to sit at, were placed next the table of Attila, so that each could take of the food on the dishes without leaving his seat. The attendant of Attila first entered with a dish full of meat, and behind him came the other attendants with bread and viands, which they laid on the tables. A luxurious meal, served on silver plate, had been made ready for us and the barbarian guests, but Attila ate nothing but meat on a wooden trencher. In everything else, too, he showed himself temperate; his cup was of wood, while to the guests were given goblets of gold and silver. His dress, too, was quite simple, affecting only to be clean. The sword he carried at his side, the latchets of his Scythian shoes, the bridle of his horse were not adorned, like those of the other Scythians, with gold or gems or anything costly. When the viands of the first course had been consumed we all stood up, and did not resume our seats until each one, in the order before observed, drank to the health of Attila in the goblet of wine presented to him. We then sat down, and a second dish was placed on each table with eatables of another kind. After this course the same ceremony was observed as after the first. When evening fell torches were lit, and two barbarians coming forward in front of Attila sang songs they had composed, celebrating his victories and deeds of valour in war. And of the guests, as they looked at the singers, some were pleased with the verses, others reminded of wars were excited in their souls, while yet others, whose bodies were feeble with age and their spirits compelled to rest, shed tears. After the songs a Scythian, whose mind was deranged, appeared, and by uttering outlandish and senseless words forced the company to laugh. After him Zerkon, the Moorish dwarf, entered. He had been sent by Attila as a gift to Aetius, and Edecon had persuaded him to come to Attila in order to recover his wife, whom he had left behind him in Scythia; the lady was a Scythian whom he had obtained in marriage through the influence of his patron Bleda. He did not succeed in recovering her, for Attila was angry with him for returning. On the occasion of the banquet he made his appearance, and threw all except Attila into fits of unquenchable laughter by his appearance, his dress, his voice, and his words, which were a confused jumble of Latin, Hunnic, and Gothic. Attila, however, remained immovable and of unchanging countenance nor by word or act did he betray anything approaching to a smile of merriment except at the entry of Ernas, his youngest son, whom he pulled by the cheek, and gazed on with a calm look of satisfaction. I was surprised that he made so much of this son, and neglected his other children but a barbarian who sat beside me and knew Latin, bidding me not reveal what he told, gave me to understand that prophets had forewarned Attila that his race would fall, but would be restored by this boy. When the night had advanced we retired from the banquet, not wishing to assist further at the potations.

Bibliography

Readers interested in learning more about Attila and the Huns should consult the works of Priscus and Jordanes.

More modern accounts include Edward Gibbon's seminal *Decline and Fall of the Roman Empire,* available for free in various translations on the internet as part of the public domain.

For the most modern takes, see John Man's *Attila: A Barbarian King and the Fall of Rome*; Ian Hughes's *Aetius: Attila's Nemesis*; and Michael Babcock's *The Night Attila Died: Solving the Murder of Attila the Hun.*

William the Conqueror

Chapter 1: The Normans

The Normans, "norsemen" or "men from the north", settled in Normandy about 150 years before the birth of William. In origin, they were essentially Vikings who arrived in their longboats and decided to stay, a pattern that the nomadic conquerors also established in northern England, Scotland and even as far afield as Russia. Those who built the Duchy of Normandy would provide the catalyst for a specific culture that came to exercise a strong political and military influence over much of Europe during the early Middle Ages.

Although they were initially pagans, the Normans soon embraced Christianity and mixed with the Saxon, Celtic and Frankish inhabitants through a combination of conquest and intermarriage, to the extent that by the early 11th century, the Normans had a distinct culture that had evolved considerably from the Viking stereotype. In William's time, the Normans were renowned for their piety, architecture and martial skills. In particular, "Romanesque" Norman churches and cathedrals remain some of the most spectacular medieval structures that have survived over the centuries, and their castles were huge stone-built fortresses that helped form today's cliched view of what a castle should look like. The one at Rochester in England is a classic example, but most original Norman castles were still made of earth and timber.

Rochester Castle's keep

As soldiers, the Normans enjoyed the traditions of aggression and bravery that had been bequeathed to them by their Viking forefathers. More importantly, by this period they had developed a sophisticated combined arms doctrine that would prove highly successful across Europe and the Middle East, and they would play important roles not just in England but also Italy and the Crusades. Several of the crusader kingdoms and castles were essentially Norman in culture and leadership.

By the 11th century, the Normans had established a reputation among outsiders, and a Benedictine monk of that era, Geoffrey Malaterra, described the people:

"Specially marked by cunning, despising their own inheritance in the hope of winning a greater, eager after both gain and dominion, given to imitation of all kinds, holding a certain mean between lavishness and greediness, that is, perhaps uniting, as they certainly did, these two seemingly opposite qualities. Their chief men were specially lavish through their desire of good report. They were, moreover, a race skillful in flattery, given to the study of eloquence, so that the very boys were orators, a race altogether unbridled unless held firmly down by the yoke of justice. They were enduring of toil, hunger, and cold whenever fortune laid it on them, given to hunting and hawking, delighting in the pleasure of horses, and of all the weapons and garb of war."

When William was born, Normandy was a powerful independent duchy with boundaries that are more or less similar to the modern French province today. At the time, France was a mosaic of such mini-states, many but not all of them owing allegiance to the French king who directly ruled what was then "France", an area based on Paris and the Isle de France. For Normandy, France was a powerful ally/threat and always a fundamental political consideration. To her north and south as well, she had significant neighbours, including Flanders and Anjou, jockeying for position and power. It was a complex, fluid and dangerous political and military situation that was most often managed through marriages, alliances, and, all too frequently, war. Notionaly sitting above this situation, and exercising varying degrees of influence at different times, was the Church. No ruler could afford to ignore the Pope or the wealthy institution of the Church within his own domain. It was into this mix, around 1027/8, that William was born.

Chapter 2: William's Early Years

At the time of William's birth, his father Robert was the second son of the existing Duke of Normandy and therefore not immediately in line to inherit the duchy. Robert had taken a woman called Herlava as his wife, but the union had not been blessed by the Church, probably because of her humble background. Thus, in the eyes of the church, baby William was technically a bastard.

Statue of William's father, Robert the Magnificent

Matters might have stayed that way - and history would have turned out quite differently - if Robert had not inherited the duchy following the suspicious death of his elder brother. It is unclear whether Robert had a hand in his brother's death, but such intrigues were not uncommon in medieval Europe. 73 years later, William's own son would to suffer a similar fate in a "mysterious" hunting accident in England, thereby losing the English throne.

Regardless of how it happened, Robert became Robert I, Duke of Normandy, and he promptly married Herlava off to another nobleman and took a legitimate wife himself. Herlava had two other sons with her new husband, Robert and Odo, and both would play an important part in William's life. Meanwhile, Robert I always made it clear that he expected William to inherit, regardless of his legitimacy, and his wishes were apparently broadly accepted by the Church and nobility.

In 1035, Robert I announced that he would make a pilgrimage to Jerusalem, and he went about carefully making arrangements for the rule of his unstable duchy while he was away. That made it all the more ironic that Robert would never return; the following year he died of a fever in

Nicaea (in present-day Turkey). He had seen Jerusalem, but in doing so he lost his life and left his duchy in the hands of ambitious noblemen, a skillful archbishop, and a boy of only seven or eight. In his biography of William, E.A. Freeman described the political situation at the time the young boy succeeded Robert:

"The reigning king, Henry the First, owed his crown to the help of William's father Robert. On the other hand, the original ground of the alliance, mutual support against the Karolingian king, had passed away. A King of the French reigning at Paris was more likely to remember what the Normans had cost him as duke than what they had done for him as king. And the alliance was only an alliance of princes. The mutual dislike between the people of the two countries was strong. The Normans had learned French ways, but French and Normans had not become countrymen. And, as the fame of Normandy grew, jealousy was doubtless mingled with dislike. William, in short, inherited a very doubtful and dangerous state of relations towards the king who was at once his chief neighbour and his overlord.

More doubtful and dangerous still were the relations which the young duke inherited towards the people of his own duchy and the kinsfolk of his own house. William was not as yet the Great or the Conqueror, but he was the Bastard from the beginning. There was then no generally received doctrine as to the succession to kingdoms and duchies. Everywhere a single kingly or princely house supplied, as a rule, candidates for the succession. Everywhere, even where the elective doctrine was strong, a full-grown son was always likely to succeed his father. The growth of feudal notions too had greatly strengthened the hereditary principle. Still no rule had anywhere been laid down for cases where the late prince had not left a full-grown son. The question as to legitimate birth was equally unsettled. Irregular unions of all kinds, though condemned by the Church, were tolerated in practice, and were nowhere more common than among the Norman dukes. In truth the feeling of the kingliness of the stock, the doctrine that the king should be the son of a king, is better satisfied by the succession of the late king's bastard son than by sending for some distant kinsman, claiming perhaps only through females. Still bastardy, if it was often convenient to forget it, could always be turned against a man. The succession of a bastard was never likely to be quite undisputed or his reign to be quite undisturbed."

12th century depiction of Henry I of France

Initially, the Archbishop of Rouen stepped in as guardian and brought stability and the rule of law, ensuring that the transition was a smooth one, but his death in 1037 ushered in a period of instability. William was still not yet a teen, and Gilbert of Brionne and then Ralph of Gace acted as guardians in turn, each using the role to further his own position. At the same time, various noblemen and landowners across Normandy also exploited the weak rule from the center to resolve long-standing disputes, and small-scale skirmishes punctuated these early years.

It is unclear whether William was in direct danger himself, but his guardians sure were. Gilbert was killed within months of becoming guardian, as was a guardian named Turchetil. A third guardian, Osbern, was killed in William's own chamber as the young boy slept. Regardless of whether he was truly faced with any danger, it was asserted by some of his contemporaries that the boy was constantly moved around and hidden for his safety.

William was unable to influence events as a boy, and precisely when he began to directly wield power himself has proven difficult for historians to determine, but it was probably around 1042, when he was still just a young teen. That year, Henry I of France moved forces towards the southern border and demanded the destruction of the castle at Tillieres, which he claimed was a threat to French security. In no position to argue, William acceded to the request, but his man on the spot refused to surrender the castle. Matters were only resolved when William arrived on the scene in person and forced the issue, after which an uneasy treaty was signed with France. While that was obviously an inauspicious start for a ruler who would come to earn the cognomen "Conqueror", it was evidence that William had courage, political insight, and a realistic understanding of the way statecraft worked, even at that young age.

Given William's lineage and youth, it was only a matter of time before he would face challenges to his power, and the first serious revolt broke out in 1046, fomented by a number of discontented noblemen led by Count Guy of Burgundy, a Frenchman who also happened to be William's cousin. Their grievances were various, but in essence they all felt they had been mistreated by the settlement that had established William as ruler of Normandy. At least that was the pretext; the likelihood is that these ambitious warlords felt able to challenge a young and inexperienced ruler and simply tried to seize their opportunity. Geographically, the rebellion was centered to the west of Normandy, in the Contentin peninsula, and there was an attempt at an ambush of the young Duke, but he escaped into the night and was able to rally his supporters and deploy a small army. The scene was set for William of Normandy's first battle.

The outcome of William's first battle would be decided by another twist of 11th century French intrigue, when Henry I of France came to William's assistance with a larger army of his own. His motives are difficult to discern, but William had been cooperative during the stand-off over Tillieres and Henry probably needed a new ally. The two met and spent the eve of battle together.

Details of the battle at Val-es-Dunes are scant, but it is believed to have taken place somewhere near Caen in the summer of 1047, and the forces involved were probably modest, even by medieval standards. It seems probable that Henry's forces were to the left of the line, with William's Normans buttressing their right. The rebels had a larger force, but lost some support when Ralph of Tesson switched sides before battle was joined. Freeman explained, "Yet one of the many anecdotes of the battle points to a source of strength which was always ready to tell for any lord against rebellious vassals. One of the leaders of the revolt, Ralph of Tesson, struck with remorse and stirred by the prayers of his knights, joined the Duke just before the battle. He had sworn to smite William wherever he found him, and he fulfilled his oath by giving the Duke a harmless blow with his glove."

The battle was mostly a mounted one, with charges and countercharges and some fierce fighting near King Henry I. Personal leadership was fundamental to medieval European warfare, and the King or commanding general was expected to show bravery and decisiveness by leading from the front. In fact, soldiers' morale was so inextricably tied to their leaders' examples that armies often collapsed and panicked if the commander fell, as would happen during William's most famous battle. While the action focused around King Henry I, William is just as likely to have fought bravely with his own knights, albeit in a subsidiary role. He was still only 20, and the Normans were the junior partners here, even though the battle was fought for the future of their duchy.

As was also common in medieval battles, the collapse, when it came, was a sudden one, and it was then that the main butchery ensued. Once their own cavalry was defeated in the attritional clashes with the French and Normans, the rebel line wavered, and Henry knew exactly when to launch the coup de grace. The allies surged forward, and the rebels fled the field. The butchery was savage, particularly at the river Orne. Here the heavily armored knights floundered and drowned by the hundreds, their bodies clogging the watermill downstream. To be trapped against a river was another grim feature which would recur in medieval warfare.

Val-es-Dunes was a turning point for William. He now had a useful alliance with the French, and he had demonstrated his military competance and his leadership. For now at least, he had a unified duchy, and his security problems became external ones. After winning the battle, Henry gave William free reign to hunt down his prey, a laborious process that would require several years. Count Guy retreated to an island bastion, where he was eventually forced to surrender and sent into exile, while Le Plessis-Grimoult was less fortunate; he was imprisoned by William for the remaining 30 years of his life. Others, such as of Haimo of Creully, were slain in battle. William, who cleaned up the rebellion with equal parts competence and ruthlessness, had come of age.

That said, what is now universally considered ruthless from a modern perspective was considered far less ruthless in medieval Europe. As Freeman's biography notes, William was considered lenient for not putting all the rebels to the sword:

"The victory at Val-ès-dunes was decisive, and the French King, whose help had done so much to win it, left William to follow it up. He met with but little resistance except at the stronghold of Brionne. Guy himself vanishes from Norman history. William had now conquered his own duchy, and conquered it by foreign help. For the rest of his Norman reign he had often to strive with enemies at home, but he had never to put down such a rebellion again as that of the lords of western Normandy.

According to his abiding practice, he showed himself a merciful conqueror. Through his whole reign he shows a distinct unwillingness to take human life except in fair fighting on the battle-field. No blood was shed after the victory of Val-ès-dunes; one rebel died in bonds; the others underwent no harder punishment than payment of fines, giving of hostages, and destruction of their castles. These castles were not as yet the vast and elaborate structures which arose in after days. A single strong square tower, or even a defence of wood on a steep mound surrounded by a ditch, was enough to make its owner dangerous. The possession of these strongholds made every baron able at once to defy his prince and to make himself a scourge to his neighbours. Every season of anarchy is marked by the building of castles; every return of order brings with it their overthrow as a necessary condition of peace."

William's confidence in himself, and his ability to inspire his subjects, may have been due in no small part to his stature. While there is no surviving portrait that sought to convey his likeness with accuracy (as opposed to depictions on the Bayeux Tapestry intended to assert his power), contemporary writers described him as being tall, athletic, and extremely powerful. Geoffrey Martel went so far as to claim William was without peers when it came to fighting and horsemanship.

Chapter 3: Consolidation

After proving himself an able soldier and leader, William next turned to diplomacy. To the north of Normandy lay Flanders and Ponthieu. The former had been a particularly bitter enemy, and Ponthieu also posed a danger. In a deft double deal, William arranged to marry Matilda, the beautiful daughter of Count Baldwin V of Flanders, while also marrying off his sister to Count Enguerrand of Ponthieu. His northern flank was thereby effectively secured in one fell swoop.

His own marriage to Matilda, which took place sometime around 1049/50, was not without controversy. Since William and Matilda were distantly related, the proposed match was rejected by the Pope and elements of the Church in Normandy itself. The fact that William went ahead with the marriage anyway is a measure of his confidence and power, and he would not secure retrospective endorsement from the papacy until 1054, thus openly defying the Church for several years. The price for this later settlement was the construction of two magnificent abbeys in Caen that still remain tourist sites today.

Though William and Matilda were married purely for political reasons, it was by all accounts a happy marriage, a rarity for royal marriages of that time. William and Matilda would have four sons and five daughters, and over the course of their marriage she became such a trusted member of William's inner circle that he would leave her to rule in Normandy when he was away, most notably during his initial invasion of England in 1066. Clearly a highly capable woman in her own right, Matilda was able to establish respect and authority in the male-dominated world of Norman politics.

The first ten years of their marriage would be characterized by political and military consolidation. In 1051, William led an army to check the expansionist ambitions of Geoffrey of Anjou to the south. At the siege of Domfront, Geoffrey declined battle, and when William captured the town, his men mutilated residents who had shouted abuse at him over the ramparts. While that was an unquestionably brutal act, it was a standard practice that turned no heads in the mid-11th century, as everyone understood it was important that the ruler be seen defending his pride and dignity.

The Anglo-Saxon Chronicle claimed that William also visited England in 1051, and it was said "William Earl came from beyond sea with mickle company of Frenchmen, and the king him received, and as many of his comrades as to him seemed good, and let him go again." He may have come to England possibly because the English King Edward had chosen him as a successor that year, but given that he was busy fighting in Anjou to the south of Normandy that same year, a trip north across the English Channel seems highly unlikely.

At the same time, Freeman noted that the situation in England and subsequent events suggest that some sort of promise was made to William around this time:

"This claim is not likely to have been a mere shameless falsehood. That Edward did make some promise to William—as that Harold, at a later stage, did take some oath to William—seems fully proved by the fact that, while such Norman statements as could be denied were emphatically denied by the English writers, on these two points the most patriotic Englishmen, the strongest partisans of Harold, keep a marked silence. We may be sure therefore that some promise was made; for that promise a time must be found, and no time seems possible except this time of William's visit to Edward. The date rests on no direct authority, but it answers every requirement. Those who spoke of the promise as being made earlier, when William and Edward were boys together in Normandy, forgot that Edward was many years older than William. The only possible moment earlier than the visit was when Edward was elected king in 1042. Before that time he could hardly have thought of disposing of a kingdom which was not his, and at that time he might have looked forward to leaving sons to succeed him. Still less could the promise have been made later than the visit. From 1053 to the end of his life Edward was under English influences, which led him first to send for his nephew Edward from Hungary as his successor, and in the end to make a recommendation in favour of Harold. But in 1051-52 Edward, whether under a vow or not, may well have given up the hope of children; he was surrounded by Norman influences; and, for the only time in the last twenty-four years of their joint lives, he and William met face to face. The only difficulty is one to which no contemporary writer makes any reference. If Edward wished to dispose of his crown in favour of one of his French-speaking kinsmen, he had a nearer kinsman of whom he might more naturally have thought. His own nephew Ralph was living in England and holding an English earldom. He had the advantage over both William and his own older brother Walter of Mantes, in not being a reigning prince elsewhere. We can only say that there is evidence that Edward did think of William, that there is no evidence that he ever thought of Ralph. And, except the tie of nearer kindred, everything would suggest William rather than Ralph. The personal comparison is almost grotesque; and Edward's early associations and the strongest influences around him, were not vaguely French but specially Norman."

Either way, it's clear that William's relationship with Edward, and the issue of his succession to the English throne, would become manifestly important 15 years later.

Shortly after William had won the campaign in Anjou, he faced rebellion from one of his most loyal noblemen, Count William of Arques, who rejected the Duke's authority. This forced the Duke to conduct a swift Norman siege at the Count's castle at Arques. As ever, the politics were as fluid as quicksilver. There is little evidence to explain just why this once erstwhile loyalist, who had fought for William in the Anjou campaign, defected, but it may have had something to do with pride and his exclusion from William's inner circle. Equally puzzling were the actions of King Henry I of France, who rushed to support Count William of Arques. For France, it is likely that Normandy, with its recent victory and new treaties, was becoming too powerful.

Nevertheless, despite the combination of forces fighting for Count William and King Henry, the Normans were able to hold off the French and secure the surrender of the castle. Count William was exiled for life, never to return.

In 1054, just two years after putting down Count William's challenge, William faced another threat, this time in the form of an alliance between King Henry of France and Geoffrey of Anjou. However, their invading forces were blunted when the vanguard was caught and massacred at Montemer, which was enough to dissuade Henry from advancing any further. Without French intervention, Anjou's threat was neutralized, at least for now, and William subsequently seized the initiative himself by taking an army into Maine, which was controlled at the time by Anjou, and building a castle at Ambrieres. This was a deliberate provocation, and Geoffrey's troops responded by laying siege to William's garrison, but they proved too weak to assault William's army and eventually gave up and withdrew to Anjou.

The next and final round followed in 1057, when Anjevin and French troops under Henry and Geoffrey thrust north once again, laying waste to the countryside round Caen. This time, they were caught on the banks of the river Dives, where William's army attacked their rear as they crossed the river. Like at Val-es-Dunes, warfare along a body of water caused heavy casualties as the encumbered enemy soldiers struggled in the swift flowing stream, and more soldiers drowned than died by the sword.

Chastened once more, Henry and Geoffrey both withdrew, and it would prove to be their last joint enterprise. The death of both men in 1060 marked a new phase in William's reign, because now it was France that had to deal with a new infant king, and in Anjou there was a dispute over succession. This ensured that there was now little immediate threat from either to his south, and William had secured his northern front with the two marriages in 1050. It had taken 10 years, but he now enjoyed security to the south.

William immediately moved to capitalize on this situation by again invading Maine in 1062, this time assaulting the powerful fortress at Le Mans. His judgment that the Anjevins would be too preoccupied with their succession crisis to intervene proved correct, and Maine became a Norman holding under William's half brother Robert. Shrewdly, Robert swore fealty to Anjou and the Normans introduced a "light touch" regime, resisting large scale colonization and potentially getting bogged down in a traditionally hostile territory.

To the west lay Brittany, until now a quiet area posing no serious challenge to William, and it had been placated by means of some skillful diplomacy between William's court and the local nobility. In fact, noblemen from Brittany were encouraged to work with William and were given modest estates inside Normandy in order to secure their allegiance. Eventually, however, this situation unraveled in 1064, when Conan Fitz Alan began raids into Norman lands. William marched straight into the heart of Brittany, and Fitz Alan favored discretion over valor by declining battle.

With that, all of Normandy's borders were firmly secured. William had been Duke of Normandy for nearly 30 years and had been in command for at least 20 of those, but it was only at the close of 1064 that he considered himself fully in control of the local situation. Through the exercise of shifting alliances, bold and rapid campaigning, and even yielding when necessary, William had beaten or neutralized all of his enemies and neighbours. It was time to turn his eyes across the Channel.

Chapter 4: A Question of Succession

In January of 1066, King Edward the Confessor of England died in his palace at Winchester around the age of 60. Though he had been married for over 20 years, Edward had not produced an heir, but he apparently promised the crown of England to several people, among them Harold Godwinson and William of Normandy.

William clearly believed that Edward had promised him the throne, and this is certainly possible. Edward had spent nearly 25 years of his youth in France, mostly under the protection of William's father Robert when he was Duke of Normandy, and in 1033 Robert had gone as far as to launch a naval expedition to place Edward on the English throne. The expedition failed, and Edward would not become King until 1042, but the alliance between the two families was at that time a strong one. Notwithstanding this, sources for the "promise" are all continental and all post-1066. Freeman explained in his biography:

"It was only for a short time that William could have had any reasonable hope of a peaceful succession. The time of Norman influence in England was short. The revolution of September 1052 brought Godwine back, and placed the rule of England again in English hands. Many Normans were banished, above all Archbishop Robert and Bishop Ulf. The death of Godwine the next year placed the chief power in the hands of his son Harold. This change undoubtedly made Edward more disposed to the national cause. Of Godwine, the man to whom he owed his crown, he was clearly in awe; to Godwine's sons he was personally attached. We know not how Edward was led to look on his promise to William as void. That he was so led is quite plain. He sent for his nephew the Ætheling Edward from Hungary, clearly as his intended successor. When the Ætheling died in 1057, leaving a son under age, men seem to have gradually come to look to Harold as the probable successor. He clearly held a special position above that of an ordinary earl; but there is no need to suppose any formal act in his favour till the time of the King's death, January 5, 1066. On his deathbed Edward did all that he legally could do on behalf of Harold by recommending him to the Witan for election as the next king. That he then either made a new or renewed an old nomination in favour of William is a fable which is set aside by the witness of the contemporary English writers. William's claim rested wholly on that earlier nomination which could hardly have been made at any other time than his visit to England."

Harold's claim to the throne appears to have been stronger and was universally accepted amongst the English nobility at the time. Made by Edward before witnesses on his death bed, there is no doubt at all that his intention was to bequeath his crown to Harold, but he probably did make the earlier promise to William, and there is evidence to suggest that the fickle Edward made similar promises to others, including King Swein of Denmark.

The issue of succession was further complicated by evidence of a loyalty oath sworn to William by Harold only two years before the Battle of Hastings, in which Harold agreed to support William's claim to the English throne. Exactly why Harold traveled to Normandy in 1064 is still in dispute among historians, but it's believed William held one or two members of the Godwinson family, possibly a brother of Harold's, as hostages. Historian and biographer Jacob Abbott speculated that it may have been one of Harold's sisters, who was held as hostage through arranging a marriage between her and a Norman chieftain. While that sounds odd, it was a common practice in European medieval diplomacy as a way of ensuring rulers did not break their promises. Harold's mission may have been an endeavor to secure their release, or to confirm his support for William's candidacy to the English throne. Given that he was shipwrecked on the coast of Ponthieu, it may even be that he was not headed for Normandy at all but instead intended to visit Flanders, where one of his other brothers (Tostig) had a marriage connection.

Either way, Harold ended up at William's court in Rouen. William had extracted him from the none too pleasant custody of Guy of Ponthieu, and Harold must have felt in debt or powerless, at least to an extent. It's known that Harold accompanied William on his last campaign in Brittany in 1064 and fought bravely on the Norman side, and he also swore allegiance to William, promising to support his candidacy and prepare a military base for him at Dover upon the death of Edward.

The Bayeux Tapestry depicting William giving Harold arms in 1064

Given what would happen in 1066, the events of 1064 seem to have been more of a charade than anything else, and that's exactly how historian Jacob Abbott interpreted them:

"Harold listened to all these suggestions, and pretended to be interested and pleased. He was, in reality, interested, but he was not pleased. He wished to secure the kingdom for himself, not merely to obtain a share, however large, of its power and its honors as the subject of another. He was, however, too wary to evince his displeasure. On the contrary, he assented to the plan, professed to enter into it with all his heart, and expressed his readiness to commence, immediately, the necessary preliminary measures for carrying it into execution. William was much gratified with the successful result of his negotiation, and the two chieftains rode home to William's palace in Normandy, banded together, apparently, by very strong ties. In secret, however, Harold was resolving to effect his departure from Normandy as soon as possible, and to make immediate and most effectual measures for securing the kingdom of England to himself, without any regard to the promises that he had made to William.

Nor must it be supposed that William himself placed any positive reliance on mere promises from Harold. He immediately began to form plans for binding him to the performance of his stipulations, by the modes then commonly employed for securing the fulfillment of covenants made among princes. These methods were three— intermarriages, the giving of hostages, and solemn oaths.

Finally, in order to hold Harold to the fulfillment of his promises by every possible form of obligation, William proposed that he should take a public and solemn oath, in the presence of a large assembly of all the great potentates and chieftains of the realm, by which he should bind himself, under the most awful sanctions, to keep his word. Harold made no objection to this either. He considered himself as, in fact, in duress, and his actions as not free. He was in William's power, and was influenced in all he did by a desire to escape from Normandy, and once more recover his liberty. He accordingly decided, in his own mind, that whatever oaths he might take he should afterward consider as forced upon him, and consequently as null and void, and was ready, therefore, to take any that William might propose.

Harold felt some slight misgivings as he advanced in the midst of such an imposing scene as the great assembly of knights and ladies presented in the council hall, to repeat his promises in the very presence of God, and to imprecate the retributive curses of the Almighty on the violation of them, which he was deliberately and fully determined to incur. He had, however, gone too far to retreat now. He advanced, therefore, to the open missal, laid his hand upon the book, and, repeating the words which William dictated to him from his throne, he took the threefold oath required, namely, to aid William to the utmost of his power in his attempt to secure the succession to the English crown, to marry William's daughter Adela as soon as she should arrive at a suitable age, and to send over forthwith from England his own daughter, that she might be espoused to one of William's nobles."

Freeman notes that among the foreigners who had potential claims to the throne, William was probably the least preferable among the English themselves:

"William's own election was out of the question. He was no more of the English kingly house than Harold; he was a foreigner and an utter stranger. Had Englishmen been minded to choose a foreigner, they doubtless would have chosen Swegen of Denmark. He had found supporters when Edward was chosen; he was afterwards appealed to deliver England from William. He was no more of the English kingly house than Harold or William; but he was grandson of a man who had reigned over England, Northumberland might have preferred him to Harold; any part of England would have preferred him to William. In fact any choice that could have been made must have had something strange about it. Edgar himself, the one surviving male of the old stock, besides his youth, was neither born in the land nor the son of a crowned king. Those two qualifications had always been deemed of great moment; an elaborate pedigree went for little; actual royal birth went for a great deal. There was now no son of a king to choose. Had there been even a child who was at once a son of Edward and a sister's son of Harold, he might have reigned with his uncle as his guardian and counsellor."

Either way, based on this complicated set of circumstances, it is clear that both William and Harold had strong personal reasons for believing they had claims on the English throne in 1066. William had presumably received an earlier undertaking from Edward and had Harold's oath of support, while Harold probably resented the oath that he had been strong-armed into swearing and had subsequently heard Edward bequeath the throne to him on his death bed. As a result, the stage was set for a battle over the throne of England, and it would end up permanently changing the course of English history.

Chapter 5: The Battle of Hastings

Not surprisingly, the coronation of Harold II of England on January 6, 1066 infuriated William, who summoned his noble advisors and secured their agreement for a Norman invasion of England, despite caution on the part of many of them. This was followed by a broader meeting at Caen, where William consulted his allies and built broader support for his plan.

By the summer of that year, William had assembled a large force, probably amounting to some 10,000 fighting men, with as many as 700 vessels in which to move them across the channel. His army was a decidedly mixed one, with contingents of men from Brittany, Flanders, Ponthieu and possibly even Norman allies in Italy as well. It enjoyed explicit support from the Church, with a papal banner sent from Rome, and was also therefore a triumph of diplomacy for William. More importantly, the army was a balanced one in terms of arms. The striking force would be about 2,000 heavy Norman cavalry equipped with lances, archers equipped with both conventional bows and more modern crossbows who could break up the English line, and simple infantrymen, who were lightly armored and carrying swords.

By contrast, Harold's Anglo-Saxon army was composed entirely of infantry, divided into two broad types. The vast mass were the fyrd, lightly armed infantry equipped with swords and battle axes who were equivalent to William's infantry and possibly superior to them in hand to hand action. The second type were the housecarls, which consisted of Harold's personal troops, noblemen and their families. These men would have heavier armor and carry large shields, an important component in English defensive tactics. The housecarls were tough, well-trained soldiers who were fanatically loyal to their King.

Aware of the threat posed by William, Harold had immediately assembled his army and used it to watch the south coast. At the same time, a powerful English fleet patroled the Channel. But unfortunately for Harold, the Normans were not his only problem, because his estranged brother Tostig had made an alliance with Harald Hadradder, King of the Norwegians. It's unclear what the basis for the alliance was, but those two men met in Scotland and invaded northern England with an army, and prior to that Tostig had caused trouble for his brother with raids on the southern and eastern coasts. Harold thus faced threats on two fronts, and Freeman would go so far as to claim, "It was the invasion of Harold of Norway, at the same time as the invasion of William, which decided the fate of England."

In the north, Harold had the support of two powerful Earls, Edwin of Murcia and Morca of Northumbria. They gathered their troops and marched to meet Tostig and Hadradder's forces near York. The battle of Fulford took place on September 20, 1066, and it was a hard-fought battle between two evenly matched armies, but eventually the invaders prevailed due to poor positioning on the part of the English army and a steady flow of reinforcements. This ultimately forced Harold to march north with the forces he had been keeping to meet William, and they caught the Norwegians off guard at Stamford Bridge a few miles from York. Although they put up a stubborn defence, the Norwegians did not have time to don their armor and were eventually were cut to pieces, with both Tostig and Hadradder falling in the melee. Harold had destroyed the first of two invasions he would be called upon to counter in 1066, but while he was in the north of the country, William had landed on the Kentish coast.

The fight for England in 1066

To a degree, the summer had been a frustrating one for the Duke of Normandy. His army, large for its time, lay in camp at Dives-sur-Mer on the Normandy coast, likely delayed in its crossing due to inclement weather and the powerful English fleet still on patrol in the Channel. Abbott described the scene in William's camp as September drew near:

> "Of course, the assembling of so large a force of men and of vessels, and the various preparations for the embarkation, consumed some time, and when at length all was ready—which was early in September—the equinoctial gales came on, and it was found impossible to leave the port. There was, in fact, a continuance of heavy winds and seas, and stormy skies, for several weeks. Short intervals, from time to time, occurred, when the clouds would break away, and the sun appear; but these intervals did not liberate the fleet from its confinement, for they were not long enough in duration to allow the sea to go down. The surf continued to come rolling and thundering in upon the shore, and over the sand-bars at the mouth of the river, making destruction the almost inevitable destiny of any ship which should undertake to brave its fury. The state of the skies gradually robbed the scene of the gay and brilliant colors which first it wore. The

vessels furled their sails, and drew in their banners, and rode at anchor, presenting their heads doggedly to the storm. The men on the shore sought shelter in their tents. The spectators retired to their homes, while the duke and his officers watched the scudding clouds in the sky, day after day, with great and increasing anxiety.

In fact, William had very serious cause for apprehension in respect to the effect which this long-continued storm was to have on the success of his enterprise. The delay was a very serious consideration in itself, for the winter would soon be drawing near. In one month more it would seem to be out of the question for such a vast armament to cross the Channel at all. Then, when men are embarking in such dark and hazardous undertakings as that in which William was now engaged, their spirits and their energy rise and sink in great fluctuations, under the influence of very slight and inadequate causes; and nothing has greater influence over them at such times than the aspect of the skies. William found that the ardor and enthusiasm of his army were fast disappearing under the effects of chilling winds and driving rain. The feelings of discontent and depression which the frowning expression of the heavens awakened in their minds, were deepened and spread by the influence of sympathy. The men had nothing to do, during the long and dreary hours of the day, but to anticipate hardships and dangers, and to entertain one another, as they watched the clouds driving along the cliffs, and the rolling of the surges in the offing, with anticipations of shipwrecks, battles, and defeats, and all the other gloomy forebodings which haunt the imagination of a discouraged and discontented soldier."

The Bayeux Tapestry depicting Norman preparations for the invasion

This expensive and logistically demanding exercise forced William to pay for the costs himself, but he had to have been worried that the troops might become undisciplined or even start to desert. Luckily, these ships were withdrawn in September, probably because Harold had cost issues of his own, or perhaps to release sailors for the herring season, but either way it presented William with an opportunity to make his move. He shifted his forces northwards to Valery-sur-Somme, nearly opposite to Dover and therefore a much shorter crossing. Once there he waited for favorable winds.

Shortly before he embarked, legend has it that William caught some of Harold's spies in Normandy as they tried to ascertain the Duke's plans. According to sources, instead of executing them, William sent them back to England and told them, "Go back to King Harold, and tell him he might have saved himself the expense of sending spies into Normandy to learn what I am preparing for him. He will soon know by other means—much sooner, in fact, than he imagines. Go and tell him from me that he may put himself, if he pleases, in the safest place he can find in all his dominions, and if he does not find my hand upon him before the year is out, he never need fear me again as long as he lives."

Moving a large force across the Channel was a hazardous operation in the 11th century, even without any interference from the English, but on September 27 the weather cleared and William set sail. He ensured that his own ship quickly pulled so far ahead of the fleet that in a calculated display surely meant to exude confidence, he relaxed with a heavy meal of meat and wine in the middle of the Channel while waiting for his troop ships to catch up.

Norman acounts claimed that William personally stumbled when he landed at Pevensy on September 28, but this is likely an apocryphal story drawing upon the similar legend that Julius Caesar had stumbled coming ashore 1100 years earlier. In fact, the landing was completely unopposed, since Harold's army was recovering near Stamford Bridge at the time. William built a small fortification and sent rading parties off to devastate the land, an unpleasant and laborious process that was designed to draw out the opposition on the assumption that they would need to fight or see their crops and wealth destroyed.

It was two weeks before Harold appeared in the area, and he arrived with his forces depleted by combat and forced marching. Despite advice to the contrary, he was determined to bring William to battle as soon as possible, and he liked the battlefield as a good spot for his infantry to fight. For his part, William had been frustrated with his inability to meet his enemy in pitched battle, so with both armies in position on October 13, the night before the battle, the battle of Hastings would be a set piece one with both sides eager to win a decisive victory.

Before the battle, it is believed William challenged Harold to a personal duel to decide the battle, as opposed to having the armies slug it out, a challenge Harold rejected. Abbott explained the ultimatums William sent to Harold before the battle:

He accordingly sent his embassy with three propositions to make to the English king. The principal messenger in this company was a monk, whose name was Maigrot. He rode, with a proper escort and a flag of truce, to Harold's lines. The propositions were these, by accepting either of which the monk said that Harold might avoid a battle. 1. That Harold should surrender the kingdom to William, as he had solemnly sworn to do over the sacred relics in Normandy. 2. That they should both agree to refer the whole subject of controversy between them to the pope, and abide by his decision. 3. That they should settle the dispute by single combat, the two claimants to the crown to fight a duel on the plain, in presence of their respective armies.

It is obvious that Harold could not accept either of these propositions. The first was to give up the whole point at issue. As for the second, the pope had already prejudged the case, and if it were to be referred to him, there could be no doubt that he would simply reaffirm his former decision. And in respect to single combat, the disadvantage on Harold's part would be as great in such a contest as it would be in the proposed arbitration. He was himself a man of comparatively slender form and of little bodily strength. William, on the other hand, was distinguished for his size, and for his extraordinary muscular energy. In a modern combat with fire-arms these personal advantages would be of no avail, but in those days, when the weapons were battle-axes, lances, and swords, they were almost decisive of the result. Harold therefore declined all William's propositions, and the monk returned."

Freeman explained how this was likely nothing more than a calculated display of gamesmanship meant to boost Norman morale ahead of the fight:

"When Harold refused every demand, William called on Harold to spare the blood of his followers, and decide his claims by battle in his own person. Such a challenge was in the spirit of Norman jurisprudence, which in doubtful cases looked for the judgement of God, not, as the English did, by the ordeal, but by the personal combat of the two parties. Yet this challenge too was surely given in the hope that Harold would refuse it, and would thereby put himself, in Norman eyes, yet more thoroughly in the wrong. For the challenge was one which Harold could not but refuse. William looked on himself as one who claimed his own from one who wrongfully kept him out of it. He was plaintiff in a suit in which Harold was defendant; that plaintiff and defendant were both accompanied by armies was an accident for which the defendant, who had refused all peaceful means of settlement, was to blame. But Harold and his people could not look on the matter as a mere question between two men. The crown was Harold's by the gift of the nation, and he could not sever his own cause from the cause of the nation. The crown was his; but it was not his to stake on the issue of a single combat. If Harold were killed, the nation might give the crown to whom they thought good; Harold's death could not make William's claim one jot better. The cause was not personal, but national. The Norman duke had, by a wanton invasion, wronged, not the King only, but every man in England, and every man might claim to help in driving him out. Again, in an ordinary wager of battle, the judgement can be enforced; here, whether

William slew Harold or Harold slew William, there was no means of enforcing the judgement except by the strength of the two armies. If Harold fell, the English army were not likely to receive William as king; if William fell, the Norman army was still less likely to go quietly out of England. The challenge was meant as a mere blind; it would raise the spirit of William's followers; it would be something for his poets and chroniclers to record in his honour; that was all."

Harold largely offset his problem of numbers and fatigue by his choice of position. For an army of his type, Senlac Hill, 10 miles north of modern Hastings, was an ideal field. A delineated ridge position with a steep hill to its front, difficult terrain on either flank and a wooded area behind it, the geographical features would serve to channel any attacks right into the center of Harold's line, and he would rely on his infantry shield wall to break up Norman attacks and win a battle of attrition. Meanwhile, William would use his mixture of arms by bringing up the archers to fire at the infantry lines before moving the infantry forward, with the cavalry serving as shock troops who could exploit a breakthrough. Harold hoped that fighting on the higher ground and his infantry's use of javelins would negate the effective use of cavalry.

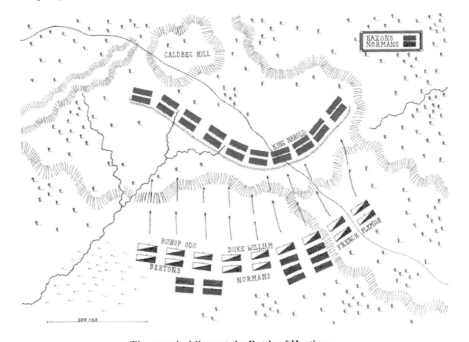

The enemies' lines at the Battle of Hastings

The Battle of Hastings would last almost all day on October 14, and though it was one of the closest battles of the era, it was also one of the most decisive. Beginning at about 8:00 or 9:00 in the morning, William's archers moved forward and attempted to weaken the English line prior to an assault. Much to William's chagrin, however, the archers had little impact as the English maintained their shield wall and suffered few casualties.

Norman infantry surged up the slope. "Out! Out! Out!" screamed the Anglo Saxon warriors. The clash was physical, loud, bloody. The English housecarls hacked ruthlessly at the panting Normans, adept in close quarter combat and with the clear advantage of position and protection. After less than an hour, the Bretons on William's left broke and streamed back down Senlac Hill in what was a critical moment in English history. Large groups of English troops, egged on by Harold's two brothers, romped down the hill in pursuit, but as they cut in to the fleeing Norman infantry, groups of Norman cavalry charged at the disorganized English pursuit and hit them in the flank and rear. Without formation or cohesion, the English infantry were badly mauled as they now became the pursued.

A scene from the Bayeux Tapestry depicting the fighting

The battle took a different shape as noon approached. Harold's line was ragged, with holes in it due to casualties and inadequate shield cover in parts. One of William's lieutenants suggested high trajectory archery, and this too began to take its toll as the arrows now fell beyond the protective wall and into the packed ranks behind. English casualties mounted, and having already noted the English propensity for undisciplined pursuit, William repeatedly tried to tempt them out of formation with feint attacks accompanied by the heavy cavalry.

Nevertheless, the ragged line of Englishmen continued to hold as the late afternoon turned to evening, and attack after attack was mounted up the hill, interspersed with the now deadly archery. It was at this time that the most famous event of the battle transpired. Accounts of Harold's death at Hastings differ; tradition has it that Harold was killed by an arrow in the eye, as depicted in the Bayeux tapestry, but more plausible research suggests that William and three or four accomplices picked out Harold in the denuded English line and cut their way through to him. This certainly would accord with practice at the time, as it was normal for a commander to seek his opposite number and kill him in person. Either way, once Harold was killed, his army began to disintegrate. Only the housecarls made a final stand behind a sunken lane in the woods, fighting to the last man.

The Bayeux Tapestry depicting Harold's death by an arrow to the eye (2nd figure from the left)

William, exhausted, spent the night on the battlefield. He had won by making his own luck, quickly learning from Harold's mistakes and shrewd enough to see the wisdom of the advice he received on archery. As an exercise in command, it had been workmanlike rather than inspired, but it had also been brave; William was unhorsed twice and had to raise his helmet in order to prove to his troops that he was still alive.

Looked at dispassionately, the main factor in the victory was the relative sophistication of the Norman army. It was the combination of cavalry, infantry and archery which won the day for William. It was the first time archers had been used in a battle in England, and it was clearly a triumph of the new model of warfare over the older, traditional one. Hastings ensured that the armies of Western Europe would use that model for their armies for the next 250 years. The next tactical revolution would be brought about by the English longbow, when, once again, Englishman fought Frenchman.

Harold has long been blamed for being too eager to fight William, as opposed to a depth-in-defense or prolonging things as winter set in, but some historians don't necessarily fault him. For example, Freeman asserted:

"Harold was blamed, as defeated generals are blamed, for being too eager to fight and not waiting for more troops. But to any one who studies the ground it is plain that Harold needed, not more troops, but to some extent better troops, and that he would not have got those better troops by waiting. From York Harold had marched to London, as the meeting-place for southern and eastern England, as well as for the few who actually followed him from the North and those who joined him on the march. Edwin and Morkere were bidden to follow with the full force of their earldoms. This they took care not to do. Harold and his West-Saxons had saved them, but they would not strike a blow back again. Both now and earlier in the year they doubtless aimed at a division of the kingdom, such as had been twice made within fifty years. Either Harold or William might reign in Wessex and East-Anglia; Edwin should reign in Northumberland and Mercia. William, the enemy of Harold but no enemy of theirs, might be satisfied with the part of England which was under the immediate rule of Harold and his brothers, and might allow the house of Leofric to keep at least an under-kingship in the North. That the brother earls held back from the King's muster is undoubted, and this explanation fits in with their whole conduct both before and after. Harold had thus at his command the picked men of part of England only, and he had to supply the place of those who were lacking with such forces as he could get. The lack of discipline on the part of these inferior troops lost Harold the battle. But matters would hardly have been mended by waiting for men who had made up their minds not to come."

Chapter 6: William the Conqueror

The Battle of Hastings is one of history's most famous and important battles, which is why it's widely forgotten that it did not immediately decide the issue of succession to the English throne. In fact, it took William another 10 weeks to finally secure his new crown. During this period, the northern Earls rallied more troops and attempted to put Edgar Aetheling on the throne, and there was resistance when William attempted to cross the Thames at Southwark. In response, he marched right around London, devastating crops and villages as far afield as Middlesex and Hertfordshire. This "harrying of the south" was later eclipsed by events in northern England, but nonetheless it was still very evident in the Domesday survey returns made 20 years later by William's orders.

Eventually, the English sued for peace, and the Earls recognized that it was in their interests to work with William. The nobility swore their loyalty to William, who was crowned William I of England on Christmas Day in 1066.

William had conquered England and remains the last person to successfully invade that nation, but in 1066 he found himself ruling two states separated by 50 miles of wild sea, with plenty of enemies in each. This posed a stiff challenge for any 11th century monarch. William's solution was to establish a team of trusted subordinates in both England and Normandy, and to share his time between the two. In England, the key players were initially William's half-brother, Bishop Odo of Bayeux, who was given significant land holdings in Kent, and Roger of Montgomery, whose stronghold became Sussex. Normandy, as noted earlier, was left with his wife Matilda and his eldest son Robert Curthose.

Both domains would see a series of security threats over the first decade of William's joint rule. William returned to Normandy only five months after Hastings in March 1067, and with him he brought a group of English Earls, including Edwin of Mercier and Morcar of Northumbria, some of whom would prove troublesome later. These were essentially hostages meant to ensure the good behavior of their fellow countrymen, particulalry the remaining noblemen.

In Normandy, matters were relatively stable for the first couple of years, as William's grip on the Norman heartland was firm. When the challenges emerged, they came from familiar quarters, beginning in Maine in 1069. Le Mans revolted, and it was not long before the Anjevins began dabbling in the area, as they had over a decade earlier. The Norman garrison was ejected, and for a time Maine was effectively self-governing itself, something William could not tolerate for long. Unfortunately, William could not take immediate action there because he was engaged in more serious disturbances across the Channel.

Matters worsened in 1070 when William's brother-in-law, Baldwin VI of Flanders, died. There was a dispute over succession, and William Fitz Obern, one of William's most loyal advisors, was killed in a skirmish while attempting to intervene. Robert the Frisian became the Count of Flanders, and although he was also related to William by marriage, his regime was at best frosty towards the Normans. William had lost control of Maine and the security of a firm alliance with Flanders to the north, and to make matters worse, 20 year old King Philip of France was beginning to come of age enough to conspire against William.

With Anjou now openly assisting Maine, the time was ripe for action, but it was not until 1073 that William felt able to lead an army in person in Normandy. He had returned briefly at the end of 1071 in order to reinforce garrisons and issue defensive instructions to his commanders, but what was needed here was a punitive expedition with William at its head. In the summer of 1073, that is precisely what he initiated. His large army, for the first time, was a composite Anglo-Norman force, which was noteworthy given what had been transpiring in England during this same period. That William felt confident enough to lead in person and to assemble such a mixed force was a testament to his self-confidence. The campaign was relatively bloodless and completely successful. Launched against Maine, the rapid capitulation of Le Mans served notice both on Anjou and on the young French King. Maine was brought back under Norman rule, and William's reputation in mainland France was restored. For the time being at least, his hold on Normandy and its borders seemed to be secure.

One reason the use of an Anglo-Norman force was surprising was because William had to spend several years after Hastings struggling to control England. Despite his Christmas coronation, and the flood of loyalty oaths that came with it, William was crowned at a time when he was only truly in control of a fraction of the land. In 1066, England was a heavily divided country, ruled in practice by local noblemen, and though some of them were new blood from Normandy, many of them were figures from the Anglo-Saxon era. Naturally, there was plenty of resentment over Norman rule, and some of the revolts that William had to deal with had a nationalist flavor; but many of these conflicts were simply power struggles between warlords. In military matters, William's approach was always decisive and ruthless, but in the political settlements that followed, he emphasized reconciliation whenever and wherever he could, fully aware that England could not be held down by force of arms alone.

Ironically, the first revolt to disturb the peace in England after William's coronation was a Norman one, beginning with the Count of Boulogne assembling his followers and attacking William's garrison at Dover. Although the attempt ended up being more of a farce than a danger, it only marked the beginning. It was followed by a revolt in Northumbria, which was resolved through diplomacy, and in the west Norman troops had to lay siege to Exeter in 1068 to defuse trouble there as well. While revolts of any type naturally make leaders uneasy, these were small-scale affairs that were relatively easily suppressed or appeased. Indeed, that same year William felt safe enough to bring Matilda across the Channel and have her crowned Queen of England.

In 1069, however, the scale of uprisings entered a new dimension when two of Harold's sons, returned from exile in Ireland, attacked Exeter. Furthermore, in the north a rebelllion coalesced around the figure of Edgar Aethelring, who had been denied the crown in 1066, and his revolt was supported by a Danish invasion. There was trouble at Stafford in the midlands, as well. It was begining to look like 1066 all over again, but this time, with William in the role of Harold.

The dangers of 1068 forced William into energetic campaigning as he led forces from one threatened sector to another. The Danes, wary of facing William in pitched battle, fled across the North Sea, but they would come back in 1070, this time teaming up with rebellious English earls Edwin and Morcar and charismatic rebel leader Hereward the Wake in his eastern bastion at Ely. Peterborough was sacked by the Danes, led by King Swein, but eventually the Normans bribed them to leave England, leaving William free to deal with Hereward's force. William built a causeway across to the island on which Ely then stood and secured the surrender of the rebels. Earl Edwin had by now fled north, only to be captured and killed by elements loyal to William, Morcar was imprisoned for life, and Hereward slipped away into the marshes and into English folklore.

Order had been restored, at least to an extent. William now marched his army into Yorkshire, the center of much of the opposition, and laid waste to a huge swathe of land. This was the famous "harrying of the north", traditionally seen as an excessive act of barbarism by English historians. Certainly hundreds or even thousands were killed, either directly or as a result of being made destitute, and many fled south through Evesham. While this episode is certainly unsavory in a modern context, again it was uncommon in medieval Europe, and William's conduct was exactly what would be expected of a ruler attempting to stamp out revolt in a troublesome area.

In 1071, William returned briefly to Normandy in an attempt to stabilize the situation there, but his priority remained England. King Malcolm of Scotland had been another thorn in his side, actively supporting several of the rebellions south of the border, so in the summer of 1072 William moved north. Marching confidently into the heart of Scotland, he secured Malcolm's capitulation and oath of loyalty without bloodshed, and by now his reputation as a warrior king at the head of a vaunted Norman military machine had become enough of a deterrence, at least for a few years. With peace established in England, William returned to France for his 1073 invasion of Maine.

In 1075, William faced yet another well coordinated revolt in England, this time led by two of his Norman noblemen, Ralph of Norwich and Roger of Hereford. Also implicated in the plot, though not active in it, was Earl Waltheof, until now one of William's most loyal Anglo-Saxon noblemen. Energetic as ever, William marched an army against Ralph in what is now Cambridgeshire, easily scattering his poorly disciplined insurgents. The revolt then collapsed, Ralph and Roger were imprisoned for life, and Waltheof was executed by local authorities at Winchester.

The Battle of Hastings had been followed by a tempestuous decade that left William constantly worried about security in both of his domains, but he also had to deal with civil matters. Despite the flare-ups, most of the time his subjects lived in relative peace, and William's style was to leave well alone.

As a result, Normandy continued to be governed much as it always had been, and in many ways so did England. The two currencies remained separate, as did the legal systems. England continued to be ruled through its system of local "sherrifs", while Normandy had its "vicomptes", who played similar but not entirely identical roles. English noblemen and churchmen, if they proved loyal, were retained; in fact, Edward the Confessor's Chancellor, Regenbald, served William in the same capacity for years, and an Englishman called Earnwig was appointed Sherrif of Nottingham in 1070. Norman noblemen and close advisors had been rewarded after Hastings with lands seized from Harold's dead courtiers, but even in those cases William allowed the families of the deceased to buy back their ancestral lands.

At the heart of William's administration was commerce. Royal holdings were effectively rented out to whoever could pay the most, allowing them to farm there as they saw fit. The "Danegeld", originally a tax levied to pay for defenses against Viking invaders, continued to be raised most years, and at a high level. Even the criminal law was used to make money; "murdrum", defined by William as the slaying of any Frenchman, resulted in a hefty fine for all of the citizens of the locality concerned. The resulting income to the Crown was not insignificant, an indication that nationalist resentment was still so high that people were willing to pay the price to spill French blood.

In addition to his lightning military campaigns, William sought to exert control by building castles, most consisting of simple log and earth structures that were bolstered with a "moat and bailey." But William also built some heavily fortified stone structures, the most famous of which is now known as the Tower of London, and it's estimated that as many as 500 castles of various types were built during William's reign.

From the mid 1070's, the circling flock of enemies which had dogged William's reign grew even bolder, and it came to include some of those closest to him. Although by medieval standards he was now an old man (in his mid-40s) and considerably overweight, his energy apparently didn't diminish, but the last decade of his life was marked less by striking military victories than by compromise and humiliation.

1076 had seen further fighting in Brittany, where Ralph of Gael was besieged by William in September, but that siege fizzled out when William, concerned at reports of a French invasion, withdrew in September. Early in 1077, Count Fulk of Anjou attacked Norman holdings in Maine, and William lacked the resources to force a decision, creating a four year military stalemate. That situation seemed to indicate William now lacked the ability to decisively enforce his will.

Perhaps sensing weakness, and clearly resenting the fact that he had no real authority of his own, William's eldest son Robert turned on him. Late in 1077, following a drunken brawl in which Robert felt he had been publicly humiliated, he rode to Rouen with a group of followers, intent on seizing William's capital. Denied access to the city, he fled to France, where the troublesome Philip was happy to give him use of a castle on the Norman border at Gerberoy. This was too much for William. At the end of 1078 he attacked his son's forces outside the castle, and in the battle itself he was wounded in a hand-to-hand fight with Robert. The Duke pulled his troops back to Rouen, and it was there a few months later that Matilda managed to broker a reconciliation between the two.

As if to prove the sincerity of this rapproachment, it was Robert who in 1080 led his father's troops into Scotland to punish yet another incursion from King Malcolm. Malcolm again swore fealty to William and this time the treaty with the Scots would hold. Meanwhile, William's half-brother Bishop Odo, still the most powerful man in England, had to deal with an uprising in Durham.

The notion of any kind of unified Norman rule in England seemed to be slipping away, and the instability continued in France as well. In 1081, William's fortress at La Fleche was besieged, and since he was unable to intervene effectively, he had to rely on a priest to negotiate a peace treaty with the Bretons.

As if to make matters worse, Odo himself fell out of favor with William in 1083 for reasons that remain unclear. It is known that Odo was actively conspiring to take over the papacy and had kept this plot from the King, which might have posed enough of a threat in William's eyes. Either way, in an astonishing act of high political theater, William arrested his half-brother in person on the Isle of Wight. Ignoring all protestations concerning the rights of the Church (theoretically Bishop Odo was only subject to Church law), William had him imprisoned for treason.

Later that year, Matilda died, and with her went possibly the last of his old inner circle that William could truly trust. Mother to his children but also a shrewd politician in her own right, Matilda had been one of the very few who had remained loyal to William throughout. It had been a remarkable royal marriage, and her death left him completely distraught, but William had little time for mourning. Within two months of Matilda's death, his son Robert Curthose again rejected his father's rule, this time fleeing to Italy. Robert would spend the rest of his father's reign conspiring against William and attempting to raise forces to oppose him. Meanwhile, Hubert, the Vicompte of Maine, attempted to establish independence once more. William was unable to suppress the revolt and relied instead on diplomacy, ultimately persuading Hubert to sue for peace.

At the start of 1085, with Normandy surrounded by enemies on its borders and William beset by disloyalty within, he learned of a twin threat to England. There were reports that the Count of

Flanders had allied with King Cnut of the Danes for a two-pronged assault on England. William's response was to levy an unprecedented Danegeld of 6 shillings per hide and to recruit a large army, which he took to England. In the end neither invasion materialized, but the extremely high taxation provoked controversy at court.

It was possibly in response to this that William initiated one of the most astonishing administrative feats of medieval Europe: the Domesday book. Domesday was effectivley a nationwide land survey conducted across Norman England in 1085-86 by seven area-based commissioners. Shrewdly, William appointed senior officials with no ties to the areas they were surveying. Its purpose may have been simply taxation to ascertain exactly what taxable lands and goods existed, or it may have been for military planning and determining the resources available for future campaigns and garrisons. Other theories as to the true purpose of Domesday abound, but regardless of its purpose, William's work left history with an extremely detailed snapshot of Norman England. For example, it was from these volumes that scholars understand the extent of the damage wrought during the "harrying of the north", or the pattern of land ownership in any given parish. It is a hugely important historic resource, and astonishingly, these detalied returns were available to William as early as the summer of 1086.

By now, with the immediate threat from Denmark and Flanders having abated, William was forced to return to Normandy to address another familiar foe: Philip of France. For much of the year and into 1087, Philip's troops ravaged the area around Evreux. Insults were exchanged, and William prepared for war, but his time was running out. He would not live long enough to restore his honour against the King of France.

It is not known precisely how William suffered the injury to his abdomen that eventually killed him, but it's likely the injury was the result of a riding accident, and that he suffered some kind of rupture which subsequently turned septic. However it happened, it quickly became apparent that the primitive medicine of the day would not save him. Taking to his bed in Rouen, he found the city too noisy, and instead had a small house built for himself just to the west. It was there that he summoned his close advisors and relatives to go about making preparations for the future of his joint realm.

William ultimately decided to split Normandy and England. His son Robert, still in open revolt, would nonetheless inherit the duchy, while the next in line, his second son William, would rule England. At the dying Duke's insistence, all of his political prisoners were to be released. Present at the death bed were the Archbishop of Rouen, his half brother Robert, and sons William and Henry. On the morning of September 9, 1087, William the Conqueror, the Duke of Normandy and King of England, died.

The funeral was, like William's life, not without controversy. It took place at the Abbey of Saint Etienne in Caen, which had been established decades earlier in exchange for the Pope's blessing to his marriage with Matilda, and a fire is said to have broken out in the city, leaving mostly clergy to bury William. Reportedly, the body proved too large for the sarcophagous, and if accounts are to be believed, the abdomen ruptured as the priests struggled with it, filling the church with a noxious odour. All of these stories may well be untrue, but accounts of William's death feel strangely undignified when considering his personal achivements.

What was William actually like personally? While that is impossible to answer, given that every contemporary source had prejudices and biases, it's clear that he was a great leader. As he proved time and again, he had fantastic diplomatic skills, he was an innovative and brave military leader, he was personally brave and strong, and he prudently managed civil affairs and finances. It's known that he became a large man over time due to a large appetite, and he is reputed to have had a brash sense of humor, which would undoubtedly have been a byproduct of his supreme self-confidence. He also proved to be compassionate for a man of his era, as evidenced by his willingness to forgive those who went against him, and he was more pious and loyal than most of those around him. Of course, it goes without saying that William was a driven man, ambitious for power and wealth.

The two states that William left behind were hardly united or at peace. Soon after his death, Odo conspired with Robert to oust his brother from the English throne and re-establish a united state, but the revolt failed, and King William "Rufus" II would rule England until his suspicious death in 1100. His younger brother Henry inherited the throne, and in 1106 he imprisoned Robert after their sibling battle at Tinchebray had achieved unity once more. During his own time as Duke of Normandy, Robert Curthose had presided over an almost anarchic collapse in Normandy, but Henry at least restored the empire his father had bulit. Still, as a politcal entity, it was not to last. The Plantagenates took the English throne by marriage in 1154, ending the short lived Norman lineage. Ironically, they were from Anjou of all places.

Although William's domains would not stay united for long, William's invasion permanently transformed English culture. Following his death, the two cultures slowly merged with each other, from modes of dress to language and political outlook. England, first under the Normans and then the Plantagenets, began to emerge as a powerful nation in its own right, rather than a divided and somewhat barbarous island off the coast of Europe, and it had an unmistakably French shading to its culture.

Moreover, although Anglo-Saxon England had been beaten by the "French" in 1066, the Norman regime installed by William sowed the seeds of longstanding disputes and warfare between England and France for hundreds of years. Queen Mary declared that she would die with Calais, the last English posession in mainland France, "inscribed on her heart" when it was lost in 1558. England and France, today the closest of allies, fought a seemingly endless series of wars, the last of which ended with Napoleon's defeat less than 2 centuries ago. Given that history, it's hardly surprising that Hastings still resonates in English pubs and classrooms.

For better or worse, all of it can be traced to the remarkable warrior king known as William the Conqueror.

Bibliography

Abbott, J. (2012) William the Conqueror

Bates, D. (1989) William the Conqueror

Bradbury, J. (2005) The Battle of Hastings

Crouch, D. (2002) The Normans: the History of a Dynasty

Curtis, H and Neveux, F. (2008) A Brief History of the Normans: The Conquests that Changed the Face of Europe

Douglas, D. (1964) William the Conqueror

Freeman, E.A. (1867-1876) William the Conqueror

Grehan, J. and Mace, M. (2012) The Battle of Hastings 1066: The Uncomfortable Truth

Hagger, M. (2012) William: King and Conqueror

Le Patourel, J. (1976) The Norman Empire

Rex, P. (2011) William the Conqueror: the Bastard of Normandy

Rowley, T. (2009) The Normans

Saladin
Chapter 1: Saladin's Early Years and Surroundings

Like all great conquerors, Saladin did not exist in a vacuum, historical or otherwise. The world he came into was greatly affected by major historical events (especially the First and Second Crusades) and his two predecessors – Zengi (c.1085-1146) and his son Nur ad-Din (1118-1174). Saladin was born in Tikrit (now in modern Iraq) circa 1138, but he spent his formative years in Damascus in Syria. Little is known about his childhood or young adult life before he joined his uncle, Shirkuh (d.1169), in his expeditions against Egypt around the age of 25 in 1163. Saladin was well-educated in ancient studies and the Qu'ran, according to the North African writer, al-Wahrani, and was fond of the city of Damascus, coming to view it as his home city rather than Tikrit.

Saladin would be a giant on the world's stage during his time, but that was not the only reason he is so well known and remembered today. His true name was not "Saladin," the westernization of his *laqab* or title, "Salah-ed-Din," ("Righteousness of the Faithful"), but the more simple "Yusuf son of Ayyub." Both hated and admired, he is one of the best-documented rulers of the Middle Ages, with two biographers who were his personal secretaries, the Kurdish historian Baha ad-Din ibn Shaddad (1145-1234) and the Persian scholar Imad-ad-Din al-Isfahani (1125-1201). Letters that he sent and received from Egypt, and later in Syria, also survive. He is frequently mentioned in in chronicles like those of Kurdish historian Ali ibn Al-Athir (1160-1233), who served for a time with Saladin's army in Syria, and William, Archbishop of Tyre (1130-1186), a Frankish crusader historian.

Depiction of Saladin burning a town, from a manuscript of the French translation of William of Tyre's *Historia*

According to legend, his father, a Kurdish mercenary named Najm ad-Din Ayyub (d.1173), was forced into exile the night of Saladin's birth. Ayyub had gone against his own lord to give refuge to Zengi and his troops in 1132 after the murder of a rival Christian by his brother Shirkuh, a favor Zengi repaid six years later by giving Saladin's family asylum after Ayyub (who later lent his name to his son's dynasty) was exiled.

Ayyub fell out of favor in 1146 with Zengi's son, Nur ad-Din, when he surrendered the castle of Baalbeck while being attacked, but he was able to get back into Nur ad-Din's good graces by negotiating the surrender of Damascus to Nur ad-Din in 1154. Saladin therefore began his military career serving Zengi and Nur ad-Din under his father and his uncle Shirkuh. Therefore, while his fortunes came from the Zengids, his loyalties remained within his own family.

The Zengids and Ayyubids were very much a product of their period and of the wave of Turkish invaders from the previous century. The Seljuq Turks had arrived in the early 11th century from Central Asia by way of Persia and quickly conquered most of the area of Anatolia, the Levant and North Africa, leaving only a small area around Constantinople to the Byzantine Empire (which had previously held Jerusalem and the Levant until the early seventh century). But the Seljuqs were not a cohesive group, and they quickly fell apart into a loosely organized empire of squabbling nobles.

When the Byzantine Emperor subsequently sent envoys to the Pope in Rome asking for aid against the Seljuqs, it is most likely that he asked for and expected mercenaries. Pope Urban II, for his own reasons, decided the Byzantines needed a new thing – a crusade - instead. In one of the most famous events in the Catholic Church's history, Urban II exhorted the faithful to take up arms for the Holy Land and promised them remission of their sins if they died in battle. In November 1095, according to Fulcher of Chartres, the pope said, "I, or rather the Lord, beseech you as Christ's heralds to publish this everywhere and to pers-e all people of whatever rank, foot-soldiers and knights, poor and rich, to carry aid promptly to those Christians and to destroy that vile race from the lands of our friends. I say this to those who are present, it is meant also for those who are absent. Moreover, Christ commands it." Fulcher of Chartres has Urban II continue:

"All who die by the way, whether by land or by sea, or in battle against the pagans, shall have immediate remission of sins. This I grant them through the power of God with which I am invested. O what a disgrace if such a despised and base race, which worships demons, should conquer a people which has the faith of omnipotent God and is made glorious with the name of Christ! With what reproaches will the Lord overwhelm us if you do not aid those who, with us, profess the Christian religion! Let those who have been accustomed unjustly to wage private warfare against the faithful now go against the infidels and end with victory this war which should have been begun long ago. Let those who for a long time, have been robbers, now become knights. Let those who have been fighting against their brothers and relatives now fight in a proper way against the barbarians. Let those who have been serving as mercenaries for small pay now obtain the eternal reward. Let those who have been wearing themselves out in both body and soul now work for a double honor. Behold! on this side will be the sorrowful and poor, on that, the rich; on this side, the enemies of the Lord, on that, his friends. Let those who go not put off the journey, but rent their lands and collect money for their expenses; and as soon as winter is over and spring comes, let them eagerly set out on the way with God as their guide."

Tens of thousands of dutiful Christians thus took up arms for what would become the first of many crusades.

A disorganized European peasant army was easily destroyed by the Turks in 1096, but the army of nobles who followed later were better supplied and better trained. They took advantage of the unique circumstances of the Seljuqs' failing empire and the power vacuum left in its wake after the Seljuqs had replaced local Arab elites and traveled down through Anatolia. They took Jerusalem and large sections of the coastal Levant in 1099, two weeks before Urban II died in July of that year.

Urban II

The Crusaders' descendants proceeded to fight a losing battle to keep the Holy Land for the next two centuries. At first, they were fairly successful due to the continuing power vacuum in the Muslim Near East. However, in the first decades of the 12th century, Imad ad-Din Zengi (no relation to Saladin's biographer) came to power and became determined to retake the Levant from the European invaders.

Zengi was born in 1085, and his early life was even more inauspicious than Saladin's, marked as it was by his father's execution as a traitor to his lord, Malik-Shah, who was nominal sultan of all the Seljuqs, when Zengi was 11. Zengi grew up in Mosul, a city on the Tigris River in what is now northern Iraq, and eventually became *atabeg* there in 1127. The following year, the *atabeg* of Damascus died, sparking a power struggle between Muslim and Christian leaders for the city. An *atabeg* was a Turkish governor (in this case, one ruling for the Sultan of Damascus in the Seljuq system). Zengi became ultimately independent, the Seljuq sultanate having fallen apart following the deaths of Malik-Shah and his highly competent vizier, Nizam al-Mulk, in 1092.

Perhaps inspired by his father, who had been the practical ruler of Syria before his execution,

Zengi set out to expand his base from Mosul to Aleppo (which his father had ruled), Homs and the former Christian county of Edessa. The chronicler Ibn 'al-Adim quotes Zengi referring to himself as a "tyrant" and discusses the strong discipline that he maintained through fear over his troops. Zengi practiced a highly effective blend of ruthlessness, alliance and treachery, which did not make him unique among his rivals so much as he was simply better at it than others. He had become both hated and admired by the time of his assassination at the hands of a Frankish slave in 1146.

One problem with the Seljuq rulers, and one reason why their empire fell apart so quickly, was that they parceled out territories to their sons, so each ruler's fiefdom easily fell apart upon the death of a ruler. This was true of Zengi, as well. He left his Syrian territories to his second son, Nur ad-Din, and his Iraq territories to his first-born son. The latter dynasty survived until the 13th century.

Nur ad-Din was more of a military leader than a game player in his father's mold. William of Tyre called Nur ad-Din a great enemy of Christian Palestine but also acknowledged him as a just and courteous enemy who became deeply religious after a major illness changed his outlook on life. Shortly after his father's death, Nur ad-Din made a change in his father's long-term strategy. He decided to conquer Egypt.

There were two reasons for this. One was that he and his older brother divided up their father's realm between them, so that the brother had Zengi's Iraq possessions and Nur ad-Din held Syria. This required that he make any future expansions to the south to avoid conflict with his brother, with whom he was on cordial terms. Second, the Crusaders had come to their own conclusions in the wake of the failure of the siege of Damascus during the Second Crusade and the final loss of the County of Edessa in the north. It became clear to them that they had little hope of making any progress in Syria. Therefore, they, too, needed to look south. Thus, both the Crusaders and Nur ad-Din now looked toward Egypt.

Egypt was a tempting prize, albeit not an easy one. The problem for the Crusaders was that they had a powerful Syria on their flank every time they tried to invade Egypt. The problem for Nur ad-Din, over and above any issue of religious conflict, was that uniting Egypt and Syria was almost impossible with the Crusader States lying in the way.

The Crusaders made their move first in the 1150s. The last Egyptian caliph, Al-Adid (1149-71), came to the throne in 1154, though the real power lay with his astute vizier, Shawar (d.1169). Shawar was in favor of allying with the Crusaders, which was not an especially popular position, and he had accrued a large fortune at the expense of the people, which was also not popular. However, he was good at manipulating the local emirs, who were characterized by crusader sources as weak and easily swayed. He also needed to do something to protect Egypt from her many enemies.

Allying with the Franks was not as odd a pairing as it might have seemed. In border regions between Islam and Christianity, like the Middle East and the Iberian Peninsula, during times when a victor was not clear and the battle went back and forth, even intense religious differences gave way to more regional and even clan or personal, differences. The gulf between the Shi'ite Fatimids, who had established their dynasty in the ninth century, and the Sunni Turkish Syrians, who had come almost as late to the scene as the Franks and were culturally almost as alien, was huge. Since the Franks had recently taken Egypt's last stronghold, Ascalon, this made them Egypt's *de facto* neighbors. It is unclear how much Shawar was aware of the ultimate goal of joining Syria with Egypt in the eyes of Syrian warlords like Nur ad-Din, but he was certainly aware that the Egyptian dynasty was as much at risk of being as completely destroyed by a Syrian Muslim invasion as by a Christian one. He therefore made the unpopular alliance with the relatively weaker and more over-stretched power.

The Syrians, for their part, were rough, violent, well-versed in war, and centered in their family loyalties. After Nur ad-Din sent his lieutenant Shirkuh (Saladin's uncle) to invade the country and break the Crusader hold, Shawar responded by expelling Shirkuh and accepting the Crusaders back, even brokering a treaty between the Franks and the young Caliph. It was not until 1169 that Shirkuh was able to invade and hold Egypt successfully, consolidating his power by executing Shawar. Shirkuh, however, did not live long to enjoy his success, for he died two months later.

Chapter 2: The Conquest of Egypt

19th-century depiction of the victorious Saladin, by Gustave Doré.

It is at this point, at the age of 31, that Saladin was finally able to shine. Though Zengi's intervention in his family fortunes had greatly affected his life, he was still just an eight year old child when Zengi was assassinated. Therefore, his main lord had always been Nur ad-Din and his main influence had been his father and his uncle, Shirkuh, both of whom served Zengi and then Nur ad-Din.

Saladin had fought with his uncle on Shirkuh's Egyptian expeditions since 1164. The Ayyubids were clannish and close-knit, so Saladin's position in his uncle's army was literal nepotism, but this familial opportunism did not detract from his ability. M.C. Lyons and D.E.P Jackson, in their definitive biography, *Saladin: The Politics of the Holy War* (1982), note that Shirkuh picked Saladin as his *aide-de-camp* over his own sons, an indication of Shirkuh's recognition of his nephew's innate abilities. Shirkuh had a reputation (reported even by his enemies, like William of Tyre) for winning the loyalty of his men by living among them and sharing their hardships. Shirkuh was a coarse, short, fat man whose fierce temper that had gotten his family exiled from Tikrit, but he was also a shrewd general and a beloved military leader.

It is probably no coincidence that Saladin, too, acquired a reputation for living with his men and rousing their undying loyalty, though his appearance and personal habits were more moderate, like his nominal lord Nur ad-Din. No account of his life definitively explains what Saladin learned from Shirkuh, but a comparison of what contemporaries thought were their respective military strengths demonstrates that Saladin's experience, shrewdness, strategy, specific skills in exciting loyalty in his troops, work ethic, and even expeditious ruthlessness did not grow in a vacuum. He probably picked much of it up from observing his uncle over the six years he served him in Egypt.

For example, in one major battle with the Franks near Giza, Saladin was given charge of the right flank. He chose to put the baggage with his uncle in the middle (contemporary Muslim sources put Saladin in the middle), giving the impression of a weak center. Allowing a soft center so that the enemy can attack it and be surrounded by a pincer movement is an old tactic and very effective with a disciplined army that will hold together while being divided. Hannibal had famously used it to destroy a Roman army at the decisive Battle of Cannae over a thousand years earlier, and generals have been trying to use it with the same success ever since. In his own battle, Saladin successfully executed his part of the pincer and helped ensure the Franks were routed. This kind of experience would serve him well when his uncle was gone.

Shirkuh had ordered the assassination of Shawar, leaving a power vacuum upon his death. The young Caliph and his advisors chose Saladin as the new governor, according to Ibn al-Athir, because Saladin was perceived to be the weakest candidate and the least likely to be able to rally the Syrian emirs. Al-Wahrani claims that Saladin was chosen out of respect for his family's prowess, while Imad ad-Din claims that the Syrian faction forced Saladin on the Caliph. Whatever the reasons, Saladin did not simply walk into his position. He was forced to earn the loyalty of the emirs and make the Caliph's faction bend to his will, though he did so in part by making small concessions and using security matters (such as the Frankish invasion) to put down revolts and execute any emirs that opposed him.

There were many such revolts, perhaps exacerbated by the Syrians' practice of confiscating the Egyptian emirs' goods at will. According to Syrian chronicler Ibn Abi Tayy, "When a Turk saw an Egyptian, he took his clothes." Ibn Abi Tayy even accused the Syrians of evicting Egyptians from their houses without cause. Soon, there were riots in Cairo, the power center of the

Caliphate. According to Abu Salih, Maqrizi and a letter by Saladin to Baghdad, Saladin was, as late as the summer of 1172, losing money to European merchants while facing sporadic-but-rising insurrection in a country in debt. Turning the situation around took far more than the nepotism that had put him at his uncle's side in the first place, and his success bode well and was a sign of his future greatness.

One of the first things Saladin did, aside from playing the Egyptian emirs against each other, was to consolidate his position by employing nepotism himself. He made the judicious appointment of trusted relatives to several important posts in his army and even got Nur ad-Din to send his father to Egypt. Unlike his later image as a patriot of Egypt (which was frequently invoked for propaganda purposes by the pan-Arab Nasser regime in the mid-20th century), Saladin did not choose to keep the old elite of Egyptian emirs, let alone the Caliphate, in place. Retaining the Caliphate would have been an option if he had chosen to remain a vassal to Nur ad-Din, but he was already moving away from that allegiance. Instead, he set out to destroy the old Egyptian Fatimid leadership and replace it completely with Syrians, encouraging his own men to have children and fathering four of his own by 1173. He did not father any children until he had passed the age of 30.

It is unknown at what point Saladin decided to defy Nur ad-Din, though he clearly engaged in a policy of expansion of power to balance out the problems going on in Egypt almost from the moment of Shirkuh's death. But it is entirely possible that he had no long-term plan at the time and only later became clear to him that expansion, especially east back into the Levant, would bring him into eventual and inevitable conflict with Nur ad-Din. Similarly, Nur ad-Din's motives for growing tired of waiting for Saladin are not entirely clear – or, at least, their origins are not clear. Some historians claimed that Nur ad-Din felt that Saladin was not sending him enough tribute from Egypt for the jihad back in Syria, but Imad ad-Din insists that Nur ad-Din did not want the money that Saladin later offered him.

Up to this point, Saladin had been no more a religious man than his uncle or Zengi, even according to his own biographers. However, the conquest of Egypt changed his outlook. Egypt was rich, fertile and chaotic enough to present him with many of the challenges that eventually made him a great general, yet also weak enough to provide him with an achievable conquest to retain. As part of this new awareness of his increased status in the world, he gave up wine and began to take the rules of Islam more seriously. This was a good thing, for he needed a clear head to deal with an assassination attempt later that year by the Egyptian faction. He then defeated a Crusader army near Damietta, before attacking Darum the following year.

In Egypt, Saladin was perhaps already trying to establish his legitimacy as a devout and just Muslim ruler who was replacing an older, corrupt elite that had fallen away from the true faith. Despite Saladin's later reputation for culture and gentility, fostered by his two biographers, even the faithful Imad ad-Din complained about his master's retainers, whom he referred to as "rough companions." Saladin therefore needed to create a basis for his right to rule that successfully counteracted both the hereditary legitimacy of those he overthrew and the rough lack of Arab culture in his own family. The intense loyalties within his own clan could only take him so far as long as they remained known solely as mercenaries and military governors.

Saladin now began to consolidate his power in Egypt, which included suppressing the local Shi'ite worship via the establishment of Sunni madrasas, pushing aside the minor Caliph (who conveniently died in 1171 and was replaced by a Sunni Abbassid Caliph after the Shi'ite emirs were massacred), and raising himself up as a virtual equal to his erstwhile lord, Nur ad-Din. All of these things were perfectly standard for an ambitious Seljuq leader and were signs that an astute leader like Nur ad-Din could not possibly miss.

Saladin soon made his intentions even clearer, first by ignoring several letters from Nur ad-Din, failing to support Nur ad-Din in wars to the north with his nephews after his older brother's death in 1170, and in attacks on Jerusalem in 1171 and 1173. His lack of support effectively announced his intention to declare independence from Nur ad-Din, and he may have been relying on the Crusader States as a buffer for protection. Recognizing the trend and worrying that the rich breadbasket of Egypt was slipping from his grasp, Nur ad-Din reluctantly decided to wage a war against Saladin before Saladin could become too powerful.

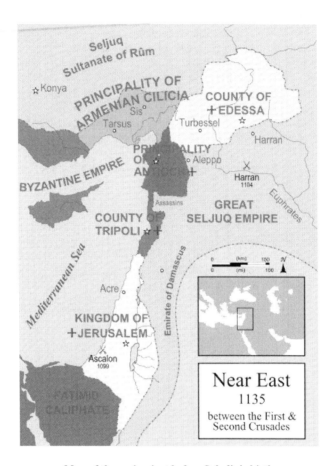

Map of the region just before Saladin's birth

However, he died on the eve of the invasion in 1174, from a similar illness to that suffered by Shirkuh. Several of Saladin's rivals or obstacles died at opportune times for Saladin, suggesting to some enemies that someone – perhaps the Assassins if not Saladin, himself – had poisoned them. Nur ad-Din left behind a minor son, As-Salih Ismail al-Malik (1163-81). Saladin immediately declared his regency over As-Salih, married Nur ad-Din's widow, and effectively replaced his former lord. Al-Malik conveniently died in 1181 at the age of 18, not having reached his majority or taken power.

Chapter 3: Civil War in Syria

This transfer of power to the new dynasty did not occur immediately. Any plans Saladin had of uniting the realms were put on hold as he engaged in a civil war with other claimants to Nur ad-Din's throne. His main difficulty arose from the fact that he had no legitimate basis for ruling in Syria, or for deposing the rightful Caliph and ruling Egypt for that matter. He was not related to Nur ad-Din, who had a living son and living adult brothers, as did Nur ad-Din's nominal lord in Baghdad. Saladin was only one of Nur ad-Din's mercenaries, and he had earned the distrust of Nur ad-Din and the Syrians concerning his devotion (or lack of it) to jihad by failing to provide financial assistance to Syria during the warring with the Christians. As such, Saladin had to pursue his goals in Syria through subterfuge and warfare.

Saladin's first break came in 1174, when the emir of Damascus reluctantly asked for his aid after being attacked by another former captain of Nur ad-Din, Gumushtigin of Aleppo. Gumushtigin had seized Nur ad-Din's heir, As-Salih, and tried to seize all of Nur ad-Din's territory. Saladin crossed the desert from Egypt with a select cavalry of 700. When he arrived in Damascus, he was welcomed as a liberator and immediately took over the castle there.

After leaving his brother to administer Damascus and taking the town of Hamah, Saladin then besieged Gumushtigin in Aleppo. Fearing Saladin's intentions, As-Salih himself begged the populace not to give in. The siege, as well as one made against the well-defended fortress at Homs, was thwarted by an attack by 13 Assassins, requested by Gumushtigin, and an opportunistic attack by the crusader Raymond III, Count of Tripoli (1140-87), who was at times both Saladin's enemy and ally. The Count of Tripoli was greatly respected in Europe, and William of Tyre described him glowingly:

"A man of slender build, extremely spare, of medium height and swarthy complexion. His hair was straight and rather dark in color. He had piercing eyes and carried his shoulders very erect. He was prompt and vigorous in action, gifted with equanimity and foresight, and temperate in his use of both food and drink, far more than the average man. He showed munificence towards strangers, but towards his own people he was not so lavish. He was fairly well-lettered, an accomplishment which he had acquired while a prisoner among the enemy, at the expense of much effort, aided greatly, however, by his natural keenness of mind. Like King [Amalric I], he eagerly sought the knowledge contained in written works. He was indefatigable in asking questions if there happened to be anyone present who in his opinion was capable of answering."

The siege had harmed Saladin's reputation in Syria because he had laid siege to a city where his former lord's son was taking refuge. This provided a propaganda boon for his Muslim enemies, but Saladin quickly raised the siege and used the crusader attack to show that he was defending the faith from the Franks. His fortunes in Syria began to change again when he was finally able to take Homs in March 1175.

His next rival was Saif ad-Din (d.1180), a nephew of Nur ad-Din, who marched against him in Hama with a superior army the following month. Worried, Saladin first tried to sue for terms, but was unable to win them. By judiciously deploying his forces on the high ground, he was able to use his battle-hardened soldiers (who had gained experienced from the civil war in Egypt) to crush the other army's superior numbers. This would not be the last time Saladin used this tactic, or that it would be successful. From this point onward, Saladin declared himself the ruler of Syria and eased as-Salih out. In Cairo, gold coins were minted with his new title: al-Malik an-Nasir Yusuf Ayyub, ala ghaya ("the King Strong to Aid, Joseph son of Job; exalted be the standard").

The Cairo Citadel, ordered constructed by Saladin in the 1170s.

Saif ad-Din and Gumushtigin were not truly crushed, however, until 1176. Saladin defeated Saif ad-Din in battle in the spring and then made a truce with Gumushtigin and As-Salih in June, only slightly deterred by a solar eclipse he considered an omen and a nearly successful assassination attempt. During intense hand-to-hand fighting that drove Saladin's left flank back, Saladin personally led a charge that helped rout the Zengids, leaving Saladin in possession of the enemy's supplies. In a cunning move designed to build loyalty, he freed the Zengid prisoners of war and spread the loot around his army without taking anything of value himself.

Saladin spent the rest of the summer punishing the Assassins for the assassination attempt by laying waste to their territory. This had little effect, and he ultimately broke a truce with the Crusaders to ally with the Assassins instead. It was this alliance, and a battle at Tell Jezer in November, that perhaps explains Saladin's later hatred of the military orders, especially the Assassins' traditional enemies, the Knights Templar. He lost the battle because the Templars were able to reach his bodyguard and cut them down. Saladin escaped, but he had learned a lesson about these Frankish enemies who were every bit as hardened and disciplined as his men. He engaged in skirmishes with the Crusaders in 1178 and then took a major Templar castle, Jacob's Ford, at the end of August in 1179. In 1180, a drought forced him to agree to a peace with Baldwin IV, the last King of Jerusalem (1161-85).

Medieval depiction of Baldwin IV's coronation

Saladin spent the summer entangled in a potentially damaging dispute between an ally, Nur al-Din (to whom he had given refuge), and Nur al-Din's father in law, the powerful Seljuq Sultan of Rum who accused Nur al-Din of abusing his daughter and demanded back her dowry. 1181 was wasted on fruitless attempts to consolidate the conquest of Yemen, but it did bring one bright spot with the death of one of Saladin's great rivals – Saif al-Din – in June.

Saladin did not marry Nur ad-Din's widow, Ismat ad-Din Khatun (d.1186), until 1176, when he defeated his Zengid rivals and became *de facto* ruler of Syria. In spite of the generally restricted status of women in medieval Islamic society, she was no shrinking violet and was the actual hereditary heir to Damascus. Despite the cold, political nature of their alliance, and his having other wives, Saladin was greatly devoted to her until her death ten years later. According to William of Tyre, she rebuffed a siege by King Amalric I of Jerusalem (1136-74) in the wake of her first husband's death, forcing him to accept her terms after a siege of two weeks.

Chapter 4: The Road to Hattin

By 1180, Saladin had consolidated his power in both Egypt and Syria, but he still could not join his two realms because of the obstacle that had once protected his Egyptian realm as a buffer zone: the Crusader States. He now decided to root out the Christian principalities from the Levant, even the Byzantines, though this was not a new goal. He had begun harrying the Crusaders and pushing them back out of Egypt even before he had finished establishing his power there. However, he had also allied with them against other Muslim rivals from time to time. With his triumph over his Muslim rivals complete, he now turned on his erstwhile Christian foes. Attacks on Muslim caravans and other violations of truces by notorious crusader, Raynald of Chatillon (c.1125-1187), beginning in 1181, gave Saladin the pretext for this change in tack.

Depiction of Raynald of Châtillon torturing Patriarch Aimery of Antioch, from the manuscript of William of Tyre's *Historia*)

How much of this new call to jihad in the 12th century was genuine religious fervor for Saladin and his predecessors, and how much was cynical political aggrandizement, remains subject to debate. Zengi, in particular, was ruthless in his pursuit of power, engaging in assassinations and betrayals of other Muslim leaders far more than engaging directly with crusaders. Nur ad-Din and Saladin both continued this pattern of accruing power. Zengi was also not portrayed as a good Muslim by some contemporaries, nor was was Shirkuh. In his hostile account of Zengi's assassination, Damascene chronicler Ibn al-Qalanisi claims that Zengi was killed while drunk, a major violation of Islamic religious code, implying that this was a common occurrence.

On the other hand, Zengi showed considerable zeal in attacking the Crusaders once he began to engage with the Crusader States and does at least appear to have seen them as major rivals for Damascus and the rest of Syria. Also, while contemporary accounts are mixed on how devout Saladin was (he never, for example, went on *hajj* – pilgrimage – to Mecca), he was reported as abstaining from alcohol and other excesses following his conquest of Egypt, and he engaged the

Crusaders far more than previous or contemporary *atabegs*.

Thus, it's probably fair to say there was a bit of both the worldly and the divine in his motivations and methods. Saladin, despite carefully cultivating the image of a holy warrior through his biographers, was no different in this respect from either his Muslim or his Christian enemies, as the Crusaders had similarly mixed motives and methods. He certainly believed, but perhaps not quite as devoutly as he claimed. Nevertheless, it was necessary to promote himself as a jihadist Sultan favored by God in order to rally other Muslims to his cause, and it was made all the more important by the fact that Saladin, like the other *atabegs*, represented a usurping class from West Asia that the old Arab elite resented and did not respect. Also, Saladin had deposed the Egyptian caliph and usurped the rightful successor of his own lord. Caliphs, as descendants of the Prophet Muhammad, were considered to be major religious leaders, even when they had been reduced to weak puppets in secular power. Thus, it was necessary for Saladin to establish himself as the legitimate leader of Syria and Egypt by playing the righteous sultan guided by God in holy war via jihad. This required the language of holy war, even when Saladin warred with other Muslims.

The Crusaders had an advantage in this kind of war, despite being decentralized in secular power and relatively weak militarily compared to their Muslim neighbors. Christian religious authority was strongly centralized in two ancient poles – the Papacy in Rome and the Patriarchate in Constantinople. Christians were also quite strict in which authority they accepted. Latins might work with the Byzantines, and the Pope might choose to correspond with the Patriarch as a fellow vicar in Christ, but this alliance was always tenuous. Latins did not recognize the authority of the Patriarch, and the Byzantines had the same view toward the Pope. This allowed secular leaders to align themselves according to clear religious authorities, and to use their endorsement to accrue support for crusades, something non-caliphate rulers struggled to do in promoting Islamic jihad. Christian religious authority, older and better organized, also had longevity that Muslim religious authority lacked. Perhaps most importantly, the Christians weren't warring with each other, whereas the division between the two main Muslim sects, majority Sunnism and minority Shi'ism, played a huge factor in the conquest of Egypt and left the two sides downright hostile towards each other. In comparison, the division between Latin and Greek Christianity was only a century old at that point.

Another trend was occurring that ultimately doomed Christian Palestine, while introducing a great long-term threat to the Islamic World of which leaders in the east like Saladin were, at best, only vaguely aware. This involved what was going on in Europe. Even as the fortunes of the Crusaders in Palestine gradually declined, other crusades and other expansions against Muslims closer to home were far more successful. By the time Saladin won the Battle of Hattin, the Muslim region of Al-Andalus had long since fragmented and was in the process of a terminal reduction and decline, despite the best efforts of two major waves of powerful jihadists from

North Africa, the Almoravids and the Almohads, and by 1130, Norman mercenaries had wrested Sicily and southern Italy from the Muslims (who had taken it from the Byzantines) and established a kingdom there. It remained in Christian hands thereafter. Thus, while Saladin and other Turkish leaders were in the process of expelling the Latin Christians from the Middle East, the Latins were expelling the Muslims from Europe and blocking them from eventual access to the Americas, gradually forming the geopolitical structure that exists today.

Focused closer to home, Saladin faced a clear threat in the Crusader States that went even beyond religion. Because they held the coastline from Byzantine Anatolia down to the Persian Gulf, Christian realms lined the entire western border of Syria. They also held the entire coastline at arm's length from Syria, even blocking it from the Gulf and any land connection with Egypt. Saladin would proceed to hound the Kingdom of Jerusalem, but at the same time, they were able to harry Egypt from both land and sea. They could also mount relief crusades from Europe by these routes.

With all of Syria under his control, Saladin could now deal with this long-term threat. He was aided by luck in the fortuitous weakening of the Frankish dynasty in Jerusalem. First, Amalric I died suddenly in 1174, while in the middle of a dispute with one of the military religious orders, the Knights Templar. His son, Baldwin IV succeeded him. Though Baldwin was an able leader in many ways, he was still a minor and had also contracted leprosy as a child. This ensured that he could never father children of his own and resulted in bitter disputes over the succession even during his lifetime. The succession eventually went to his sister, Sibylla (1160-90), and her second husband, Guy de Lusignan (1150-94). His immediate successor was Sibylla's eight-year-old son by her first husband. However, Baldwin V only lived until 1186.

13ᵗʰ century depiction of Amalric I

Though an able leader, Baldwin was excoriated by the Andalusian traveler, Ibn Jubayr (1145-1217), as a "pig," despite the writer's reluctant admission that Muslims under Latin rule in the area did better than those under Muslim rule in Syria. Writing about his trip to Palestine in 1185, Ibn Jubayr, a great supporter of Saladin, also referred to Baldwin's mother, Agnes of Courteney, an able regent after his father's sudden death, as a "sow." Though this harsh attitude was partly due to Baldwin being Christian, and the natural animosities between the two faiths, it also stemmed from Muslim disgust at Baldwin's leprosy, which they perceived as a sign of God's displeasure. Despite loyal support from writers like William of Tyre, the strength of the King's power over his own subjects was also weakened by the Franks' own disgust at his condition, about which they had similar feelings. In spite of this, Baldwin served as ably as he could until his death in March 1185.

Medieval depiction of the traveler Ibn Jubayr, who met and wrote about Saladin.

Shortly after her son's death, Sibylla was crowned and her husband, Guy, became King Consort, since women like Sibylla were not expected to lead men into battle. Guy was an affable man but not perceived as a very good military leader. In fact, he had angered Baldwin by allowing Reynaud de Chatillon to pillage Muslim territories in violation of treaties and had been deposed as Baldwin's successor in favor of Guy's stepson, Baldwin V.

Guy was so unpopular in the Kingdom that the Frankish nobles demanded the more politically astute Sibylla divorce him before she could be crowned. She agreed to do so on the condition that she be allowed to choose her next husband herself. They agreed, not expecting her to be like Odysseus' wife Penelope in cunning. She divorced Guy and then promptly chose him all over again as her husband, crowning him as her consort. She bore him two daughters, who died along with her of fever in 1190 while they were on crusade. The title passed to her sister, continuing down the female line for the next century.

Unfortunately for the Kingdom of Jerusalem, Guy was no Odysseus. Taking poor advice from Reynaud de Chatillon and an unusually fanatical Grand Master of the Templars, Gerard de Ridefort, he engaged Saladin at a place called the Horns of Hattin, not far from Jerusalem, on July 4, 1187. Gerard, having arrived in the country in the late 1170s, was still filled with a crusader's zeal and lacked the more usual sense of regional *realpolitik* that his predecessors, Arnold de Torroja and Odo de St. Amand, had possessed. He advocated a reckless attack uphill against the Muslim forces between two ridges (the "horns") that doomed the Crusader effort.

The Horns of Hattin today

Saladin was not passive in the encounter. He had drawn out the Crusaders from their water source by besieging and taking the nearby castle of Tiberias as a feint. Then he deliberately set himself on the ridge at Hattin and had built fires on either side of the Crusader army's passage to cut them off from water. This made the Crusaders hot and thirsty, weakening them even further when Saladin's army swept down upon them. One of Saladin's biographers, Baha ad-Din ibn Shaddad, explained that the Franks "were closely beset as in a noose, while still marching on as though being driven to death that they could see before them, convinced of their doom and destruction and themselves aware that the following day they would be visiting their graves."

Medieval illustration of the battle

With their access to water and retreat line cut off, the crusaders made one last desperate attempt to break through. Ibn al-Athir wrote the following account based off the recollections of Saladin's son, al-Afdal:

"When the king of the Franks was on the hill with that band, they made a formidable charge against the Muslims facing them, so that they drove them back to my father. I looked towards him and he was overcome by grief and his complexion pale. He took hold of his beard and advanced, crying out "Give the lie to the Devil!" The Muslims rallied, returned to the fight and climbed the hill. When I saw that the Franks withdrew, pursued by the Muslims, I shouted for joy, 'We have beaten them!' But the Franks rallied and charged again like the first time and drove the Muslims back to my father. He acted as he had done on the first occasion and the Muslims turned upon the Franks and drove them back to the hill. I again shouted, 'We have beaten them!' but my father rounded on me and said, 'Be quiet! We have not beaten them until that tent [Guy's] falls.' As he was speaking to me, the tent fell. The sultan dismounted, prostrated himself in thanks to God Almighty and wept for joy."

With that, the Crusader army was destroyed. Both Gerard and Guy were captured, as well as the noble brigand, Raynald, and they were all brought to Saladin's tent. Saladin let the thirsty men drink water, but he quickly turned his attention to Raynald and accused him of violating his oaths. In response, Raynald stated, "Kings have always acted thus. I did nothing more." After that response, Saladin grabbed his sword and personally beheaded Raynald, shocking his other prisoners and no doubt leaving them thinking it would soon be their turn. He then explained, "It is not the wont of kings, to kill kings; but that man had transgressed all bounds, and therefore did I treat him thus. This man was only killed because of his maleficence and perfidy."

The remaining Templars and Hospitallers were executed on Saladin's orders. Saladin's secretary explained, "Saladin ordered that they should be beheaded, choosing to have them dead rather than in prison. With him was a whole band of scholars and sufis and a certain number of devout men and ascetics, each begged to be allowed to kill one of them, and drew his sword and rolled back his sleeve. Saladin, his face joyful, was sitting on his dais, the unbelievers showed black despair". Members of the military religious orders were not allowed to offer ransom beyond their own belts and swords, and all of them refused to apostasize. Gerard and Guy were both eventually ransomed at great cost, and Gerard died in battle on October 1.

It is estimated that only about 3,000 of the Christians survived the battle, leaving Palestine at Saladin's mercy. A number of outposts quickly fell, and Saladin then moved on to Jerusalem, which negotiated a surrender to him via a knight named Balin on October 2, 1187. Saladin had considered attacking the city and slaughtering its inhabitants, but the surrender avoided this. Even so, thousands of poor Christians who could not afford to ransom themselves were sold into slavery, but Saladin also allowed Jews back into the city for the first time in nearly a century. Saladin was at the very height of his power and seemed to have triumphed utterly. Save for one port, Tyre, all of the Crusader States had been conquered.

Chapter 5: The Third Crusade

Unfortunately for Saladin, three factors wrecked his plans, though not completely. First, the defeat at Hattin and the loss of Jerusalem galvanized the Franks in Europe in a way that previous defeats, and even the loss of Ascalon (which had precipitated the Second Crusade) had not done.

Though interest had been flagging in the Crusades to that point, suddenly, with such a clear enemy, it revived and crystallized. Second, Tyre held out against Saladin's forces and provided an entry for the Crusaders to land and establish a beachhead. Ironically, Saladin had overlooked the more important strategic target of Tyre to go after Jerusalem first. Now, he could not take it.

Third, there was a leader in Europe that would prove to be Saladin's equal in mettle and desire to fight in religious war. Richard I of England (1157-1199) did not originally want to go, since he was focused on consolidating his own power base in his mother, Eleanor's, vast grand duchy in Aquitaine in southwestern France. Eleanor, a powerful and controversial figure, was later accused in 13th and 14th century histories like the *Chronique abrégé* and the *Chronique de Flanders* of having had an affair with Saladin, even though he was only 11 when she and her first husband were in Palestine during the Second Crusade. Richard was not motivated by racy stories about his mother's sojourn on crusade to go, himself.

The shock of the news about Hattin, however, was. The exhortation of some chroniclers, a mixture of shaming and flattery, cast him as the knight to defeat Saladin and revive the Crusader States. Unlike some Frankish writers in Palestine, like the now-departed William of Tyre, who had written with grudging admiration about their Muslim foes, many European chroniclers felt quite differently about Saladin. Joachim de Fiore, a Calabrian monk, prophesied that the seven heads of the dragon in the Book of Revelation were seven historical figures who had threatened or would threaten the world, with Saladin being the sixth, the last herald before the Antichrist. Richard was strongly urged to go to Palestine and engage with Saladin. Finally, in 1189, two years after the Battle of Hattin and the fall of Jerusalem, he did. Part of what allowed him to do so was the death of his father Henry that year, as well as his ability to leave his youngest brother behind in England as regent and his mother to administer Aquitaine.

17th century portrait of Richard the Lionheart

Richard was not the only leader to go, though he was arguably the best in military matters, and the two that went with him were also great leaders in their own right. The aged Frederick I Barbarossa, Holy Roman Emperor (1122-1190), was already a legendary knight when he set out for the Holy Land. Unfortunately, he drowned in a river accidentally on the way, dealing a great blow to the crusade before it had even began in earnest. Second was Philip Augustus of France (1165-1223), a shrewd and politically astute ruler who would end up diplomatically worming his way into possession of most of his Norman rival's possessions from Richard's brother and successor John after Richard's death. Richard and Philip were allies, even friends, but also strong personalities who distrusted each other. Also, Philip resented being in the shadow of Richard's military prowess, which was regarded more highly than Philip's diplomacy. Still, he was intelligent enough not to show it, or to keep from going on crusade with Richard. In fact, both kings had desired to go but did not want to if it would leave the other rival at home.

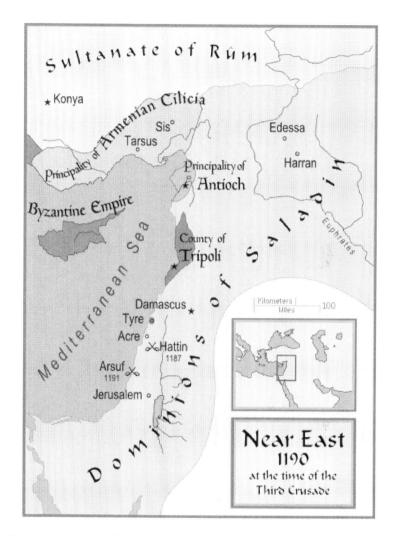

Saladin greeted the news with wariness, but he still felt confident that he could wreck the crusade, especially after Frederick Barbarossa's death. After all, English and French rulers could not stay in the Holy Land forever.

By now, however, Saladin was also running on borrowed time. Now in his 50s, he had been campaigning almost constantly for over a quarter of a century and it was taking its toll. He was old, while Richard was still young and vigorous, the same age as Saladin had been when he had subdued and conquered Egypt. Saladin was finally about to meet his match.

Richard and Philip's arrival at Acre with a large army on June 8, 1191 was greeted with joy and relief by the remaining Latin Christians living there, especially when Richard, still sick from scurvy, oversaw the siege and successful capitulation of the city.

Depiction of Philip (right) and Richard accepting the keys to Acre; from the Grandes Chroniques de France.

As the crusaders took Acre, Saladin himself employed delaying tactics, including saddling Richard with 2700 prisoners and their families near Acre. Perceiving them (probably correctly) as a major security threat that could retake the town if he left them behind, and unable to take them with or provision them, Richard engaged in the most ruthless and brutal act of his life. He massacred them all, including their families, in front of Saladin's horrified army. Saladin's soldiers attempted to break through the crusader lines to save them, but Richard's troops held them back. All told, the crusaders killed an estimated 3,000 Muslims, including women and children. Saladin biographer Baha ad-Din ibn Shaddad wrote of the slaughter, "The motives of this massacre are differently told; according to some, the captives were slain by way of reprisal for the death of those Christians whom the Musulmans had slain. Others again say that the king of England, on deciding to attempt the conquest of Ascalon, thought it unwise to leave so many prisoners in the town after his departure. God alone knows what the real reason was."

Alhough Baha ad-Din reports that Saladin retaliated by killing all Frankish prisoners between August 28 and September 10, Saladin had learned a harsh lesson about his new enemy. He had at last encountered a leader who was as ruthless, if not more so, than he was, and it sent a clear signal to Saladin that he could not expect to play on Richard's very conditional mercy. Even so, the two rulers treated each other with courtesy and respect, exchanging gifts and correspondence, though they never met in person.

Richard next moved his forces to Arsuf, where the last major battle of the Third Crusade would be fought on September 7. During the morning fighting, Richard's left flank began to waver. Richard was able to rally those men and then decided that instead of reinforcing his left, he would use his right to attack Saladin's left. According to the *Itinerarium Regis Ricardi*, a Latin prose account of the Third Crusade, "King Richard pursued the Turks with singular ferocity, fell upon them and scattered them across the ground. No one escaped when his sword made contact with them; wherever he went his brandished sword cleared a wide path on all sides. Continuing his advance with untiring sword strokes, he cut down that unspeakable race as if he were reaping the harvest with a sickle, so that the corpses of Turks he had killed covered the ground everywhere for the space of half a mile."

Depiction of Richard the Lionheart at the Battle of Arsuf, by Gustave Doré.

After routing Saladin's army at Arsuf, Richard wanted to retake Jerusalem immediately, but he was strongly advised against it. Though he had won a victory, his force was now too small and could not be replenished. Once the centerpiece of the Crusader States and the prize for which the entire First Crusade had fought, Jerusalem was now a strategic albatross that could not be properly defended or held by a visiting army. Richard very reluctantly turned away from his greatest goal.

Also thwarted in an attempt to invade Egypt, Richard eventually used his victories to negotiate with Saladin, and the correspondence they carried out became legendary for its chivalry, and it helped make and cement Saladin's legacy in the West. Having heard that Richard lost a horse at Arsuf, Saladin personally sent him two horses as a replacement. Richard even went so far as to solve the issue of Jerusalem by proposing that his sister marry Saladin's brother.

Ultimately, the leaders agreed on a three-year truce on September 2, 1192 that would leave Jerusalem in Muslim hands but allow Christian pilgrims into the city as well. With that, Richard headed back home, where he was facing the prospect of collusion between Philip and his brother back in Europe. Indeed, he was captured and held for ransom by Frankish enemies on the way home, despite returning in the company of friends, the Templars.

Chapter 6: Death and Legacy

Though defeated in battle, Saladin essentially scored a strategic victory by retaining Jerusalem during the Third Crusade, but the leader was too weary to savor the victory, and the damage Richard had done during his year in Palestine was just enough to revive the Crusader States. Saladin returned to Damascus and fell ill from a fever, which killed him on March 4, 1193. Shortly before his death, he drew up his will and gave away all of his possessions to the poor, retaining just a few piece of gold and silver for himself. This was a traditionally humble death for a pious prince, and he was buried in a simple wooden box.

As soon as Saladin was buried, his great empire began to fall apart. He left behind 17 sons and various brothers who squabbled over his realm. In the traditional Turkish way, he had divided up leadership of the various areas among his relatives, which proved disastrous as his once large empire was quickly ripped asunder by fratricidal war. The competence of his sons ranged from the foolish (Al-Afdal, who only ruled Damascus for three years before being deposed) to the destructive (Al-Aziz Uthman, who took Egypt and tried to tear down the Pyramids before dying in a hunting accident in 1198). The much-reduced Ayyubid sultanate eventually fell to a brother, Al-Adil. He continued the line until the dynasty was destroyed by a combination of revolt among its slave soldiers, the Mamluks, and invasion by the Mongols in the 1250s. Since Al-Adil and his sons had little interest in continuing Saladin's attacks on the Crusaders, it fell to the Mamluks to destroy the last of the Crusader States in 1291.

Despite his many successes, Saladin was rather quickly forgotten by his Muslim contemporaries after his death. Only 42 years after Saladin had captured the much-fought-over Jerusalem, his nephew, Al-Kamil, was willing to give it back, and the Crusaders themselves were not especially willing to take it. His empire almost immediately fell apart, and the Christians returned to and rebuilt many of their former possessions. Within six decades, his dynasty was replaced by one of former slaves, the Mamluks. Very few of his building works now survive. As with most rulers of the Middle East, Saladin's successes during his lifetime were largely ephemeral.

A century later, the Islamic Ottoman Empire replaced the Seljuq Empire, and the Ottoman Turks remained in power in the Levant and the eastern part of the Mediterranean until the 20th century. Constantinople fell to an Ottoman sultan in 1453. Blocked in the east, the Franks centralized power into various kingdoms and turned their attention back west to Europe and the New World. With no Christian enemies to fight anymore, the historical memory of the Crusades largely faded for Muslims in the Middle East, and Saladin's memory faded with it.

It's often said that the winners write the history books, but it's very rare for the winners to have such a positive view of the enemy. For Saladin, however, this was exactly the case. It would be the European Christians who kept his name and reputation alive, and they even admired him, though this admiration should be seen in the context of their using him as a foil for their own great leaders, especially Richard the Lionheart. It was a common trope in Medieval Europe to set up a great enemy as a chastisement from God for wicked Christian leaders. Admiring Saladin was perhaps also a way for the Franks to portray themselves as having the superior religion because they could see quality in an enemy and to show that chivalry was a universal code in all upper classes through the world.

This does not mean that any of the Christians who admired Saladin as a good villain and a model of chivalry thought that his religion was better than theirs. In fact, after Britain took Jerusalem from the Ottoman Empire, rumors of leaders like British General Allenby and French General Henri Gouraud proclaiming their final victory in the Crusades over Saladin became popular. These reflected both Arab resentment of European colonialism and European feelings of superiority over the Middle East.

Still, for the most part the European view of Saladin was positive. Dante portrayed him as a virtuous pagan in *The Divine Comedy*, as did the *chansons*. Sir Walter Scott cast him as a mysterious helper for the Scottish hero knight of his novel, *The Talisman* (1825). Scott used his characterization of Saladin's civilized nature as a way to accentuate the vices of his evil Templar villains.

As pan-Arab nationalism arose in the wake of the failure of the Ottoman Empire and the rise of European colonialism in the Middle East, Muslims took this romanticized view of Saladin to heart. Anti-Crusades ideology has fueled much anti-Western anger in the past century, culminating in Osama bin Laden's illogical call to jihad, and Saladin became the symbol and hero for those who sought to fight the West, just as Saladin had done so successfully so long ago.

Saladin has been especially honored in Egypt, where he has been erroneously hailed as a homegrown hero ever since Gamal Abdel Nasser took Saladin's eagle standard as the symbol for Nasserism. He is also extremely popular in Iraq, where he was born. Despite being secular rulers,

Egyptian strong man Nasser (1918-1970) and Iraqi dictator Saddam Hussein (1937-2006) both played up their associations with Saladin to increase their popularity (Hussein, like Saladin, was born in Tikrit). Hussein also favored another conqueror of Jerusalem as his historical idol: the biblical Nebuchadnezzar. As with most historical comparisons, those who have taken Saladin as their historical role model have said more about themselves than about Saladin.

Today, Saladin is an extremely popular idol in the Middle East, one that obscures the true man and shrewd general behind the myth. Saladin's personality was a complex one, but many have tried to simplify it for good or ill. To his biographers and to many of his Christian rivals, he was the soul of chivalry and also in a more condescending sense a medieval version of the "Noble Savage" in European literature. This version of Saladin appeared, with no trace of irony, in works as diverse as William of Tyre, Jan Lievens' fanciful 17th century portrait of a dark-skinned African Saladin holding a pious Guy de Lusignan captive in golden chains after Hattin, Sir Walter Scott's *The Talisman*, and the recent film *Kingdom of Heaven* (2005). In these, he is portrayed as a mild-mannered pacifist, even a healer, reluctantly turning to war in the face of obstinate and savage Christian foes.

Lievens' portrait of Saladin and Guy

The religion of the source is important in this view. In the Christian view, Saladin is intended to show up Christian hypocrites who kill in the name of their religion, violating their own beliefs (*If a pagan can act like this, Christian knights should be ashamed to sink so much lower,* goes the lesson), but he is not intended to show that Islam is superior to Christianity. He is portrayed as an embarrassing example, or a weapon of God, but not really a human hero to be emulated.

The opposite is the case in the Islamic world, where Saladin is raised to truly mythic heights. Many of the less comfortable aspects of his background and life have been completely ignored, including the important facts that he was not an Arab, that he conquered Egypt and destroyed her independence, that he was a rebellious vassal, that some of the things attributed to him were the accomplishments of others who may even have been his enemies, and that he spent as much of his career fighting other Muslims as he did fighting Christians. Like everyone else who is turned into a symbol after death, the inconvenient stuff is simply altered or ignored for the sake of the narrative.

The negative sources are fewer, but vociferous. In them, Saladin is a savage Kurd, a usurper, even a plotter and a poisoner who was vicious to his enemies and even a precursor to the Antichrist. In some sources, such as Ibn al-Athir (who wrote after Saladin's death and was not entirely contemporary), Saladin is portrayed as weak and irreligious, gaining power mainly through nepotism.

This portrayal is obviously not fully accurate, either, but it must be considered. Saladin was educated and cultured in many ways. There is considerable evidence that he respected Islamic learning and certain aspects of Arab culture, that he showed mercy when he did not have to and diplomacy even with his enemies. And he did end his life humbly. But he also has a darker side.

He did not rise to power through his education or his culture. He rose through the connections of his family, and through force and guile, which were common tools of his time though they may appear distasteful today. Several notable and brutal examples exist to show that Saladin's mercy could be arbitrary and affected by his personal feelings. There were times when he chose to dehumanize entire groups of people through his rhetoric, even civilians, which he then massacred or enslaved if they angered him. Contrary to some of the mythmaking, his actions show high ambition, and he was frequently the aggressor on his campaigns. These are all things that were indicative of his contemporaries, both Muslim and Christian, as well, and Saladin does not appear to have been as brutal as a Zengi or a Reynaud de Chatillon. But he was nonetheless far more bloody than the myth. This is an important consideration when placing him in the context of his times. He was often a great hero, but he could also be a great villain, and not all of his victims deserved their fates.

One thing that does shine through in most sources is that he was a great general and a well-respected leader. His enemies respected his military prowess and his own army loved him. And though he died before completing his goal of destroying the Crusader states in Palestine, and though it would take another century before his descendants accomplished this, he did succeed in breaking the backs of the Crusader States and uniting, however briefly, Egypt with Syria. These things were not small accomplishments. After Saladin, the Crusaders attempted to continue on, and did for quite some time, but a combination of unfortunate events, waning interest in Europe, and the effectiveness of Saladin's campaigns ultimately doomed Christian Palestine. It is, in large part, Saladin who is responsible for Islam dominating the Middle East today.

It is still difficult at this point to discern his true motivations under the layers of diplomacy, political expediency and pious propaganda, especially at critical moments of his career, such as his sudden rise in Egypt in the wake of his uncle's death. But Saladin was no more paradoxical than any other great ruler in history, and he is generally considered, both by his contemporaries and by subsequent writers, to be one of the most remarkable figures of his age. His dream was to conquer all of the Levant and bring it back, both under Muslim rule and under a strong Muslim ruler. For him, strong Muslim rule meant a single ruler. He came very close to succeeding, and he laid the foundations for his descendants to complete his dream, albeit at a cost none of them could foresee.

Saladin's entire career was affected by the nature of medieval Islamic politics, where there was little administrative continuity between one secular ruler and the next, even within a hereditary dynasty. Unlike Christian Europe, the Qur'an laid out strict rules on how individuals and groups in the *ummah* (the community of Islam) should treat each other, but there was no secular, or even larger religious, power to enforce this. Thus, there was no legal mechanism to deter a Muslim ruler from becoming a tyrant. This also meant that a ruler could institute very quick and decisive reforms, but these reforms were dependent on his (or her, since a few female Muslim rulers did exist) force of personality. They could easily be reversed or allowed to fade by a weak or hostile successor.

Saladin lived in a militarized culture of Turkish mercenaries, where the strongest rulers fought on the field of battle and jockeyed for position with their rivals as much as they allied with them. Minors or religious leaders like the caliphs (descendants of the Prophet Muhammad) were used as puppets. A strong ruler could easily eliminate the previous government of his predecessor and institute his own. In Saladin's culture, a king ruled by decree.

It is perhaps the greatest paradox of Saladin's life and career that he excelled at exploiting this idiosyncrasy of Islamic politics, yet the same aspect ultimately destroyed his own legacy in the Middle East within a century of his death. Amazingly enough, it would be his foremost adversaries that helped keep his name and legacy alive.

Bibliography

Barber, Malcolm. *The Crusader States*. Yale University Press, 2012.

Eddé, Anne-Marie. *Saladin*. Belknap Press of Harvard University Press, 2011.

Hindley, Geoffrey. *Saladin: Hero of Islam*. Pen and Sword, 2010.

Kedar, B.Z. *The Horns of Hattin*. Variorum, 1992.

Maalouf, Amin. *The Crusades through Arab Eyes*. Schocken Books, 1984.

Nicolle, David. Saladin: *The Background, Strategies, Tactics and Battlefield Experiences of the Greatest Commanders of History*. Osprey Publishing, 2011.

Online Resources

Ed-Din, Beha. *The Life of Saladin*. Palestine Pilgrims' Society, 1897.
http://archive.org/details/libraryofpalesti13paleuoft

Gibb, Sir Hamilton. *The Life of Saladin: From the Works of Imad ad-Din and Baha ad-Din*. Clarendon Press, 1973. http://www.ghazali.org/books/gibb-73.pdf

Lawson, Rich. *Richard and Saladin: Warriors of the Crusade*. (Retrieved 8/31/2012)
http://www.shadowedrealm.com/articles/exclusive/richard_saladin_warriors_third_crusade

Lev, Yaacov. *Saladin in Egypt*. Brill, 1999.
http://books.google.com/books/about/Saladin_in_Egypt.html?id=v22DckibeIUC

Lyons, M.C. and Jackson, D.E.P. *Saladin: The Politics of the Holy War*. Cambridge University Press, 1982.
http://books.google.com/books?id=hGR5M0druJIC&printsec=frontcover#v=onepage&q&f=false

Genghis Khan
Chapter 1: Rags to Riches

One of the most amazing aspects of the empire Genghis Khan would conquer and consolidate is its humble origins. History's great conquerors have, by and large, had the advantage of a leg up in kick-starting their careers. Alexander the Great inherited an almost pitch-perfect military machine from his father, the great reformer of the Macedonian army. Julius Caesar had the benefit of a centuries-old warrior society dedicated to conquest and expansion at his back. Napoleon could call upon the resources of a state which, though impoverished and recently revolutionized, was still one of the oldest and most powerful in Europe. Genghis Khan had none of this. His starting point was a loosely scattered collection of warrior nomad tribes, some organized into federations, all fiercely independent, and almost all hostile to all outsiders. It would require strong will and genius to forge these steppe warriors into one of history's greatest fighting forces.

Hard places breed hard men, and the steppes of Mongolia, where Genghis Khan was born, are such a place. The "sea of grass" was populated by the Mongols, fiercely independent tribal nomads who wondered from place to place in search of forage and food. They were renowned archers and horsemen, and the horse was revered in Mongolian culture as a central part of an individual's existence; horses provided transportation in a land where distances were colossal and food in the form of dried horseflesh, fermented mare's milk and milk curds, all staples of the Mongolian diet. Their way of life was simple, that of hunter-gatherers and tribal warriors, and even their prayers, which revolved around worship of the sky, seem crude today.

The Mongols were inured to extraordinary hardship and were reputed to be able to endure days on end in the saddle, subsisting solely on scraps of food and blood from their own horses, which were just as tough as themselves, if not tougher. Soft life was despised in Mongolia as being both effeminate and beyond contemplation, and those who practiced it (i.e. other cultures) were regarded as effeminate and weak. It was into this harsh land that Genghis Khan was born, sometime between 1160 and 1170 A.D., not far from the modern Mongolian capital of Ulaan-Bataar. Sources for his early life are fragmentary and uncertain because it was only when Genghis Khan came into contact with cultures with a strong written tradition that his historical narrative became more authoritative, but historians have been able to piece together much of his childhood and early achievements with reasonable accuracy.

The Onon River in Mongolia, the region where Genghis Khan was born and grew up.

Genghis Khan was born with the name Temujin at birth, the son of Yesugei Khan of the Borjigin tribe and Holeun of the Olkhunut, and he was apparently named after a Tatar warlord that Yesugei had defeated in battle. He was Yesugei's third son (his first with Holeun), with two olderer brothers named Hasar and Haciun, and he was later joined by a younger brother named Temuge. He also had a sister, Temulen, and two half-brothers, Behter and Belgutei. There is no reliable record of what Temujin actually looked like, as most of the portraits of him that survive were produced after his lifetime and accounts describing him are in all likelihood fraught with symbolism and represent popular and prophetic conceptions of a foreign conqueror more than Temujin's actual appearance. One of the most authoritative and comprehensive descriptions of his appearance comes from the Persian historian Rashid-ad-Din, who somewhat incongruously describes him as being tall in stature with red hair and green eyes. Those were not the physical attributes of a typical Mongol at the time, but it is possible Temujin possessed these physical characteristics since they do occur among Mongolian people to this day.

Several portents are said to have surrounded his birth, though these are most likely largely apocryphal. The most popular one claims that Temujin emerged from Holeun's womb with a blood clot clutched in his fist, an ancient omen which signified he would grow to become a ruler. However, this fate was not immediately apparent because when Temujin was around six years old, his mother Holeun gave birth to another boy, Temuge. According to Mongol tradition it was Temuge who would inherit the larger portion of Yesugei's wealth and his title, as the youngest son of a ruler traditionally inherited. This system, of course, is in stark contrast with the Western world's more familiar custom of having the eldest son inherit.

Despite the fact that Yesugei apparently did not intend for Temujin to be his successor, he did not intend to leave him penniless either, and a fitting match was arranged for him at a very young age as was common among the Mongols. When Temujin was just nine he was sent by his father to the nearby Onggirat tribe, where he was taken in by the family of Borte, a girl who was to be his future wife. As was customary, her family looked after his upbringing until he reached the age of twelve, when it was expected he would marry. Once they did marry, Borte would bring Temujin a sizeable dowry in return for the honor of being married to a Khan's son, but until then Temujin was expected to serve Borte's family.

Much of his education had already taken place at this point, for he would be considered a man at 12, and at that age Temujin was already a proficient rider, wrestler, archer and hunter. As fate would have it, these skills would be of crucial importance to his family and himself in the following years because, unbeknownst to him as he watched his father ride away, the first crisis of a life full of them was approaching.

On his way back from delivering Temujin to the Onggirat, Yesugei met a party of travelling Tatars, his erstwhile enemies, and he agreed to eat with them. During the encounter, however, the Tatars poisoned him, and Yesugei died shortly thereafter. When news of this reached Temujin, he immediately left the Onggirat and hurried home, where he presented himself before the Borjigin and announced he would take Yesugei's place as Khan. Not surprisingly, the young teen was scorned by the Borjigin, who reckoned he was too young and untested to fill Yesugei's shoes. In a cruel but not uncommon turn of events, he, his mother, his brothers, his sister and his half-brothers were abandoned by the Borjigin, left to fend for themselves with virtually nothing but the clothes on their backs during a winter on the steppes without horses or the support of a tribe.

This rapid turn of events was made all the more devastating by the fact that the tribal system meant a Mongol's tribe was everything to him. Without it, he was an outcast, a nothing, in danger not merely of starvation on the unforgiving sea of grass but also of consequence-free enslavement or killing. Temujin endured this life for years, barely scraping by as an outcast with the constant threat of starvation always staring him in the face, and it was during this time that his mother drummed one of the lessons that would come to dominate Temujin's future policies into him: the tribe was all, and alliances were vital to escape the outcast's life. Holeun and her children survived on scraps, the leavings of other tribes, and what they could hunt, dressing themselves in animal skins and living in shelters they built themselves. While these were obvious hardships, it was during this difficult time that Temujin's natural resourcefulness and inclination to leadership led him to become the virtual head of the household, a position for which he competed with his elder half-brothers Behter and Belgutei, who resented him as an upstart. Temujin, however, was made of stronger stuff than they, and he proved that even as a pre-teen he was old and ruthless beyond his years when he killed Behter after the older boy had refused to hand over the animals he had hunted for the common pot. And despite their position as outcasts, it appears as though even the small happenings of Temujin's renegade family still attracted attention among the Mongol tribes, for this killing seems to have been noticed, and it formed the first tassel of what was to be a fearsome reputation.

In 1182 Temujin and his family's solitary existence was rudely shattered when the Tayichiud, a local tribe who shared bonds of ancestry with the Borjigin and had been allies of Yesugei, seized Temujin in a raid and made him a slave. Temujin was forced to endure hardships even greater than those he had struggled through as an outcast, spending most of his days in a portable stock similar to an ox's yoke. In fact, his predicament was apparently so dire that one of his guards became sympathetic enough to his plight to help him escape the Taychiud. Temujin fled from captivity into the night and hid underneath a riverbank before managing to discard his yoke. This became yet another crucial part of is reputation, and his daring escape from the Taychiud led him to acquire a significant measure of notoriety on the plains, where such piratical acts were held in high regard.

Shortly after his escape Temujin met Jelme and Borchu, two warriors who agreed to enter his service and support his claim as Khan of the Borjigin. He was also joined by Jamukha, a young Mongol nobleman who was the son of his tribe's Khan, around this time, and Jamukha eventually became Temujin's blood-brother and closest friend. With renewed confidence following his growing status, Temujin presented himself to the Onggirat at age 16, demanding that Borte's father honour the agreement he had made to Yesugei and give him Borte's hand in marriage, something which the older man was honourable enough – or far-seeing enough – to do. Despite the fact that their marriage had been arranged, Temujin seems to have been truly in love with Borte, who was his one queen for life; though he did take lesser wives, as was expected of him, he never allowed any to replace Borte.

Shortly after his marriage, Temujin and his followers swore service to Toghrul Khan, Khan of the Kerait, a mighty confederation of Mongol tribes. Toghrul had been Yesugei's blood-brother, and it was because of that bond, and the young man's growing reputation, that he took Temujin's vow.

Genghis Khan and Toghrul Khan. Illustration from a 15th century Jami' al-tawarikh manuscript

Temujin would not regret taking the vow, because shortly afterwards Borte was kidnapped by the Merkits, a rival federation, and given as wife to one of their warriors. Temujin was distraught, but Toghrul Khan reportedly gave him 200,000 (almost certainly an inflated number) of his warriors and sent him to destroy the Merkits and, in so doing, get Borte back. Toghrul evidently recognized Temujin was a natural leader, and he took him under his wing and also encouraged Temujin to get help from his blood-brother Jamukha, who had risen to become Khan of the powerful Jadaran tribe while Temujin and Borte had been enjoying their married life.

The campaign – Temujin's first major war – was brief, bloody and extraordinarily successful. The Merkits were virtually annihilated in a series of battles and Temujin was able to recapture Borte unharmed, though not, if rumor is to be believed, untouched. Borte's first son, Jochi, was inconveniently born nine months after her ordeal, and though she and Temujin steadfastly refused to deny his parentage, doubt dogged him all through his life. At the same time, the campaign against the Merkits also marked the beginning of a falling-out with Jamukha despite their earlier bond of blood-brotherhood, and the rift would develop into an ever-greater rivalry.

In addition to getting his wife back, the victorious campaign against the Merkits brought Temujin vast amounts of power, prestige, and followers, and he began to be regarded as a serious warlord in his own right. With Toghrul's blessing, Temujin embarked upon a campaign in the following years to unify the tribes of central Mongolia under his own command. The tribes of the area, unlike the vast federations to the east and west, were largely disunited, allowing Temujin to swallow them up piecemeal despite the fact they were brave fighters. Temujin proved adept at playing the alliance game as well, persuading some tribes to yield bloodlessly to him and pitting some tribes against each other.

Temjuin also implemented policies that were nothing short of revolutionary. Traditionally, defeated tribes could look forward to a future of enslavement, summary execution or diaspora, but Temujin, possibly because he had been an outcast and slave himself, instead incorporated the vanquished into his own tribe, even going so far as having his mother Holeun adopt war orphans as her own in order to make children of the defeated tribe his half-brothers. This generous, humane approach won Temujin the appreciation and love of people who would otherwise revile him, and when defeated warriors realized that he would take them under his wing and grant them a share in the future spoils of victory, they flocked willingly to his banner. The institution of a system of promotion and rank within Temujin's fledgling army that was based not on blood and family but upon merit alone also meant that Temujin's generals and captains were among the very best the Mongols could produce, for they made their reputations and maintained them by the sword alone.

By 1190 Temujin had succeeded in bringing the entire region of central Mongolia under his direct control, forging its disparate, quarrelsome tribes into a single administrative and military entity. He was also a father at least three times over, as his wife had given birth to sons Chagatai, Ogadai and Tolui in the interim. It is unclear if other children died in infancy, or how many daughters he had if any, a clear indication that daughters were less important to chroniclers than sons.

Temujin's success did not go unnoticed, and it began to worry Toghrul, who still believed Temujin would stay faithful to him despite the fact he was blossoming into a powerful warlord who used "radical" policies that made his subjects far more loyal to him than usual. Toghrul's apprehension was exacerbated by his jealous son Sengum, who was bitterly resentful of Temujin. Sengum felt temujin was usurping his place in his father's affections, and he wasted no time in pouring poison into Toghrul's ear, warning him that Temujin would soon be powerful enough to depose him. Sengum suggested that his father should rid himself of Temujin right away, and it appears Sengum and his faction made an attempt on Temujin's life around this time. The attempt almost certainly occurred with Toghrul's tacit consent, and Temujin certainly suspected as much, for the relationship between the two, which had previously been amicable, became frosty. In order to attempt to repair the strained relationship, Temujin went so far as to offer to marry Jochi to one of Toghrul's daughters, but Toghrul refused. It was a gross and calculated insult, though also possibly a consequence of the doubts men harbored about Jochi's parentage, and it drove Temujin into a fury. Instead of an amicable settlement of the dispute, there would be war.

Toghrul was wary of Temujin's new Mongol federation and of Temujin's ability as a commander, so he sought to even the odds by allying himself with Jamukha. Though Jamukha maintained respect and affection for his blood-brother, the two had been rivals for quite some time, even if this was to be the first major clash between the two. However, Jamukha proved to be as intractable an ally for Toghrul as he had been for Temujin, and the two rapidly fell out, their situation worsened by the fact a number of important tribes notionally loyal to their newly formed coalition deserted to Temujin. Toghrul and Jamukha were defeated, and though Jamukha and a sizeable number of his followers managed to flee, the Kerait as an independent federation wase finished. They were incorporated into the new Mongol federation, and their surviving warriors went on to swell the ranks of Temujin's ever-burgeoning army.

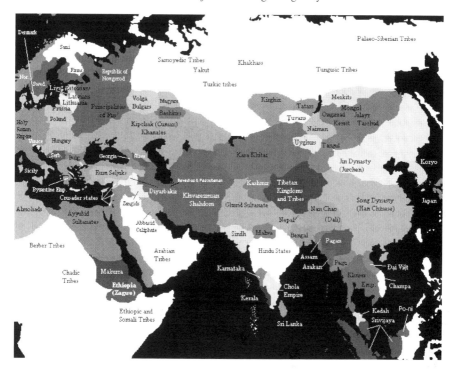

Map of Asia before the Mongolian invasions.

Temujin now turned his attention to Jamukha, who had fled west into the lands of the Naiman federation along with what was left of his army and followers. The Naimans, led by Kuchlug, along with what remained of the Merkits, convened a kurultai (council of Khans) and elected Jamukha their Gur Khan (Great Leader). Temujin, with his well-publicised aspirations of Mongolian unification, could not ignore such a deliberate slap in the face, and in 1201 he marched on Jamukha and his new allies. Before battle was even joined, his ranks were swollen by thousands of deserters who reckoned they would benefit from serving in Temujin's new, meritocratic army. Among these deserters was Subotai, a general and a notorious soldier who was also the younger brother of Jelme, one of Temujin's generals and earliest supporters.

In another unusual custom, Temujin's army accepted deserters and treated them better than defeated warriors and captured enemies. While deserters were welcomed, defeated warriors and captured enemies were, for apparently the first time, treated ruthlessly; they were "measured against the linchpin", which meant they were forced to march past a wagon wheel. If they were taller than the wagon wheel (meaning they were fully grown and not yet stooped by age), they were beheaded, ostensibly to prevent tribal rivalries that might be nourished by not-easily-indoctrinated adults.

Temujin clashed with Jamukha in half a dozen battles, and though none of them were decisive Jamukha nonetheless racked up a string of defeats over the years that led his frustrated followers to hand him over to Temujin in 1206. This move backfired, as Temujin, declaring that he would not abide disloyal men in his army, had Jamukha's betrayers publicly executed. He also offered to renew his friendship with Jamukha, promising a place of high regard in his army, but Jamukha, humbled by his defeat, instead begged for an honorable execution. According to Mongolian tradition, an honorable execution had to be a bloodless one, and Temujin granted his wish.

The war was not yet over with Jamukha's defeat, but it was almost done. What was left of the Merkits were defeated piecemeal by Subotai, newly promoted to the rank of general in Temujin's army and quickly justifying the trust reposed in him and the reputation as an able commander he had acquired among the ranks of Temujin's enemies. The Khan of the Naiman federation, Kuchlug, realized that all hope was lost and fled west to the lands of the Kara-Khitai Khanate, which still remained independent and hostile to Temujin. However, they must have felt quite lonely, for they were virtually alone in retaining their independence. In the space of just a few years, by hook or by crook, Temujin had united the Naimans, the Merkits, the Tatars, the Uyghurs, and the Keraits into a single Mongol federation, a feat unheard of in living memory. At a kuruldai sometime after 1206 A.D., Temujin was proclaimed by the assembled Khans to be Genghis Khan, Great Khan of all the Mongols.

Genghis Khan proclaimed Khagan of all Mongols. Illustration from a 15th century Jami' al-tawarikh manuscript

Having already accomplished something none of his contemporaries had thought possible, Genghis could have been content with what he had achieved. But he was far from done. He had promised his people more, including the plunder of China, and he would make good on that promise.

Chapter 2: The Terror from the Steppes

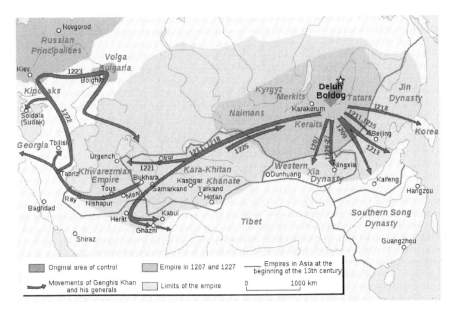

Original area of control	Empire in 1207 and 1227
Movements of Genghis Khan and his generals	Limits of the empire

Empires in Asia at the beginning of the 13th century

0   1000 km

Though there seems to have been some earlier contacts with Chinese dynasties through Toghrul Khan, and the Chinese were certainly aware of and probably worried by Temujin's activities, his involvement in the affairs of the ever-feuding Chinese dynasties began directly (in 1205 when a group of renegade Mongols from the Kerait tribe took refuge with the Xi Xia Dynasty in what is now north-western China. Because the Xi Xia had agreed to give the Keraits aid, Genghis launched an attack on their territory, forcing several of the local noblemen to acknowledge him as overlord. However, at the time Genghis was still preoccupied with defeating Jamukha and uniting Mongolia, so this initial incursion into Chinese territory was aborted.

Once he had united the Mongols, however, Genghis returned to the domains of the Xi Xia in 1207, and this time he came with a vengeance. He quickly sacked the fortress of Wulahai, one of the main Xi Xia garrisons, after capturing it by subterfuge and annexing the surrounding region. There was a lull in the fighting between 1207-1209, but hostilities were violently renewed when Genghis launched an invasion with a host of around 70,000 Mongol infantry and cavalry, the core of which were his feared horse archers, warriors that conventional forces had significant trouble dealing with. Their double-curved bows were immensely powerful despite their compact size, almost as much as English longbows, and they could shoot them as easily from the saddle as they could from foot. Just as importantly, the horse archers were so skilled on horses that they could ride in at a gallop to shower slow-moving formations with a hail of arrows before veering quickly out of the way of a counter-attack. They were devastating in the open field and could be counted upon to destroy any enemy no matter how heavily armored, for heavy armor just made them slower to maneuver. However, the Mongol cavalry was useless in attacking fortifications, and the Xi Xia were quick to seize upon this fact and try to use it to their full advantage.

Despite their belligerence, and the fact that they could field an army of more than 150,000 men, Genghis successfully seized Wulahai in 1209, this time for good, the Xi Xia evidently having learned little from his previous sacking of the fortress. He then marched his army down the Huang River into the Xi Xia heartland and besieged their capital, Zhongxing. The Mongol army encircled the city and cut off supply routes, but it quickly found itself stumped. Genghis Khan had never faced fortifications such as those at Zhongxing, which included massive bastions bristling with catapults and other artillery, as well as bowmen armed with repeating crossbows. It was a colossal and formidable obstacle requiring highly scientific and modern siege engines to reduce. The walls could not be carried by escalade, so Genghis would need siege towers to approach them, or catapults and trebuchets to batter a breach, and his army possessed neither the technical expertise to construct them or the knowledge to use them effectively if they had.

Seemingly at a loss, Genghis devised an ingenius strategy; he would use the vast manpower at his disposal to dam and divert the Huang River, thereby flooding Zhongxing and forcing its surrender. Unfortunately, the ambitious plan backfired, and though Genghis did manage to dam the river, he did not succeed in diverting its course in the desired direction. In fact, he actually managed to inadvertently obliterate the Mongol camp with the river's sudden spate. However, the monumental scale of his undertaking persuaded the Xi Xia ruler, Li Anquan, to surrender Zhonxing to him, having persuaded himself that nothing would stop Genghis from having his way. Li Anquan offered one of his daughters in marriage, as well as other tokens of submission and a vast amount of tribute quickly swallowed up by the ever-hungry Mongol army, and he agreed to accept the presence of a Mongol garrison in Zhonxing. In one fell swoop, Genghis had reduced Xi Xia, with all its wealth and mighty army, to a client state.

Despite Genghis's lightning victory, the other Chinese states did not appear to take particular notice other than to rejoice at the humbling of a rival. In 1210, the Jin, a powerful state to the south of Xi Xia that had long been involved in keeping Mongolian tribes destabilized to prevent them from unifying, sent an embassy to Genghis. The ambassador declared that a new Jin emperor had been announced, and he haughtily advised that Genghis offer tokens of submission to what he should consider his overlord. Not surprisingly, Genghis was far from impressed. At the same time, when high-ranking Jin officials took advantage of the embassy to desert to his side and encouraged him to wage war on the Jin, he distrusted their advice for fear of treachery. His reply to the Jin ambassador was to spit at his feet and gallop away. It would be war.

In 1211, Genghis Khan summoned a kurultai to confirm the declaration of war, and that same year he launched his great army, numbering around 100,000 warriors, against the Jin, who were rumored to have as many as a million men under arms themselves. Genghis Khan's army was entirely cavalry, either armored heavy cavalry or horse archers, and it traveled with no commissariat or supply train, meaning it was immensely mobile.

The Mongols first fought a series of indecisive clasheswith the vastly superior (around 400,000 men) Chinese forces which, though not important to the war's outcome, nonetheless allowed generals like Jebe The Arrow, Muqali and Subotai ample opportunity to distinguish themselves alongside Tolui and Ogadai, two of Genghis's sons who had been entrusted with armies of their own.

Eventually, the Mongol army advanced towards the narrow defile of Badger Pass in the Zhangjiakou region. The Mongols, in typical fashion, had scourged and harrowed all the lands west of Badger Pass, which was the last natural defensive position of any strength west of the vast city of Zhongdu (modern Beijing, and the seat of the Jin Emperor). Heisilie Hushashu, the general in charge of the Jin forces, which thanks to an emergency call-up from every town and garrison in the Jin domains now numbered 500,000 men, knew his business: Badger Pass would negate the advantage of Mongol maneuverability by forcing the horse archers to loose their volleys and ride their horses within tight confines. This would force the fight into a hand-to-hand struggle, which would favor Jin's tactics and weaponry.

Depiction of fighting at Badger Pass

However, by this time the Mongols had started equipping themselves with Chinese steel cuirasses and even manufacturing their own, and their cavalry was heavily armored and protected enough to engage in hand-to-hand fighting. Moreover, prior to the battle's commencement, Genghis, displaying magnificent tactical acumen, dispatched lightly armored men to scale the heights around Badger Pass and encircle the enemy army, attacking them from the rear at the same time Genghis advanced the main bulk of his army up the Pass. Despite the lack of space to manuever, the Mongol warriors proved their superiority to the Jin conscripts and professionals and the encircled Jin army was utterly destroyed, the scattered survivors harried by the rampaging Mongol cavalry for more than 30 miles. The Jin general fled to Zhongdu, where he murdered the Jin Emperor and assumed control of the city, naming his nephew Wanyang Xun Emperor.

Meanwhile, Genghis detached a force under Jebe to invade and harry Manchuria, where they captured the city of Shenyang. By 1212, even though Genghis had suffered a wound in the interim, the Mongols were masters of Manchuria and were ready to lay siege to Zhongdu itself in the very center of the Jin heartland. Despite some of his detachments suffering a defeat against a scratch mobile column of Jin forces, Genghis and his generals smashed the Jin armies in the field to shreds and ravaged the now undefended Chinese plains before besieging Zhongdu in 1214.

Once again, Genghis found it difficult to invest a Chinese stronghold. Throughout a protracted siege, Genghis was unable to reduce the city walls, but the situation inside of them got so desperate that the defenders were eventually forced to the point of starvation and began eating their own dead. On top of that, their general, Heishilie Husashu, lost his life. Eventually the Jin surrendered Zhongdu and agreed to pay Genghis a colossal tribute, the likes of which had never been seen, and the Jin also presented him with a princess in marriage. Satisfied, enriched, and having proven who was the better ruler, Genghis withdrew his army.

Persuaded that Zhongdu was not the impregnable stronghold he had envisaged, Wanyang Xun moved the Jin capital further from the ravages of the Mongols to the southern city of Kaifeng. However, in 1215 one of the Jin armies defected to Genghis's side, and apparently without instigation they launched an attack on Zhongdu. Taking advantage of the situation, Genghis sent a fresh Mongol army against Zhongdu, and the city was ruthlessly sacked in May of that year. The loss of Zhongdu and the surrender of one of the larger Jin field armies in the area broke the back of the Jin resistance, and in the following years (1215-1217) the Mongol armies mopped up what was left of their resistance in most of the northern Jin territories, adding them to the burgeoning Mongol Empire.

Depiction of Mongol cavalry fighting Jin warriors

Though the mopping up would take years, Genghis was now effectively in control of most of the region, and in addition to territorial gains and a vast amount of wealth, Genghis and his army also gained a massive wealth of invaluable experience and expertise. The subjugation of western China brought better armor and better blacksmithing techniques for Mongol warriors, a host of logicians and supply experts who could provide Genghis's army with lines of communication and supply stretching for thousands of miles, and hundreds if not thousands of vastly skilled Chinese military engineers who knew how to manufacture and operate siege weapons the like of which the Mongols had never seen before. No fortress, no matter how large or sophisticated, would ever again be a match for them.

Returning to the Mongolian heartland with an army that was laden down with the fruits of their plunder but also weary from almost a decade of vicious, relentless warfare, Genghis turned his attention elsewhere. To the west of the Mongols was yet more of the sea of grass, stretching to unknown horizons, but ruling it was the vast and bellicose Khara-Kitai Khanate. The Khara-Kitai, horse nomads like the Mongols, were governed by Kuchlug, Genghis Khan's erstwhile enemy. Kuchlug had usurped the throne of the Khan who had first given him and the broken remnants of his army shelter when he had fled west from Genghis's vengeance. The Khara-Kitai were enemies ruled by a treacherous and ruthless leader who had already shown himself to be no friend of Genghis, and as far as the Great Khan was concerned they were next on the list. However, Genghs knew that he could not ask much more of his army, the core of which was exhausted and extremely satisfied with the plunder they had obtained in their ravaging of the Jin heartland, not to mention the vast amount of tribute the Chinese had agreed to pay. Many of the Mongol soldiers wanted the leisure to enjoy the fruits of their decade's worth of campaigning, and more wanted to retire outright. Others had been left behind on garrison duty in the Jin and Xi Xia territories. Nonetheless, Genghis still had a significant number of troops available, his youngest and most adventurous at that, and he could count on fresh levies of trained warriors who had been children when he had first headed off to China. Genghis also had plenty of ambitious generals in his service who hungered for more advancement and wealth.

In the end, Genghis chose Jebe, who had already distinguished himself in the campaigns against the Xi Xia and the Jin, to lead a small army of 20,000 men into the lands of the Khara-Kitai. It was a sizeable gamble, as Genghis knew that Jebe could never hope to defeat the much larger forces of Kuchlug, which were as proficient at steppe warfare as Genghis's warriors. However, he trusted the younger general's judgment, and Jebe did not disappoint him. Rather than attempting to take Kuchlug's warriors head on, Jebe engaged him in guerrilla warfare, striking suddenly and then vanishing out of the steppe, and all the while growing more powerful. The cannier among Kuchlug's chiefs realized that if Jebe were defeated they would in all likelihood incur the wrath of the Great Khan himself and face a far vaster Mongol army in the future, so they defected to Jebe's side.

Jebe's ranks had swelled to such an extent by 1218 that he was finally confident enough to face Kuchlug in open battle. The resulting clash, which took place near Kashgar, was a complete disaster for Kuchlug, who was defeated and forced to flee for his life. However, he did not run for long; Kuchlug and a few of his battered followers were hunted down by Jebe and his men in the aftermath of battle and he was killed, bringing an end to the mighty Khara-Kitai Khanate, which was folded into the Mongol Empire. Genghis Khan now ruled a vast region that stretched from Beijing to modern Afghanistan.

By all accounts, Genghis Khan could have been content to stop there. He had accomplished his stated goal of bringing all the steppe peoples together and uniting the warrior tribes and confederations of the sea of grass under his own banner. In addition to forging a new and mighty Mongol nation, he had also humbled the Chinese, who had meddled in Mongol affairs for centuries, and reduced much of their western kingdoms to the status of conquered vassals.

Genghis could have rested upon his laurels and enjoyed his plunder, but it was not to be. To the west, his domains now bordered those of the Shah of Khwarezm, a mighty ruler who controlled all the land from the Arabian Peninsula to Afghanistan and south to the Himalayas and who was about to make the biggest mistake of his life.

Chapter 3: Total War

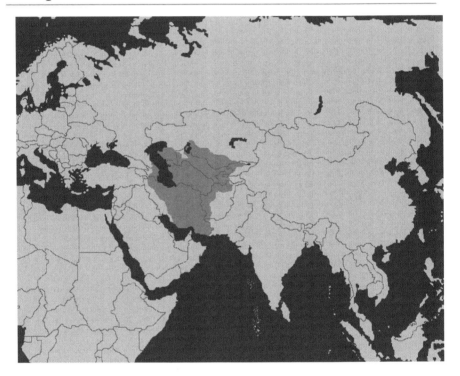

The Khwarezmid Empire circa 1220

The Shah of Khwarezm, Ala-ud-Din Muhammad, was by all accounts a confrontational man. He had already been in trouble with the Caliph of Baghdad, his notional overlord, who expected a "gift" in return for confirming his appointment as Sultan, something which Ala-ud-Din had not seen fit to provide. And he had every reason to be leery of Genghis Khan and the Mongols, having had an ambassador at Zhongdu who had told him firsthand of the Mongol atrocities within the city. Accordingly, he was extremely suspicious when word reached him that Genghis

Khan wanted to amicably extend an offer of alliance to Khwarezm, and his suspicions were further compounded when Genghis sent a caravan into Khwarezm in 1218. The caravan, a trade mission numbering some five hundred men composed largely of Muslim vassals as a mark of respect for Khwarezm's faith, reached the city of Otrar. The governor of Otrar, an arrogant man named Inalchuq, decided that the small minority of Mongols accompanying the caravan were spies, and threw them into jail as well as seizing the caravan's goods.

Needless to say, Genghis Khan was not pleased by this reception. Mongol couriers traveled unusually fast for the time period, changing horses at specially established waystations and sometimes getting as far as 100 miles a day, so news reached Genghis back on the steppe relatively quickly. Upon receiving the news, Genghis dispatched an urgent diplomatic mission comprised of two Mongol dignitaries and one Muslim (as a sop to the Shah's faith) to go before the Shah and demand the release of the Mongols captured with the caravan, as well as Inalchuq's immediate arrest and his delivery to Genghis Khan's justice for the insult. Ala-ud-Din, however, flew into a rage at what he deemed insolent demands from an uncultured savage half the world away, and he ordered the heads of the two Mongol ambassadors shaved as an insult. The Muslim was beheaded and his head delivered to the two shaven-headed dignitaries, who were then unceremoniously booted back whence they had come. The other caravan members were also executed.

Genghis reacted to this intentional affront and demonstration of barbarism with predictable fury. He amassed the largest army he had ever fielded, a total of 200,000 men based around a core of heavy and light cavalry and horse archers, with support units including Chinese medical personnel, siege warfare experts, military engineers, a commissariat corps and a siege train that included everything from giant crossbows and mortars to catapults and trebuchets capable of hurling gunpowder bombs. Genghis also summoned his ablest generals - Subotai, Jebe, Mukali, Jelme, his brother Hasar, his sons Jochi, Chagatai, and Tolui - and marched across the steppe. By 1219, he was poised on the border of Khwarezm.

Before invading, Genghis split up his force into multiple units, which allowed them all more mobility. One army, led by Jochi and numbering around 25,000 men, was sent directly against the Shah himself as soon as he took the field, with the objective of harrying him, and if possible killing him, but above all preventing him to act as a rallying point for the entire Khwarezmid forces. Jochi's men succeeded in ravaging the Khwarezmid heartland, routing several contingents that were hurrying to join the Shah, but it turned out there was no need to worry about the Khwarezmid forces massing together. Though the Khwarezmid army totaled some 400,000, it appears that the Shah was fearful his army would betray him if he amassed it entirely in one place. In fairness to the Shah, this was a reasonable concern, since his armies consisted of units with diverse loyalties, but it would essentially allow the Mongols to set about his smaller armies with superior numbers and beat them piecemeal.

As Jebe's forces marched to the southeast of the empire and Jochi operated in the northeast, Genghis marched northwest at the head of the Mongol main force, some 50,000 men, and he set about besieging Otrar through the winter of 1219-1220. Though the city stubbornly resisted any attempt at breaching the walls, the Mongols managed to penetrate the walls when they discovered an open gate that may have been treacherously unlocked. They then besieged the citadel, which held out for another month until it inevitably fell. Inalchuq, the governor who had instigated the war in the first place, was captured hurling tiles from the roof at the rampaging Mongols and was executed by having molten gold poured down his throat. The city itself was ravaged, with Genghis personally ordering the massacre and enslavement of many of its people.

Genghis then fully demonstrated his brilliance by marching his army on from Otrar and concealing them in the remote vastness of the Kyzil-Kum desert, which the Khwarezmids reckoned to be utterly impassable by any force of reasonable size. However, by enduring unimaginable hardship and moving from oasis to oasis, Genghis Khan was able to emerge from the desert within striking distance of the major city of Bokhara. The garrison was completely unprepared and caught by a masterful surprise attack, and after just three days of siege they attempted a sally and were massacred in the open field. Genghis then took possession of the city, much of which was burnt to the ground, and proclaimed, "I am the flail of God, sent to punish you for your sins". Genghis drafted young men into the Mongol army, executed what was left of the garrison, sent any valuable craftsmen and marriageable women as slaves to Mongolia and executed the rest.

Genghis next turned his army towards Samarkand, capital of Khwarezm and arrived there in 1220, in time for his army to be promptly reinforced by the troops of Chagatai and Ogadai before laying siege to the city. Despite his impressive Chinese siege experts, Genghis was facing an army of 100,000 men safely ensconced behind colossal walls bristling with catapults, but he was not inclined to be wary or merciful. The Khwarezmids had incited the Great Khan's wrath, and they would rue the day they had offended him. Genghis launched an attack on the city using captured civilians as human shields, and after just a few days of fighting the garrison, which might well have outnumbered the besieging Mongols, was incensed enough to sally forth in a counterattack. Genghis feined a retreat to draw more than 50,000 enemy soldiers out of the city, and once they were outside the walls he turned his army around and mauled them. Around 50,000 of the garrison were killed, and a few days later most of the survivors, possibly as many as 40,000, surrendered to Genghis Khan. The Mongols then fought their way into the city and stormed the citadel. After that, he broke his earlier assurances to those who had surrendered and executed every man who had borne arms against him. But that was not all. Genghis then marched the entire civilian population out of the city and executed them to the last man, woman and child, a massacre which numbered tens and possibly hundreds of thousands of people. The Mongols topped it all off by erecting a large pyramid made out of the severed heads.

Ala-ud-Din, who had attempted to come to the city's rescue but been headed off by Jochi's forces, was so horrified that he fled for safety, closely hounded by a force under Subotai and Jebe. The Shah took refuge in a remote island in the Caspian Sea with a handful of loyalist soldiers and his son Jalal-ad-Din, where he died (according to the ancient accounts, of a broken heart) in 1220.

Genghis, however, was still not content. He marched his army towards Urgench, another vast and wealthy trading city governed by the Shah's mother. She fled as the Mongol armies approached, but she was eventually captured and sent as a prisoner to Mongolia while Genghis's army invested the city. It was quickly joined by forces under Jochi, Ogadai and Chagatai, but the siege proved difficult; the city was surrounded by water and marshland, making siege works a nightmare to construct. Once Genghis and his men did manage to break through the walls, the garrison still opposed them, fighting house by house and street by street in a grim gutter brawl that negated the skills of the fast-hitting steppe horsemen and forced them to engage in hand-to-hand fighting in narrow, barricaded streets. Losses were heavy on both sides, but it resulted once again in an inevitable victory for Genghis. A quarrel between Jochi, who had been promised the city's spoils, and Chagatai, who reckoned Jochi was being too soft on Urgench because he was afraid it would ruin his share of the plunder if it were damaged too much, resulted in Genghis awarding the city to Ogadai. The decision would create a years-long estrangement between himself and Jochi, exacerbated as always by the fact Jochi's parentage was still in doubt despite the Khan's recognition of him as his own.

Medieval depiction of Ogadai

Genghis Khan had already shown his savage side during these campaigns, but the capture of Urgench was notorious for a massacre of unprecedented magnitude. The city's entire population, minus nubile women and skilled craftsmen, was put to the sword, with one Middle Eastern scholar claiming that each one of the 50,000 soldiers in Genghis's army was given the responsibility of executing 24 people. If true, that would be a total of more than a million dead, which even if greatly exaggerated almost certainly indicates the destruction of Urgench was one of the grimmest massacres in history. The Mongols went on to devastate Khwarezm, depopulating entire regions, razing whole cities to the ground, diverting rivers to flood them or giving them to the flames, obliterating vast stretches of farmland, and even diverting a river to completely destroy Ala-ad-Din's birthplace. It was essentially the systematic annihilation of an entire empire.

While Genghis and the main Mongol force were engaged in these atrocities, he sent a force of 50,000 under his youngest son Tolui into the Khorasan region, the Khwarezmid heartland, which still possessed plenty of hostile fortresses and garrisons. Tolui's army had a relatively small number of Mongol soldiers, being mostly composed of foreign auxiliaries and a vast siege train designed specifically for reducing hostile cities to rubble, and it proved adept at doing so. Termez and Balkh quickly fell to Tolui's men before they marched on the vast and populous city of Merv, the "jewel of Khorasan", which despite the small size of its garrison was hugely wealthy. Despite initial stiff resistance, the garrison of Merv agreed to surrender when Tolui promised the city would be spared if they did. As the pattern set by Genghis indicated, this was merely a ruse, and Tolui went back on his promise and massacred everyone within the walls, again killing as many as an estimated million civilians.

Tolui then moved on to Nishapur, which had the bad fortune of being the site where Tokuchar, a son-in-law of Genghis, was killed while leading an attack during the siege. Tolui was so furious that he ordered the execution of every living thing within Nishapur's walls, including cats, dogs and other animals, all while Tokuchar's widow looked on. He then marched on Herat, but after witnessing Nishapur's fate the inhabitants surrendered without a fight and were spared. Tolui then smashed Bamian, Tush and Mashad and, in 1221, with Khorasan a depopulated and cowed husk, he rejoined Genghis's forces.

As the Mongolians ravaged the empire, Jalal-ad-Din, taking up his father's mantle, had fled into the remote mountains of Afghanistan, where he was gathering the remnants of the Khwarezmid armies to fight Genghis and his invading Mongols. However, Genghis disdained to fight Jalal-ad-Din and instead sent an army under Shihihutag, only to have it routed in 1221 near Parwan by Jalal-ad-Din. Genghis, driven into a rage at Shihihutag's incompetence, marched into Afghanistan himself and annihilated Jalal-ad-Din's forces on the Indus River, forcing him to flee into India.

Illustration depicting Genghis Khan watching as Jalal ad-Din prepares to ford the Indus.

With that, the Khwarezmid Empire had been defeated and destroyed with unthinkable savagery. The Chinese could already attest to the potential brutality of Genghis Khan, but the Khwarezmids clearly brought out the worst in him as a result of their ruler's arrogance. The destruction of the country had been incredibly violent, even by Mongol standards, though it is worth noting that only cities that resisted before surrendering were destroyed, whereas Heart saw the writing on the wall and was spared).

Genghis returned to Mongolia, but his conquests were not yet done. In the west, yet more territories and yet more strange enemies awaited him. Moreover, the recent campaign had also sown the seeds of an internecine warfare which would threaten Genghis's empire once he was gone. After Urgench, Genghis officialy named Ogadai his successor which infuriated Jochi and induced him to march with his followers into the remoteness of Northern Mongolia and refuse to answer his father's increasingly angry summons. At the time, however, Genghis had other problems to distract his attention besides wayward sons. There were rumblings of revolt in the Jin and Xi Xia regions, signaling that China was about ready to erupt into all-out war. The Mongol hordes would again have to ride into battle.

Chapter 4: The Last Campaign

It was time to go home, but Genghis Khan decided his army would march through Afghanistan and the northernmost part of India to return to Mongolia, allowing him to subdue previously untouched territory and gather yet more plunder. However, even though there were reports that the Jin and Xi Xia were being bellicose, Genghis was persuaded to divide his army at the suggestion of Jebe and Subotai, his two most able and most ambitious generals, who suggested that he dispatch a force of 20,000 riders to the west and take a circuitous route home. Subotai and Jebe, at the head of their 20,000 warriors, rode through Persia and into modern Azerbaijan, sacking Zanjan, Qazvin and Rey and plundering Hamadan, which wisely opened its doors to the Mongols and spared itself an undue amount of bloodshed. Ozbeg, the ruler of Azerbaijan, cannily managed to spare Tabriz, his country's capital, and the still undamaged portions of his domains, by offering Subotai and Jebe a colossal bribe that included vast amounts of replacement horses, which the Mongols prized above all other gifts. Jebe and Subotai moved on, their ranks swelling as thousands of Kurd and Turcoman warriors, nomad horse archers like the Mongols, joined for the promise of plunder and adventure.

Subotai and Jebe then turned north and west into the Kingdom of Georgia, where their vanguard suffered heavy casualties at the hands of a force of 10,000 men commanded by King George IV near Tbilisi, but in a later engagement they succeeded in smashing the Georgian army and driving them from the field. Jebe and Subotai pulled back from Georgia and diverted their attention to the cities of Maghareh and Hamadan, which this time refused to surrender peaceably and was destroyed for its defiance.

A fresco depicting George IV in the Betania monastery in Georgia.

In the autumn of 1221, the Mongol army raided into Georgia again, and though George IV tried to contest their passage with an army of 60,000 men, he fell for Genghis Khan's old tactic of feigning retreat and then savaging his pursuers. George IV's his army was completely destroyed, and he himself suffered a serious wound in the process. Much of Georgia was ravaged by the Mongols after George IV was defeated, but Jebe and Subotai were not satisfied with this success. In a daring move, they marched their army across the Caucasus in the depths of winter, and though the harsh terrain claimed scores of lives and most of their siege train, it was successful. However, word of their coming must have reached the local population, for Jebe and Subotai's forces, now numbering around 30,000 men, were met by a coalition of Alans, Cherkeks, Lezgians, Khazars, Bulgars and Cumans, a force more than double what the Mongols could muster. Nevertheless, Jebe and Subotai succeeded in persuading the Cumans to stand down and destroyed the remainder of the coalition forces. Once again, they reneged on their promises; once victorious, they promptly carved the Cuman host to pieces and sacked one of their main cities, Astrakhan. The remnants of the Cuman forces fled north, with the Mongols in hot pursuit, while Jebe and Subotai took the time to meet with a Venetian delegation and enter into an alliance which saw them destroy any forces (chiefly Genoese) hostile to Venetian interests in the Crimean peninsula.

The Mongols then advanced into modern Russia, where they were met by a hastily assembled force composed of various contingents from the principalities of Kiev and Rus, supported by what was left of the Cuman armies anxious for revenge. The Russians were lured by Subotai and Jebe into a nine-day pursuit that was the result of a feigned retreat, and once they were thoroughly disordered the Mongols turned around and destroyed them. Their leader, Mstislav the Bold of Kiev, held out with the remnants of his army within his fortified camp for several days but was eventually forced to surrender in return for safe conduct. In the end, however, Jebe and Subotai ignored their promises and gave him an honorable (bloodless) death by crushing him and his most prominent nobles under their feasting platform at a victory banquet.

25 years later, a papal legate traveling through the countryside took note of the devastation: "They attacked Rus, where they made great havoc, destroying cities and fortresses and slaughtering men; and they laid siege to Kiev, the capital of Rus; after they had besieged the city for a long time, they took it and put the inhabitants to death. When we were journeying through that land we came across countless skulls and bones of dead men lying about on the ground. Kiev had been a large and heavily populated town, but now it has been reduced almost to nothing, for there are at the present time scarce two hundred houses there and the inhabitants are kept in complete slavery."

The Millennium of Russia Monument depicting Mstislav (left) and his son-in-law, Daniel of Galicia.

With Kievan Rus now open to them, the Mongols plundered much of the surrounding region before turning back east in 1223. They also, however, suffered a notable defeat at the hands of the Volga Bulgars, who sometime in 1223 managed to surprise either a Mongol detachment or the Mongol vanguard, numbering some 15,000 warriors, and use their own tactics against them by luring them into a pursuit with a false retreat before attacking them. Thousands were killed and around 4,000 taken prisoner in what was the first major defeat for a Mongol force in the field. Tthe Volga Bulgars, according to one ancient chronicler, displayed remarkable business acumen by ransoming the 4,000 Mongol prisoners for 4,000 head of cattle, which ultimately helped Subotai and Jebe. That defeat also did not tarnish what was in all respects a truly stunning achievement; their three-year cavalry raid crossed over 9,000 miles and shattered the combined armies of half a dozen countries, bringing Azerbaijan, Georgia, Armenia and Kievan Rus into the Mongol orbit and providing vast amounts of plunder. Genghis Khan had every reason to be pleased with his generals' performance.

Genghis's army, which had battled its way through stiff resistance all the way back to the Mongol heartland, was battle-weary, and the troops under Jebe and Subotai who eventually rejoined him on the steppe were even more tired. But there could be no respite, because the Tangut emperor of Xi Xia, despite being a vassal to Genghis, was now in open revolt and had allied with the Jin in a bid to regain independence. Reinforced by levies of young warriors anxious to share in their older relatives' glory, in 1226 Genghis marched on the Jin and Xi Xia once again. 1226 was also the year that Jochi, still estranged from his father, died under mysterious but convenient circumstances, leading some scholars to assume he was poisoned on Genghis's orders since he had refused to respond to an official summons and was thus virtually in rebellion himself. If Genghis grieved, he did not show it.

Genghis now launched his army into Xi Xia, smashing the cities of Ganzhou, Shuzou, Heisui and Xiliang-Fu before crushing a Tangut army sent to oppose him near Helanshan. He then besieged Lingzhou on the Yellow River and annihilated a Tangut relief force sent to rescue the city. The following year his men took the new Tangut capital, Ning Hia, and then ravaged vast stretches of the enemy-held countryside. He forced the surrender of several provinces within the Tangut heartland, and eventually his seemingly unstoppable progress persuaded the Tangut emperor to sue for peace, hoping Genghis would show leniency. Naturally, he did not; the entire royal family was put to death and their dynasty was wiped out.

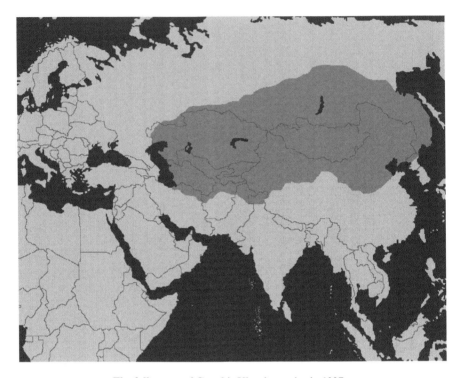

The full extent of Genghis Khan's empire in 1227

In late 1227, following the destruction of the Tangut dynasty, Genghis Khan himself died. His death is shrouded in mystery and hounded by controversy, but several popular theories exist. One ancient account claimed a Tangut princess whom Genghis had either been given in marriage or was intent on assaulting pulled out a knife she had concealed and stabbed him in the groin or leg, leading to his death from blood loss or gangrene. The princess was then said to have thrown herself into the Yellow River afterwards to preserve her virtue. This extremely demeaning death is most likely a fiction, the result of negative propaganda from hostile chroniclers after Genghis's death.

Other more likely accounts suggest that Genghis was killed in a final battle against the Tanguts or suffered a fall from a horse, either during a military action or during a hunt, and that it aggravated his old wounds and eventually killed him. Some believe he suffered from some debilitating disease, such as pneumonia or tuberculosis, which eventually finished the elderly Khan off. It is worth noting that at this point Genghis was in his mid-to-late 60s and had been fighting virtually uninterruptedly for the better part of 50 years, so it is highly likely that decades of campaigning would have taken their toll, making even a trivial injury or illness potentially life-threatening.

After Genghis Khan's death, his body was brought east to the Mongolian heartland, where pursuant to his wishes he was buried near his birthplace in a secret, unmarked location, per Mongolian custom. His funeral guard killed anyone they met on the way to his burial site, so no one would know where Genghis's bones lay, and then stampeded their horses repeatedly over the spot to give no indication of where he was buried. Some versions of this story even suggest a river was diverted over the site.

Following his death, Genghis's sons enacted the provisions laid out by his will, which he had planned meticulously in the years following the campaign against the Khwarezmid Empire. The Mongol army, numbering over 130,000 men, was split up among his family, with the bulk (around 100,000 men) going to Tolui as the youngest, while the remaining 30,000 men went to his other male children (who all had sizeable forces of their own already). Genghis's empire was also split up, though it remained a Mongol empire with intimately connected family and cultural ties, in accordance to his wishes. Ogadai, his favourite son, received the title of Great Khan and the Empire of the Great Khan, comprising most of Eastern Asia and China; Tolui, the youngest, received the Mongolian Heartland; Genghis's grandsons Batu and Orda, Jochi's sons, received the western Eurasian territories, including eastern Rus; and Chagatai was given Central Asia and Khwarezm. All of them would build upon Genghis's legacy, using the Yassa code of governance and the administrative and military infrastructure he had created to expand his territories further than they had ever stretched. In 1279, about 50 years after Genghis's death, the empire he had started and built from scratch stretched from Poland to Korea.

Genghis Khan was by all accounts and by any objective standard an extraordinary man, but that is far different than being a celebrated one. His ethical code can be difficult to swallow, and it is virtually impossible for any civilized individual to condone what he and his generals did to the Khwarezmid Empire through repeated breaches of trust and the wholesale massacre and destruction not just of great cities but of entire regions.

Naturally he is celebrated in Mongolia as the founder of that nation, but his legacy is far more negative in other places. For centuries, much of the Middle East has despised him and viewed him as nothing less than genocidal. As historian Steven Ward noted of the havoc wreaked by Genghis in the region, "Overall, the Mongol violence and depredations killed up to three-fourths of the population of the Iranian Plateau, possibly 10 to 15 million people. Some historians have estimated that Iran's population did not again reach its pre-Mongol levels until the mid-20th century."

For their part, the Chinese have a more nuanced view of Genghis Khan. While he ravaged vast swaths there, he never subdued the entire region. Moreover, when his grandson Kublai Khan did conquer all of China, he ruled as a relatively enlightened leader and would be credited for founding the Yuan Dynasty that ultimately united the whole nation. And though Genghis Khan is scorned by people as far and wide as Iraq and Russia, his conquests also ensured that the Mongols mixed with the region's native inhabitants. Countless numbers of individuals spread across the hemisphere are descendants of Genghis and his men.

Genghis Khan Monument in Hulunbuir, Inner Mongolia (which despite the name is an autonomous region in China)

With all of that said, Genghis Khan must be placed in the context of his own era, during which war and conquest was far more brutal and still centuries removed from concepts like war crimes. Moreover, despite his barbarity, Genghis Khan was also a remarkably progressive monarch who developed an intricate administrative system and promoted men to military and government positions of exceptionally high seniority based exclusively on merit and regardless of provenance, social background, and nationality. In the end, disregarding questions of morality, his legacy is ultimately that of an illiterate and impoverished son of a murdered tribal leader who rose from being a tribeless vagrant and a slave to become the ruler of the greatest land empire in the history of the world, commanding forces of hundreds of thousands of men and presiding over the daily lives of millions. Just as noteworthy, Genghis Khan did it all in the face of constant opposition and entirely on his own merit.

Bibliography

Readers interested in learning more about Genghis Khan should consult Jack Weatherford's excellent *Genghis Khan and the Making of the Modern World*, or John Man's *Genghis Khan*. Other contemporary accounts include Leod de Hartog's *Genghis Khan, Conqueror of the World* (1989) and Paul Ratchnevsky's *Genghis Khan, his Life and Legacy* (1991).

Older 20th century titles on Genghis Khan include Peter Brent's *The Mongol Empire: Genghis Khan: His Triumph and His Legacy* and Harold Lamb's *Genghis Khan: The Emperor of All Men*.

A more contemporary medieval account is Rashid al-Din Tabib's *A Compendium of Chronicles: Rashid al-Din's Illustrated History of the World*

His life is also the subject of the enjoyable (albeit heavily fictionalized) Conqueror series of novels by Conn Iggulden.

Napoleon Bonaparte

The Imperial Standard of Napoleon Bonaparte

Chapter 1: Early Life, 1769-1793

Napoleon was born in Ajaccio, Corsica, on August 15th, 1769, as Napoleone di Buonaparte. This Italian-sounding name was no coincidence, as Corsica had been owned by the Republic of Genoa until 1768, when the Genoese sold the island wholesale to France. The Buonapartes were an ancient, noble, and affluent family, and when in 1777 Napoleon's father, Carlo Buonaparte, was named Corsica's envoy to the throne of France, this opened up even more avenues for the Buonapartes. In accordance with the family's ambitions to expand into the circles of power on the mainland, in 1779, at the age of eleven, Napoleon was sent to school in France. He was first enrolled in a Catholic school in Autun but soon left for the military academy at Brienne-le-Chateau.

Military talents are sometimes apparent in a man from the very beginning; Robert E. Lee graduated first in his class at West Point without a single demerit. But for a man heralded as one of the greatest military leaders of all time, it may be somewhat surprising that Napoleon struggled mightily at the military academy. By all accounts, he had a miserable few years. Far away from home and from everything that was familiar to him, the young Napoleon was forced to endure constant teasing from other students who mocked his strong Corsican accent and poor

French.

It was a difficult time for Napoleon, but rather than become despondent he chose to dedicate himself utterly to his studies, showing a particular aptitude for mathematics, possibly because his poor command of French made the humanities a more difficult subject for him to tackle. Given his knack for mathematics, authorities at the school initially thought he'd be best suited as a sailor, and when Napoleon graduated from Brienne-le-Chateau in 1784 he briefly considered joining the British Royal Navy, a career choice that would have undoubtedly changed the course of European history forever.

Of course, a life on the high seas was not to be. Instead of joining the Royal Navy, Napoleon was also accepted by the highly prestigious *Ecole Militaire* in Paris, which he graduated from with full honors in 1785, a whole year before most other students. During his time at the *Ecole*, likely because of his skill with mathematics, Napoleon chose to become a gunner. Upon graduation, he was commissioned a second lieutenant in *La Fere*, an artillery regiment of the Royal French Army. Between 1785 and 1789, when revolution broke out in France, Napoleon was posted on garrison duty with his regiment around the country, although, obviously homesick, he spent almost half of that period in Corsica on leave.

Napoleon at 23

Napoleon will always be associated as one of France's greatest legends, but before the French Revolution, every indication suggests not only that Napoleon missed Crosica but that he genuinely identified himself as a Corsican nationalist. In 1789 he went so far as to write to Pasquale Paoli, the Corsican separatist leader, that France had "drowned the throne of [Corsica's] liberty in waves of blood". Moreover, young Napoleon actually actively opposed

French forces on Corsica.

However, in the ensuing revolutionary turmoil that engulfed France – and, by extension, Corsica – Napoleon appears to have changed his opinion and aligned himself with the Revolutionary Jacobin party, going so far as to change his name to the more French-sounding Napoleon Bonapart. With the backing of the Jacobins, Napoleon rose to the rank of Captain, but in so doing came into direct conflict with Pasquale Paoli, who had attempted to use the chaos of the Revolution to emancipate Corsica from the mainland. To escape Paoli's revenge, Napoleon was forced to leave Corsica with his entire family in June 1793. He would never return to his homeland.

Chapter 2: Napoleon the Revolutionary, 1793-1799

Napoleon was not blind to the opportunities that the revolution could bring an ambitious and talented young man. In 18th century Europe, a rise through the ranks of the military was one of the surest routes to prominence in society, and with the complete destabilisation of a centuries-old social order under way, Napoleon could hope to rise much further than the younger son of a provincial aristocrat from a hardscrabble island could ever have aspired to under the *ancien regime*. France was beset by enemies, both without and within: royalists and counter-revolutionaries of every faction riddled the country, and Britain, Prussia, Austria, Spain, Portugal, the Netherlands, the Ottoman Empire and the Italian states had all declared war on France and were massing armies on her borders. There was plenty of work to be had for soldiers. Having turned his back for good on Corsica, Napoleon set about securing his place in the new France. A month after he had fled his homeland, Napoleon published a semi-autobiographical pamphlet, *Le Souper de Beaucaire*, in which a soldier, over dinner, persuades some moderate merchants to abandon their counter-revolutionary sentiments. This pamphlet firmly established Napoleon as a young man of sound and unimpeachable revolutionary ideals, and it caught the eye of Augustin Robespierre, younger brother of Revolution and Reign of Terror leader Maximilien Robespierre. This by no means insignificant patronage meant that Napoleon, with the help of another influential friend, fellow Corsican Antoine Cristophe Saliceti, was able to secure an appointment as artillery commander at the Siege of Toulon, despite the resentment of many older officers, who viewed the young Corsican as a thruster and an upstart.

Through the particular blend of relentless work and expert use of his highly-placed connections which characterised his early career, Napoleon, despite being a junior commander, was able to firmly put his mark on the siege, conducted between September and December of 1793. It was imperative that Toulon, an anti-revolutionary city which had risen with the backing of the British, be taken, and Napoleon managed to purloin, borrow, or redirect vital artillery from half a dozen nearby French armies and impress infantrymen from the besieging army into service as gunners. He then placed this mishmash of forces under the command of retired artillery officers who happened to live in the area, who he rousted back into service. With a keen eye for artillery, Napoleon identified the necessary high point from which to unleash artillery and force the besieged British forces to quit the city. During the attack, this massed force of guns, and their deployment, proved vital in the capture of the city and Napoleon – who suffered a thigh wound wound in the leg for his pains – was promoted first to Colonel during the siege itself and, immediately afterwards, to Brigadier-General of the artillery and commander of the newly created Army of Italy's gunners. He was just 24 years old.

Depiction of Napoleon at Toulon

Napoleon's star was on the rise, especially as his new appointment and connections meant that he was *de facto* commander of the Army of Italy. The nominal commander of the army, Pierre Dumberbion, was a supine man who was wary of Napoleon's influence with the Robespierres and actively deferred to him, allowing Napoleon to plan a series of engagements which increased French territorial gains along the Italian border. However, Napoleon suffered a serious setback when, in July of 1794, the Thermidorian reaction put an end to the dominion of Robespierre. Robespierre lost his head, and Napoleon initially lost his freedom, being imprisoned for his association with the family. Yet again, Napoleon managed to distance distancing himself from the Robespierres sufficiently to secure his relief, even though the new revolutionary government distrusted him. For over a year Napoleon, demoted from artillery general to infantry commander, was shuffled from insignificant posting to insignificant posting, including a brief spell in the Bureau of Topography. When he flatly refused to take a further demotion to serve with the Army of the West in the Vendee uprising, he was removed from the active duty list.

Napoleon's career, it seemed, was over before it had truly begun.

Napoleon was, for all intents and purposes, permanently sidelined. However, on October 3rd, 1795, following their exclusion from the newly created Directory, the royalist party launched an attempted coup against the National Convention, the revolutionary legislative assembly. Napoleon, who happened to also be in Paris at the time, was hastily summoned by Paul Barras, then a key figure in the revolutionary government, and placed in charge of the scratch force assigned to defend the National Convention at the Tuileries Palace. With the help of a young cavalryman, Joachim Murat – who would later become one of Napoleon's Marshals and be rewarded for his service with the throne of the Kingdom of Naples – Napoleon was able to defeat the royalists and, in one stroke, erase any negative marks his association with Robespierre and less than stellar record during the previous year's service might have earned him.

For his services in the Directory's hour of need, Napoleon was promoted to Commander of the Interior and given command of the Army of Italy, though this appointment was not as prestigious as it might seem, as the Army of Italy was then in poor fighting condition. In a bizarre twist, he also began courting a former mistress of Barras's, Josephine de Beaurnais, whom he married the following year, in March of 1796. Josephine was no stranger to powerful men, nor generals at that. 6 years Napoleon's senior, Josephine had already been widowed when her husband, general Alexandre de Beaurnais, was beheaded during the Reign of Terror. Josephine was keenly aware that a woman's social advancement was best secured through powerful men, and her enormous spending habits have even led some to speculate that Barras foisted her upon Napoleon to preserve his own wealth.

Josephine

Never one to rest on his laurels – or on his marital bed, for that matter – just two days after marrying Josephine, Napoleon left for the front, taking over command of the Army of Italy and almost immediately launching it in an all-out invasion across the Alps. Napoleon had at his disposal 37,000 half-trained and unmotivated soldiers, along with 60 guns, and he could expect no reinforcements. He faced upwards of 50,000 enemy troops, but that prospect seems not to have daunted him.

It was during the Italian Campaign that Napoleon began showing off his prodigious military talents, utilizing tactics that soundly defeated his opponents. Not yet 30, Napoleon led a decisive campaign across Italy, defeating the Austrians at the Battle of Montenotte and then again at Dego, and crushed the Piedmontese (at the time, Italy was not yet a unified country) at Mondovi'. Piedmont capitulated soon thereafter and sued for peace, defeated in just two weeks after having fought the French for more than three years.

These early victories galvanised Napoleon's men, and with new reinforcements Napoloen pushed southwards, defeating the Austrians again at Lodi on May 10th, then pushed south after investing the strategically vital city of Mantua, occupying Tuscany and the Papal States and crushing the Austrians again at Lonato and Castiglione and forcing their commander, Field Marshal Wurmser, to retreat back into the Alps. Once reinforced, Wurmser again tried to push southwards again to relieve Mantua, but was defeated by Napoleon at Rovereto and then again at Bassano, losing more than three quarters of his army in the process. The Austrians were determined not to abandon Mantua, however, and launched another relief effort under Marshal Alvinczy, but despite some small initial successes he too was defeated by Napoleon at Arcole and then again at Rivoli. Unable to hold out any longer, Mantua fell shortly thereafter, allowing the French to push forward into Austria itself, advancing to within less than 100 miles of Vienna.

Faced with annihilation, Austria was forced to capitulate and, soon thereafter, to sign the Treaty of Campo Formio, declaring peace with France and effectively destroying the coalition which had threatened the Republic for so long. As a result, Napoleon returned to France to a veritable hero's welcome, having captured over 150,000 enemy soldiers, not to mention almost 600 guns and 200 enemy battle-flags. Napoleon had won dozens of battles, revolutionizing the use of mobile artillery and employing pincer movements that attacked both flanks of an enemy army as it advanced forward on his army's center. Even as a young adult, Napoleon's military strategies were generations ahead of his opponents, and he would later explain, "I have fought sixty battles and I have learned nothing which I did not know at the beginning. Look at Caesar; he fought the first like the last."

Now France's foremost general, Napoleon had what effectively amounted to free rein when it came to planning the Republic's military campaign, but he had made sure not to neglect his involvement in politics in Paris while he was campaigning against the Austrians, dispatching one of his generals to crush the resurgent royalists in the capital and establish his patron Barras and the other Republicans firmly in their positions of power.

Bonaparte Before the Sphinx, by Jean-Léon Gérôme, 1868

Napoleon's next planned campaign was even more ambitious: an attack against none other than France's age-old enemy, Britain. However, an initial review of France's naval forces led Napoleon to conclude his navy could not hope to outfight the power of the Royal Navy, which had been the dominant naval power for centuries, so he was forced to look elsewhere. After months of planning, Napoleon crafted a scheme to attack and conquer Egypt, denying the British easy access to their colonies in India, with the ultimate goal of linking up with the Sultan Tipoo in India itself and defeating the British in the field there.

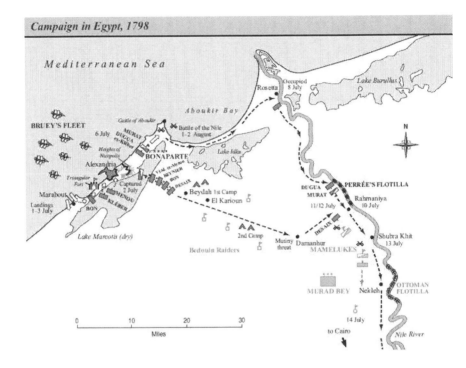

Campaign in Egypt, 1798

With this grand plan in mind, Napoleon left France with an army of about 25,000 men and crossed the Mediterranean, narrowly eluding British naval pursuit. He landed at Alexandria on July 1st, 1798, and defeated the Egyptian forces at the Battle of Subra Khit and then again, two weeks later, at the famous Battle of the Pyramids, where modern European infantry tactics – most notably the square formation – proved to be completely invulnerable to attacks by unsupported Egyptian cavalry. French losses were less than 30, while the Egyptians lost 2000 men killed, further cementing Napoleon's status in the minds of his troops as an invincible general.

However, despite Napoleon's successes on land, his navy continued to be a letdown, and his fleet was almost completely destroyed by Admiral Horatio Nelson at the Battle of the Nile. In addition to being unable to be reinforced or supplied by sea, his ambitions to establish a permanent presence in Egypt were further frustrated by a number of uprisings. Early in 1799, Napoleon advanced against France's erstwhile enemy, the Ottoman Empire, invading modern Syria (then the province of Damascus) and conquering the cities of Gaza, Jaffa, Arish and Haifa. However, with the plague running rampant through his army and his lines of supply from Egypt stretched dangerously thin, Napoleon was unable to destroy the fortified city of Acre and was forced to retreat. The retreat cost him almost all of his wounded as, harassed by enemy forces, he was forced to abandon most of his casualties to the Ottomans' mercy, or lack thereof. Most of the wounded were tortured and beheaded.

Upon returning to Cairo, Napoleon finally received dispatches from France which, with the Mediterranean rife with Royal Navy vessels, had been severely delayed. The dispatches told of renewed hostilities with Austria and her allies, and a series of defeats in Italy which had virtually annihilated all of Napoleon's previous hard-won gains in the Italian peninsula. Leaving his army under the command of his subordinate General Kleber, Napoleon took advantage of a lull in the Royal Navy blockade and embarked upon one of his remaining ships. He set sail for France, determined to rescue her from this fresh wave of enemies.

Chapter 3: Becoming Emperor Napoleon I, 1799-1805

Napoleon on the Throne, by Jean Auguste Dominqiue Ingres (1806)

By the time Napoleon arrived in France, the situation had become somewhat less dire. A series of French victories on the country's borders, including a crucial one against the Austrians in the Alps at the hands of one of Napoleons' pupils, General Massena, had removed the immediate danger of invasion. Still, the country remained rife with political tension. The recently constituted Directory was viewed as supine and ineffective by the people, and their situation was worsened by a combination of years of internal and external war which, coupled with an enemy naval blockade, had virtually bankrupted the country. France was ready for change.

Napoleon was offered a chance to be a part of that change when one of the Directors, Emmanuel Sieyes, included him in his scheme to stage a coup against the Directory and seize power. Never one to turn down a chance for advancement, Napoleon agreed, and on November 9th, as false rumours of a Jacobin uprising (started by the plotters themselves) spread through the city, he took charge of a detachment of troops and escorted key members of the Directory away from their seat in Paris, to the nearby residence of Chateau Saint-Cloud. When members of the Directory realised that something suspicious was afoot, they attempted to protest, at which point Napoleon ordered his men to advance on them with bayonets. With the majority of the legislators thus dispersed, Napoleon was able to coerce or convince the remainder to name himself, Sieyes and another of the plotters, Roger Ducos, temporary Consuls and effective rulers of France.

Emmanuel Sieyes had always imagined Napoleon would take a subordinate role in the governing of the country and be grateful for being involved in the plot, but Sieyes had severely underestimated who he was dealing with. Just a little over a month after the coup, Napoleon drafted a constitution, known as the Constitution of the Eighth Year of the Republic, which placed virtually all legislative and executive powers in the hands of the First Consul and relegated the remaining two to subordinate roles. Having already outfoxed foes on the battlefield, Napoleon displayed his skills in the political realm by now outwitting Sieyes badly; Napoleon managed to get himself elected First Consul, and thus by extension he had become the *de facto* monarch of France.

Early in 1800, with his political place in Paris firmly established, Napoleon led an army into Italy, in a brief campaign which culminated with his triumph over the Austrian forces at the Battle of Marengo, an unusually closely-run engagement whose outcome was decided by timely French reinforcements arriving at the eleventh hour. If there was any doubt how important Napoleon considered this victory, one need only look at his postwar plans for Marengo. Napoleon placed subordinates in charge of constructing a pyramid dedicated to his victory, with streets to be built and named after his other victories in Italy. Ultimately, the plans fell through, but the importance of the victory stayed close: Napoleon would name the horse he used there Marengo, and he would ride Marengo at momentous battles like Austerlitz and Waterloo.

This campaign effectively ended any Austrian belligerence, although a further campaign, led by one of Napoleon's generals in Austria itself, was necessary to completely quell all resistance and impose the Treaty of Luneville on the Austrians, which confirmed all French territorial advances before and after the Treaty of Campo Formio. Bereft of one of her strongest allies in the mainland, Britain also chose to cease hostilities and signed the Treaty of Amiens, though this peace would prove exceedingly short-lived.

It was not like Napoleon to sue for peace, but he had little choice in the matter. Despite his victories, France was still debt-ridden and vulnerable, and Napoleon's position itself was far from secure. Napoleon's political maneuvering had secured him power, but it had also made him enemies on all sides, from Jacobins to Royalists, and he foiled two plots on his life in 1800. Moreover, Napoleon had re-instituted slavery in France's colonies in 1802, but this legislature proved ill-advised as, later that year, slaves in Saint Domingue and Haiti rose up in a bloody revolt. An army, dispatched to crush the rebellion, was decimated by yellow fever and Napoleon, mindful of the Clausewitzian maxim that a general must never reinforce failure, was forced to abandon those possessions to the rebels. Still desperate for money and realizing that overseas colonies were indefensible without a strong navy, Napoleon sold much of the French holdings in North America to President Thomas Jefferson's United States in an effort to fill France's dwindling coffers. At less than 3 cents per acre (about 40 cents in today's currency), the Louisiana Purchase doubled the size of the United States, and it still comprises over 20% of America today. Napoleon was looking for ways to finance his empire's expansion, and he also had geopolitical motives for the deal. Upon completion of the agreement, Napoleon stated, "This accession of territory affirms forever the power of the United States, and I have given England a maritime rival who sooner or later will humble her pride."

The last thing Napoleon wanted in 1803 was another protracted and expensive war, at least until he had been given time to revitalise France's finances, but he was given no choice. In May 1803 Britain broke the terms of the Treaty of Amiens and declared war on France. Furious at this turn of events, Napoleon decided it was time to punish Britain once and for all and began massing a colossal army of about 200,000 men – his first *Grande Armee* – at Boulogne, with the intent of crossing the Channel and invading England. Napoleon organized the army into seven corps, each with its own artillery units, as well as a cavalry reserve that was organized into divisions. This military organization would come to be adopted and closely mimicked across the world, still in use during the Crimean War and the American Civil War over half a century later.

Despite this mobilization, Napoleon remained acutely aware that his position in France was far from stable. In 1804 his spies foiled a Bourbon plot to murder him, taking revenge on the Bourbons by executing the Duke of Enghien, who had not even been part of the plot. The decision to take that drastic step was made on the advice of France's famous and erstwhile Foreign Minister Talleyrand, who would become one of Napoleon's most important advisers. In order to make future Bourbon accession to the throne more difficult – and of course to satisfy his own ambition – in December of 1804, Napoleon had himself crowned Emperor of France at Notre Dame, adopting the title Napoleon I. A few months later, Napoleon held another grand coronation in Milan, crowning himself King of Italy. These steps also allowed him to give titles to his top generals, naming them Marshals of the Empire to ensure their loyalty.

Coronation of Napoleon I and Empress Josephine by Jacques-Louis David, 1804.

Chapter 4: War of the Third Coalition

The newly anointed *Empereur* shook the European *ancien regime* to the core. All across Europe, monarchs sat up and took notice. An upstart might become the leader of a country, but for him to declare himself royalty was unthinkable. Austria, Russia and Portugal eventually joined Britain in declaring war on France, but Napoleon remained focussed on Britain itself. Destroy Britain, he believed, and Austria and Russia would lose heart and withdraw their armies.

With this plan in mind, Napoleon dispatched his navy southwards down the Channel, attempting to persuade the Royal Navy that they were headed for the British West Indies. However, the Royal Navy intercepted the French fleet and brought it to battle off Cape Finisterre in July 1805. The engagement was inconclusive, but the French Admiral, Pierre-Charles Villeneuve, chose to retreat for the safety of the allied Spanish port of Cadiz, where he was promptly blockaded along with the Spanish fleet. Unfortunately for Napoleon, though he was able to discover and cultivate a large number of excellent soldiers – his Marshals chief among them – he was never able to do so with regards to sailors, and the timid and hidebound Villeneuve was a textbook example of this failure.

With his navy bottled up in Cadiz, Napoleon had to cancel his plans for the invasion of Britain. Furious, he marched his *Grande Armee* towards Bavaria, where reports indicated a large Austrian army under General Mack was headed. A Russian reinforcement army was not far behind Mack, but Napoleon marched his army between the two of them on October 9, cutting off Mack's line of advance and forcing him to fall back on Ulm. By separating the two Coalition forces, he was able to confront them piecemeal, and after a brilliant series of movements, Napoleon completely enveloped Mack's army and then utterly annihilated it on October 20th, 1805, killing or wounding 12,000 Austrians and capturing 30,000 more.

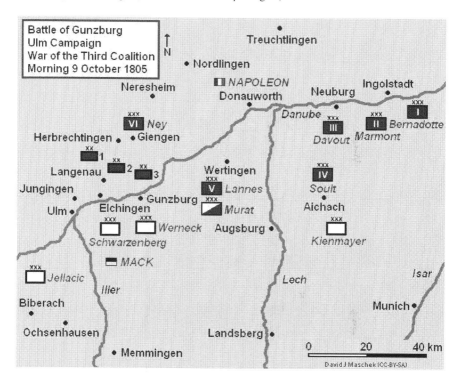

Dividing the Russians and Austrians during the Ulm Campaign

The use of quick movements to interpose his own army between allied armies and then defeat them in detail individually would become a hallmark of Napoleon's military campaigns, allowing his often outmanned armies to fight on more favorable terms. It was a strategy made possible both by Napoleon's genius and by his trusted and competent subordinates, particularly Marshal Ney and Marshal Murat.

Marshal Murat

Marshal Ney

This triumph was given a slightly sour note by what was happening at sea, however. Although he did not know it at the time, the following day Napoleon's ambitions for the invasion of Britain were crushed once and for all. Villeneuve left Cadiz with the combined French and Spanish fleets, only to be surprised by the Royal Navy under the command of Admiral Nelson. Despite having an advantage in number of ships, Nelson's masterful performance resulted in the destruction of half the French and Spanish fleets, and the loss of over 13,000 sailors. Famously dressed in his military best, Nelson made for a very conspicuous target on deck, and the man who had already lost an eye in battle was mortally wounded at the height of his victory. Nelson and Trafalgar are still celebrated as one of Britan's greatest military heroes and triumphs respectively, and the Battle effectively restricted Napoleon to land-based operations for the foreseeable future.

Trafalgar may have been a permanent setback for the French, but it was not necessarily a bad thing that Napoleon was relegated to land-based campaigns, because Napoleon clearly excelled at it. And six weeks after Ulm, Napoleon scored one of his most legendary victories, the kind generals' dreams are made of, at the Battle of Austerlitz, where he faced a combined army of Russian and Austrian soldiers under the command of Czar Alexander I and Holy Roman Emperor Francis II.

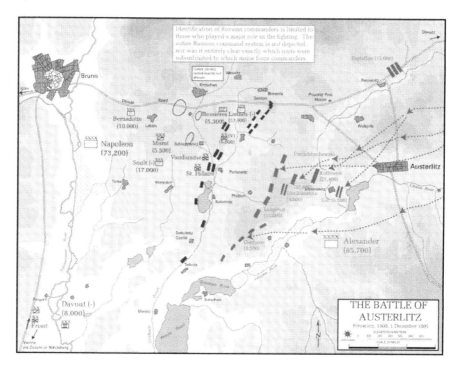

The Allied forces retreated in the face of Napoleon's army as it crossed the Rhine and advanced, refusing to give battle. In an attempt to bring about battle, Napoleon occupied Austerlitz with only 50,000 of his men, hoping it would entice the Coalition's nearly 90,000 man army to attack. Unbeknownst to the Russians and Austrians, Napoleon concealed reserve troops that could march in support and bring his numbers up to nearly 80,000. Moreover, Napoleon sent out entreaties suggesting he desired to negotiate peace, which he correctly assumed would be interpreted as a sign of weakness.

Napoleon wasn't entirely confident of his success, but his ruse worked, and the Coalition army advanced to give battle on December 2, 1805. Napoleon invited an attack on his right flank by intentionally giving up high ground, the Prazen Heights, with the intention of using a hidden attack force that would counterattack the Heights and then slice into the rear of the Coalition's advancing attack. As he ordered the counterattack, Napoleon stated, "One sharp blow and the war is over."

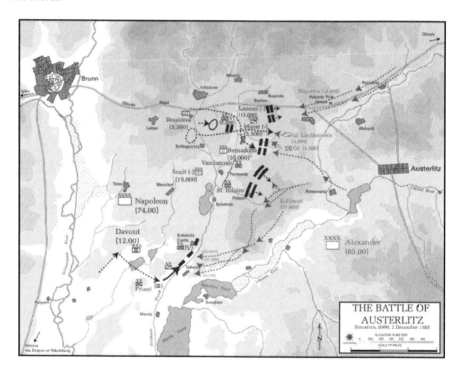

Napoleon's counterattack went perfectly, with his troops advancing invisibly under the cover of mist. When they retook the Prazen Heights, it had the effect of slicing the Coalition army in two, while ensuring that the French forces on the center of the field were now along the rear of the Coalition's attack on their right flank. After severe fighting to hold the center, Napoleon swung his men to the right to attack the Coalition's left flank, which was already in a fighting retreat. With the French now sweeping the field, panic ensued among the Coalition army, which was routed in two parts with the French inbetween them.

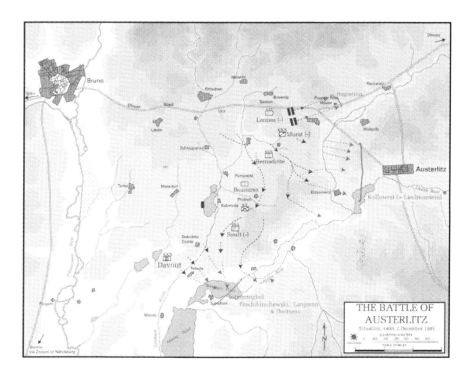

To say the Battle of Austerlitz was a complete victory would be an understatement; it was one of the most important battles in Europe's history. As a result of Napoleon's smashing victory, which resulted in the destruction of the Coalition's army, the French would occupy Vienna in the coming months, force the disbandment of the Third Coalition, dissolve the Holy Roman Empire, and come to occupy much of the European continent. It was a dazzling success for Napoleon, one so great that it seems around this time that his hubris began to spiral out of control. According to some, he began to genuinely believe the legend of his invincibility – a mistake he would come to regret in later years.

Chapter 5: War of the Fourth Coalition

After his victory over the Third Coalition, there was a year of relative peace in Europe, but it was little more than an illusion. The Peace of Pressburg, ratified after Austerlitz, technically held, but all the while the defeated members of the Coalition were licking their wounds and massing their armies again in preparation of resuming the fight against the French. After barely a year, in 1806, Prussia and Russia, with support from several other minor European states, declared war on France.

The Fourth Coalition may have been a formal alliance, but when the fighting started, the Russians were still way too far away to support the Prussians, who were now faced with the prospect of opposing the French singlehandedly. Napoleon acted quickly, striking out into modern Germany and defeating the Prussians at the twin battles of Jena-Auerstedt, another amazing victory that featured one French corps under Marshal d'Avout defeating the brunt of the Prussian Army, an event that shocked even Napoleon. By the time the Russians could take the field, the Prussian army, which had once numbered nearly 250,000, was in tatters. When Napoleon entered Berlin in October 1806 and visited Frederick the Great's tomb, he remarked to his marshals, "If he were alive we wouldn't be here today."

The disaster spurned both civil and military reforms among the Prussians, who realized the need to cast off archaic systems that had allowed inexperienced and unskilled aristocrats to assume important military positions. Moreover, some of the most famous Prussians took part in the campaign, including Carl von Clausewitz (whose military treatise, *On War*, made him perhaps second only to Napoleon in 19th century military influence), and General Gebhard Leberecht von Blücher, who would feature more prominently at Leipzig and Waterloo.

After a winter lull, a common occurrence in Napoleonic campaigns, hostilities resumed and Napoleon fought a blood-soaked and inconclusive battle with the combined Russian and Prussian forces at Eylau, where both sides fought each other to a standstill. The combined casualty toll for Eylau was about 30,000, divided equally between the French and the Russo-Prussians. Despite the stalemate at Eylau, Napoleon pushed forward undaunted, and later that summer he defeated the Russian forces at the Battle of Friedland, where he inflicted almost 40,000 casualties on them between enemy soldiers killed, wounded and captured, a figure compounded by the fact the Russians fought with their backs to a river and hundreds drowned in the panicked retreat that ended the battle. Friedland left Napoleon in such a powerful position that in July 1807 he was able to impose the Treaty of Tilsit upon Russia and Prussia, ending hostilities with Russia and stripping Prussia of over half of its territories.

After this treaty, the only major Coalition power still actively at war with Napoleon was Britain, which had still not been defeated in the field and had earlier succeeded in virtually destroying French naval power. Realizing he could not cross the English Channel to invade Britain itself, Napoleon resolved to strangle Britain's lifeblood: trade. Shortly after the Treaty of Tilsit, he published decrees that instituted a Continental Blockade, banning all British imports into mainland Europe. With no navy to enforce the Blockade it was a largely symbolic gesture, but reducing the British to smuggling must have afforded Napoleon a certain degree of satisfaction. Though the Continental Blockade was not as effective as Napoleon could have hoped, a widely forgotten aspect of it is that the "Napoleonic Codes" he drafted and put in place along with the Continental System were later implemented into societies and nations across the European continent long after Napoleon himself was gone.

Furthermore, the Continental System also provided a useful pretext for further conquering across the part of the European continent not yet under France's control. Portugal, a long-standing British ally, had been flaunting the Blockade with impunity, not least because it had the allegedly neutral Spain as a buffer to shield it from France. Napoleon decided to punish the Portuguese for their defiance and, in the autumn of 1807, he marched across Spain, whose government had granted him free passage, and invaded Portugal. The Portuguese had been unprepared for an invasion from Spain, and Napoleon's army, moving with the lightning speed that characterised the majority of his campaigns, was able to push forward and secure Lisbon in a matter of weeks. However, his hopes of capturing the Portuguese royal family were frustrated. The Portuguese royals managed to board a ship for Rio de Janeiro, from where they governed the country's overseas colonies for over a decade.

Napoleon could have contented himself with conquering Portugal, but his characteristic thirst for conquest prompted him to attempt an even more daring plan. In the early spring of 1808, French armies began filing quietly into Spain, ostensibly on the way to reinforce the garrisons still subduing the last pockets of resistance in Portugal. These armies excited no particular suspicion, as the Spanish were sure of Napoleon's good faith. However, they were to receive a rude awakening when, with his forces placed in key positions throughout the country, Napoleon proceeded to seize key cities and garrisons all across Spain. By May, the entire country was virtually in his hands, with the Spanish armies either defeated or scattered and leaderless. Napoleon, it seemed, had won an almost bloodless victory.

Chapter 6: The War of the Fifth Coalition and the Invasion of Russia

Napoleon was now master of almost all of Western Europe, and his French empire was at the height of its power. But Napoleon's longtime adversaries were still hoping to defeat him.

In early May of 1808, Napoleon forced the King of Spain to abdicate, taking him and his son prisoner, and installed his brother Joseph Bonaparte on the throne. Napoleon believed, wrongly, that the relatively supine reaction to his conquest was a symptom of Spain's desire for political change, and so instead of reducing the nation to a client state and allowing it to preserve at least some face, he made the key error of instituting a regime change. The reaction to the coronation of Joseph was instantaneous and awe-inspiring: the entire country of Spain rose in open revolt. It was a nationwide popular uprising, the first guerrilla war ("guerrilla" is Spanish for "little war") and it caught Napoleon almost completely unprepared. He had thought Spain subdued, and suddenly his garrisons were being murdered in their beds all across the Iberian Peninsula by a ruthless enemy who promised him, "war to the knife!"

For the first time, Napoleon had encountered a military problem beyond his comprehension. He was the master of conventional warfare, but this asymmetric conflict baffled him, as it has scores of great generals ever since. Mistaking the cheerful reports of his generals in the field, who told of battles won against superior Spanish forces, for a sign of victory, Napoleon felt comfortable enough to leave the country despite the insurrection. What he did not realise was that though the Spanish field armies were being made short work of, the fact that the entire country was up in arms against the French meant literally every Spanish peasant could be an enemy – and probably was. Without Napoleon's presence to bolster their morale and bereft of his tactical acumen, his troops in Spain soon blundered. In the summer of 1808, General Dupont's entire army, totalling more than 24,000 men, was obliged to surrender to the Spanish at Bailen. Bereft of the necessary troops to keep his fragile hold on Spain, Joseph panicked and ordered his high command to institute a general retreat. This was an event of truly momentous proportions: Napoleon's veterans, it seemed, could be beaten after all. News of the victory resonated across Europe, prompting Austria and Prussia to take up arms against France once again.

Napoleon's woes were further compounded by his old enemies, the British. Even as Spain was rising, a British army under the command of Sir Arthur Wellesley, the man who would later become the Duke of Wellington, landed in Portugal and, in a dashing display of soldiering that made even Napoleon sit up and take notice, proceeded to liberate the country from the French.

Duke of Wellington

Furious at this new turn of events, Napoleon decided it was time for him to show his generals how it was done. Massing more than 280,000 troops on the Spanish border, 100,000 of which were his dreaded veterans of the *Grande Armee*, Napoleon swept into Spain in October of 1808. The Spanish armies, plagued by poor organisation and indecision, were powerless to resist him; every force that tried to stand its ground was annihilated, and Napoleon won a spectacular series of victories at Burgos and Tudela, forcing what little was left of the Spanish armies to scatter throughout the country. His best Marshals also performed admirably: in the north, Marshal Soult defeated Sir John Moore's British army, harried it across half the country, and forced it to embark and flee the Iberian Peninsula. Despite being held up by a ruthless defence organised by General Palafox at Saragossa, in little over two months the French had succeeded in subduing the entire Spanish peninsula once again, leaving tens of thousands of dead and entire cities reduced to rubble in their wake. It was a textbook example of Napoleon's military genius and his remarkable callousness, but once again he was to win the war and lose the peace.

With his armies poised to conquer Portugal once again, Napoleon felt secure enough to leave the Iberian Peninsula, again ignoring the threat posed by the thousands of Spanish irregulars, now bolstered by the remnants of the dispersed Spanish armies, that were scattered across the Peninsula. It was a mistake that would cost him dearly, for the British took advantage of the vulnerable situation of the French in Spain and, shortly after Napoleon's departure, landed a new army in Portugal, an army that would go on to shatter, at Bussaco and Badajoz, San Sebastian and Vitoria, Fuentes d'Onoro and Salamanca, the myth of French invincibility.

All that was still in the future, however. In the spring of 1809 Napoleon's most pressing concern was the newly belligerent Austria, who, galvanised by the Spanish victory at Bailen, broke their alliance with France and threatened to invade. Napoleon first pushed the enemy forces back towards the Danube and then smashed them at the Battle of Wagram in July 1809. At that battle, Napoleon's grand plan involved using part of his force to pin down the Austrian army in place while using the bulk of his army to wheel around into that army's flank, allowing him to envelop the army without a direct assault. It was a strategy that would be attempted many times unsuccessfully during the rest of the century, including at the first major battle of the American Civil War, the First Battle of Bull Run. Sensing their predicament, the Austrians were induced to make a frontal assault themselves, which disrupted Napoleon's strategy but nevertheless resulted in a decisive French victory, which forced Austria into a new treaty with France.

After subduing Austria, there followed a period of aggressive expansion for Napoleon's Empire: the Kingdom of Sweden, a former enemy of France, was annexed and its throne granted to one of Napoleon's Marshals, Bernadotte. Once again using the pretext of non-compliance with the Continental Blockade, Napoleon occupied the Papal states and had the Pope abducted, keeping him in captivity for nearly five years. It was also around this time that Napoleon's marriage with Josephine, which had never been particularly sound considering he abandoned her marriage bed just two days after their union to go to war, deteriorated completely. Though Napoleon's love letters to Josephine remained and are a testament to his strong feelings, he was bitterly frustrated by her failure to provide him with an heir with which to continue his Imperial dynasty. It is possible that he privately felt the inability to father children was his shortcoming, but given Napoleon's nature, he had to portray it as Josephine's problem. In 1810 Napoleon divorced Josephine. To cement his alliance to Austria, he married the Arch-Duchess Marie Louise of Austria, which temporarily brought a measure of peace to the two warring countries.

The French Empire in 1811

Always restless, Napoleon was not a man made for peacetime. He had succeeded in subduing most of his enemies – though in Spain, the British continued to be a perpetual thorn in his flank that drained the Empire of money and troops – but his relationship with Russia, never more than one of mutual suspicion at best, had now grown downright hostile. At the heart of it, aside from the obvious mistrust that two huge superpowers intent on dividing up Europe felt for one another, was – once again – the Continental Blockade. Russia had initially agreed to uphold the Blockade in the Treaty of Tilsit, but they had since taken to ignoring it altogether. Napoleon wanted an excuse to teach Russia a lesson, and in early 1812 his spies gave him just that: a preliminary plan for the invasion and annexation of Poland, then under French control.

Napoleon wasted no time attempting to defuse the situation. He increased his *Grande Armee* to 450,000 fighting men – diverting much needed reinforcements from Spain to do so – and prepared it for invasion. On July 23rd, 1812, he launched his army across the border, despite the protestations of many of his Marshals. The Russian Campaign had begun. It was to be Napoleon's greatest blunder, the final act of hubris of a man who thought himself invincible.

Russia's great strategic depth already had a habit of swallowing armies, a fact which many would-be conquerors learned the hard way, and Napoleon, exceptional though he was in so many regards, proved that even military genius can do little in the face of the might of Russia's greatest strategist, General Winter, combined with the indestructible resilience of its people. Initially, the campaign seemed to be going in Napoleon's favor. He met with little opposition as he pushed forwards into the interior with his customary lightning speed, but gradually this lack of engagements became a hindrance more than a help; Napoleon needed to bring the Russians to battle if he was to defeat them.

Moreover, the deeper Napoleon got his army sucked into Russia, the more vulnerable their lines of supply, now stretched almost to breaking point, became. The *Grande Armee* required a prodigious amount of material in order to keep from breaking down, but the army's pace risked outstripping its baggage train, which was constantly being raided by Cossack marauders. Moreover, Napoleon's customary practice of subsisting partially off the land was proving to be ineffective: the Russians were putting everything along his line of advance, including whole cities, to the torch rather than offer him even a stick of kindling or sack of flour for his army. The horses, in particular, were having the worst of it, with the relentless pace and poor forage killing them in ever greater numbers. Like all armies of the time, moreover, Napoleon's force had acquired a slew of camp-followers, a motley collection of soldiers' wives, servants, prostitutes, and merchants of every description, who were horribly vulnerable to the hit-and-run attacks of the Cossacks.

Napoleon, like a man punching at shadows, was getting increasingly desperate. The more he advanced, the more he needed a battle, to get a chance to rest his troops in the aftermath, plunder the surrounding countryside, and above all lessen the number of enemies harrying his advance. On September 7th, 1812, he must have thought his prayers had finally been answered. The Russians had decided to stand and fight almost at the very gates of Moscow. Battle was promptly joined, with horrific effect: the Battle of Borodino, as it was later called, resulted in a combined casualty toll of over 75,000, a hideously long butcher's bill that crippled the *Grande Armee*. The Russian army retreated and Napoleon was able to occupy Moscow, hoping this would persuade the Tsar to sue for peace. However, even as his advance guard pushed into the city, the retreating Russians put the capital to the torch. The Russian Army's retreat also ensured that it would live to fight another day, if necessary.

This was a crippling blow for Napoleon, who had been sure that taking Moscow would prompt the Russians to surrender. Instead, with winter on the way, they appeared more bellicose than ever. Napoleon and his army lingered for several weeks in the burnt shell of Moscow but then, bereft of supplies and facing the very real threat of utter annihilation, Napoleon gave the order to retreat.

What followed was one of the most gruelling and horrific ordeals ever endured by an army in recorded history. The retreat from Moscow to the safety of the Berezina river, a march of 400 miles which almost all Napoleon's men had to carry out on foot (most of the horses had long since perished of cold, hunger, or simply been eaten) in the middle of the merciless Russian winter, was a nightmare worse than Napoleon could ever have imagined. One can only speculate as to what his thoughts could have been as he watched his men torn apart by the sabers of marauding Cossacks or simply killed where they lay or sat by the cold, but doubtless he must have rued the day he ever set foot into Russia. In some units, discipline broke down completely, with reports of cannibalism and other atrocities running rife. Others managed to keep their order, but discipline could do little against hunger and the relentless cold. By the time the *Grande Armee* had reached the Berezina, it had been decimated: of the over 450,000 fighting men that had invaded Russia that autumn, less than 40,000 remained.

Napoleon's retreat from Moscow, by Adolf Northern (1845)

Chapter 7: The War of the Sixth Coalition

For Napoleon, the nightmare was far from over. The customary winter lull in campaigning, not to mention the casualties the Russians had sustained at Borodino, bought him time to raise another conscript army, boosting the *Grande Armee*'s numbers to 350,000. However, these new troops were a mere shadow of the ones he had lost in Russia, and Napoleon was acutely aware these raw, untried recruits could be unreliable in battle.

Napoleon also rightly anticipated that a battle was coming. Following the *Grande Armee*'s annihilation, Napoleon's enemies all across Europe had taken heart and risen up in arms again: Russia, Prussia, Austria, Britain, Spain, Portugal, even Sweden, governed by Napoleon's erstwhile Marshal Bernadotte. All the European powers were fielding their armies, determined to rid themselves of Napoleon once and for all.

Napoleon would not let himself be so easily subdued, however. Despite news of fresh reversals in Spain that had seen the French forced out of their strongholds and back to the Franco-Spanish border in the Pyrenees by Wellington's British forces and their Spanish and Portuguese allies, Napoleon rallied his new *Grande Armee* and proceeded to ravage the advancing Prussian,

Austrian and Russian forces on the German front, defeating their combined armies at the Battle of Dresden in 1813. Once again, Napoleon managed to slice the enemy army in two, this time using a turning movement along one of the flanks and using a cavalry charge to follow it up. Napoleon inflicted 4 times more casualties than his army suffered, but ailment forced him from the field, and he was unable to follow up this success.

The French had been outnumbered nearly 2 to 1 at Dresden, and even after their victory they remained heavily outnumbered. The Sixth Coalition was capable of putting a million men into fields across Europe, and Napoleon couldn't possibly defend the entire French Empire against that number. Duke Wellington once famously said Napoleon alone was worth 50,000 men in the field, but even genius must bow to the laws of mathematics, and there was little Napoleon could do about the fact that he was consistently outnumbered by 2 or 3 to 1. And Napoleon had defied odds while commanding seasoned veterans, but most of those had been lost on the plains of Russia.

Fate eventually caught up to Napoleon at the Battle of Leipzig in October 1813, also fittingly known as the Battle of Nations. After Dresden, the Coalition's commanding generals actually implemented a strategy that sought to give battle against the French only in fields where Napoleon was not present, thereby fighting only against his marshals. Austrian, Prussian, Russian, and Swedish forces began advancing on a wide front against Napoleon. After weeks of marching and counter-marching, Napoleon was confronted at Leipzig by an army twice his army's size.

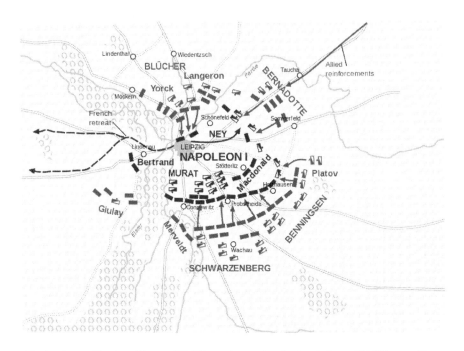

The battle was bloody, with over 600,000 combatants involved and almost 100,000 casualties, but Napoleon escaped complete encirclement and was able to retreat with 70,000 men in good fighting order, leaving approximately 40,000 scattered stragglers to fend for themselves. Napoleon had finally suffered a decisive defeat in a pitched battle, and his retreat ceded French control of Prussia permanently.

France was now an island in a storm. British, Spanish and Portuguese armies pressed through the Pyrenees in the south and attacked Bordeaux, while Russians, Austrians and Prussians closed in from the north and west. Napoleon lashed out, winning a series of minor victories inside France proper, but he was powerless in the face of ever growing enemy forces. The barrel of French conscription had been scraped dry, and there were no more troops to be had. In March 1814, the allied forces took Paris. Napoleon hoped to use the remnants of his army to attack the Coalition forces in Paris itself, but his generals threatened mutiny. A few days later, under considerable pressure from his Marshals, Napoleon was forced to abdicate. At first, he attempted to secure the succession for his young son borne by Marie Louise, but this was refused by the Coalition, whose rulers were still European royalty and fully intended to ensure the restoration of the ousted Bourbons in France. Napoleon was forced to abdicate unconditionally.

For the first time, Napoleon found himself on the losing end of a treaty. The terms of the Treaty of Fontainebleau denied him and his heirs any claim to the throne of France, assigned his wife and son to the Austrian court, and banished Napoleon himself, with a small honor guard, to the small island of Elba, a lick of land home to some 10,000 inhabitants off the Italian coast. Napoleon, seemingly resigned to his fate, bid an extremely moving farewell to his veterans of the Old Guard which left many of the hard-bitten soldiers in tears. Having bid his most loyal soldiers goodbye, Napoleon took ship for Elba, and exile.

Portrait of Napoleon, by Jacques-Louis David (1812)

Chapter 8: The Hundred Days

Although Napoleon was exiled, he was allowed to retain the title of Emperor and was given de facto control over Elba. But it is not surprising the man who once ruled Europe was not content with the island of Elba. Separated from his family and cast away on a small island, Napoleon attempted suicide by taking a poison pill. However, he had first carried the pill with him on the retreat from Moscow, rightly concerned about an uncertain fate at the time. The age of the pill had fatally weakened the pill, which stopped it from fatally weakening Napoleon.

Though the Emperor had busied himself developing the island's industries and had established a miniature army and navy, he must still have found time to brood upon his situation and could not have helped but think of himself as reduced to laughing stock. The "Emperor of Elba" was a poor title for a man who had once ruled over more than half of mainland Europe. Even some of Napoleon's old Marshals, like Murat, now controlled more territory than the man who had raised them in the first place. To add insult to injury, the salary he had been promised in the Treaty of Fontainebleau and that was meant to keep him in relative luxury was often late and sometimes failed to arrive at all. Coupled with his deteriorating health and the express refusal of the Austrian court to let him speak or write to his wife and son, Napoleon must have felt himself well and truly slighted. Beaten, but not defeated, he resolved to show the Coalition powers he could still make Europe tremble.

Napoleon's return from Elba, by Karl Stenben

Of all the incredible military feats Napoleon accomplished, none were more impressive than his escape from Elba and his return to France, which was literally a bloodless revolution. On February 26th, 1815, Napoleon escaped from Elba. In a desperate gamble, he landed on the

French mainland with less than a thousand men and marched on Paris.

What happened next was truly remarkable. An infantry regiment was sent to intercept Napoleon and his men, but Napoleon rode up to them alone and shouted, "Here I am. Kill your Emperor, if you wish." Upon seeing their once invincible Emperor before them, the soldiers mutinied and went over to his side *en masse.* Other corps soon followed, and in no time at all Napoleon found himself at the head of an army marching on Paris. The newly reinstituted Bourbon monarch fled the city and so, with barely a shot fired, Napoleon found himself enthroned as Emperor once more.

Naturally, Napoleon's enemies were not as excited about his return as the French, and the reaction of the Coalition nations was predictable. They branded Napoleon an outlaw and declared war, not on France but on Napoleon himself, and readied their armies. It would be the Seventh Coalition of nations to oppose Napoleon in less than 15 years.

The Coalition's nations were capable of putting over half a million men in the field, and Napoleon had already learned his math lessons at Leipzig. However, the Coalition's forces were widespread, and Napoleon, never one to submit passively to fate, decided to go on the offensive before the allies could consolidate their forces and overwhelm him. Gathering an army of 100,000 men, he marched into what is now Belgium, intent on driving his force between the advancing British army under the Duke of Wellington and the Prussian forces under Marshal Blucher. Napoleon's forces fought two separate engagements on June 16th, one at Quatre Bras against the British and the other at Ligny against the Prussians. The Prussians were beaten at Ligny, forcing the British to retreat from Quatre Bras and take up a defensive position at Waterloo. Napoleon dispatched one of his commanders, Marshal Grouchy, to harry the Prussians with 30,000 men, with orders to stop Blucher from linking up with Wellington. Then he himself turned against the British.

Blucher

Napoleon desperately needed to keep the British and Prussians from linking up, so he had to give battle at Waterloo on June 18th, 1815. Realizing he would have to take the offensive, Napoleon waited during the early morning hours for the ground to dry in anticipation of infantry and cavalry charges, giving Duke Wellington time to emplace his men firmly in a strong defensive position, the vulnerable points in his line guarded by fortified farms, and Napoleon's troops, who had to wait until late afternoon for the ground to be dry enough to deploy infantry and artillery properly, were unable to drive the British from the high ground. For hours, Napoleon's men attempted to dislodge the British, most notably on the British right at the Château of Hougoumont.

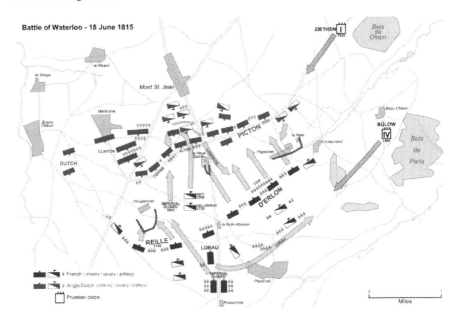

As the British repulsed attacks, Wellington waited for the right time to deliver a massed cavalry charge, counterattacking the center of the French line. Napoleon was also fully aware that Blucher's Prussians were on the move, in an effort to link up with the British, and eventually the first Prussians began arriving around 4:30 in the afternoon, 5-6 hours into the fight, representing a fresh threat to the French's right flank.

Desperate to avoid the linking of the two armies, Napoleon ordered in his final reserves and ultimate crack unit, the Imperial Guard. Around 7:30 at night, the Guard mounted one of the most famous charges in military history, attempting to break the center of the British line and interpose itself between the British and Prussians. As the attack faltered, the French were met with a counterattack by 1,500 British soldiers who Wellington had skillfully hid behind high ground by lying down to avoid artillery fire. This counterattack sent the Imperial Guard into a rout, and the sight of their retreat unnerved the rest of the French army. Napoleon had just met his Waterloo.

Chapter 9: Exile to St. Helena and Death

In terms of casualties, Waterloo was not one of the bloodiest battles of the Napoleonic Era, but it was unquestionably the most decisive, and even today it remains one of the most famous battles in history. The Belgians themselves were well aware of its import, as tourism to the battlefield started the very next day. By then, of course, Napoleon was in flight to Paris, but there, with the mood of popular opinion turning against him, he abandoned the city and attempted to catch a ship to the United States. He surrendered himself to a ship of the Royal Navy blockade when he realised his situation was hopeless, on June 29th, 1815. This time, the allies were less inclined to be as generous with Napoleon as they had been at Fontainebleau. Napoleon was stripped of all wealth and titles and banished to the remote British island of Saint Helena in the Atlantic, thousands of miles away from Europe.

The Longwood House, Napoleon's home on St. Helena

Napoleon was banished to the Longwood House, a damp, dank place, but the British were still worried about a potential escape. At one point in 1818, false rumors that Napoleon had escaped panicked Londoners Napoleon's British custodian, Hudson Lowe, treated him notoriously poorly, curtailing guests from visiting Napoleon unless they stayed indefinitely. For his part, Napoleon began dictating memoirs, but he continued to have machinations of escape, with contacts in South America and even old Imperial Guards members plotting a potential empire in Southwest America. Napoleon also hoped sympathetic British politicians might eventually release him.

The poor conditions at Longwood began to take their toll, and Napoleon's health began to decline sharply in 1821. There was nothing British doctors could do, and on May 5th, 1821, Napoleon finally succumbed to the poor health that had dogged him for much of his later years, dying in exile on the island of Saint Helena.

Given his treatment at the hands of his captors, and the fact he was only 51 when he died, controversy has often surrounded the Emperor's death, and many scholars have gone out of their way to attempt to prove that Napoleon was poisoned, with autopsy studies and chemical analysis showing that he had abnormal levels of arsenic in his hair. However, it has also been suggested that most people at that time would have been exposed to arsenic and other toxic substances throughout their lives, so these findings are to be expected. Other findings suggest peptic ulcers or perhaps even stomach cancer as the cause of Napoleon's death at the early age of 51, though doubtless depression also played a part in his demise.

Napoleon's Tomb at Les Invalides

Many great generals and many great rulers have carved their names into the annals of history, but the men who succeeded in mastering both politics and warfare are few and far between. Of this handful of gifted statesmen-soldiers, perhaps the most famous – or infamous - was the man who came to be known as His Imperial Majesty Napoleon I, By the Grace of God and the Constitutions of the Republic, Emperor of the French. In less than fifteen years of rule he dramatically altered the world's map, conquering or bringing under French control Spain, Switzerland, Belgium, the Netherlands, Italy, much of modern Germany, the Balkans, and Poland, smashing the armies of half a dozen great powers into kindling in the process. Never before or since had France's borders been pushed so far in mainland Europe, but the glory of his conquests exacted a grim price: over a decade and a half of near-continuous warfare resulted in a combined civilian-military death toll of around six million, the devastation of much of the continent and the near-complete bankruptcy of France herself, not to mention the loss of all her overseas colonies.

"The great thief of Europe" has always been a polarizing figure, not least because his stance on so many issues has always been so ambivalent. The ultimate politician, he was fond of remarking, "It is by making myself Catholic that I brought peace to Brittany and Vendée. It is by making myself Italian that I won minds in Italy. It is by making myself a Moslem that I established myself in Egypt. If I governed a nation of Jews, I should reestablish the Temple of Solomon". Ever aware of his listeners and always keeping an eye set firmly on posterity, Napoleon almost never spoke his mind, no matter how small his audience might be. Any attempt to extricate the man from his policies is an exercise in futility, and idle speculation at best.

Even towards his death, Napoleon remained vague about a great many of his personal issues, not least his religiosity: in letters to his friends he expressed a sympathy for Islam and doubted Christ's divinity, yet on his deathbed he was anointed following Roman Catholic precepts. Perhaps the only subject on which Napoleon always expressed absolute certainty was warfare, and with good reason. His roll-call of triumphs –Jena, Marengo, Ulm, Austerlitz, Borodino, the Pyramids – is the one achievement even Napoleon's many detractors cannot deny. Revered by much of France to his dying day and beyond, admired by many forward-thinking humanists throughout Europe, loathed as an upstart tyrant by the *ancien regime* and hated by thousands more across the continent for his imperialistic ambitions, it was impossible not to have a strong opinion about Napoleon.

Regardless of what might have finally killed Napoleon in 1821, it is fitting that his death, like most of his life, should be surrounded by controversy. Love or hate him, it is undeniable that in less than half a century Napoleon was able to forge a legacy that will likely last for thousands of years. He modelled himself on Caesar and, like him, tried to grasp too much and ended up losing everything, and with it his life. Yet doubtless the diminutive Corsican would be pleased to know that we are still writing about him today, almost two centuries since his armies made the whole of Europe shake, and the man who always concerned himself with posterity forged a legacy that endures to this day.

Chapter 10: Common Myths about Napoleon's Life

Given the staggering importance of the man, it isn't surprising that a number of myths about Napoleon have permeated popular culture, some of which continue to be widely believed today. The myth that Napoleon was poisoned to death by the British has been scientifically refuted, but what about some of the others?

Was Napoleon Short? The myth that has had the longest staying power in the nearly 200 years since Napoleon's death is that he was unusually short for his time. This, of course, has given rise to the phrase "Napoleonic Complex", used to explain why short men overcompensate by being overly ambitious.

In fact, the myth that Napoleon was short likely comes from differences in height measurement between the British and French. In 1802, a French doctor measured Napoleon at 5 feet 2 inches, which would be uncommonly short, except in American or British terms, that measurement meant Napoleon was 5'6 or 5'7, an average height. Moreover, as a title of affection, his Imperial Guard, which had a height requirement, called him "The Little Corporal".

Thus, a myth was born.

Was Napoleon a Good Chess Player? Chess was growing in popularity across Europe during the 19th century, as the first true grandmasters of the game began to master the art of chess. And given the fact that chess is the ultimate game of strategy, many people figured it would make sense that the greatest military strategician of his day would be great at chess too.

Napoleon did in fact play chess, even in exile on St. Helena, and some of his games were even recorded for posterity. But even though both war and chess require strategy and forward thinking, they are two wholly different things. Garry Kasparov probably wouldn't be a great general, and Napoleon was certainly no Kasparov.

According to contemporary sources, Napoleon was a fairly average player, which shouldn't be surprising considering he was too busy conquering entire armies than capturing kings on a chessboard. A detailed discussion of Napoleon's chess history can be found at http://www.chesshistory.com/winter/extra/napoleon.html

Did Napoleon's Men Shoot the Nose off the Sphinx? One of the more colorful legends that still exists today accuses Napoleon and his men of shooting the nose off the famous Sphinx in Egypt, presumably with a cannonball. Variations of that legend have accused other soldiers of destroying it, including British soldiers.

The Sphinx's nose was purposely removed, but it appears to have been done several centuries before Napoleon landed there. Archaeologists have discovered chisels were used to remove the nose, and a 14th century Egyptian historian mentions the removal of the Sphinx's nose, attributing it to religious practices.

Bibliography

Readers interested in learning more about Napoleon should consider some of these excellent books:

Napoleon's Wars: An International History – Charles Esdaile. Penguin, 2008.
Napoleon – Vincent Cronin. Harper Collins, 2005.
Napoleon: A Political Life. – Steven Englund. Harvard University Press, 2005.
The Campaigns of Napoleon – David Chandler. W&N, 1995.

Robert E. Lee
Chapter 1: Early Years

Robert Edward Lee was born on January 19, 1807, at Stratford Hall Plantation in Westmoreland County, Virginia, near Montross, the fifth child to Major General Henry "Light Horse Harry" Lee III (1756–1818) and his second wife, Anne Hill Carter (1773–1829). Though his year of birth has traditionally been recorded as 1807, historian Elizabeth Brown Pryor has noted Lee's writings indicate he may have been born the previous year. Lee's family had Norman-French lineage that could trace itself back to one of Virginia's pioneering families; Robert's great-great grandfather, Henry Lee I, was a prominent Virginian colonist originally arriving in Virginia from England in the early 1600s with Richard Lee I.

Light Horse Harry

Lee's well-regarded family also boasted his father's accomplishments. Lee's father had served with distinction as a cavalry officer under General George Washington in the American Revolution, and after the war Light Horse Harry served as a member of the Virginia legislature and as Governor of Virginia. His mother, daughter of Charles Carter (whose father Robert was one of the first wealthy men in America) and Anne Butler Moore, grew up in an idyllic life at Shirley Plantation, Tyler, one of the most elegant mansions in all Virginia. Both the Lees and Carters were prominent in Virginia's political affairs, with family members regularly sitting in the House of Burgesses, and serving as speakers and governors. Two Lees signed the Declaration of Independence.

By the time of Robert's birth, Light Horse Harry, 17 years Anne's senior, was in deep financial trouble and scandal loomed over his family. Having retreated to Stratford Hall after failing as both a tobacco farmer and land speculator, Henry was aggressively hounded by creditors and subsequently stripped of property and servants to satisfy his mounting debts. Today "Light Horse Harry" is best remembered as Robert E. Lee's father, but at the time he was so absorbed in his own financial woes that he couldn't even be bothered to name his new son.

In 1809, Henry was arrested twice for debt and imprisoned in Westmoreland County jail, forcing Anne to deliver him food herself for lack of servants. Though offered asylum for herself and her children by her brother-in-law, husband of her late sister, Mildred, Anne refused to abandon her husband, choosing to maintain her home and family despite Henry's imprisonment. Upon his release, however, she insisted they move to Alexandria, Virginia, where she had numerous family members nearby and her children were assured an education at their neighboring plantations, and later, Alexandria Academy.

In 1813, Henry Lee's career and life in America came to a quiet (if not covert) end when he slipped off to Barbados in the West Indies after sustaining serious internal wounds--and by most reports, nearly killed--in a political riot in Baltimore, Maryland. Left to fend for herself, Anne spent her inheritance to provide for her children, writing infrequently to Henry, who was said to have spent little time at home even when things were going well. In 1818, when Robert was just 11, Anne was informed of her husband's death by a letter from her brother-in-law, two weeks after it occurred.

Though little has been written about Robert's boyhood, which was not something he discussed in his personal writings, by all accounts, Robert knew his father only as a shadowy, distant figure who had once been a great soldier and man of social standing. For Robert, it was Light Horse Harry's reputation as a man of apparent dignity, poise, and charm that could serve as a role model. And like any proud Virginian of the period, Light Horse Harry insisted that all his sons learn to swim, ride, shoot, box, dance, and use a sword--but only in self-defense--like every fine Virginia gentleman.

The tragedies of his father's later life, however--and the disgrace it brought his family-- invariably drew Robert close to his mother and in many ways shaped the man he became. It would not be unfair to say Robert was his mother's boy.

Chapter 2: Education and West Point

Young Robert began his formal education in Alexandria, Virginia, at a private school maintained by the wealthy Carter family for their numerous offspring on one of their numerous plantations, then transferred to nearby Alexandria Academy. Today Lee's letters are of great interest to historians and casual readers alike, but amazingly, Robert was only formally instructed in French, not English, resulting in a writing style that consistently utilized uncustomary spelling such as *honour* and *agreable*, with proper names like *french*, *english*, and *yankee* written in lowercase. These linguistic oddities would be well illustrated in countless letters sent to friends and family throughout his life.

Young Robert was also familiar with hard work at a young age. After his eldest brother, William, left for Harvard, brother Sidney Smith joined the U.S. Navy, and sister Anne was away most of the time seeking medical attention for a chronic illness (believed to be tuberculosis), it fell upon Robert as the eldest remaining sibling to assist his mother around the home, forcing him to develop a strong sense of responsibility while still very young.

Following his natural aptitude for mathematics, Robert applied for admission into the United States Military Academy at West Point in early 1825. Today West Point is considered the country's elite military academy, and Lee's fantastic academic record there is still the stuff of legends, but when Lee applied to West Point, it was a highly *unimpressive* school consisting of a few ugly buildings facing a desolate, barren parade ground. Accepted in March of that year, Robert began his formal career as a soldier in July at the age of 18.

Upon Robert's departure for West Point, his mother moved with her two remaining daughters, Elinor and Elizabeth, from Alexandria to Georgetown, Washington D.C. Later, as her health quickly deteriorated, she moved to the home of Henry Lee's grandson, William Henry Fitzhugh, at Ravensworth in Fairfax County, Virginia.

Quickly demonstrating his aptitude for leadership and devotion to duty, Robert ranked high among his West Point classmates from the very beginning of his stint. Never insubordinate, always impeccably dressed, and never receiving even a single demerit; he became the template for his fellow cadets, who referred to him as "The Marble Model." While studying there he made many life-long friends, including fellow Virginian Joseph E. Johnston, as well as Albert Sidney Johnston, Leonidas Polk, Jefferson Davis, John B. Magruder, and William N. Pendleton-- all of whom would come to play critical roles for the Confederacy during the Civil War.

Excelling in both mathematics and military exercises (particularly tactics and strategy), Robert studied engineering, science, and drawing, among other subjects. In his free time, he was known to pore over Alexander Hamilton's autobiography, Napoleon's memoirs, and *Confessions* by the renowned 18th-century Genevan political philosopher and writer, Jean-Jacques Rousseau. Awarded the highest rank in the Corps--cadet adjunct--his senior year, Robert graduated with high honors in 1829, ranked first in his class in artillery and military tactics and second in overall standing. He was immediately commissioned brevet lieutenant in the U.S. Army Corps of Engineers, considered the elite of the army in 1829.

Immediately after graduation, Robert went to visit his mother who was by this time dying of advanced tuberculosis. Tending her to her final day, Anne passed away on June 29, 1829. Robert the boy then became Lee the military man.

Chapter 3: Early Military Service and Personal Life

Although Lee's position in the U.S. Army Corps of Engineers was a prestigious one, Lee's first military assignment was at a remote army post at Fort Pulaski on Cockspur Island, Georgia (on the Savannah River). Though not yet receiving full lieutenant's pay, he was tasked with full responsibility for seeing to it that the groundwork for the construction of a new fort was laid--a job requiring him to spend much of his time immersed in mud up to his armpits.

Though he was now away from Virginia, Lee's time spent in Georgia also represented perhaps the most social period of his life. Lee managed to find sufficient distraction from his less-than-pleasant duties in the home of West Point friend, Jack Mackay, whose family home was located in Savanna and where Lee often spent time with Jack's two sisters Margaret and Eliza. Said to have enjoyed dancing, gossip, and parties, Lee, the Southern gentleman, was in his element, conversing and cavorting with Georgia's social elites. Still, even though Lee was often the charming "life of the party" and was sharing the company of many eligible women, he seems to have fancied few.

After serving 17 months at Fort Pulaski, Robert was transferred to Fort Monroe, Virginia, where he was made assistant to the chief of engineers. While stationed there, Lee met his second cousin, Mary Anna Randolph Custis. Mary was the pampered and frail daughter of Mary Lee Fitzhugh and famously wealthy but slovenly agriculturalist George Washington Parke Custis (grandson of Martha Washington). Although they outwardly had very little in common--he was elegant, admired stoicism, and relished social gatherings, while she was dull, complained incessantly, and loathed parties--Lee proposed marriage. Some historians believe the attraction was at least in part based on Mary's profession to having a religious epiphany the year before, damning the keeping of slaves. On July 5, 1831, the two were wed. The 3rd U.S. Artillery served as honor guard.

In that Lee could scarcely support Mary in the style she'd been accustomed, he agreed to move into her family home, which still stands on a hill overlooking Washington, D.C. Even so, beginning in August of 1831, the couple shared Lee's cramped junior officer's quarters at the fort for a period of two years, during which Mary brought along one of her slaves, Cassy, to tend to her personal needs. A little more than a year later, Mary gave birth to their first child, George Washington Custis--who Lee nicknamed "Boo." In the years that followed, the Lees would produce six more children: Mary, William H. Fitzhugh, Eleanor Agnes, Annie, Robert Edward Jr., and Mildred. All three sons would serve in the Confederate Army under their father during the Civil War.

1854 engraving of Mary

From 1834 to 1837, Robert served as assistant engineer in Washington, but spent the summer of 1835 helping survey the boundary line between the states of Ohio and Michigan. In 1836 he was given his first solo project, that of finding a way to control the course of the "Mighty" Mississippi River, which was constantly threatening to destroy the burgeoning commerce of the city of St. Louis. Through the ingenious accomplishment of this daunting project involving the moving of 2,000 tons of rock to build strategically-placed dikes, an engineering feat in itself, Lee established once and for all his professional standing. Recognition for this monumental accomplishment came in the form of promotion to first lieutenant of engineers, assigned to supervise the engineering work for the St. Louis harbor, thus becoming a member of the board of engineers for U.S. Atlantic coast defenses. But while his professional life excelled during these years, his family life began to falter.

Shortly after giving birth to their second child, Mary Curtis, in 1835 (whom Lee would refer to simply as "Daughter"), his wife's health began a downward spiral that would plague her throughout her life. Chronic pelvic infection, abscesses of the groin, and rheumatism would come to define her day-to-day existence, and her physical limitations and mental state weighed heavily on Lee. In May 1837, Lee's third child, William Henry Fitzhugh was born, followed by Anne Carter in 1839, and Eleanor Agnes in 1841--with whom Lee kept in constant contact through letters while away performing his duties. That same year, he was promoted to captain and transferred to Fort Hamilton in New York Harbor, where he was put in charge of building fortifications. A short time later his family came to join him, and for the first time he was able to spend more than a few days at a time with them.

Ironically, as his family grew in size, despite his preference for spending his time close to home, Lee began hoping hostilities would erupt somewhere in the U.S. territories. Even on a captain's salary, soon the basic upkeep and education of his children would reach a critical point, and military men were seldom promoted above the rank of captain in peace time.

Lee with his son William, circa 1845

Chapter 4: The Mexican-American War

When the United States declared war on Mexico on May 13, 1846, Lee thought the opportunity to prove himself as a field officer had finally arrived. But the growing sentiment in the North was that the annexation of Texas was just a slaveholders' ploy to seize more territory for the further expansion of slavery. Ulysses S. Grant, one of the first American soldiers to cross the disputed border, believed the Army was being sent there just to provoke a fight, and a young Congressman from Illinois named Abraham Lincoln first gained national attention for sponsoring legislation demanding that President Polk show the spot where Mexicans had fired on American troops, believing that "President Polk's War" was full of deception.

Regardless, in September of 1846, Lee was sent to San Antonio de Bexar, Texas, with orders to report to Brigadier General John E. Wool. Considering that he might not return from this mission, Lee made out his will, leaving everything to his wife Mary, before setting off. There he was tasked with selecting travel routes for the troops and supervision of the construction of bridges for Wool's march toward Saltillo, the capital city of the northeastern Mexican state of Coahuila, just south of Texas.

On January 16, 1847, Lee was then attached to General Winfield Scott's command at Brazos, Texas. Scott was planning to take the war deeper into Mexico, to Veracruz (in east-central Mexico) and then Mexico City. Immediately acknowledged for his excellent intuition as a scout, Lee became a member of Scott's staff and experienced his first active combat while taking part in the capture of Veracruz.

During the march to Mexico City, Lee was promoted to brevet major, receiving high praise for his insightful reconnaissance and choice of artillery placement that ultimately made the capture of Mexico's capital possible. It was also Lee's engineering skills that enabled American troops to cross the treacherous mountain passes leading to the capital. General Scott's official reports raved about Lee's war-time efforts, declaring that his "success in Mexico was largely due to the skill, valor, and undaunted courage of Robert E. Lee," calling him "the greatest military genius in America." Diaries of many of his fellow officers showed how impressed they all were with the brave "Virginian."

Chapter 5: After the Mexican-American War

When the Mexican-American War ended in 1848, Lee returned to service with the U.S. Army Corps of Engineers. After spending three years at Fort Carroll in Baltimore harbor, Lee was made superintendent of West Point in 1852, a tribute to both his exemplary military record and his natural ability to lead. Although he voiced his preference for field duty rather than a desk job, he assumed his new position with zeal. Lee made numerous improvements to the buildings, revamped the curriculum, and was known to spend a great deal of time with the cadets, gaining him a reputation as a fair and kind superintendent.

Lee had proven himself at West Point a second time, but his destiny was not to remain there. With dissension mounting between the North and South, exacerbated by the Mexican-American War, it wasn't long before Lee would find himself in the middle of an insurgence.

In early 1855, Lee was promoted to lieutenant colonel of the newly organized 2nd Cavalry and stationed at Jefferson Barracks in St. Louis, Missouri. Much of his time spent during the next few years at his new post were spent in court-martial service or with the 2nd Cavalry on the Texas frontier, where local Native American tribes posed an ongoing threat to settlers.

During this time, Lee continued to demonstrate his talent as both soldier and organizer, but as would later be revealed in his letters, these were not happy years for Lee. He disliked being separated from his family and felt guilty for not being available to his wife, who by now had become a chronically-ill invalid. Indeed, for nearly two decades, Lee found himself constantly being pulled in opposite directions by his wife's needful requests and his sense of duty to the job he was assigned. In one famous letter in 1834, Lee responded to one of Mary's requests to return by writing to her, "But why do you urge my immediate return, & tempt one in the strongest manner... I rather require to be strengthened & encouraged to the full performance of what I am called on to execute."

Lee in 1850

Although Lee returned to Washington at every opportunity, it was the death of his father-in-law in October of 1857 that would ultimately lead him to request an extended leave from the Army. Having to deal with the settlement of her father's estate exacerbated Mary's already frail condition, prompting Lee to find a way to remain at her side. And as it would happen, Lee was home in 1859 tending to family matters when he received orders from Washington to hurry to Harpers Ferry, West Virginia.

John Brown was a preacher and an abolitionist who believed that slavery could not be ended without violence, and he proved his convictions in Kansas, becoming a nationally recognized figure while fighting against pro-slavery militias in Kansas. But Brown was far from done.

John Brown

After his activities in Kansas, Brown spent the next few years raising money for his agenda in New England. He had previously organized a small raiding party that succeeded in raiding a Missouri farm and freeing 11 slaves, but he set his sights on far larger objectives. In 1859, Brown began to set a new plan in motion that he hoped would create a full scale slave uprising in the South.

Brown's plan relied on raiding Harper's Ferry, a strategically located armory in western Virginia that had been the main federal arms depot after the Revolution. Given its proximity to the South, Brown hoped to seize thousands of rifles and move them south, gathering slaves to his group as he went. The slaves would then be armed and ready to help free more slaves, inevitably fighting Southern militias along the way. Brown went so far as to inform Frederick Douglass of his plans. Douglass was the prominent black abolitionist of his era, but he attempted to dissuade freed blacks from joining Brown's group because he believed it was doomed to fail.

In July 1859, Brown traveled to Harper's Ferry under an assumed name and waited for his recruits, but he struggled to get even 20 people to join him. Rather than call off the plan, however, Brown went ahead with it. That fall, Brown and his men used hundreds of rifles to seize the armory at Harper's Ferry, but the plan went haywire from the start, and word of his attack quickly spread. Local pro-slavery men formed a militia and pinned Brown and his men down while they were still at the armory.

After being called to Harpers Ferry, Lee took decisive command of a troop of marines stationed there, surrounded the arsenal, and gave Brown the opportunity to surrender peaceably. When Brown refused, Lee ordered the doors be broken down and Brown taken captive, an affair that reportedly lasted just three minutes. A few of Brown's men were killed, but Brown was taken alive. Acknowledged for accomplishing this task so quickly and efficiently, Lee was sent back to resume his duties in Texas. By most accounts, Lee already knew what was on the wind.

The fallout from John Brown's raid on Harper's Ferry was intense. Southerners had long suspected that abolitionists hoped to arm the slaves and use violence to abolish slavery, and Brown's raid seemed to confirm that. Meanwhile, much of the northern press praised Brown for his actions. In the South, conspiracy theories ran wild about who had supported the raid, and many believed prominent abolitionist Republicans had been behind the raid as well.

On the day of his execution, Brown wrote, "I, John Brown, am now quite *certain* that the crimes of this *guilty land* will never be purged away but with *blood*. I had, as I now think vainly, flattered myself that without very much bloodshed it might be done."

Chapter 6: Going to War

While West Point was decidedly an institution where political discussion was freely intertwined with all areas of military discussion and most Southern men were politically oriented, Lee was known as fundamentally apolitical. To the extent that he resigned himself to commit to party politics, he was a neo-Federalist, which by default made him a Whig. It would not be incorrect, however, to say that since his work in Washington involved official correspondence and lobbying of Congress regarding the U.S. Army Corps of Engineers budget, he developed a deep dislike for Democrat bureaucracy. Nevertheless, Lee had never envisioned a time that would require a choosing of political sides.

In the wake of the Mexican-American War and the John Brown insurgence, Lee began to seriously consider the discontentment growing among his fellow countrymen across the United States. While many Southerners began discussing secession even before Republican candidate

Abraham Lincoln won the presidential election in 1860, Lee did not favor slavery (though his family maintained many, he had freed what slaves he'd inherited several years before) and did not support secession. He felt that slavery had an evil effect on both master and slave, with both sacrificing elements of their soul to maintain the balance, and could see nothing solved by disunion, conflict, or civil war.

Despite having virtually zero support in the slave states, Abraham Lincoln ascended to the presidency at the head of a party that was not yet 10 years old, and one whose stated goal was to end the expansion of slavery. Although Lincoln did not vow to abolish slavery altogether, southerners believed Lincoln's presidency constituted a direct threat to the South's economy and political power, both of which were fueled by the slave system. Southerners also perceived the end of the expansion of slavery as a threat to their constitutional rights, and the rights of their states, frequently invoking northern states' refusals to abide by the Fugitive Slave Act.

Lincoln's predecessor was among those who could see the potential conflict coming from a mile away. While still in office, President James Buchanan instructed the federal army to permit the Confederacy to take control of forts in its territory, hoping to avoid a war. Conveniently, this also allowed Southern forces to take control of important forts and land ahead of a potential war, which would make secession and/or a victory in a military conflict easier. Many Southern partisans in federal government in 1860 took advantage of these opportunities to help Southern states ahead of time.

Several Southern states began to secede in the months after November, and when Texas seceded from the Union in 1861, Lee was recalled to Washington to await orders while an appropriate response was formulated. A devout admirer of George Washington and the monumental self-sacrifice he'd made to establish the Union, Lee hated the idea of a divided nation. Thus, he began to see his destiny as protecting the freedom, liberty, and legal principles for which Washington had so gallantly risked his life. Even so, he suffered great trepidation in choosing between standing with his native Virginia and the Northern Union, should it come down to a civil war, especially when President Lincoln would offer Lee command of the United States Army.

In a letter to his sister Lee wrote, " ...in my own person I had to meet the question whether I should take part against my native state...with all my devotion to the Union, and the feeling of loyalty and duty of an American citizen, I have not been able to make up my mind to raise my hand against my relatives, my children, my home. I have therefore resigned my commission in the army, and, save in defense of my native state--with the sincere hope I may never be called upon to draw my sword."

Lee grieved his choice to break with his men, and particularly General Scott, whom he considered a close, personal friend. Ultimately, however, just as Washington had chosen to separate himself from the British Empire, Lee chose to separate from the Union to fight what the South regarded a second war of independence. And once he chose sides, Lee never looked back.

One of the forts in the South was Fort Sumter, an important but undermanned and undersupplied fort in the harbor of Charleston, South Carolina. Buchanan attempted to resupply Fort Sumter in the first few months of 1860, but the attempt failed when Southern sympathizers in the harbor fired on the resupply ship.

In his First Inaugural Address, Lincoln promised that it would not be the North that started a potential war, but he was also aware of the possibility of the South initiating conflict. After he was sworn in, Lincoln sent word to the Governor of South Carolina that he was sending ships to resupply Fort Sumter, to which the governor replied demanding that federal forces evacuate it. Southern forces again fired on the ship sent to resupply the boat, and on April 12, 1861, Confederate artillery began bombarding Fort Sumter itself. After nearly 36 hours of bombardment, Major Robert Anderson called for a truce with Southern forces led by P.G.T. Beauregard, and the fort was officially surrendered on April 14. No casualties were caused on either side by the dueling bombardments across the harbor, but, ironically, two Union soldiers were killed by an accidental explosion during the surrender ceremonies.

After the attack on Fort Sumter, support for both the northern and southern cause rose. President Lincoln requested that each loyal state raise regiments for the defense of the Union, with the intent of raising an enormous army that would subdue the rebellion. However, four states which had been avoiding seceding or declaring support for the Union seceded after Lincoln's call for volunteers. The Confederate States of America now consisted of South Carolina, Mississippi, Florida, Alabama, Georgia, Louisiana, Texas, Virginia, Arkansas, North Carolina and Tennessee. The border states of Kentucky, Maryland, and Delaware remained in the Union, but the large number of southern sympathizers in these states buoyed the Confederates' hopes that those too would soon join the South.

Despite the loss of Fort Sumter, the North expected a relatively quick victory. Their expectations weren't unrealistic, due to the Union's overwhelming economic advantages over the South. At the start of the war, the Union had a population of over 22 million. The South had a population of 9 million, nearly 4 million of whom were slaves. Union states contained 90% of the manufacturing capacity of the country and 97% of the weapon manufacturing capacity. Union states also possessed over 70% of the total railroads in the pre-war United States at the start of the war, and the Union also controlled 80% of the shipbuilding capacity of the pre-war United States.

The firing on Fort Sumter and Lincoln's call to arms brought events quickly to a head. Now Virginia, which had delayed commitment as long as possible, had to choose sides, and with its secession in April 1861, Lee was called to join the military command in Virginia.

Serving first as military advisor to Confederate President Jefferson Davis in Richmond, Lee initially had no troops under his command. In May 1861, he was appointed a full general of the Confederate Army but spent much of his time preparing Virginia for immanent invasion--not fighting in the field. Strategic posts along the borders from Norfolk to Harpers Ferry were seized, troops and supplies amassed, and Lee's phenomenal ability to organize was put to use.

The emphasis on land battles during the Civil War ultimately doomed hundreds of thousands of soldiers on each side. This is because the Civil War generals began the war employing tactics from the Napoleonic Era, which saw Napoleon dominate the European continent and win crushing victories against large armies. However, the weapons available in 1861 were far more accurate than they had been 50 years earlier. In particular, new rifled barrels created common infantry weapons with deadly accuracy of up to 100 yards, at a time when generals were still leading massed infantry charges with fixed bayonets and attempting to march their men close enough to engage in hand-to-hand combat.

The first realization of this problem occurred at the First Battle of Manassas or Bull Run in July 1861. After Fort Sumter, the Lincoln Administration pushed for a quick invasion of Virginia, with the intent of defeating Confederate forces and marching toward the Confederate capitol of Richmond. Lincoln pressed Irvin McDowell to push forward. Despite the fact that McDowell knew his troops were inexperienced and unready, pressure from the Washington politicians forced him to launch a premature offensive against Confederate forces in Northern Virginia. His strategy during the First Battle of Bull Run was grand, but it proved far too difficult for his inexperienced troops to carry out effectively.

McDowell's army met Fort Sumter hero P.G.T. Beauregard's Confederate army near a railroad junction at Manassas on July 21, 1861. Located just 25 miles away from Washington D.C., many civilians from Washington came to watch what they expected to be a rout of Confederate forces. Instead, Confederate reinforcements under General Joseph E. Johnston arrived by train in the middle of the day, a first in the history of American warfare, and troops led by Thomas Jonathan "Stonewall" Jackson helped turn the tide. As the battle's momentum switched, the inexperienced Union troops were routed and retreated in disorder back toward Washington in an unorganized mass.

With over 350 killed on each side, both the Confederacy and the Union were quickly served notice that the war would be much more costly than either side had believed.

Stonewall Jackson, who Lee would later call his army's "right hand".

Today Lee is remembered as the Civil War's greatest general, and George B. McClellan is often derided as one of the Union's most ineffective generals. And most associate Lee with the Army of Northern Virginia, which he came to command in the summer of 1862 and defeat McClellan in the Seven Days Battles. However, in 1861, it was McClellan that got the best of Lee.

Though Lee took no direct part in the first battle at Manassas (Bull Run) in July of 1861, he was tasked with saving western Virginia from Union forces under General George B. McClellan who'd defeated Confederate troops in Kanawha Valley. Bad weather, poorly trained men, and lack of cooperation among his officers, however, ultimately led to a dismal defeat for Lee. With the Union taking control of western Virginia, Lee considered the campaign a miserable, personal failure, and western Virginia would formally become the new state of West Virginia and part of the Union in 1863.

Given such a crushing defeat at the beginning of the war, that might have been the end of Lee's Civil War career. However, Jefferson Davis's faith in Lee's abilities ensured it was just the beginning. It's quite possible that Lee was saved by his past association with Davis at West Point. History has accorded Abraham Lincoln a spot in the pantheon of American politics for the manner in which he steered the Union to victory and into the Reconstruction period after the war. In turn, Davis has been heavily criticized. While Jefferson Davis had personal favorites like Lee and Albert Sidney Johnston, Davis constantly clashed with other Confederate generals like Joseph Johnston, which led to often discombobulated war strategy. At the same time, part of the Confederacy's raison d'etre was that the federal government was too centralized, so the decentralized nature of the Southern states hampered Davis's ability to manage and coordinate the war effort.

Jefferson Davis

Though only a few months into the war, by August 1861, things were already going badly for the South. Although eyes remained intently focused on the Eastern theater, with the two capitals (Washington D.C. and Richmond) located within 100 miles of each other, several forts to the west had fallen to General Ulysses S. Grant, most of Kentucky and a large portion of Tennessee were all but abandoned, and Confederate general Joseph E. Johnson was planning a draw back from Manassas after the battle there. Equally disheartening, European recognition didn't come as expected, and supplies were already running dangerously low.

At this point, Jefferson Davis put Lee in command of the southeastern coast of the Confederacy, an area under imminent threat from a Union unit out of Hampton Roads near Norfolk. Mustering what was becoming Lee's trademark determination, he took decisive action by enlisting more troops, establishing blockades at all access points, and establishing an inner line of defense beyond the reach of Union naval guns. Lee quickly and decisively brought an abrupt halt to the advance of Union forces.

Chapter 7: The Peninsula Campaign and Seven Days Battles

Called to Richmond in March 1862, Lee became part of Jefferson Davis's inner circle. At this time, his primary job was to mediate between feuding generals. While some Southern generals, including Lee, believed troops should be shifted as needed to meet new threats, General Johnston insisted that all troops should be concentrated around Richmond as preparation for a final showdown.

During the Civil War, one of the tales that was often told among Confederate soldiers was that Joseph E. Johnston was a crack shot who was a better bird hunter than just about everyone else in the South. However, as the story went, Johnston would never take the shot when asked to, complaining that something was wrong with the situation that prevented him from being able to shoot the bird when it was time. The story is almost certainly apocryphal, used to demonstrate the Confederates' frustration with a man who everyone regarded as a capable general. Johnston began the Civil War as one of the senior commanders, leading (ironically) the Army of the Potomac to victory in the Battle of First Bull Run over Irvin McDowell's Union Army. But Johnston would become known more for losing by not winning. Johnston was never badly beaten in battle, but he had a habit of "strategically withdrawing" until he had nowhere else to go.

General Johnston

Despite Union successes in the Western theater, the focus of the Lincoln Administration remained concentrated on Richmond. The loss at Bull Run prompted a changing of the guard, with George McClellan, the "Young Napoleon", put in charge of reorganizing and leading the Army of the Potomac. McClellan had finished second in his class at West Point and was a well-regarded engineer, not to mention a foreign observer at the siege of Sevastopol during the Crimean War. This experience made him fit for commanding an army, but it also colored his military ideology in a way that was at odds with a Lincoln Administration that was eager for aggressive action and movement toward Richmond.

Under McClellan, and at Lincoln's urging, the Army of the Potomac conducted an ambitious amphibious invasion of Virginia in the spring of 1862. McClellan hoped to circumvent Confederate defenses to the north of Richmond by attacking Richmond from the southeast, landing his giant army on the Virginian peninsula. McClellan originally surprised the Confederates with his movement, but the narrow peninsula made it easier for Confederate forces to defend. One heavily outnumbered force led by John Magruder famously held out under siege at Yorktown for nearly an entire month, slowing the Army of the Potomac down. Magruder used a tactic of marching his men up and down the siege lines repeatedly to give the appearance he had several times more men than he actually had.

Lee advised Davis to consider a compromise that would protect Richmond from the North and keep Union generals McDowell and McClellan from joining forces. While Johnston's army would stay between McClellan and Richmond, Lee suggested that General "Stonewall" Jackson be ordered to muster all his units and drive toward the Potomac, striking heavily at whatever stood in his path.

Jackson would go on to lead an army to one of the most incredible campaigns of the war in the Shenandoah Valley in 1862. Known as the Valley Campaign, Jackson kept 3 Union armies occupied north of Richmond with less than 1/3 of the men. Jackson's forces marched about 650 miles in just 3 months, earning the nickname "foot cavalry."

Unbeknownst to both Lee and Davis, however, Johnston had already taken it upon himself to pull his troops back to a line of defense nearer Richmond as McClellan advanced. Several weeks later after word of General Jackson's startling victories over McDowell and his subsequent retreat were received, Johnston learned that McClellan was moving along the Chickahominy River. McClellan's Army of the Potomac got close enough to Richmond that they could see the city's church steeples. It was at this point that Johnston got uncharacteristically aggressive.

Johnston had run out of breathing space for his army, and he believed McCellan was seeking to link up with McDowell's forces. Therefore he drew up a very complex plan of attack for different wings of his army, and struck at the Army of the Potomac at the Battle of Seven Pines on May 31, 1862. Like McDowell's plan for First Bull Run, the plan proved too complicated for Johnston's army to execute, and after a day of bloody fighting little was accomplished from a technical standpoint. However, McClellan was rattled by the attack, and Johnston was seriously wounded during the fighting, resulting in Lee being sent to assume command of the Army of Northern Virginia.

From his first day in command, Lee faced a daunting, seemingly impossible challenge. McClellan had maneuvered nearly 100,000 troops to within seven miles of Richmond, three Union units were closing in on General Jackson's Confederates in Virginia's Shenandoah Valley, and a fourth Union army was camped on the Rappahannock River ostensibly ready to come to McClellan's aid.

In a series of confrontations known as the Seven Days' Battle, Lee instructed Jackson to move as if to advance back through the Shenandoah Valley but then secretly bring his entire force by train back to the Richmond sector as reinforcements. Jackson had successfully tied up the Union armies in the Valley before returning to Richmond. Lee immediately took the offensive, attacking the Army of the Potomac repeatedly in a flurry of battles known as the Seven Days Battles. Fearing he was heavily outnumbered, McClellan began a strategic retreat, and despite badly defeating the Confederates at the Battle of Malvern Hill, the last battle of the Seven Days Battles and the Peninsula Campaign, it was clear that the Army of the Potomac was quitting the campaign. The failure of McClellan's campaign devastated the morale of the North, as McClellan had failed to advance despite originally having almost double the manpower.

In a characteristically audacious manner that came to define his generalship, Lee's bold offensive tactics had seen his army engage in bloody hand-to-hand combat that ranged from Mechanicsville to Fraser's Farm to Malvern Hill. By themselves, none of the battles could be called pivotal or even tactical victories for the Confederates, and Malvern Hill was a debacle, but from a strategic standpoint Lee succeeded in forcing McClellan and his back-up forces to retreat, while Jackson's tactics proved effective in the Shenandoah. Lee had prevented McClellan from capturing Richmond.

Lee had become a bona fide war hero, but he was just getting started.

Chapter 8: The Second Battle of Manassas or Bull Run

Even before McClellan had completely withdrawn his troops, Lee sent Jackson northward to intercept the new army Abraham Lincoln had placed under Maj. General John Pope, formed out of the scattered troops in the Virginia area. Pope had found success in the Western theater, and he was uncommonly brash, instructing the previously defeated men now under his command that his soldiers in the West were accustomed to seeing the backs of the enemy. Pope's arrogance turned off his own men, and it also caught the notice of Lee.

Once certain McClellan was in full retreat, Lee joined Jackson, planning to strike Pope before McClellan's troops could arrive as reinforcements. In late August 1862, in what is described in military annals as a "daring and unorthodox" move, Lee divided his forces and sent Jackson northward to flank them, ultimately bringing Jackson directly behind Pope's army and supply base. This forced Pope to fall back to Manassas to protect his flank and maintain his lines of communication. Recognizing Lee's genius for military strategy, General Jackson quickly became Lee's most trusted commander, and he would later say that he so trusted Lee's military instincts that he would even follow him into battle blindfolded.

When Pope's army fell back to Manassas to confront Jackson, his wing of Lee's army dug in along a railroad trench and took a defensive stance. The Second Battle of Manassas or Bull Run was fought August 28-30, beginning with the Union army throwing itself at Jackson. While Jackson's men defended themselves, Lee used Longstreet's wing to deliver a devastating flank attack before reinforcements from the retreating Army of the Potomac could reach the field. The strategy, which came to be referred to as the "anvil and hammer", saw Longstreet's men sweep Pope's army off the field. Fought on the same ground as the First Battle of Manassas nearly a year earlier, the result was the same: a decisive Confederate victory that sent Union soldiers scrambling back to the safety of Washington.

General Longstreet, who Lee would later call his "Old Warhorse"

After two days' fighting, Lee had achieved another major victory, and he now stood unopposed 12 miles away from Washington D.C. While Johnston and Beauregard had stayed in this position in the months after the first battle, Lee determined upon a more aggressive course: taking the fighting to the North.

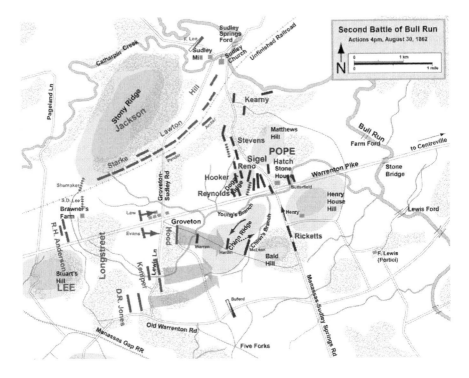

Chapter 9: The Maryland Campaign

In the summer of 1862, the Union suffered more than 20,000 casualties, and Northern Democrats, who had been split into pro-war and anti-war factions from the beginning, increasingly began to question the war. As of September 1862, no progress had been made on Richmond; in fact, a Confederate army was now in Maryland. And with the election of 1862 was approaching, Lincoln feared the Republicans might suffer losses in the congressional midterms that would harm the war effort. Thus, he restored General McClellan and removed General Pope after the second disaster at Bull Run. McClellan was still immensely popular among the Army of the Potomac, and with a mixture of men from his Army of the Potomac and Pope's Army of Virginia, he began a cautious pursuit of Lee into Maryland.

In early September, convinced that the best way to defend Richmond was to divert attention to Washington, Lee had decided to invade Maryland after obtaining Jefferson Davis's permission. Today the decision is remembered through the prism of Lee hoping to win a major battle in the

North that would bring about European recognition of the Confederacy, potential intervention, and possible capitulation by the North, whose anti-war Democrats were picking up political momentum. However, Lee also hoped that the fighting in Maryland would relieve Virginia's resources, especially the Shenandoah Valley, which served as the state's "breadbasket". And though largely forgotten today, Lee's move was controversial among his own men. Confederate soldiers, including Lee, took up arms to defend their homes, but now they were being asked to invade a Northern state. An untold number of Confederate soldiers refused to cross the Potomac River into Maryland.

Historians believe that Lee's entire Army of Northern Virginia had perhaps 50,000 men at most and possibly closer to 30,000 during the Maryland campaign. However, Lee sized up George McClellan, figured he was a cautious general, and decided once again to divide his forces throughout Maryland. In early September, he ordered Jackson to capture Harpers Ferry while he and Longstreet maneuvered his troops toward Frederick. With McClellan now assuming command of the Northern forces, Lee expected to have plenty of time to assemble his troops and bring his battle plan to fruition.

However, the North was about to have one of the greatest strokes of luck during the Civil War. For reasons that are still unclear, Union troops in camp at Frederick came across a copy of Special Order 191, wrapped up among three cigars. The order contained Lee's entire marching plans for Maryland, making it clear that the Army of Northern Virginia had been divided into multiple parts, which, if faced by overpowering strength, could be entirely defeated and bagged. The "Lost Order" quickly made its way to General McClellan, who took several hours to debate whether or not it was intentional misinformation or actually real. Once he decided it was accurate, McClellan is said to have famously boasted, "Here is a paper with which if I cannot whip *Bobby Lee*, I will be willing to go home."

To Lee's great surprise, McClellan's army began moving at an uncharacteristically quick pace, pushing in on his Confederate forces at several mountain passes at South Mountain, including at Turner's Gap and Crampton's Gap. While Jackson's wing was forcing the Harpers Ferry garrison to surrender, Lee regathered his other scattered units around Sharpsburg near Antietam Creek. McClellan's army, which may have outnumbered Lee's forces by about 50,000 men, confronted the Confederates around the night of September 16.

As fate would have it, the bloodiest day in the history of the United States took place on the 75th anniversary of the signing of the Constitution. On September 17, 1862, Lee's Army of Northern Virginia fought McClellan's Army of the Potomac outside Sharpsburg along Antietam Creek. That day, nearly 25,000 would become casualties, and Lee's army barely survived fighting the much bigger Northern army. The fighting that morning started with savage fighting on the Confederate left flank near Dunker church, in a corn field and forests. The Confederates barely held the field in the north sector.

Lee's army may have been saved by the Northern army's inability to cross the creek near "Burnside's Bridge". Ambrose Burnside had been given command of the "Right Wing" of the Army of the Potomac (the I Corps and IX Corps) at the start of the Maryland Campaign for the Battle of South Mountain, but McClellan separated the two corps at the Battle of Antietam, placing them on opposite ends of the Union battle line. However, Burnside continued to act as though he was a wing commander instead of a corps commander, so instead of ordering the IX corps, he funneled orders through General Jacob D. Cox. This poor organization contributed to the corps's hours-long delay in attacking and crossing what is now called "Burnside's Bridge" on the right flank of the Confederate line.

General Burnside

Making matters worse, Burnside did not perform adequate reconnaissance of the area, which afforded several easy fording sites of the creek out of range of the Army of Northern Virginia. Instead of unopposed crossings, his troops were forced into repeated assaults across the narrow bridge which was dominated by Confederate sharpshooters on high ground across the bridge. The delay allowed General A.P. Hill's Confederate division to reach the battlefield from Harpers Ferry in time to save Lee's right flank that afternoon. Fearing that his army was badly bloodied and figuring Lee had many more men than he did, McClellan refused to commit his reserves to continue the attacks. The day ended in a tactical stalemate.

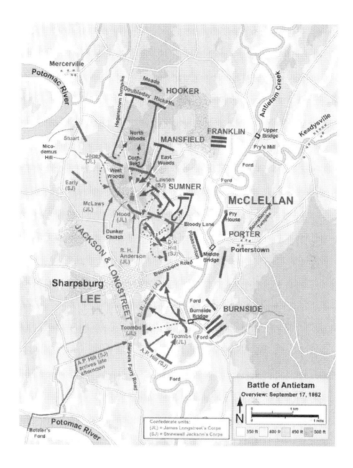

Battle of Antietam
Overview: September 17, 1862

Confederate units:
(JL) = James Longstreet's Corps
(SJ) = Stonewall Jackson's Corps

N

Though badly beaten and out of supplies, Lee somehow managed to withdraw his troops across the Potomac and back to safety. Though his invasion of Maryland had been a total failure, to his credit, it was only by his military prowess that he was able to save his army and maintain the integrity of the Confederate forces. Nevertheless, Antietam is now widely considered a turning point in the war. Although the battle was tactically a draw, it resulted in forcing Lee's army out of Maryland and back into Virginia, making it a strategic victory for the North and an opportune time for President Abraham Lincoln to issue the Emancipation Proclamation.

Chapter 10: The Battle of Fredericksburg

Despite heavily outnumbering the Southern army and badly damaging it during the battle of Antietam, McClellan decided not to pursue Lee across the Potomac, citing shortages of equipment and the fear of overextending his forces. General-in-Chief Henry W. Halleck wrote in his official report, "The long inactivity of so large an army in the face of a defeated foe, and during the most favorable season for rapid movements and a vigorous campaign, was a matter of great disappointment and regret." Lincoln had also had enough of McClellan's constant excuses for not taking forward action, and he relieved McClellan of his command of the Army of the Potomac on November 7, effectively ending the general's military career.

In place of McClellan, Lincoln appointed Burnside, who had just failed at Antietam. Burnside didn't believe he was competent to command the entire army, a very honest (and accurate) judgment. However, Burnside also didn't want the command to fall upon Joe Hooker, who had been injured while aggressively fighting with his I Corps at Antietam in the morning. Thus, he accepted.

Under pressure from Lincoln to be aggressive, Burnside laid out a difficult plan to cross the Rappahannock and attack the Confederates near Fredericksburg. The plan was doomed from the very beginning. On December 12, Burnside's army struggled to cross the river under fire from Confederate sharpshooters in the town. The next day, the Army of the Potomac could not dislodge Stonewall Jackson's men on the right flank. The battle is mostly remembered however for the piecemeal attacks the Union army made on heavily fortified positions Longstreet's men took up on Marye's Heights. The Northern soldiers were mowed down again and again. As men lay dying on the field that night, the Northern Lights made a rare appearance. Southern soldiers took it as a divine omen and wrote about it frequently in their diaries. The Union soldiers saw less divine inspiration in the Northern Lights and mentioned it less in their own. The Battle of Fredericksburg also spawned one of Lee's most memorable quotes. During the battle, Lee turned to Longstreet and commented, "It is well that war is so terrible, otherwise we would grow too fond of it."

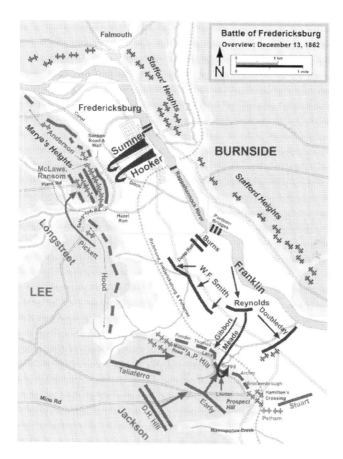

After the virtual slaughter (with the dead said to have been stacked up in rows), the Union army retreated across the river in defeat. Although Lee had accomplished a decisive victory over Burnside's forces, the Union general had positioned his reserves and supply line so strategically that he could easily fall back without breaking lines of communication--while Lee had no such reserves or supplies. And since Lee didn't have the men to pursue and completely wipe out Burnside's army (and simply holding them would ultimately prove too costly), Lee chose not to give chase. Some military strategists contend this was a military blunder, but either way, the fighting in 1862 was done.

Chapter 11: Chancellorsville – Lee's

Greatest Victory

Lee had concluded an incredibly successful year for the Confederates in the East, but the South was still struggling. The Confederate forces in the West had failed to win a major battle, suffering defeat at places like Shiloh in Tennessee and across the Mississippi River. As the war continued into 1863, the southern economy continued to deteriorate. Southern armies were suffering serious deficiencies of nearly all supplies as the Union blockade continued to be effective as stopping most international commerce with the Confederacy. Moreover, the prospect of Great Britain or France recognizing the Confederacy had been all but eliminated by the Emancipation Proclamation.

Given the unlikelihood of forcing the North's capitulation, the Confederacy's main hope for victory was to win some decisive victory or hope that Abraham Lincoln would lose his reelection bid in 1864, and that the new president would want to negotiate peace with the Confederacy. Understandably, this colored Confederate war strategy, and unquestionably Lee's.

After the Fredericksburg debacle and the "Mud March" fiasco that left a Union advance literally dead in its tracks, Lincoln fired Burnside and replaced him with "Fighting Joe" Hooker. Hooker had gotten his nickname from a clerical error in a newspaper's description of fighting, but the nickname stuck, and Lee would later playfully refer to him as F.J. Hooker. Hooker had stood out for his zealous fighting at Antietam, and the battle may very well have turned out differently if he hadn't been injured at the head of the I Corps. Now he was in command of a 100,000 man Army of the Potomac, and he devised a complex plan to cross the Rappahannock River with part of his force near Fredericksburg to pin down Lee while using the other bulk to turn Lee's left, which would allow his forces to reach the Confederate rear.

Hooker's plan initially worked perfectly, with the division of his army surprising Lee. Lee was outnumbered two to one and now had to worry about threats on two fronts. Incredibly, Lee once again decided to divide his forces in the face of the enemy, sending Stonewall Jackson to turn the Union army's right flank while the rest of the army maintained positions near Fredericksburg. The Battle of Chancellorsville is one of the most famous of the Civil War, and the most famous part of the battle was Stonewall Jackson's daring march across the Army of the Potomac's flank, surprising the XI Corps with an attack on May 2, 1863. Having ignored warnings of Jackson's march, the XI Corps was quickly routed.

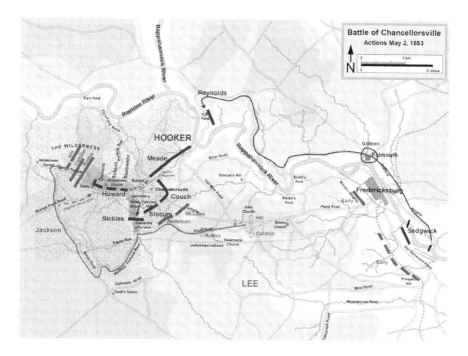

The surprise was a costly success however. Jackson scouted out ahead of his lines later that night and was mistakenly fired upon by his own men, badly wounding him. Jackson's natural replacement, A.P. Hill, was also injured, so Lee had cavalry leader J.E.B. Stuart assume command of Jackson's corps with Jackson out of action. On May 3, Stuart fiercely attacked the Union army, attempting to push them into the river, while on the other flank, the Confederates evacuated from Fredericksburg but ultimately held the line. Hooker began to lose his nerve, and he was injured during the battle when a cannonball nearly killed him. Historians now believe that Hooker may have commanded part of the battle while suffering from a concussion.

By the end of the battle, the Army of the Potomac had once again been defeated, retreating across the river. But Lee would also lose his "right hand". After Jackson's left arm was amputated, he seemed to be recovering, but his doctors were unaware of his symptoms that indicated oncoming pneumonia. Jackson would die May 10, eight days after his brilliant attack.

Chapter 12: The Pennsylvania Campaign

In the spring of 1863, General Lee discovered that McClellan had known of his plans and was able to force a battle at Antietam before all of General Lee's forces had arrived. General Lee now believed that he could successfully invade the North again, and that his defeat before was due in great measure to a stroke of bad luck. In addition, General Lee hoped to supply his army on the unscathed fields and towns of the North, while giving war ravaged northern Virginia a rest. After Chancellorsville, Longstreet and Lee met to discuss options for the Confederate Army's summer campaign. Longstreet advocated detachment of all or part of his corps to be sent to Tennessee, citing Union Maj. General Ulysses S. Grant's advance on Vicksburg, the critical Confederate stronghold on the Mississippi River. Longstreet argued that a reinforced army under Bragg could defeat Rosecrans and drive toward the Ohio River, compelling Grant to release his hold on Vicksburg. Lee, however, was opposed to a division of his army and instead advocated a large-scale offensive (and raid) into Pennsylvania. In addition, General Lee hoped to supply his army on the unscathed fields and towns of the North, while giving war ravaged northern Virginia a rest.

Knowing that victories on Virginia soil meant little to an enemy that could simply retreat, regroup, and then return with more men and more advanced equipment, Lee set his sights on a Northern invasion, aiming to turn Northern opinion against the war and against President Lincoln. With his men already half-starved from dwindling provisions, Lee intended to confiscate food, horses, and equipment as they pushed north--and hopefully influence Northern politicians into giving up their support of the war by penetrating into Harrisburg or even Philadelphia. Given the right circumstances, Lee's army might even be able to capture either Baltimore or Philadelphia and use the city as leverage in peace negotiations.

In the wake of Jackson's death, Lee reorganized his army, creating three Corps out of the previous two, with A.P. Hill and Richard S. Ewell "replacing" Stonewall. Hill had been a successful division commander, but he was constantly battling bouts of sickness that left him disabled, which would occur at Gettysburg. Ewell had distinguished himself during the Peninsula Campaign, suffering a serious injury that historians often credit as making him more cautious in command upon his return.

In early June, the Army of Northern Virginia occupied Culpeper, Virginia. After their victories at Fredericksburg and Chancellorsville against armies twice their size, Confederate troops felt invincible and anxious to carry the war north into Pennsylvania. Assuming his role as Lee's "Eyes of the Army" for the Pennsylvania Campaign, Stuart bivouacked his men near the Rappahannock River, screening the Confederate Army against surprise Union attacks. Taken with his recent successes, Stuart requested a full field review of his units by General Lee, and on June 8, paraded his nearly 9,000 mounted troops and four batteries of horse artillery for review, also charging in simulated battle at Inlet Station about two miles southwest of Brandy Station. While Lee himself was unavailable to attend the review, some of the cavalrymen and newspaper reporters at the scene complained that all Stuart was doing was "feeding his ego and exhausting the horses." He began to be referred to as a "headline-hunting show-off."

Despite the critics, Stuart basked in the glory. Renowned Civil War historian Stephen Sears described the scene, "The grand review of June 5 was surely the proudest day of Jeb Stuart's thirty years. As he led a cavalcade of resplendent staff officers to the reviewing stand, trumpeters heralded his coming and women and girls strewed his path with flowers. Before all of the spectators the assembled cavalry brigade stretched a mile and a half. After Stuart and his entourage galloped past the line in review, the troopers in their turn saluted the reviewing stand in columns of squadrons. In performing a second "march past," the squadrons started off at a trot, then spurred to a gallop. Drawing sabers and breaking into the Rebel yell, the troopers rush toward the horse artillery drawn up in battery. The gunners responded defiantly, firing blank charges. Amidst this tumult of cannon fire and thundering hooves, a number of ladies swooned in their escorts' arms."

However much Stuart enjoyed "horsing around", there was serious work to be done. The following day, Lee ordered Stuart to cross the Rappahannock and raid Union forward positions, shielding the Confederate Army from observation or interference as it moved north. Already anticipating this imminent offensive move, Stuart had ordered his troops back into formation around Brandy Station. Here, Stuart would endure the first of two low points in his military career: the Battle of Brandy Station, the largest predominantly cavalry engagement of the Civil War.

Union Maj. General Joseph Hooker interpreted Stuart's presence around Culpeper as a precursor to a raid on his army's supply lines. In response, he ordered his cavalry commander, Maj. General Alfred Pleasonton, to take a combined force of 8,000 cavalry and 3,000 infantry on a raid to "disperse and destroy" the 9,500 Confederates. Crossing the Rappahannock River in two columns on June 9,1863 at Beverly's Ford and Kelly's Ford, the first infantry unit caught Stuart completely off-guard, and the second surprised him yet again. Suddenly the Confederates were being battered both front and rear by mounted Union troops.

In addition to being the largest cavalry battle of the war, the chaos and confusion that ensued across the battlefield also made Brandy Station unique in that most of the fighting was done while mounted and using sabers. One account of the battle noted, "Of the bodies that littered the field that day, the vast majority were found to have perished by the sword."

After 10 hours of charges and countercharges that swept back and forth across Fleetwood Hill (where Stuart had headquartered the night before) involving drawn sabers and revolvers, Pleasonton decided to withdraw his exhausted men across the Rappahannock River. Stuart immediately claimed a Confederate victory because his men had managed to hold the field and inflicted more casualties on the enemy while forcing Pleasonton to withdraw before locating Lee's infantry. But Stuart was trying to save face, and nobody else, including Lee, took his view of the battle. The fact was, the Southern cavalry under Stuart had not detected the movement of two large columns of Union cavalry and had fallen prey to not one but *two* surprise attacks. Two days later the Richmond *Enquirer* reported, "If Gen. Stuart is to be the eyes and ears of the army we advise him to see more, and be seen less. Gen. Stuart has suffered no little in public estimation by the late enterprises of the enemy."

Lee was now painfully aware of the increased competency of the Union cavalry, as well as the decline of the seemingly once-invincible Southern mounted armed forces under Stuart. Moreover, Stuart was now smarting from the negative publicity and the hit his reputation had taken at Brandy Station. The prideful, vainglorious cavalry leader hoped to bring glory to himself.

During the first weeks of summer of 1863, as Stuart screened the army and completed several well-executed offenses against Union cavalry, many historians think it likely that he had already planned to remove the negative effect of Brandy Station by duplicating one of his now famous circumnavigating rides around the enemy army. But as Lee began his march north through the Shenandoah Valley in western Virginia, it is highly unlikely that is what he wanted or expected.

Before setting out on June 22, the methodical Lee gave Stuart specific instructions as to the role he was to play in the Pennsylvania offensive: as the "Eyes of the Army" he was to guard the mountain passes with part of his force while the Army of Northern Virginia was still south of the Potomac River, and then cross the river with the remainder of his army and screen the right flank of Confederate general Richard Stoddert Ewell's Second Corps as it moved down the Shenandoah Valley, maintaining contact with Ewell's army as it advanced towards Harrisburg.

But instead of taking the most direct route north near the Blue Ridge Mountains, Stuart chose a much more ambitious course of action.

Stuart decided to march his three best brigades (under Generals Hampton and Fitzhugh Lee, and Col. John R. Chambliss) between the Union army and Washington, north through Rockville to Westminster, and then into Pennsylvania--a route that would allow them to capture supplies along the way and wreak havoc as they skirted Washington. In the aftermath, the *Washington Star* would write: "The cavalry chief [Stuart] interpreted his marching orders in a way that best suited his nature, and detached his 9000 troopers from their task of screening the main army and keeping tabs on the Federals. When Lee was in Pennsylvania anxiously looking for him, Stuart crossed the Potomac above Washington and captured a fine prize of Federal supply wagons . . . ."

But to complicate matters even more, as Stuart set out on June 25 on what was probably a glory-seeking mission, he was unaware that his intended path was blocked by columns of Union infantry that would invariably force him to veer farther east than he or Lee had anticipated. Ultimately, his decision would prevent him from linking up with Ewell as ordered and deprive Lee of his primary cavalry force as he advanced deeper and deeper into unfamiliar enemy territory. According to Halsey Wigfall (son of Confederate States Senator Louis Wigfall) who was in Stuart's infantry, "Stuart and his cavalry left [Lee's] army on June 24 and did not contact [his] army again until the afternoon of July 2, the second day of the [Gettysburg] battle."

According to Stuart's own account, on June 29 his men clashed briefly with two companies of Union cavalry in Westminster, Maryland, overwhelming and chasing them "a long distance on the Baltimore road," causing a "great panic" in the city of Baltimore. On June 30, the head of Stuart's column then encountered Union Brig. General Judson Kilpatrick's cavalry as it passed through Hanover--reportedly capturing a wagon train and scattering the Union army--after which Kilpatrick's men were able to regroup and drive Stuart and his men out of town. Then after a twenty-mile trek in the dark, Stuart's exhausted men reached Dover, Pennsylvania, on the morning of July 1 (which they briefly occupied).

Late on the second day of the battle, Stuart finally arrived, bringing with him the caravan of captured Union supply wagons, and he was immediately reprimanded by Lee. One account describes Lee as "visibly angry" raising his hand "as if to strike the tardy cavalry commander." While that does not sound like Lee's style, Stuart has been heavily criticized ever since, and it has been speculated Lee took him to task harshly enough that Stuart offered his resignation. Lee didn't accept it, but he would later note in his after battle report that the cavalry had not updated him as to the Army of the Potomac's movements.

Given great discretion in his cavalry operations before the battle, Stuart's cavalry was too far removed from the Army of Northern Virginia to warn Lee of the Army of the Potomac's movements. As it would turn out, Lee's army inadvertently stumbled into Union cavalry and then the Union army at Gettysburg on the morning of July 1, 1863, walking blindly into what became the largest battle of the war.

Though he had privately confided to his wife that he desired command of the Army of the Potomac, Meade never publicly expressed his wishes to those in charge, thus avoiding the political squabbling among generals. On June 28, however, he got his wish.

Before sunrise on that morning, a messenger entered Major General George Meade's field headquarters, shook the sleeping general and said, "I'm afraid I've come to give you some trouble, General." Jumping to his feet, Meade's first thought was that he was being arrested-- probably for arguing with Hooker on the battlefield. Informed that he had replaced Maj. General Joseph Hooker as commander of the Army of the Potomac (Lincoln had passed over his friend, the more qualified John F. Reynolds), Meade at first protested, stating that he didn't want the job. Informed that his promotion was not a "request," Meade hitched up his sagging long underwear, ran his fingers through his thinning hair and said, "Well, I've been tried and condemned without a hearing, and I suppose I shall have to go to the execution." Historians have also speculated that it may well have been Mead's foreign birth that got him selected over Reynolds. As such, he was excluded from running for the U. S. Presidency and therefore posed no future threat to Lincoln, as Reynolds may have if successful. Of course, that doesn't square with reports that Reynolds turned the offer down.

In addition to being informed by Hooker that he was in command, Meade received a telegram from general-in-chief Henry Halleck:

"General:

You will receive with this the order of the President placing you in command of the Army of the Potomac. Considering the circumstances, no one ever received a more important command; and I cannot doubt that you will fully justify the confidence which the Government has reposed in you.

You will not be hampered by any minute instructions from these headquarters. Your army is free to act as you may deem proper under the circumstances as they arise. You will, however, keep in view the important fact that the Army of the Potomac is the covering army of Washington, as well as the army of operation against the invading forces of the rebels. You will therefore manoeuvre and fight in such a manner as to cover the Capital and also Baltimore, as far as circumstances will admit. Should General Lee move upon either of these places, it is expected that you will either anticipate him or arrive with him, so as to give him battle.

All forces within the sphere of your operations will be held subject to your orders.

Harper's Ferry and its garrison are under your direct orders.

You are authorized to remove from command and send from your army any officer or other person you may deem proper; and to appoint to command as you may deem expedient.

In fine, General, you are intrusted with all the power and authority which the President, the Secretary of War, or the General-in-Chief can confer on you, and you may rely on our full support.

You will keep me fully informed of all your movements and the positions of your own troops and those of the enemy, so far as known.

I shall always be ready to advise and assist you to the utmost of my ability.

Very respectfully,

Your obedient servant,

H. W. Halleck, General-in-Chief."

Meade then issued General Orders No. 67:

By direction of the President of the United States, I hereby assume command of the Army of the Potomac.

As a soldier, in obeying this order—an order totally unexpected and unsolicited—I have no promises or pledges to make.

The country looks to this army to relieve it from the devastation and disgrace of a foreign invasion. Whatever fatigues and sacrifices we may be called upon to undergo, let us have in view, constantly, the magnitude of the interests involved, and let each man determine to do his duty, leaving to an all-controlling Providence the decision of the contest.

It is with great diffidence that I relieve in the command of this army an eminent and accomplished soldier, whose name must ever appear conspicuous in the history of its achievements; but I rely upon the hearty support of my companions in arms to assist me in the discharge of the duties of the important trust which has been confided to me.

George G. Meade, Major General, commanding.

When word of Meade's promotion spread around camp, it certainly surprised many men. After all, Meade lacked charisma, did not exude confidence, and did not arouse enthusiasm among his men by his presence. In fact, considering the many times he'd been wounded (or nearly wounded), many considered him a danger to his men and to himself. Even his trusty horse "Old Baldy" had been wounded under him at Second Bull Run and again at Antietam. Ultimately, the best thing his men could say about him was that at least he had never made any ruinous mistakes.

Assuming command of the Army of the Potomac on June 28 at Prospect Hall in Frederick, Maryland, (with his second son, George, now part of his staff), Meade had his work cut out for him, though few apparently considered his position. Having to first locate his forces, he then had to review Hooker's strategy, study the most recent intelligence reports, and then determine the appropriate course of action, all the while keeping an eye fixed on Lee. Ultimately disregarding Hooker's plans to strike into the Cumberland Valley, Meade opted to march on Harrisburg, Pennsylvania to move toward the Susquehanna River, keeping his troops between Lee's army and Washinton.

Upon taking command, Meade began drawing up defensive positions around northern Maryland about a dozen miles south of Gettysburg. His proposed line would be referred to as the Pipe Creek Circular, but it would never be implemented due to actions outside of Meade's control.

It is believed that one of the first notices Lee got about the Army of the Potomac's movements actually came from a spy named "Harrison", a man who apparently worked undercover for Longstreet but of whom little is known. Harrison reported that General George G. Meade was now in command of the Union Army and was at that very moment marching north to meet Lee's army. According to Longstreet, he and Lee were supposedly on the same page at the beginning of the campaign. "His plan or wishes announced, it became useless and improper to offer suggestions leading to a different course. All that I could ask was that the policy of the campaign should be one of defensive tactics; that we should work so as to force the enemy to attack us, in such good position as we might find in our own country, so well adapted to that purpose—which might assure us of a grand triumph. To this he readily assented as an important and material adjunct to his general plan." Lee later claimed he "had never made any such promise, and had never thought of doing any such thing," but in his official report after the battle, Lee also noted, "It had not been intended to fight a general battle at such a distance from our base, unless attacked by the enemy.

Without question, the most famous battle of the Civil War took place outside of the small town of Gettysburg, Pennsylvania, which happened to be a transporation hub, serving as the center of a wheel with several roads leading out to other Pennsylvanian towns. Lee was unaware of Meade's position when an advanced division of Hill's Corps marched toward Gettysburg on the morning of July 1.

The battle began with John Buford's Union cavalry forces skirmishing against the advancing division of Heth's just outside of town. Buford intentionally fought a delaying action that was meant to allow John Reynolds' I Corps to reach Gettysburg and engage the Confederates, which eventually set the stage for a general battle.

The I Corps was led by Pennsylvanian General John F. Reynolds, an effective general that had been considered for command of the entire army in place of Hooker and was considered by many the best general in the army. Since Lee had invaded Pennsylvania, many believe that Reynolds was even more active and aggressive than he might have otherwise been. In any event, Reynolds was personally at the front positioning two brigades, exhorting his men, "Forward men! Forward for God's sake, and drive those fellows out of the woods."

As he was at the front positioning his men, Reynolds fell from his horse, having been hit by a bullet behind the ear that killed him almost instantly. With his death, command of the I Corps fell upon Maj. Gen. Abner Doubleday, the Civil War veteran wrongly credited for inventing baseball. Despite the death of the corps commander, the I Corps successfully managed to drive the Confederates in their sector back, highlighted by sharp fighting from the Iron Brigade, a brigade comprised of Wisconsin, Indiana, and Michigan soldiers from the "West". In an unfinished railroad cut, the 6th Wisconsin captured the 2nd Mississippi, and regimental commander Rufus Dawes reported, "The officer replied not a word, but promptly handed me his sword, and his men, who still held them, threw down their muskets. The coolness, self possession, and discipline which held back our men from pouring a general volley saved a hundred lives of the enemy, and as my mind goes back to the fearful excitement of the moment, I marvel at it."

Around noon, the battle hit a lull, in part because Confederate division commander Henry Heth was under orders to avoid a general battle in the absence of the rest of the Army of Northern Virginia. At that point, however, the Union had gotten the better of the fighting, and the

Confederate army was concentrating on the area, with more soldiers in Hill's corps in the immediate vicinity and Ewell's corps marching from the north toward the town.

As the Union's I Corps held the line, General Oliver O. Howard and his XI Corps came up on the right of the I Corps, eager to replace the stain the XI Corps had suffered at Chancellorsville thanks to Stonewall Jackson. As a general battle began to form northwest of town, news was making its way back to Meade several miles away that Reynolds had been killed, and that a battle was developing.

Meade had been drawing up a proposed defensive line several miles away from Gettysburg near Emmitsburg, Maryland, but when news of the morning's fighting reached him, Meade sent II Corps commander Winfield Scott Hancock ahead to take command in the field, putting him in temporary command of the "left wing" of the army consisting of the I, II, III and XI Corps. Meade also charged Hancock with determining whether to fight the general battle near Gettysburg or to pull back to the line Meade had been drawing up. Hancock would not be the senior officer on the field (Oliver Howard outranked him), so the fact that he was ordered to take command of the field demonstrates how much Meade trusted him.

As Hancock headed toward the fighting, and while the Army of the Potomac's I and XI Corps engaged in heavy fighting, they were eventually flanked from the north by Ewell's Confederate Corps, which was returning toward Gettysburg from its previous objective. For the XI Corps, it was certainly reminiscent of their retreat at Chancellorsville, and they began a disorderly retreat through the streets of the small town. Fighting broke out in various places throughout the town, while some Union soldiers hid in and around houses for the duration of the battle. Gettysburg's citizens also fled in the chaos and fighting.

After a disorderly retreat through the town itself, the Union men began to dig in on high ground to the southeast of the town. When Hancock met up with Howard, the two briefly argued over the leadership arrangement, until Howard finally acquiesced. Hancock told the XI Corps commander, "I think this the strongest position by nature upon which to fight a battle that I ever saw." When Howard agreed, Hancock replied, "Very well, sir, I select this as the battle-field."

As the Confederates sent the Union corps retreating, Lee arrived on the field and saw the importance of the defensive positions the Union men were taking up along Cemetery Hill and Culp's Hill. Late in the afternoon, Lee sent discretionary orders to Ewell that Cemetery Hill be taken "if practicable", but ultimately Ewell chose not to attempt the assault. Lee's order has been criticized because it left too much discretion to Ewell, leaving historians to speculate on how the more aggressive Stonewall Jackson would have acted on this order if he had lived to command this wing of Lee's army, and how differently the second day of battle would have proceeded with Confederate possession of Culp's Hill or Cemetery Hill. Discretionary orders were customary for General Lee because Jackson and Longstreet, his other principal subordinate, usually reacted to them aggressively and used their initiative to act quickly and forcefully. Ewell's decision not to attack, whether justified or not, may have ultimately cost the Confederates the battle. Edwin Coddington, widely considered the historian who wrote the greatest history of the battle, concluded, "Responsibility for the failure of the Confederates to make an all-out assault on Cemetery Hill on July 1 must rest with Lee. If Ewell had been a Jackson he might have been able to regroup his forces quickly enough to attack within an hour after the Yankees had started to retreat through the town. The likelihood of success decreased rapidly after that time unless Lee were willing to risk everything."

With so many men engaged and now taking refuge on the high ground, Meade, who was an engineer like Lee, abandoned his previous plan to draw up a defensive line around Emmittsburg a few miles to the south. After a council of war, the Army of the Potomac decided to defend at Gettysburg.

Day 1 by itself would have been one of the 25 biggest battles of the Civil War, and it was a tactical Confederate victory. Union casualties were almost 9,000, and the Confederates suffered slightly more than 6,000. But the battle had just started, and thanks to the actions of Meade and Hancock, the largest battle on the North American continent would take place on the ground of their choosing.

By the morning of July 2, Major General Meade had put in place what he thought to be the optimal battle strategy. Positioning his now massive Army of the Potomac in what would become known as the "fish hook", he'd established a line configuration that was much more compact and maneuverable than Lee's, which allowed Meade to shift his troops quickly from inactive parts of the line to those under attack without creating new points of vulnerability. Moreover, Meade's army was taking a defensive stance on the high ground anchored by Culp's Hill, Cemetery Hill, and Cemetery Ridge. Meade also personally moved the III Corps under Maj. General Daniel Sickles into position on the left of the line.

On the morning of July 2, Meade was determined to make a stand at Gettysburg, and Lee was determined to strike at him. That morning, Lee decided to make strong attacks on both Union flanks while feinting in the middle, ordering Ewell's corps to attack Culp's Hill on the Union right while Longstreet's corps would attack on the Union left. Lee hoped to seize Cemetery Hill, which would give the Confederates the high ground to harass the Union supply lines and command the road to Washington, D.C. Lee also believed that the best way to do so would be to use Longstreet's corps to launch an attack up the Emmitsburg Road, which he figured would roll up the Union's left flank, presumed to be on Cemetery Hill. Lee was mistaken, due in part to the fact Stuart and his cavalry couldn't perform reconnaissance. In fact, the Union line extended farther south than Cemetery Hill, with the II Corps positioned on Cemetery Ridge and the III Corps nearly as far south as the base of Little Round Top and Round Top. Moreover, Ewell protested that this battle plan would demoralize his men, since they'd be forced to give up the ground they had captured the day before.

As it turned out, both attacks ordered by Lee would come too late. Though there was a controversy over when Lee ordered Longstreet's attack, Longstreet's march got tangled up and caused several hours of delay. Lost Cause advocates attacking Longstreet would later claim his attack was supposed to take place as early as possible, although no official Confederate orders gave a time for the attack. Lee gave the order for the attack around 11:00 a.m., and it is known that Longstreet was reluctant about making it; he still wanted to slide around the Union flank, interpose the Confederate army between Washington D.C. and the Army of the Potomac, and force Meade to attack them. Between Longstreet's delays and the mixup in the march that forced parts of his corps to double back and make a winding march, Longstreet's men weren't ready to attack until about 4:00 p.m.

Longstreet's biographer, Jeffrey Wert, wrote, "Longstreet deserves censure for his performance on the morning of July 2. He allowed his disagreement with Lee's decision to affect his conduct. Once the commanding general determined to assail the enemy, duty required Longstreet to comply with the vigor and thoroughness that had previously characterized his generalship. The concern for detail, the regard for timely information, and the need for preparation were absent." Edwin Coddington, whose history of the Gettysburg Campaign still continues to be considered the best ever written, described Longstreet's march as "a comedy of errors such as one might expect of inexperienced commanders and raw militia, but not of Lee's ' War Horse' and his veteran troops." Coddington considered it "a dark moment in Longstreet's career as a general."

Writing about July 2, Longstreet criticized Lee, insisting once again that the right move was to move around the Union flank. "The opportunity for our right was in the air. General Halleck saw it from Washington. General Meade saw and was apprehensive of it. Even General Pendleton refers to it in favorable mention in his official report. Failing to adopt it, General Lee should have gone with us to his right. He had seen and carefully examined the left of his line, and only gave us a guide to show the way to the right, leaving the battle to be adjusted to formidable and difficult grounds without his assistance. If he had been with us, General Hood's messengers could have been referred to general Headquarters, but to delay and send messengers five miles in favor of a move that he had rejected would have been contumacious. The opportunity was with the Confederates from the assembling on Cemetery Hill. It was inviting of their preconceived plans. It was the object of and excuse for the invasion as a substitute for more direct efforts for the relief of Vicksburg. Confederate writers and talkers claim that General Meade could have escaped without making aggressive battle, but that is equivalent to confession of the inertia that failed to grasp the opportunity."

As Longstreet's men began their circuitous march, Union III Corps commander Dan Sickles took it upon himself to advance his entire corps one half mile forward to a peach orchard, poising himself to take control of higher ground. Some historians assert that Sickles had held a grudge against Meade for taking command from his friend Joseph Hooker and intentionally disregarded orders. It has also been speculated by some historians that Sickles moved forward to occupy high ground in his front due to the devastation unleashed against the III Corps at Chancellorsville once Confederates took high ground and operated their artillery on Hazel Grove. Sickles and Meade would feud over the actions on Day 2 in the years after the war, after Sickles (who lost a leg that day) took credit for the victory by disrupting Lee's attack plans. Historians have almost universally sided with Meade, pointing out that Sickles nearly had his III Corps annihilated during Longstreet's attack.

Whatever the reasoning for Sickles' move, this unauthorized action completely undermined Meade's overall strategy by effectively isolating Sickles' corps from the rest of the Union line and exposing the Union left flank in the process. By the early afternoon of July 2, nothing but the fog of war was preventing the Confederates from turning and crushing Sickles' forces, then moving to outflank the entire Union Army.

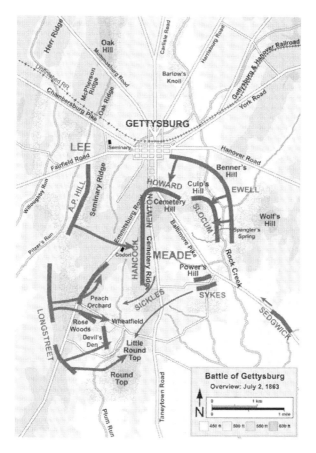

Battle of Gettysburg
Overview: July 2, 1863

With General George Meade once again in command, General Hancock and the II Corps was positioned on Cemetery Ridge, roughly in the center of the Union line. Since Lee intended to strike at both Union flanks, theoretically Hancock's men should very well not have been engaged at all on the second day of the battle. But as a result of the fact Sickles had moved his men so far out of position, it created a major gap in the Union line and brought the III Corps directly into Longstreet's path. It was 4:00 p.m. by the time Longstreet's two divisions were in position for the attack, and they were taken completely by surprise whent hey found the III Corps in front of them on the Emmitsburg Road. Division commander John Bell Hood lobbied Longstreet to change up the plan of attack, but at this late time in the day Longstreet refused to modify Lee's orders.

Thus, in the late afternoon, the fighting on Day 2 began in earnest, and Longstreet's assault commenced by smashing into Sickles III Corps, engaging them in a peach orchard, wheat field, and Devil's Den, an outcropping of boulders that provided the Confederates prime cover.

When it became obvious that Sickles' III Corps was in dire straits, the chaos in that sector acted like a vacuum that induced both sides to pour more men into the vicinity. Moreover, when Sickles was injured by a cannonball that nearly blew off his leg, command of the III Corps fell upon II Corps commander Hancock as well. As Meade tried to shuffle reinforcements to his left, Hancock sent in his II Corps' First Division (under Brig. General John C. Caldwell) to reinforce the III Corps in the wheat field. The fighting in the wheat field was so intense that Caldwell's division would be all but annihilated during the afternoon.

At the same time, men from Confederate General A. P. Hill's corps made their advance toward the Union center, forcing the Army of the Potomac to rally defenses and rushed unit to critical spots to patch the holes. With Hill in his front and Longstreet's attack to his left, Hancock was in the unenviable position of having to attempt to resist Confederate advances spread out over a few miles, at least until more and more reserves could be rushed over from the other side of the Union line to the army's left flank. At one point, Hancock ordered a regiment to make what was essentially a suicidal bayonet charge into the face of Hill's Confederates on Cemetery Ridge. Hancock sent the First Minnesota to charge a Confederate brigade four times its size. One of the Minnesota volunteers, one William Lochren later said, "Every man realized in an instant what the order meant -- death or wounds to us all; the sacrifice of the regiment to gain a few minutes time and save the position, and probably the battlefield -- and every man saw and accepted the necessity of the sacrifice." While extremely costly to the regiment (the Minnesotans suffered 87% casualties, the worst of any regiment at Gettysburg), this heroic sacrifice bought time to organize the defensive line and kept the battle from turning in favor of the Confederates. Hancock would write of them, "I cannot speak too highly of this regiment and its commander in its attack, as well as in its subsequent advance against the enemy, in which it lost three-fourths of the officers and men engaged."

As Longstreet's assault on the Union left continued, his line naturally got more and more entangled as well. As Longstreet's men kept moving to their right, they reached the base of Little Round Top and Round Top, two rocky hills south of Gettysburg proper, at the far left. When Meade's chief engineer, Brig. General Gouverneur Warren, spotted the sun shining off the bayonets of Longstreet's men as they moved toward the Union left, it alerted the Army of the Potomac of the need to occupy Little Round Top, high ground that commanded much of the field.

With Warren having alerted his superiors to the importance of Little Round Top, Strong Vincent's brigade moved into position, under orders from Warren to "hold this ground at any costs," As part of Strong Vincent's brigade, Chamberlain's 20th Maine was on the left of the line, and thus Chamberlain's unit represented the extreme left of the Army of the Potomac's line.

In front of Vincent's brigade was General Evander Law's advancing Alabama Brigade (of Hood's Division). Law ordered 5 regiments to take Little Round Top, the 4th, 15th, and 47th Alabama, and the 4th and 5th Texas, but they had already marched more than 20 miles just to reach that point. They were now being asked to charge up high ground on a muggy, hot day.

Nevertheless, the Confederates made desperate assaults against Little Round Top, even after being repulsed by the Union defenders several times. In the middle of the fighting, after he saw Confederates trying to push around his flank, Chamberlain stretched his line until his regiment was merely a single-file line, and he then had to order his left (southernmost) half to swing back, thus forming an angle in their line in an effort to prevent a flank attack. Despite suffering heavy losses, the 20th Maine held through two subsequent charges by the 15th Alabama and other Confederate regiments for nearly 2 hours.

Chamberlain

Even after repulsing the Confederates several times, Chamberlain and his regiment faced a serious dilemma. With casualties mounting and ammunition running low, in desperation, Chamberlain *claimed* to have ordered his left wing to initiate an all-out, pivoting bayonet charge. With the 20th Maine charging ahead, the left wing wheeling continually to make the charging line swing like a hinge, thus creating a simultaneous frontal assault and flanking maneuver, they ultimately succeeded in not only taking the hill, but capturing 100 Confederate soldiers in the process. Chamberlain suffered two slight wounds in the battle, one when a shot ricocheted off his sword scabbard and bruised his thigh, another when his right foot was struck by a piece of shrapnel. With this success, Chamberlain was credited with preventing the Union flank from being penetrated and keeping the Confederates from pouring in behind Union lines.

Ultimately, it was the occupation and defense of Little Round Top that saved the rest of the Union line at Gettysburg. Had the Confederates commanded that high ground, it would have been able to position artillery that could have swept the Union lines along Cemetery Ridge and Cemetery Hill, which would have certainly forced the Army of the Potomac to withdraw from their lines. Chamberlain would be awarded the coveted Congressional Medal of Honor for "daring heroism and great tenacity in holding his position on the Little Round Top against repeated assaults, and carrying the advance position on the Great Round Top", and the 20th Maine's actions that day became one of the most famous attacks of the Battle of Gettysburg and the Civil War as a whole.

But did it really happen that way? Though historians have mostly given Chamberlain the credit for the order to affix bayonets and make the charge down Little Round Top, and Chamberlain received the credit from Sharaa's *The Killer Angels* and the movie *Gettysburg*, some recent researchers have claimed that Lt. Holman S. Melcher initiated the charge. According to Chamberlain however, Melcher had requested permission to make an advance to help some of his wounded men, only to be told by Chamberlain that a charge was about to be ordered anyway.

While Chamberlain's men held the extreme left, the rest of Vincent's brigade struggled desperately to the right, and Vincent himself would be mortally wounded in the fighting. The Confederates had advanced as far as Devil's Den, but Warren continued to bring reinforcements to Little Round Top to hold off Confederate attempts on the high ground. For the rest of the battle, even after the Confederates were repulsed from Little Round Top, their snipers in Devil's Den made the defenders of Little Round Top miserable. Confederate sharpshooters stationed around Devil's Den mortally wounded General Stephen Weed, whose New York brigade had arrived as reinforcements, and when his friend, artilleryman Lt. Charles Hazlett leaned over to comfort Weed or hear what he was trying to say, snipers shot Hazlett dead as well.

The fighting on the Union left finally ended as night fell. George Sykes, the commander of the V Corps, later described Day 2 in his official report, "Night closed the fight. The key of the battle-field was in our possession intact. Vincent, Weed, and Hazlett, chiefs lamented throughout the corps and army, sealed with their lives the spot intrusted to their keeping, and on which so much depended.... General Weed and Colonel Vincent, officers of rare promise, gave their lives to their country."

Ewell's orders from Lee had been to launch a demonstration on the Union right flank during Longstreet's attack, which started at about 4:00 p.m. as well, and in support of the demonstration by Hill's corps in the center. For that reason, Ewell would not launch his general assault on Culp's Hill and Cemetery Hill until 7:00 p.m.

While the Army of the Potomac managed to desperately hold on the left, Ewell's attack against Culp's Hill on the other end of the field met with some success in pushing the Army of the Potomac back. However, the attack started so late in the day that nightfall made it impossible for the Confederates to capitalize on their success. Due to darkness, a Confederate brigade led by George H. Steuart was unaware that they were firmly beside the Army of the Potomac's right flank, which would have given them almost unlimited access to the Union army's rear and its supply lines and line of communication, just 600 yards away. the main line of communication for the Union army, the Baltimore Pike, only 600 yards to their front. Col. David Ireland and the 137th New York desperately fought to preserve the Union army's flank, much the same way Chamberlain and the 20th Maine had on the other side, and in the process the 137th lost a third of their men.

Ewell's men would spend the night at the base of Culp's Hill and partially up the hill, in positions that had been evacuated by Union soldiers after Meade moved some of them to the left to deal with Longstreet's attack. It would fall upon the Confederates to pick up the attack the next morning.

That night, Meade held another council of war. Having been attacked on both flanks, Meade and his top officers correctly surmised that Lee would attempt an attack on the center of the line the next day. Moreover, captured Confederates and the fighting and intelligence of Day 2 let it be known that the only Confederate unit that had not yet seen action during the fighting was George Pickett's division of Longstreet's corps.

If July 2 was Longstreet's worst day of the Civil War, July 3 was almost certainly Robert E. Lee's. After the attack on July 2, Longstreet spent the night continuing to plot potential movements around Little Round Top and Big Round Top, thinking that would again get the Confederate army around the Union's flank. Longstreet himself did not realize that a reserve corps of the Union army was poised to block that maneuver.

Longstreet did not meet with Lee on the night of July 2, so when Lee met with him the following morning he found Longstreet's men were not ready to conduct an early morning attack, which Lee had wanted to attempt just as he was on the other side of the lines against Culp's Hill. With Pickett's men not up, however, Longstreet's corps couldn't make such an attack. Lee later wrote that Longstreet's "dispositions were not completed as early as was expected."

When Lee learned Longstreet couldn't commence an attack in the early morning, he attempted to stop Ewell from launching one, but by then it was too late. Ewell's men engaged in fighting along Culp's Hill, until the fighting fizzled out around noon. By then, Lee had already planned a massive attack on the Union center, combined with having Stuart's cavalry attack the Union army's lines in the rear. A successful attack would split the Army of the Potomac at the same time its communication and supply lines were severed by Stuart, which would make it possible to capture the entire army in detail.

There was just one problem with the plan, as Longstreet told Lee that morning: no 15,000 men who ever existed could successfully execute the attack. The charge required marching across an open field for about a mile, with the Union artillery holding high ground on all sides of the incoming Confederates. Longstreet ardently opposed the attack, but, already two days into the battle, Lee explained that because the Army of the Potomac was here on the field, he must strike at it. Longstreet later wrote that he said, "General, I have been a soldier all my life. I have been with soldiers engaged in fights by couples, by squads, companies, regiments, divisions, and armies, and should know, as well as any one, what soldiers can do. It is my opinion that no fifteen thousand men ever arrayed for battle can take that position." Longstreet proposed instead that their men should slip around the Union forces and occupy the high ground, forcing Northern commanders to attack them, rather than *vice versa*.

Realizing the insanity of sending 15,000 men hurtling into all the Union artillery, Lee planned to use the Confederate artillery to try to knock out the Union artillery ahead of time. Although old friend William Pendleton was the artillery chief, the artillery cannonade would be supervised by Edward Porter Alexander, Longstreet's chief artillerist, who would have to give the go-ahead to the charging infantry because they were falling under Longstreet's command. Alexander later noted that Longstreet was so disturbed and dejected about ordering the attack that at one point he tried to make Alexander order the infantry forward, essentially doing Longstreet's dirty work for him.

As Longstreet had predicted, from the beginning the plan was an abject failure. As Stuart's cavalry met its Union counterparts near East Cavalry Field, a young cavalry officer named George Custer convinced division commander Brig. General David McMurtrie Gregg to allow his brigade to stay and fight, even while Custer's own division was stationed to the south out of the action.

The fighting at East Cavalry Field turned out to be Custer's best known action of the Civil War, and it was his brigade that bore the brunt of the casualties in repulsing Stuart's cavalry. Right as the Confederates were starting the artillery bombardment ahead of Pickett's Charge, Stuart's men met Gregg's on the field.

After Stuart's men sent Union skirmishers scurrying, Gregg ordered Custer to counterattack with the 7th Michigan Cavalry Regiment. Custer led the charge personally, exhorting his men with the rallying cry, "Come on you Wolverines!" In the ensuing melee, which featured sabers and close range shooting, Custer had his horse shot out from under him, at which point he took a bugler's horse and continued fighting. Ultimately, his men sent Stuart's cavalry retreating, forcing Stuart to order in reinforcements.

Stuart's reinforcements sent the 7th Michigan in retreat, but now Custer rallied the 1st Michigan regiment to charge in yet another counterattack, with the same rallying cry, ""Come on you Wolverines!" Both sides galloped toward each other and crashed head on, engaging in more fierce hand-to-hand combat. Eventually, the Union held the field and forced Stuart's men to retreat.

Custer's brigade lost over 200 men in the attack, the highest loss of any Union cavalry brigade at Gettysburg, but he had just valiantly performed one of the most successful cavalry charges of the war. Custer wasn't exactly humble about his performance, writing in his official report after the battle, "I challenge the annals of warfare to produce a more brilliant or successful charge of cavalry."

As Stuart was in the process of being repulsed, just after 1:00 p.m. 150 Confederate guns began to fire from Seminary Ridge, hoping to incapacitate the Union center before launching an infantry attack. Confederate brigadier Evander Law said of the artillery bombardment, "The cannonade in the center ... presented one of the most magnificent battle-scenes witnessed during the war. Looking up the valley towards Gettysburg, the hills on either side were capped with crowns of flame and smoke, as 300 guns, about equally divided between the two ridges, vomited their iron hail upon each other."

However, the Confederate artillery they mostly overshot their mark. The artillery duel could be heard from dozens of miles away, and all the smoke led to Confederate artillery constantly overshooting their targets. Realizing that the artillery was meant for them as a way of softening them up for an infantry charge, Hancock calmly rode his horse up and down the line of the II Corps, both inspiring and assuring his men with his own courage and resolve.

During the massive Confederate artillery bombardment that preceded the infantry assault, Hancock was so conspicuous on horseback reviewing and encouraging his troops that one of his subordinates pleaded with him that "the corps commander ought not to risk his life that way." Hancock reportedly replied, "There are times when a corps commander's life does not count."

Eventually, Union artillery chief Henry Hunt cleverly figured that if the Union cannons stopped firing back, the Confederates might think they successfully knocked out the Union batteries. On top of that, the Union would be preserving its ammunition for the impending charge that everyone now knew was coming. When they stopped, Lee, Alexander, and others mistakenly concluded that they'd knocked out the Union artillery.

A short time later, Confederate General George Pickett, commander of one of the three divisions under General Longstreet, prepared for the charge that would forever bear his name, even though he commanded only about a third of the force and was officially under Longstreet's direction. Today historians typically refer to the charge as the Pickett-Pettigrew-Trimble Assault or Longstreet's Assault to be more technically correct. Since A.P. Hill was sidelined with illness, Pettigrew's and Trimble's divisions were delegated to Longstreet's authority as well. To make matters worse, Hill's sickness resulted in organizational snafus. Without Hill to assign or lead troops, some of his battle-weary soldiers of the previous two days were tapped to make the charge while fresh soldiers in his corps stayed behind.

The charge was to begin with Pickett's division of Virginians, and shortly after the Union guns fell silent, with his men in position, Pickett asked Longstreet to give the order to advance. Longstreet could only nod, fearing that "to verbalize the order may reveal his utter lack of confidence in the plan." With that, around 2:00 p.m. about 12,500-15,000 Confederates stepped out in sight and began their charge with an orderly march starting about a mile away, no doubt an inspiring sight to Hancock and the Union men directly across from the oncoming assault.

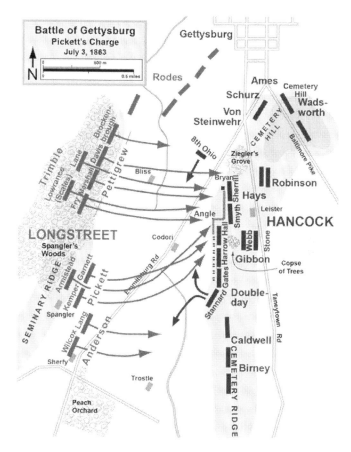

As the Confederate line advanced, Union cannon on Cemetery Ridge and Little Round Top began blasting away, with Confederate soldiers continuing to march forward. One Union soldier later wrote, "We could not help hitting them with every shot . . . a dozen men might be felled by one single bursting shell." By the time Longstreet's men reached Emmitsburg Road, Union artillery switched to firing grapeshot (tin cans filled with iron and lead balls), and as the Confederate troops continued to approach the Union center, Union troops positioned behind the wall cut down the oncoming Confederates, easily decimating both flanks. Lt. Col. Franklin Sawyer of the 8th Ohio reported, "They were at once enveloped in a dense cloud of smoke and dust. Arms, heads, blankets, guns and knapsacks were thrown and tossed in to the clear air. ... A moan went up from the field, distinctly to be heard amid the storm of battle."

While some of the men did manage to advance to the Union line and engage in hand-to-hand combat, it was of little consequence. In the midst of the fighting, as he was conferring with one of his brigadier generals, General Stannard, Hancock suddenly felt a searing pain in his thigh. He had just been severely wounded when a bullet struck the pommel of his saddle and entered his inner right thigh, along with wood splinters and a large bent nail. Helped from his horse by his aides, he removed the saddle nail himself and applied a tourniquet, colorfully swearing at his own men while demanding that they not let him bleed to death. Nevertheless, he refused to remove himself to the rear until the offensive had concluded.

After about an hour, nearly 6,500 Confederates were dead or wounded, five times that of the Union, with all 13 regimental commanders in Pickett's division killed or wounded. In the aftermath of the defeat, General Longstreet stated, "General Lee came up as our troops were falling back and encouraged them as well as he could; begged them to reform their ranks and reorganize their forces . . . and it was then he used the expression . . . 'It was all my fault; get together, and let us do the best we can toward saving which is left to us.'"

Today Pickett's Charge is remembered as the American version of the Charge of the Light Brigade, a heroic but completely futile march that had no chance of success. In fact, it's remembered as Pickett's Charge because Pickett's Virginians wanted to claim the glory of getting the furthest during the attack in the years after the war. The charge consisted of about 15,000 men under the command of James Longstreet, with three divisions spearheaded by Pickett, Trimble, and Pettigrew. Trimble and Pettigrew were leading men from A.P. Hill's corps, and Hill was too disabled by illness that day to choose the men from his corps to make the charge. As a result, some of the men who charged that day had already engaged in heavy fighting.

The charge suffered about a 50% casualty rate, as the Confederates marched into hell. The men barely made a dent in the Union line before retreating in disorder back across the field, where Lee met them in an effort to regroup them in case the Union counterattacked. At one point, Lee ordered Pickett to reform his division, to which Pickett reportedly cried, "I have no division!" Pickett's post-battle report was apparently so bitter that Lee ordered it destroyed. Though the charge was named Pickett's Charge by newspapers for the purpose of praising Pickett's Virginians for making the furthest progress, Pickett felt the charge had tarnished his career, and he remained upset that his name remained associated with the sharply repulsed attack.

Pickett

One of the Virginians who marched straight into Hancock's II Corps was his old friend Lewis A. Armistead, who was leading one of Pickett's brigades. Armistead famously led his brigade with his hat atop his sword, serving as a visual cue for his men, and they actually breached the II Corps' line, making it about as far as any Confederate got. In the fighting, Armistead was mortally wounded and captured, dying days later. Armistead's dying wishes were to deliver his Bible and other personal valuables to Hancock's wife Almira, which Longstreet had done.

Trimble and Pettigrew, the other two leaders of the charge, were both wounded in the fighting, with Trimble losing a leg and Pettigrew suffering a minor wound to the hand. All of Pickett's brigadiers were injured. In addition to Armistead's mortal wounding, Kemper was seriously wounded and captured. Meanwhile Richard Garnett, whose courage had been impugned and challenged by Stonewall Jackson unfairly in 1862, had suffered a previous leg injury and insisted on riding his horse during the charge, despite the obvious fact that riding a horse clearly indicated he was an officer. Garnett was killed during the charge, and it's unknown where he fell or where he was buried.

Pickett's Charge is the most memorable charge of July 3, but it wasn't the only fateful one made that day. As the Union cavalry repulsed Stuart, cavalry officer Hugh Judson Kilpatrick gave the order for some of his cavalry to charge north into the Confederates' right flank, Evander Law's brigade (which had opposed Chamberlain the day before). It's believed that the order was given as part of a plan by Meade to possibly follow up a repulse of Pickett's Charge with a flank attack that might lead to a rolling up of the Confederate line.

However, Kilpatrick was ordering the attack just as Pickett's infantry was starting the charge, not during its repulse, and he ordered an attack to be made piecemeal instead of one united assault.

West of Emmitsburg Road, Merrit's cavalry dismounted and began an attack on the Confederate flank, only to run into a brigade of Georgians, which easily repulsed the attack. The plan then called for Elon Farnsworth to attack, but this time Kilpatrick ordered a mounted cavalry charge. By now, with Merrit's attack having failed, the Confederate infantry was positioned behind a stone fence with wooden fence rails piled high above it to prevent horses from being able to jump into their lines. In essence, the Union cavalry would have to make a mounted charge, dismount right at the battle line, and then attempt a concerted attack. Historians have since accused Kilpatrick of shaming Farnsworth into making the suicidal chare, and Farnsworth allegedly told his superior, "General, if you order the charge I will lead it, but you must take the awful responsibility."

Farnsworth's charge began with a charge by the 1st West Virginia Cavalry that immediately devolved into confusion once they came under heavy fire. Eventually they dismounted near the wall, where they engaged in hand-to-hand fighting with sabers, rifles, and even rocks. The second part of the attack came from the 18th Pennsylvania, supported by companies of the 5th New York, but they were immediately repulsed.

Next, it fell upon the 400 man 1st Vermont Cavalry to charge forward, heading into a slaughter. As they rode forward, one lieutenant in an Albama regiment yelled, "Cavalry, boys, cavalry! This is no fight, only a frolic, give it to them!" All three battalions of the 1st Vermont were quickly repulsed. With that, the final attack was to be led by Farnsworth himself, which came upon the 15th Alabama. In the middle of the charge, Farnsworth fell dead from his horse, hit by 5 bullets. Kilpatrick's poorly designed attack resulted in Farnsworth and his men making a "Charge of the Light Brigade", and as it turned out, they would end up being the last major action of the Battle of Gettysburg.

From a military perspective, Meade had made efficient use of his subordinates (particularly Generals John F. Reynolds and Winfield S. Hancock) during this three-day, course-changing battle, ultimately executing some of the most effective battleline strategies of the War. In short, Meade had successfully commanded the forces that repulsed Lee's Army and effectively won what most historians consider the battle that changed the course of the Civil War and ultimately resulted in a Confederate defeat.

While nobody questions that Meade's strategy at Gettysburg was strong, he was heavily criticized by contemporaries for not pursuing Lee's army more aggressively as it retreated. Chief-of-staff Daniel Butterfield, who would call into question Meade's command decisions and courage at Gettysburg, accused Meade of not finishing off the weakened Lee. Meade would later state that as his army's new commander, he was uncertain of his troops' capabilities and strength, especially after a battle that had just resulted in over 20,000 Union casualties. Moreover, heavy rains made pursuit almost impossible on July 4, and Lee actually invited an attack during the retreat, hoping Meade would haphazardly attack strongly fortified positions.

Though historians now mostly credit Meade with making proper decisions in the wake of the battle, Lincoln was incredibly frustrated when Lee successfully retreated south. On July 14, Lincoln drafted a letter that he ultimately decided not to send to Meade, who never read it in his lifetime:

"I have just seen your despatch to Gen. Halleck, asking to be relieved of your command, because of a supposed censure of mine. I am very--very--grateful to you for the magnificent success you gave the cause of the country at Gettysburg; and I am sorry now to be the author of the slightest pain to you. But I was in such deep distress myself that I could not restrain some expression of it. I had been oppressed nearly ever since the battles at Gettysburg, by what appeared to be evidences that yourself, and Gen. Couch, and Gen. Smith, were not seeking a collision with the enemy, but were trying to get him across the river without another battle. What these evidences were, if you please, I hope to tell you at some time, when we shall both feel better. The case, summarily stated is this. You fought and beat the enemy at Gettysburg; and, of course, to say the least, his loss was as great as yours. He retreated; and you did not, as it seemed to me, pressingly pursue him; but a flood in the river detained him, till, by slow degrees, you were again upon him. You had at least twenty thousand veteran troops directly with you, and as many more raw ones within supporting distance, all in addition to those who fought with you at Gettysburg; while it was not possible that he had received a single recruit; and yet you stood and let the flood run down, bridges be built, and the enemy move away at his leisure, without attacking him. And Couch and Smith! The latter left Carlisle in time, upon all ordinary calculation, to have aided you in the last battle at Gettysburg; but he did not arrive. At the end of more than ten days, I believe twelve, under constant urging, he reached Hagerstown from Carlisle, which is not an inch over fifty-five miles, if so much. And Couch's movement was very little different.
    Again, my dear general, I do not believe you appreciate the magnitude of the misfortune involved in Lee's escape. He was within your easy grasp, and to have closed upon him would, in connection with our other late successes, have ended the war. As it is, the war will be prolonged indefinitely. If you could not safely attack Lee last Monday, how can you possibly do so South of the river, when you can take with you very few more than two thirds of the force you then had in hand? It would be unreasonable to expect, and I do not expect you can now effect much. Your golden opportunity is gone, and I am distressed immeasurably because of it.
    I beg you will not consider this a prosecution, or persecution of yourself As you had learned that I was dissatisfied, I have thought it best to kindly tell you why."

Still, Meade was promoted to brigadier general in the regular army and was officially awarded the Thanks of Congress, which commended Meade "... and the officers and soldiers of [the Army of the Potomac], for the skill and heroic valor which at Gettysburg repulsed, defeated, and drove back, broken and dispirited, beyond the Rappahannock, the veteran army of the rebellion."

Hancock was unquestionably one of the Union heroes at Gettysburg, but his recognition was slow in coming. In the months after the battle, the U.S. Congress thanked Meade and Howard without listing Hancock. Eventually, Major General Hancock later received the Thanks of the U. S. Congress for "gallant, meritorious, and conspicuous share in that great and decisive victory."

As usual, Hancock shared the credit with his men, writing in his post-battle report:

"To speak of the conduct of the troops would seem to be unnecessary, but still it may be justly remarked that this corps sustained its well-earned reputation on many fields, and that the boast of its gallant first commander, the late Maj. Gen. E. V. Sumner, that the Second Corps had "never given to the enemy a gun or color," holds good now as it did under the command of my predecessor, Major-General Couch. To attest to its good conduct and the perils through which it has passed, it may be stated that its losses in battle have been greater than those of any other corps in the Army of the Potomac, or probably in the service, notwithstanding it has usually been numerically weakest."

From almost the moment the Civil War ended, Gettysburg has been widely viewed as one of the decisive turning points of the Civil War. As renowned Civil War historian described Gettysburg, "It might be less of a victory than Mr. Lincoln had hoped for, but it was nevertheless a victory—and, because of that, it was no longer possible for the Confederacy to win the war. The North might still lose it, to be sure, if the soldiers or the people should lose heart, but outright defeat was no longer in the cards." While some still dispute that labeling, Lee's Army of Northern Virginia was never truly able to take the strategic offensive again for the duration of the war.

Naturally, if Gettysburg marked an important turning point in the Civil War, then to the defeated South it represented one of the last true opportunities the South had to win the war. After the South had lost the war, the importance of Gettysburg as one of the "high tide" marks of the Confederacy became apparent to everyone, making the battle all the more important in the years after it had been fought. Former Confederate comrades like Longstreet and Jubal Early would go on to argue who was responsible for the loss at Gettysburg (and thus the war) in the following decades. Much of the debate was fueled by those who wanted to protect Lee's legacy, especially because Lee was dead and could not defend himself in writing anymore. However, on July 3, Lee insisted on taking full blame for what occurred at Gettysburg, telling his retreating men, "It's all my fault." Historians have mostly agreed, placing the blame for the disastrous Day 3 on Lee's shoulders. Porter Alexander would later call it Lee's "worst day" of the war.

Ironically, though he had no use for post-war politics, Lee's legacy was crafted and embroiled in it. Though Lee accepted the South's loss, unreconstructed rebels continued to "fight" the Civil War with the pen, aiming to influence how the war was remembered. Much of this was accomplished by the Southern Historical Society, whose stated aim was the homogenization of Southern white males. But longstanding feuds between former generals found their way into the papers, and the feuds were frequently based on regional differences. These former Confederates looked to their idealized war heroes as symbols of their suffering and struggle. Based in Richmond, the Society's ideal Southern white male embodied the "Virginian" essence of aristocracy, morality and chivalry. The Society's ideal male, of course, was Robert E. Lee. David Blight credits the Society for creating a "Lee cult" that dominates public perception to this day. Writing about this perception of Lee, Charles Osbourne described the perception as "an edifice of myth built on the foundation of truth…the image became an icon."

Still, Lee was far from perfect, despite the attempts of the Southern Historical Society to defend his war record as fault free, at the expense of some of his subordinates. Given that the Confederacy lost the war, some historians have pointed out that Lee was often too eager to engage in offensive warfare. After all, Lee scored large and smashing victories at places like Chancellorsville that deprived him of more manpower against opponents that could afford casualties more than he could. Moreover, for the engineer who used tactics to successfully defend against typical Civil War tactics, he all too often engaged in the same futile offensive tactics himself, none more costly than Pickett's Charge.

However, after the war, former Confederates would not accept criticism of Lee, and blame for the loss at Gettysburg was thus placed upon other scapegoats. Although it was not immediately apparent where the blame rested for such a devastating loss, not long after the Battle of Gettysburg two names kept surfacing: cavalry leader General "Jeb" Stuart and General James Longstreet; Stuart blamed for robbing Lee of the "eyes" he needed to know of Union movement, and Longstreet for delaying his attack on Round Top Hills the second day and acting too slowly in executing the assault on the Union left flank.

Long before Gettysburg, Longstreet was characterized by his men and commanders as "congenitally resistant to hurry himself," resistant to change of orders (even from his supreme commander, Lee), and disliked to overextend his men (once bivouacked, he allowed his men to prepare three-days' rations before breaking camp, even when they were supposed to stick to a timetable). In fact, his designation as Lee's "old reliable" appears to have been bestowed by someone who had never actually worked with him or had to rely upon him.

Similarly, Longstreet's clash with A. P. Hill, then Jackson, Hood and Toombs, were indicative of his unwillingness to accept that he was not the center of attention; not the one destined for greatness. And, of course, as the War progressed, Longstreet's propensity to find fault (and start feuds) with Lafayette McLaws (who he tried to have court-martialed), Evander Law (who he tried to have arrested), Charles Field, and ultimately, Lee himself, was highly indicative of the self-possessed illusion Longstreet was living (and fighting) under. While always quick to reprimand any subordinate who questioned his orders, he clearly hesitated to resist orders from his superiors on occasions. In his Gettysburg account, Longstreet had the impudence to blame Lee for "not changing his plans" based on Longstreet's "want of confidence in them."

After General Robert E. Lee died in October of 1870, a group of ex-Confederates led by General Jubal Early (who had led a division in Ewell's corps at Gettysburg) publicly criticized Longstreet for ignoring orders and delaying his attack on the second day of the Battle on July 2, 1863. But while many former Confederates held Longstreet accountable for not following orders, Early took it one step further, arguing that Longstreet -- not Lee -- was responsible for the Confederate defeat (deemed a "tactical disaster" by most) that by most accounts was the beginning of the end for the Confederacy.

In his memoirs, however, Longstreet defended himself, saying that the blistering post-War attacks concerning Gettysburg were merely "payback for supporting Black suffrage", thus shifting the blame back to Lee. He wrote, "[Lee] knew that I did not believe that success was possible . . . he should have put an officer in charge who had more confidence in his plan." He went on to say that Lee should have given the responsibility to Early, thus justifying his insubordination.

On the other hand, Longstreet's reputation has mostly been on the upswing in the past few decades, due in no small part to Michael Shaara's 1974 novel *The Killer Angels*, which portrayed Longstreet in a more flattering light. That novel was the basis for the 1993 film *Gettysburg*, which has also helped rehabilitate Longstreet's legacy and helped make clear to the public how instrumental he was during the war. In 1982, Thomas L. Connolly and Barbara L. Bellows published *God and General Longstreet*, which took the Lost Cause proponents like Early to task for their blatant fabrications (such as the one that Lee ordered Longstreet to attack in the early morning of Day 2 of Gettysburg), helping make clear the extent of historical revision propagated by the Lost Cause. In doing so, they cast Longstreet as a sympathetic victim of circumstances and sectional and political hostility.

It's also important to note that Lee himself never made any post-War statements to suggest that he held Longstreet responsible for the Confederacy's demise.

Outwardly, Stuart was the embodiment of reckless courage, magnificent manhood, and unconquerable virility; a man who could wear--without drawing suspicion of instability--the flamboyant adornments of a classic cavalier. It was once written that his black plume and hat caught up with a golden star, seemed the proper frame for a knightly face. In that same vein, people were always aware that Stuart was engaging in public relations even then, and Civil War historian Jeff Wert captured it well: "Stuart had been the Confederacy's knight-errant, the bold and dashing cavalier, attired in a resplendent uniform, plumed hat, and cape. Amid a slaughterhouse, he had embodied chivalry, clinging to the pageantry of a long-gone warrior. He crafted the image carefully, and the image befitted him. He saw himself as the Southern people envisaged him. They needed a knight; he needed to be that knight." Stuart, in effect, was the very essence of the Lost Cause.

It has been widely presumed that those same vainglorious traits led Stuart on a glory-seeking mission near the end of June 1863, which badly damaged Lee's abilities in Pennsylvania and directly led to the Army of Northern Virginia stumbling into a general battle Lee wished to avoid. Though credited with devoting his full attention to the Confederate cause upon his arrival, many historians attribute the catastrophic loss to the absence of Stuart and his cavalry. Immediately becoming the most devastating event of Stuart's military career, in his official report General Lee's wrote, " . . . the absence of the cavalry rendered it impossible to obtain accurate information. By the route [we] pursued, the Federal Army was interposed between [my] command and our main body, preventing any communication with [Stuart] until his arrival at Carlisle. The march toward Gettysburg was conducted more slowly than it would have been had the movements of the Federal Army been known." Some of Stuart's subordinates would come to his defense after the war, and Lee deserves some blame for allowing his subordinates so much discretion, which may have worked with Stonewall Jackson but backfired spectacularly with Ewell and Stuart. After the war, Stuart's subordinate, General Thomas L. Rosser stated what many were already convinced of, "On this campaign, [Stuart] undoubtedly, make the fatal blunder which lost us the battle of Gettysburg."

To a great extent, the Confederates' search for scapegoats is a product of the fact that they were so used to being successful that a defeat had to be explained by a Southern failure, not a Northern success.

In casting about for Southern deficiencies, it is often overlooked that Meade and his top subordinates fought a remarkably efficient battle. Meade created an extremely sturdy defensive line anchored on high ground, he held the interior lines by having his army spread out over a smaller area, and he used that ability to shuffle troops from the right to the left on July 2. Moreover, Meade was able to rely on his corps commanders, especially Hancock, to properly use their discretion. Before the battle, Lee reportedly said that Meade "would commit no blunders on my front and if I make one ... will make haste to take advantage of it." If he said it, he was definitely right.

Perhaps none other than George Pickett himself put it best. When asked (certainly ad nauseam) why Pickett's Charge had failed, Pickett is said to have tersely replied, "I've always thought the

Yankees had something to do with it."

Chapter 13: The Overland Campaign: Lee Meets Grant

When Lee retreated from Pennsylvania without much fight from the Army of the Potomac, Lincoln was again discouraged, believing Meade had a chance to end the war if he had been bolder. Though historians dispute that, and the Confederates actually invited attack during their retreat, Lincoln was constantly looking for more aggressive fighters to lead his men.

Lincoln had found one in Ulysses S. Grant, once famously explaining, "I cannot spare this man. He fights." Grant had led Union forces to several victories out west, including the siege of Vicksburg that split the Confederacy in two and gave the North complete control of the Mississippi. Now, Lincoln called Grant east to be commander in chief of all armies, while William Tecumseh Sherman became the principal commander in the West.

By 1864, the South's war strategy was simply to ensure Lincoln lost reelection that November. With Grant's appointment, Lee now intended only to stand between Grant's army and Richmond, the heart of the Confederacy. And with virtually unlimited manpower and resources at his dispose, Grant need not be concerned with the cost of at all-out advance.

In April, Grant attached himself to Meade's Army of the Potomac and began marching it to meet Lee's army. On May 4, 1864, Grant launched what has come to be known as the Overland Campaign, during which he crossed the Rapidan River with 100,000 men near Fredericksburg. Grant's aims were simple: advance toward Richmond while fighting the enemy wherever he was. Lee could only assemble 60,000 men to meet the oncoming Army of the Potomac, and Grant's aggressive nature and advantage in manpower deprived Lee of any real ability to take a strategic initiative.

Nevertheless, Lee proved more than capable on the defensive. From May 5-6, Lee's men won a tactical victory at the Battle of the Wilderness, which was fought so close to where the Battle of Chancellorsville took place a year earlier that soldiers encountered skeletons that had been buried in (too) shallow graves in 1863. Both armies sustained heavy casualties while Grant kept attempting to move the fighting to a setting more to his advantage. The heavy forest made coordinated movements almost impossible, and when Lee used Longstreet to counterattack on the second day, Longstreet was nearly killed by a shot to the neck, disabling him for the rest of the campaign. Finally, Grant's army disengaged and moved to the southeast, attempting to lure Lee into open-field fighting.

Grant continued to maneuver his men toward Richmond, and Lee continued to parry. The next major battle took place at Spotsylvania Court House, where a salient in the Confederate line nearly spelled disaster. Nevertheless, Lee's army continued to stoutly defend against several attacks by the Army of the Potomac, and massive casualties were inflicted on both sides. As luck would have it, the only time Lee had a chance to take the initiative during the Battle of North Anna, he was heavily debilitated with illness. Grant nearly fell into Lee's trap by splitting his army in two along the North Anna before avoiding it.

Aware of the North's advantage in resources and men, Grant continued to push the army south. Despite Grant's failure to win any of the major battles in April and May 1864, Grant thought Lee's army was on the verge of destruction when he ordered a frontal assault at Cold Harbor. Grant was dead wrong, literally. Although the story of Union soldiers pinning their names on the back of their uniforms in anticipation of death is apocryphal, they did suffer thousands of casualties in about half an hour.

By the end of Cold Harbor, Grant had lost more men than Lee had in his whole army, and Grant had not won a single victory during the Overland Campaign. He was accused of butchery by losing tens of thousands of men, but he knew he could win a war of attrition. After Cold Harbor, Grant stole a day's march on Lee and crossed the James River, attacking the Confederacy's primary railroad hub at Petersburg, which was only a few miles from Richmond. By the time Lee's army reached Petersburg, it had been defended by P.G.T. Beauregard. The two armies dug in, as Grant prepared for a long term siege of the vital city.

Chapter 14: The Siege of Petersburg

The siege lines of Petersburg kept Lee completely pinned down and stretched his army. As Lee continued to maintain a tenuous grip there, Sherman's men in the West defeated Joseph E. Johnston and John Bell Hood in the Atlanta Campaign and then marched to sea, capturing Savannah by Christmas. Sherman's successes helped ensure Lincoln was reelected, ensuring the war would go on.

Lee had almost no initiative, at one point futilely sending Jubal Early with a contingent through the Shenandoah Valley and toward Washington D.C. in an effort to peel off some of Grant's men. Though Early made it to the outskirts of Washington D.C. and Lincoln famously became the only president to come under enemy fire at Fort Stevens, the Union's "Little Phil" Sheridan pushed Early back through the Valley and scorched it.

Petersburg dragged on through the winter of 1864 as Grant continually advanced his frontline, slowly exhausting Lee's resources. The most famous battle during this time took place when

Union engineers burrowed underneath the Confederate siege lines and lit the fuse on a massive amount of ammunition, creating a "crater" in the field. But even then, the Battle of the Crater ended with a Union debacle.

Entering 1865, the Confederacy was in utter disarray. Lee's Army of Northern Virginia had tenuously defended against Grant's siege at Petersburg for nearly six months. The main Confederate army in the West had been nearly destroyed at the Battle of Franklin weeks earlier. And Sherman's army faced little resistance as it marched through the Carolinas. By the time Lincoln delivered his Second Inaugural Address in March 1865, the end of the war was in sight.

Although Confederate leaders remained optimistic, by the summer of 1864 they had begun to consider desperate measures in an effort to turn around the war. From 1863-1865, Confederate leaders had even debated whether to conscript black slaves and enlist them as soldiers. Even as their fortunes looked bleak, the Confederates refused to issue an official policy to enlist blacks. It was likely too late to save the Confederacy anyway.

Lee's siege lines at Petersburg were finally broken on April 1 at the Battle of Five Forks, which is best remembered for Pickett enjoying a cod bake lunch while his men were being defeated. Historians have attributed it to unusual environmental acoustics that prevented Pickett and his staff from hearing the battle despite their close proximity, not that it mattered to the Confederates at the time. Between that and Gettysburg, Pickett and Lee were alleged to have held very poor opinions of each other by the end of the war, and there is still debate as to whether Lee had ordered Pickett out of the army during the Appomattox campaign.

Chapter 15: Appomattox

After fighting on April 2, the Army of Northern Virginia quit Petersburg, and with it Richmond. Lee's battered army began stumbling toward a rail depot in the hopes of avoiding being surrounded by Union forces and picking up much needed food rations. While Grant's army continued to chase Lee's retreating army westward, the Confederate government sought to escape across the Deep South. On April 4, President Lincoln entered Richmond and toured the home of Confederate President Jefferson Davis.

Fittingly, the food rations did not arrive as anticipated. As the retreat continued, Grant communicated a desire to stop the fighting and asked Lee for terms of surrender. When Lee proposed to hear the terms, the communications continued until April 9, when the two met at Appomattox Court House.

When Lee and Grant met, the styles in dress captured the personality differences perfectly. Lee was in full military attire, while Grant showed up casually in a muddy uniform. The Civil War's two most celebrated generals were meeting for the first time since the Mexican-American War.

The McLean Parlor in Appomattox Court House. McLean's house was famously fought around during the First Battle of Bull Run, leading him to move to Appomattox.

The Confederate soldiers had continued fighting while Lee worked out the terms of surrender, and they were understandably devastated to learn that they had surrendered. Some of his men had famously suggested to Lee that they continue to fight on. Porter Alexander would later rue the fact that he suggested to Lee that they engage in guerrilla warfare, which earned him a stern rebuke from Lee. As a choked-up Lee rode down the troop line on his famous horse Traveller that day, he addressed his defeated army, saying, "Men, we have fought through the war together. I have done my best for you; my heart is too full to say more."

Appomattox is frequently cited as the end of the Civil War, but there still remained several Confederate armies across the country, mostly under the command of General Joseph E. Johnston, who Lee had replaced nearly 3 years earlier. On April 26, Johnston surrendered all of his forces to General Sherman. Over the next month, the remaining Confederate forces would surrender or quit. The last skirmish between the two sides took place May 12-13, ending ironically with a Confederate victory at the Battle of Palmito Ranch in Texas. Two days earlier, Jefferson Davis had been captured in Georgia.

Although the surrender of the Army of Northern Virginia to General Ulysses S. Grant and the Army of the Potomac at Appomattox Courthouse did not officially end the long and bloody Civil War, the surrender is often considered the final chapter of the war. For that reason, Appomattox has captured the popular imagination of Americans ever since Lee's surrender on April 9, 1865. After surrendering, Lee wrote one last order to his army and a report to Confederate President Jefferson Davis, before heading home to Virginia to live out the rest of his days.

Chapter 16: Final Years, 1865-1870

As a civilian for the first time in 40 years, the Proclamation of Amnesty and Reconstruction of 1865 prevented citizen Lee from holding public office even though he was many times encouraged to enter politics; he was, after all, a celebrity.

Even so, he applied for a complete personal pardon as provided for by the proclamation, hoping to set an example for other leading Southerners. In a paperwork snafu involving the required Oath of Allegiance, however, Lee did not receive his pardon in his lifetime, but a general amnesty did restore his right to vote. It wasn't until 1975 that a National Archive employee ran across Lee's sworn oath and Congress retroactively restored his American citizenship.

Although offered many prestigious positions, Lee opted to spend his final years as president of Washington College in Lexington, Virginia. While there, he raised the school's level of scholarship and established schools of commerce and journalism. With a growing fan club of sorts, young men from all across the South flocked to what became known as "General Lee's school," later christened Washington and Lee University.

While many statesmen of the South remained "unreconstructed" and spread bitterness, resentment, and hatred after the Confederacy's defeat, Lee openly urged his students and friends to maintain the peace and accept the outcome of the war. As a true "Washingtonian" and believer in what America represented as a whole, he spent his final years doing what he could to restore the political, economic, and social life of the South, urging all to "Make your sons Americans."

Lee had frequently been ill during the Civil War, and though he began collecting papers and records with which to write memoirs about the Civil War, his health began to quickly fail in early 1870. Lee died on October 12, 1870 of a stroke, outlived by his frail wife Mary, who died November 5, 1873. Lee was buried in the chapel he built on campus in Lexington, Virginia, along with his other family members; a building often referred to as "The Shrine of the South," a spot visited by thousands each year.

Lee's home has been preserved in Arlington National Cemetery, near Washington, D.C. Lee's birthday, January 19, is observed as a legal holiday in most Southern states. Lee represents Virginia in Statuary Hall in the Capitol in Washington.

Lee's Arlington House

Chapter 17: Lee, a Man of Contradictions

History speaks of Robert E. Lee as man of peace, a man of compassion, a man responsibility. But above all, it speaks of a pragmatic man with an all-pervasive sense of duty.

Although Lee saw war as a disintegrating and largely unnecessary response to social disapproval--an act of disloyalty that fundamentally undermines a society's stability--as a military man, Lee spent most of his mature life waiting for the next war; the next battle.

Lee hadn't chosen a career in law or politics or even farming (as he'd often said he'd prefer), he'd chosen the life of a soldier; a military strategist whose job it was to enable his side to overcome the opposition through cunning, ingenuity, and deception. And for all his moral and ethical aversion to armed dissention, in reality, his natural abilities and formidable training in accomplishing these goals weren't fully utilized in times of peace, only in times of war.

As a practical man who as a boy had watched his family suffer and disintegrate due to his father's irresponsibility, Lee had vowed never to subject his family to the same financial embarrassment and social indignation. And although history records Lee as a man of principles, more to the heart it seems, he was a man of duty. A man of peace who relied upon conflict. And it seems likely that he was torn between these two principles for most of his life.

Modern history describes Lee as a man who gave his loyalty, his industry, to the causes of the

South although fundamentally, he opposed the enslavement of his fellow man. More flattering accounts emphasize that he'd actually given up his slaves long before the Civil War began.

More accurately, however, it wasn't so much that he'd "given up" his slaves as participated in slave-rental. And while Lee was never known to refer to human chattel as "slaves" or even the more popular, "darkies" (preferring instead, "the people"), Lee is quoted as saying, "The best men of the South have long desired to do away with the institution [of slavery] and were quite willing to see it abolished. But the question has ever been, 'What will you do with the freed people?'"

As records show, in late 1857, Lee inherited 63 slaves from his father-in-law, George Washington Parke Curtis. Though technically the property of his wife, Mary, responsibility for their care and maintenance ultimately fell to Lee as Master of the plantation. And while the principled Lee may have been repulsed by the idea of further subjugating these men, woman, and children under his charge, the pragmatic Lee, the dutiful Lee, knew that he could never provide for his family in the true Southern spirit--the way his wife Mary had long been accustomed-- without supplementing his officer's pay.

He needed to not only make certain that his wife and children wouldn't be left to their own devices should he die or be killed, but consider the immediate issues at hand: by the time his son Curtis started boarding school, tuition cost three hundred dollars a year; nearly a fourth of a captain's pay. Thus, as his family grew in size, so too did the necessity to compromise his principles. But as one story from his younger days demonstrates, for Lee, the issue couldn't have been nearly that cut and dry.

As the account is told, following the passing of his mother Anne, Lee's sister Mildred inherited responsibility for Nat, an elderly house servant and coachman, who in his old age, apparently suffered tuberculosis. On the advise that warmer climate might make Nat's final days more pleasant, the twenty-two year old Lee took Nat along with him to his post on Cockspur Island, where he is said to have nursed him with all the tenderness of a son through his final days. Thus, it seems that Lee's sense of responsibility and humanity rose far beyond simply supporting or opposing slavery. He genuinely saw his charges as *people*.

In the end, while the principled Lee may have seen slavery as an abomination against mankind--something he'd put an end to and something that would have pleased his wife who by this time had become an anti-slavery advocate--the practical Lee saw it as a necessary evil; a means to an end. The dutiful Lee found a way to compromise.

Chapter 18: Lee's Legacy

Ironically, though he had no use for post-war politics, Lee's legacy was crafted and embroiled in it. Though Lee accepted the South's loss, unreconstructed rebels continued to "fight" the Civil War with the pen, aiming to influence how the war was remembered. Much of this was accomplished by the Southern Historical Society, whose stated aim was the homogenization of Southern white males. But longstanding feuds between former generals found their way into the papers, and the feuds were frequently based on regional differences. These former Confederates looked to their idealized war heroes as symbols of their suffering and struggle. Based in Richmond, the Society's ideal Southern white male embodied the "Virginian" essence of aristocracy, morality and chivalry. The Society's ideal male, of course, was Robert E. Lee. David Blight credits the Society for creating a "Lee cult" that dominates public perception to this day. Writing about this perception of Lee, Charles Osbourne described the perception as "an edifice of myth built on the foundation of truth...the image became an icon."

With Lee being pushed forward as the quintessential Southern man, he began to be treated as the ideal man and ideal leader. This sentiment eventually began to influence Northern views of the man as well. An equestrian statue of Lee that was unveiled in Richmond in 1890 sparked an outburst of sentimentality that affected the North as well as the South. Reporting on the unveiling of the Lee statue, the *New York Times* referred to the memory of Lee as a "possession of the American people" and called the monument a "National possession." As far west as Minnesota, it was noted that the "Lee cult" was "in vogue." Not all Northerners shared the sentimental appreciation of the Lee cult. Frederick Douglass found that he could "scarcely take up a newspaper...that is not filled with nauseating flatteries of the late Robert E. Lee."

Few men in American history--perhaps, General George Armstrong Custer, General Douglas MacArthur, and General George S. Patton--can be so clearly defined by their military accomplishments as Robert E. Lee. Though by most accounts he was a loving and attentive husband and father, a family man with tiny feet who loved to have his children tickle them, that part of him pales in comparison to his demonstration of duty. Even as the leader of a failed cause, his sense of humility and selflessness gives him an extraordinarily unique and unparalleled place in American history.

As a soldier, Lee's strongest attribute was his natural ability to access a military situation and quickly devise an effective strategy. He excelled in his capacity to anticipate an opponent's moves and then outmaneuver them--often with inferior numbers and resources at his dispose. Never did he settle to meet the enemy on even tactical terms, and by most measure, he was unparalleled in American military history as a battlefield strategist.

Although field entrenchments had been used as a method of defense long before the founding of America, Lee refined this ancient science into a fine, fluid, and adaptive art--one that's studied today on university campuses across the land. He was a guerilla fighter with the mental agility of a ballerina; the optimal warrior in this place and time in American history when that was precisely what was called for. This, added to his power to arouse unparalleled devotion in his men, provided--quite handily--the South's greatest chance to end their war victoriously. Quite remarkable for a man who'd often remarked that all he really ever wanted to be was a farmer.

Still, Lee was far from perfect, despite the attempts of the Southern Historical Society to defend his war record as fault free, at the expense of some of his subordinates. Given that the Confederacy lost the war, some historians have pointed out that Lee was often too eager to engage in offensive warfare. After all, Lee scored large and smashing victories at places like Chancellorsville that deprived him of more manpower against opponents that could afford casualties more than he could. Moreover, for the engineer who used tactics to successfully defend against typical Civil War tactics, he all too often engaged in the same futile offensive tactics himself, none more costly than Pickett's Charge.

More objective analysts, including those among Lee's contemporaries like Longstreet and Porter Alexander, pointed out that despite these kinds of criticisms, it was Lee's daring tactics and successes that extended the Civil War so many years. Pointing out how many more casualties Lee's armies inflicted compared to those he lost, many of his subordinates compared him favorably to Napoleon, even if Lee never won the necessary complete victory.

One can only wonder what Lee would've accomplished with equal manpower and resources.

Much of what we know today about the Civil War comes from letters, government correspondences, and journal entries made by the soldiers involved, both Confederate and Union. Although Lee was never able to write memoirs, he was prolific letter writer, contributed abundantly to all three. Even in the heat of battle, it seems, his first impulse was to document his thoughts; express in words the complexities of his emotional state, mental reasoning, and assessment of the situation as he saw it. These correspondences provide invaluable insight not just into Lee the man, Lee the soldier, and Lee the husband and father, but insight into a period of American history which for the most part only received serious, unbiased reporting years after the fact.

Described by biographer Roy Blount, Jr. as "a sort of precursor-cross between England's Cary Grant and Virginia's Randolph Scott"--and perhaps the most beautiful person in America-- Robert E. Lee is perhaps the most written-about character of the Civil War era, next to President

Lincoln himself. Depicted as a handsome war hero, unifying national figure in the aftermath of a war-torn country, and a symbol of what is noble and just in the American spirit, Lee's image has evolved over time.

After Lee's death, former Maryland slave, writer, and statesman Frederick Douglass wrote, "[I]t would seem . . . that the soldier who kills the most men in battle--even in a bad cause--is the greatest Christian and entitled to the highest place in heaven." Some 37 years later on the eve of the Celebration of the Hundredth Anniversary of Lee's birth, President Theodore Roosevelt wrote, "[Lee] stood that hardest of all strains, the strain of bearing himself well through the gray evening of failure; and therefore out of what seemed failure he helped to build the wonderful and mighty triumph of our national life, in which all his countrymen, north and south, share." And now approaching a century and a half after his death, history has shown an iconic evolution from mere post-war personality to what biographer Thomas L. Connelly terms a man considered a "military genius and a spiritual leader, the nearest thing to a saint that the white South has possessed."

There can be no doubt that Lee's lasting legend is a combination of both fact and fiction; myth and understatement. As was common in 19th century America, heroes weren't always born--they were sometimes made. And it seems likely that what we now know of Lee was a carefully constructed conglomeration of both. In fact, immediately following his death, a group of Virginians led by general Jubal Early began a campaign to make Lee a national idol, a campaign that undoubtedly flavored 19th century biographies attempting to paint a fair yet colorful portrait of the iconic war hero. Immediately after the war, Grant was initially the most *popular* Civil War figure, but he was soon eclipsed.

As someone once astutely observed, 'Desperate times call for desperate measures,' and for many, America suffered no more desperate times than when brothers were called upon to take arms against bothers. And if survival of such an unnatural ordeal required the glorification--even exaggeration--of one who seemed to do it best, then we can hardly condemn those who may have sought to assure their success. But by any measure, Robert E. Lee was indeed an extraordinary individual who demonstrated through actions what we have come to define as the "American Spirit." In the face of unprecedented adversity, he repeatedly stood up, stepped forward, and sacrificed himself for the greater good. And that's why he holds the place in American history that he does.

Bibliography

Freeman, Douglas Southall. *R.E. Lee: A Biography*, 1934-5.

Blount, Jr., Roy. *Robert E. Lee*. New York: Penguin Books, 2003.

Connelly, Thomas L. *The Marble Man: Robert E. Lee and His Image in American Society*. New York: Alfred A. Knopf, 1977.

Dowdey, Clifford (editor). *The Wartime Papers of R. E. Lee*. New York: Bramhall House, 1961.

Fellman, Michael. *The Making of Robert E. Lee*. New York: Random House, 2000.

Flood, Charles. *Lee: The Last Years*. New York: Houghton, 1981.

Horn, Stanley F. (editor). *The Robert E. Lee Reader*. New York: Konecky & Konecky, 1949.

Nagel, Paul C. *The Lee's of Virginia*. New York: Oxford University Press, 1990.

Pryor, Elizabeth Brown (October 29, 2009). "Robert Edward Lee (ca. 1806-1870)," *Encyclopedia Virginia*. Retrieved March 11, 2012.

Thomas, Emory M. *Robert E. Lee: A Biography*. New York: W. W. Norton & Company, 1995.

Van Doren Stern, Philip. *Robert E. Lee: The Man and the Soldier*. New York: Bonanza Books, 1963.

George Patton
Chapter 1: Patton's Early Years

"By perseverance, study, and eternal desire, any man can become great". George S. Patton

George Patton was born into a comfortable background on November 11, 1885, the son of a wealthy family settled in California but with roots in both Virginia and New Mexico. Patton's father, George Smith Patton Sr., was a successful lawyer, District Attorney and then City Attorney for Pasadena, but he gave up his legal and nascent political careers however, in order to take over the struggling business affairs of his deceased brother-in-law. They moved from central Los Angeles to Lake Vineyard when George was still a young boy. The large estate had been built up by his frontiersman maternal grandfather, and the family holdings included a tannery, fruit plantations and a winery. Nevertheless, Patton's father struggled for the remainder of his professional life with the shambling business empire which he had inherited. Although the family remained wealthy, competition and several disastrous harvests were to lead to a steady decline and the sale of much of the land.

While his father struggled to try to get a grip on his new work, for young Georgie his surroundings provided a seemingly idyllic rural existence, with plenty of riding, fishing and other outdoor pursuits in which he excelled. He was a strong and healthy boy, quiet at times but with a stubborn determination which was to dominate his make-up. He adored his younger sister Anne ("Nita"), as well as his parents, particularly his father.

At school however, things were more problematic: Georgie struggled to read or write. Ruthlessly teased, and growing up in a society which did not yet understand dyslexia, he was often regarded as stupid. His parents stood solidly behind him, at times keeping him out of school and patiently working with him to improve on his literacy skills. Above all, both father and mother refused to acknowledge that their son was in any way slow and that his early difficulties should be allowed to hold him back in life. In turn he responded by deciding that what did not come naturally could nonetheless be developed through sheer hard work and grit; Patton, for all his reputation as America's "Blood and Guts" general, worked hard enough to evolve from dyslexic boy to prolific writer and sensitive poet.

Just as importantly, this first struggle revealed the strength of character which was to dominate his life. It was not long before he had absorbed his family's military history, which included a number of relatives that had fought for the Confederacy in the Civil War and had died in battles like Gettysburg, and his dad regaled him with tales about the legendary Confederate cavalryman John Mosby. It didn't take long for Patton to determine that it was his destiny to be a soldier.

Destiny was a central theme in Patton's life, and it was part of his psychology. In fact, he constantly sensed powerful intuitions and incidents of deja vu throughout his life, some of which made him believe in the idea of reincarnation. In 1918, arriving after dark at a new base in France, he imagined himself near a "theater", only to discover when he awoke the following day that his new camp was adjacent to a Roman amphitheater. He believed he had been there before, and he would write to his mother, "I wonder if I could have been here before as I drive up the Roman road the Theater seems familiar — perhaps I headed a legion up that same white road... I passed a chateau in ruins which I possibly helped escalade in the middle ages. There is no proof nor yet any denial. We were, we are, and we will be."

Patton's paternal grandfather had died on the battlefield the day he was promoted to Brigadier General in the Confederate Army. His grandmother had remarried, and his step-grandfather also had served the same cause with distinction. There were many others on his father's side. The Patton's were a distinguished Virginian family, awash with romantic military values which made a big impression on young George. Somehow, he never felt the same admiration for those on his mother's side. It was true that her brother-in-law had mismanaged the family business prior to his death, probably due to heavy drinking. It was also apparent that the life of a rough and self-made frontiersman (her father - Benjamin Wilson) lacked the sophisticated cachet of the

Virginian gentleman. There may even be a hint of racism in this attitude, as there was also Mexican blood on that side of the family. But for all that there was a lot of Wilson in young Georgie. It was surely from him that Patton inherited his courage and unquenchable energy.

Benjamin Wilson

Be that as it may, by the age of 10 Patton was keen to emulate his eastern forbears and become a noble warrior. This would become the root of his defining internal struggle, for he worried that he was not up to the task. He thought he might be a coward, or that "effeminate" interests such as poetry could hold him back. The result was a tension that manifested itself from a very early age in an iron-willed self discipline, a deliberately bullish demeanor and an ascetic lifestyle. Patton may not have all of the inherent attributes of the natural military leader, but nobody could work harder than him in developing them. He would win by force of will. His early battle with dyslexia and his parents' unstinting support in winning it was to be the making of the man.

1902 was a pivotal year for the 16 year old George Patton. He had resolved on a career as an army officer, and he sat down to discuss his options with his father. West Point was the place to be for anyone with Patton's ambitions. A small number of army officers were recruited from other academies but by far the majority of the annual intake was comprised of graduates of the famous Academy on the banks of the Hudson river. The question, therefore, was how to secure a place, because entry was effectively by patronage, and Patton therefore needed a sponsor. The likeliest bet, according to his father, was Senator Thomas Bard of California. Bard had nomination rights for one student and he made his selection on the basis of competitive examination. This was clearly a tall order for Patton, who by now could read and write but without the fluency expected at his age and not under exam conditions.

Still, Patton had more than a year to prepare, so his father proposed a two-pronged plan that would prove worthy of his more famous son. Patton's father suggested that he should attend the Virginia Military Institute (VMI) for a year. VMI, where Stonewall Jackson himself taught before the Civil War, had been his own alma mater and that of George's grandfather as well, meaning there would be little difficulty in securing a place.

Patton at the Virginia Military Institute

The year at VMI would accomplish several things, including building his maturity, his academic skills, and his understanding of the military life. Meanwhile his father would pull as many political strings as he could in California, lobbying Bard through every contact he could think of - and there were many. As a fallback, if the Bard idea misfired, George might still qualify for West Point from VMI or even secure appointment directly to the army as a junior officer. It A great deal of hard work would be required, but Patton's father knew he did not need to worry about his son in that regard.

That same summer marked another important turning point in his life. Staying as he always did on Catalina island for the family vacation, George met Beatrice Ayer, an elegant and attractive girl his age from a wealthy family in Massachusetts. Although very different in temperament and background, the two hit it off, and Beatrice became George's first "girlfriend." When Beatrice returned East, they began to correspond regularly, and though his continuing education and early career meant that they were often separated, "Bea" had seen something in young George Patton. She became his most loyal supporter, never wavering in her confidence in him. As maturity pulled Patton away from his parents, it was Bea who would become the rock to which he anchored as he continued with his internal turmoil. They would marry in 1910.

Perhaps not surprisingly, VMI proved to be a fantastic experience for Patton, who reveled in the military discipline, made many friends, and worked fiendishly hard at his studies. In early 1904 he travelled back to California to take Senator Bard's exam, and along with only two other candidates, Patton passed the exam and then endured an agonizing wait while Bard considered which of the three young men would receive his nomination. He ultimately chose Patton, based in no small part on the hard work that both he and his father had put into the project. They celebrated at his father's club with champagne.

West Point would be a more challenging environment than VMI, and it would require Patton's determination to see him through. He failed his first year due to his struggles with the academic component, particularly math. In other matters, including appearance, discipline, attitude and application, he was a model student. He was a fantastic swordsman and horseman; and he had a flair for shooting and tactics, so it was with some reluctance that his tutors slated him to repeat the first year. Bea and his parents were still unwavering in their support. It was therefore June 1909 before Second Lieutenant Patton graduated and was enrolled in the 15th US Cavalry, reporting for duty at Fort Sheridan, Illinois that September. Despite repeating his year as a "plebe", he had excelled in the end and even spent his final year as adjutant, thereby taking the parade as class leader.

By now Bea and George had an informal agreement to marry, but she remained in Boston while he plunged into his new job, quickly establishing a reputation for strict but fair discipline. At Fort Sheridan he once continued to drill his troopers even after having fallen from his horse and with blood streaming down his face (he would later explain his insistence on the importance of drilling in a letter during World War II, writing "A pint of sweat will save a gallon of blood."). On another occasion he apologized in public for having sworn at one of his men. The legend was building.

Beatrice and George were married at a big society event outside Boston in May 1910 and honeymooned in England before returning to officers' quarters at Fort Sheridan. Their first daughter (also named Beatrice), was born in March of the following year. The new father itched for promotion and influence, and by pulling any strings he could, Patton secured a staff job near Washington in December 1911. Once there the Pattons lived lavishly, with George engaging in horse racing, polo and a great deal of influential socializing.

In May of 1912 Patton was selected to represent his country in the first modern Olympic pentathlon, taking place in Stockholm. He came fifth, after a mix-up in the pistol shooting competition, where he finished 20th. Patton used a pistol with a larger caliber than other shooters, which left bigger holes in the target paper, and during the competition the judges ruled that he missed some shots while Patton insisted that the shots had actually gone straight through holes previously left in the paper by earlier shots. The judges wouldn't budge, but Patton was still magnanimous, stating, "The high spirit of sportsmanship and generosity manifested throughout speaks volumes for the character of the officers of the present day. There was not a single incident of a protest or any unsportsmanlike quibbling or fighting for points which I may say, marred some of the other civilian competitions at the Olympic Games. Each man did his best and took what fortune sent them like a true soldier, and at the end we all felt more like good friends and comrades than rivals in a severe competition, yet this spirit of friendship in no manner detracted from the zeal with which all strove for success."

More importantly for Patton's future career, he took the opportunity to travel to France. Beatrice spoke fluent French, and George took to the language and culture with his customary enthusiasm and dedication. It was not long before he could speak the language, and his affinity for the French would serve him well in years to come.

In France he paid for personal tuition at the celebrated French cavalry school at Saumer, where he learned under the tutelage of Adjutant Clery, one of Europe's leading swordsmen. During this time, Patton began to consider the use of the saber in U.S. cavalry regiments, and when he got back to the United States he wrote a paper advocating the French approach: the adoption of a straight saber and a new emphasis on attacking with the point, rather than the British or American slashing attack. Patton wrote in the paper, "In the Peninsula War the English nearly always used the sword for cutting. The French dragoons, on the contrary, used only the point which, with their long straight swords caused almost always a fatal wound. This made the English protest that the French did not fight fair. Marshal Saxe wished to arm the French cavalry with a blade of a triangular cross section so as to make the use of the point obligatory. At Wagram, when the cavalry of the guard passed in review before a charge, Napoleon called to them, "Don't cut! The point! The point!" The paper saw publication in the prestigious Army and Navy Journal, and in 1913 his design for a new weapon was taken up by the U.S. Army. It is not a little ironic that America's pioneer of tank warfare first made his name writing about and advocating for an already obsolete weapon system.

Notwithstanding this, he returned to Saumer (again at his own expense) for more tuition and was subsequently appointed Master of the Sword at the Mounted Service School. In this he was both tutor and student, spending two years on the prestigious cavalry course, and during this period Patton wrote regulations for the use of his new saber, as well as further articles on military affairs.

Of course, Patton had always wanted to be a soldier, and a soldier's place was on the battlefield. While studying doctrine and even writing it interested him, he craved real action. In February 1914 the United States occupied Vera Cruz on the Mexican coast, and Patton hoped that war with Mexico would ensue, but war would actually start across the Atlantic. In August Europe plunged into global conflict, and Patton seriously considered resigning from the army and volunteering for the French cavalry. Beatrice kept him in check - they now had a second daughter (Ruth, born in 1915) and he had a career to pursue - but Patton would not be kept on the sidelines for much longer.

Chapter 2: A Taste for Command

"Do everything you ask of those you command." - George S. Patton

Patton's chance came with the deteriorating security situation along the Texas-Mexican border. Brigadier General John Pershing was about to establish his cavalry brigade at Fort Bliss in response to the crisis, and Patton secured a posting to a regiment in the new command.

Pershing

With his regimental commander tending to indolence, Patton had the freedom to lead his own patrols into the wild country along the border. He enjoyed the rough-hewn settlers that he met and the fine opportunities for hunting, but he still had no military action. Matters were to evolve quickly however, and fate took a hand in placing Patton in the right place at the right time.

Days after his transfer to Bliss, Pershing suffered an appalling family tragedy when a catastrophic fire at his home had killed his wife and three children. A strong man, he immersed himself in his new job and settled down to build a brigade capable of securing northern Mexico should the circumstances require it. Patton, meanwhile, hosted an extended stay at the fort by Beatrice and the children, together with his sister Nita. Nita and Pershing became close.

When Pancho Villa turned against the U.S. by massacring civilians in early March 1916, Pershing was ordered to cross the border and strike south. He would leave one regiment to garrison the fort: Patton's. Patton was distraught, but he played his cards well, having already befriended Pershing and made it very clear that he was hungry for action. Aware also of the general's fondness for his sister, he volunteered to serve as an aide on his staff. Pershing accepted, and Patton rode south with the expeditionary force.

He was tireless in his new role, anticipating Pershing's every need and always on hand. The cavalry moved forward in what was potentially a sensitive political situation and a frustrating military one. Patton's role was centered on Pershing's headquarters but he found the opportunity to get out of camp whenever he could. By May however, Pershing had failed to trap Villa's elusive guerillas, even though he now had a divisional sized force and had penetrated hundreds of miles into Mexican territory. Making matters worse was the weather, with frequent storms blowing down tents and creating flash floods.

On May 14th, Patton was tasked with leading a small expedition in three Dodge touring cars to purchase supplies from nearby settlements. Extending their remit, Patton decided to investigate reports that one of Villa's commanders (Cardenas) was hiding in a local hacienda at San Miguelito. The cars approached the walled farm and Patton gave orders for an encirclement on foot. As this was underway, several guerillas broke cover attempting to escape on horseback and a firefight ensued, during which all of the Mexicans were killed. Patton himself had shot at least one soldier and the dead included Cardenas. Always with an eye on showmanship, Patton had the corpses latched on to the bonnets of the Dodges and drove proudly back to the camp. Indeed, the American media loved it; the New York Times carried the story prominently and Pershing was delighted. Within weeks he was promoted to First Lieutenant, though in fairness it should be noted that he had already worked hard to pass the promotion examination while he was still at Fort Bliss.

Patton had tasted action for the first time, and in doing so he had led the first American motorized attack in history. This was to be the highlight of his time in Mexico. Pressed by his wife on what it was like to be involved in combat and in particular to kill, he was blasé. He had, it seemed, found his calling in more ways than one.

Eventually Pershing's expedition began petering out, and Patton involved himself briefly in his father's unsuccessful candidacy for the U.S. Senate before being incapacitated with serious face burns following a blaze in his tent. Pershing was eventually recalled to the United States and Patton returned to normal duties at Fort Bliss, but he was again longing for action. It seemed that events in Europe would pass him by until April 1917, the United States entered World War I on the side of the Triple Entente. Pershing, the hero of the hour, was tasked with assembling an expeditionary force. Still involved with Nita and admiring of Patton's dash and expertise, it was no surprise that he selected Patton to join his advance party, which sailed for France on May 17th, 1917.

Beatrice wisely remained in Massachusetts with her young family, although for many months Patton would urge her to find a means of joining him in Europe. They were based at Chaumont, on the Lorraine front, busy with the huge organizational task of scaling up the expeditionary force from divisional to army strength. The war was tantalizingly close, and Patton sought Pershing's advice on how best to get into action. Eventually he applied to work with the Tank Corps, a new formation which was to be set up in France on the back of French and British success with the new weapon.

It was a brave and decisive move. Patton knew about engines and mobile warfare, and he was deeply interested in the evolution of his craft. He also had direct and recent combat experience, which made him eminently qualified (at least among Americans), yet he remained unsure as to whether this would be the right choice. An infantry posting would guarantee him immediate combat on the front line, and with it the chance for promotion. So it was with mixed emotions that he learned he was to head America's first tank training center at Langres; with it came promotion to Major. His immediate commander was Colonel Samuel Rockenbach.

Rockenbach and Patton began on a tricky footing but soon learned that their differing skills could complement one another. Rockenbach had overall charge of the nascent American tank force while Patton built the training school in France. Rockenbach was a skilled staff man, politically astute and ideally placed to negotiate with the British and French for supplies of the scarce tanks. American tank production had barely commenced, so the U.S. needed to rely on her allies.

Two different approaches to tank warfare were already beginning to emerge: the British had invested in heavy machines with large crews, whereas the French Renault tanks were smaller and lighter, carrying only two men. The Americans bought both types, but it would be the Renaults which were delivered first and thus would be the tanks with which the new Tank Corps would train and undertake their first attack. Meanwhile, in November the British used mass tanks at Cambrai, securing a 5 mile breakthrough and demonstrating the potential of the new weapon system. Patton had made the right choice. He had not only switched from yesterday's arm of service - the cavalry - into that of the future, but he had secured his promotion as well. A firm believer in his own destiny, fortune seemed to be smiling on him now.

Shrewdly, Patton advocated the tank as an elite supporting arm, contending that its role was to supplement the infantryman rather than replace him. This stance recognized the limitations of the technology at the time but also the prevailing army politics: there was a lot of hostility and suspicion towards the new arm. Even before the arrival of his new tanks, he set about building a well motivated and highly competent force by traditional means through strict but fair discipline, extensive training, and drilling. Emulating Pershing and building on his growing reputation, he would strut around exuding and inculcating confidence. Patton's ability to motivate the fighting man was at least as important as his strategic insight and was to serve his country well on numerous occasions. Even at the training college he led from the front, personally reversing the first of the Renaults off their railway wagons, though that was also a byproduct of the fact that he was one of the few soldiers present actually able to drive one.

Patton in France, 1918

By the end of April 1918 Patton had sufficient men to assemble his first battalion, and in August he secured 25 French tanks with which to equip them. It could not be long now before his force was deployed on the front; but he worried that the war would end too soon. Bea's parents had both died within weeks of one another earlier in the Spring and he regretted that he could not be by her side, but he was working characteristically hard in addition to establishing and running America's first tank training school, he attended the General Staff College in Langres to keep his broader skills up to date and to ensure that he remained visible where it counted.

By September they were ready to go, and when the American 1st Army would attack the St. Mihiel salient, Patton's tanks were to have the chance to prove themselves. He had been promoted to Lieutenant Colonel and now had his own brigade, with two battalions of American-manned tanks and one of French under his command. Patton was in charge of a total of nearly 150 of the tiny Renaults.

The attack went in on the 12th and lasted for two days, during which Patton was everywhere, mostly working on foot but on one notable occasion actually riding on the back of one of his tanks as he urged his men forward. He had decided that he needed to be right at the front with the actual vehicles, an approach that provided inspiration and took great courage but at the expense of command control over such a widely spread force. Notwithstanding this, Patton's battalions fought well, often ahead of the infantry or even advancing when the infantry remained pinned down.

For his part Patton learned a huge amount at St. Mihiel about the need for lavish oil reserves, about the vulnerability of those early tanks to rough terrain, and above all the need to maintain momentum. Patton's troops also learned a lot about him; he would share all of their risks and more, but he would not tolerate any slacking. The performance of the corps again attracted media attention and inevitably, Patton's ride on the back of a tank went down in military folklore. Here was a colorful, slightly eccentric leader who achieved results, just the kind of individual the American public wanted to hear about.

Two weeks later Patton's unit attacked again, this time at Cheppy, near Verdun. But this time Patton's luck ran out. Towards the end of the morning he was leading a team of six men on foot, liaising with and urging forward the tanks. If a tank was stationary and he didn't like it he would rap on the back of the turret with his walking stick and remonstrate with the surprised commander. But there were bullets flying everywhere, and Patton and his team had no protection. One by one they were hit until it was just Patton and his orderly moving between the vehicles. He took a bullet in the thigh and went down, bleeding heavily. When later asked by someone how he maintained his calmness under fire, Patton responded, "I had the same experience every day which is for the first half-hour the palms of my hands sweat and I feel depressed. Then, if one hits near you, it seems to break the spell and you don't notice them anymore. Going back in the evening over the same ground and at a time when the shelling and bombing are usually heavier, you become so used to it you never think about it." In this case, the orderly, Joe Angelo, bound the wound and saved Patton's life. Patton would never forget it, and he took the trouble to visit Angelo in his hometown after the war.

The armistice that ended the Great War took effect on November 11, 1918, Patton's 33rd birthday. Deeply superstitious as always, he saw this as a good omen. Still recovering from his wound at Cheppy, Patton received the Distinguished Service Cross for his bravery, and he was also awarded the Distinguished Service Medal for his establishment and leadership of the Tank Training School. Promoted again to full Colonel in October, it was clear that Patton had a "good" war. But how would he handle peace?

Chapter 3: Planning for the Next One

"There is only one kind of discipline, perfect discipline." George S. Patton

In the immediate aftermath of the war, Patton and his brigade remained in France pending shipment back to the U.S., but he was far from idle. He immersed himself in the problems and opportunities for tank warfare, from the bottom to the top. It was obvious that command control needed improvement, and Patton was the first to install radios that would function in a moving tank. He concluded that there was a huge potential for independent tank-based formations, something theorists such as Liddle-Hart and Guderian would envision over the coming decades, but the environment in the U.S was hardly receptive to ambitious military thinking at a time when history's deadliest war had just ended.

Moving back with his men in mid 1919, he was on the East Coast in time for the debates surrounding what became the National Defense Act of 1920, which shrunk the army radically. The League of Nations promised peace, and America was in no mood for further large scale adventures abroad. Worst of all for him, the Act abolished the infant Tank Corps, subsuming it within the infantry, which he knew would lead to a support-only role for tanks, a hugely limiting approach given the potential of more modern designs. This was to be the same mistake made by both the British and the French, who would be punished so brutally by Hitler's panzer divisions in 1940, but at this time Patton was powerless to stop it.

Agonizing over his future and that of the Army, Patton decided to rejoin the cavalry. If, as he suspected, war was coming with Mexico, then there would still be ample scope for a mounted arm in that inhospitable border terrain that he knew so well. Besides, he loved horses and all sport associated with them, racing occasionally and still playing polo. This fast paced team game, leavened with a dose of danger, was considered ideal by Patton for military leaders.

In fact, it may have been polo that had caused a marked change in his personality. Over the years he had suffered from many blows to the head, including kicks and falls, and during these years his moods became extremely mercurial, swinging from anger or depression to joyfulness or sadness in minutes. Modern writers have speculated that he may have had an undiagnosed subdural hematoma, but either way he was not an easy man to live with.

Resigned to a life in a cavalry outfit, Patton continued to study and write. He was briefly a Captain again (his substantive pre-war rank) before being promoted to major and given command of a battalion at Fort Myer, outside Washington D.C. In early 1923 he attended the Field Officers' course at Fort Riley, where his grades were excellent, a sure sign that Patton had by now conquered the dyslexia which had been such an encumbrance during his early years. Then there was the Command and General Staff College at Fort Leavenworth, Kansas, where Patton was determined to get on even in the shrunken peacetime army years. He passed as an Honor Graduate and was rewarded with a staff posting near Boston. At the end of 1923 his son (George Patton IV) was born.

After Boston, Patton was then posted to the Hawaiian Islands as head of intelligence and personnel, which was much more to his liking. Although he would have preferred command of a combat unit, in Hawaii he enjoyed the polo, fishing and company of the wealthy elite. It suited his temperament at this stage of his life, but he also took to drinking, and there were other women as well.

In 1927 Patton's father died, leaving him distraught but unable to travel back to California in time for the funeral. He made his own pilgrimage to the grave site and wrote an extended homage in the form of a letter to his departed dad. The following year his mother died too. Patton was now 43, entering middle age and less sure of himself and his future. His wife and children were thousands of miles away, his parents were dead, and his sister Nita lived the life of a spinster. For her, the relationship with Pershing had not worked out, and she would live the rest of her life alone. She would never be poor though, for George insisted that she retain all of their parents' wealth by signing over his own inheritance.

Patton's abrasive style and mood swings ultimately cost him professionally when he was relieved of the planning brief in Hawaii following impolitic criticism of senior officers. The dispirited Patton welcomed the chance to return to the mainland in 1928, this time to cavalry headquarters near Washington, but once there he became embroiled in debates over the future of the horse. Patton's head told him that the cavalry's days were numbered, but his heart and fondness for horses said otherwise, and there was also the fact that he was now a cavalry officer. Given he was a senior cavalry officer, he needed to use uncharacteristic discretion in voicing opinion over the future of the tank and armored car.

During the 1920s Patton became close to another man who would become a hero during World War II: Dwight D. Eisenhower. Eisenhower himself was now a rising star and a huge admirer of Patton's, having borrowed his course notes for the General Staff College, which helped him finish first in class. Like Patton, Eisenhower had yearned to see combat, but his initial appeals for an assignment overseas at the height of World War I were denied, and instead he remained in the infantry at home, moving to various bases in the United States. Stuck stateside, he gradually rose in rank while gaining experience with tanks, a novelty piece of military equipment at the time. Incredibly, Ike would not see combat until he was a commander during World War II. While Patton was actually leading tanks on the front, Eisenhower was at home training other members in the use of tanks, which he had mastered, and he trained young men in tank warfare in places like Texas, Georgia, and most famously at Gettysburg, Pennsylvania, where the camp was situated on the spot where Pickett's Charge had taken place over 50 years earlier.

Eisenhower

Meanwhile, Beatrice had been lobbying her constantly moving husband for a permanent home and significant independent means of her own, and she eventually bought a large estate at Green Meadows in Massachusetts. For Patton, life settled down into the routine of peace time staff work, the whirl of Washington socializing, and the challenge of the polo field. He kept himself robustly fit, beginning already to worry about his age.

In 1931 he attended college for the last time: the Army War College, its most prestigious establishment. Again he excelled, and the following year he was back at Fort Myer, this time as Executive Officer of the Third Cavalry regiment. The country was in the grip of an economic recession and army pensioners marched on Washington. It became ugly, and Patton's cavalry outfit was deployed on the streets. Although order was quickly restored, it left him with a bitter taste in his mouth; he loathed having to take action against former comrades from World War I.

Shortly afterward he was promoted to Lieutenant Colonel, now only one rank off what he had achieved during the war. The routine at the cavalry regiment continued much as before, with Patton watching events unfold in Europe and wondering whether the U.S. would become involved.

1935 brought another posting to Hawaii, and he was glad to go. This time he took his family, sailing them over from California on the family yacht, but once again he slipped into a wild lifestyle, with a series of affairs and heavy drinking in the company of the wealthier sections of Hawaiian society. It was during this period that he began an affair with his niece, Jean Gordon, the daughter of Beatrice's older sister. The two spent several days together, ostensibly buying horses for the army, but it proved to be a strong relationship that would be marred by tragedy. All of this was, of course, painful for Bea and difficult for the rest of the family. She was relieved when in 1937 they were transferred back to Massachusetts.

While resting and residing at Green Meadows, Patton took a savage kick from one of his horses that broke his leg in three places, after which he contracted phlebitis, which was life threatening. Off duty for six months, he was dismayed to be judged fit for "limited service" only. With war clouds now gathering in Europe, once again it seemed that Patton would likely miss any action. Instead he was posted to Fort Myers on staff duty, narrowly missing a cavalry command in Texas. Emotional as ever, Patton broke down in tears. His recent promotion to full Colonel was no consolation 52 years old and unfit for active service, it seemed his dreams of greatness were now behind him.

This time, it would be the enemy that proved the necessity for Patton's services and his method of warfare. The catastrophic Battle of France in 1940, following the Nazi blitzkrieg through Poland the year before, finally convinced American military planners of the need for armored divisions. Although they had plenty of tanks, most of them superior to those used by Hitler's Wehrmacht, the British and French had been defeated largely because they had failed to concentrate them in specialist divisions. If the United States were to enter the war, they at least had the time to remedy this shortcoming, and of all the senior officers in the U.S. Army, none knew more about the tank and its development than Patton. An armored corps was to be built, consisting of two full divisions, under General Chaffee, and Patton was offered command of a brigade of the newly formed 2nd Armored Division based at Fort Benning, Georgia.

Given the chance to build a new tank unit again from scratch, Patton was once more in his element. Not long after his arrival, Chaffee (who was ill with cancer) switched roles and Patton moved up to take command of the full division. Importantly he was now a general, receiving his first star that year. As with World War I, he determined to build an elite unit and to lead it personally in combat. If war came, and he believed it would, he would be able to prove the ideas he had been contemplating since those wild days with the clanking Renault tanks of 20 years before. It looked as if Patton's time had finally come.

Patton threw himself into this initial task with characteristic energy, eccentricity and flair. He had his own specially painted tank, and his staff car mounted huge klaxons, which he was fond of using. His young troopers need never have any doubt about who the commanding general was and whether he was in the vicinity. He told his men that the tank division was the most powerful organization so far devised by man, but he also impressed upon them the need for speed, maneuverability, and discipline.

Patton also happened to believe what he was telling his men, and he characteristically played the part, strutting around with his trademark ivory handled pistols and reveling in his maverick image. His men may not have realized it was mostly an act, and that it was a façade behind which lay a once shy boy who had been teased at school and worried about being considered a coward, but in any case it worked. Patton was also constantly thinking of new tactics and went so far as to buy his own plane, single-handedly inventing the art of command by radio from the air, a concept that is now taken for granted by modern armies around the world. His men worshipped him and began to believe in themselves. An elite unit had been built by Patton's force of personality.

The proof came with a series of exercises during 1941. These were competitively scored, and the 2nd Armored excelled time after time, usually beating their sister division the 1st Armored. When war finally came in December that year, it quickly became apparent that the armored corps would be one of the first deployed, and Patton was made Major General and given command of the entire corps.

It sounded like a crucial step toward combat, except Patton's command left him tasked with establishing a desert training facility for armored warfare. In early 1942, when President Roosevelt was debating where to put American forces, the Allies, which now included the Soviet Union by necessity, did not agree on the war strategy. The Germans and British were fighting in North Africa, and the British lobbied for American help in North Africa, where British General Montgomery was fighting the legendary "Desert Fox," General Erwin Rommel. At the same time, Soviet premier Josef Stalin vehemently argued for the Allies to open up another front in Europe that would help the Soviets, who were facing the brunt of the Nazi war machine in Russia. President Roosevelt ultimately sided with the British and sent American troops to North Africa, so they could help the British oppose Rommel. While this left Russia to handle the Nazis on the European continent singlehandedly, it placed a brand new army to the west of Rommel, ultimately threatening his rear.

Patton, however, was understandably nervous that his corps would participate in the fighting while he sat in the desert training the next generation of tankers. Always dutiful though, Patton scouted a suitable swathe of land in the far west and built the camp in weeks. His armored divisions were the first to use the site, learning the peculiarities of high tempo operations in desert terrain. And then things began to fall into place. The British were struggling against the Axis in North Africa, and Patton's advice was sought on the feasibility of reinforcing them directly when it was finally decided to merely send tanks across, which would assist the British much quicker than fully equipped divisions of infantry. Thus, in August 1942, he was instructed to plan for an autumn invasion of French North Africa. Patton's armored corps would be the first American combat troops to enter the Western Theater.

Chapter 4: Imperfect Hero

"May God have mercy upon my enemies, because I won't." George S. Patton

The huge naval convoy crawled through the night, lights doused, heading for the African coast. Over 100 ships in all, led by the flagship USS *Augusta*, approached Morocco to deposit Patton's 1st Armored Corps on the beaches in three places. Their mission was to secure the country as quickly as possible at minimal loss. Facing them were 100,000 French and colonial troops, who might or might not fight. Further north other American and British forces would attack Algeria. Patton would have the toughest fight; he liked it that way.

On the early morning of November 8, 1942, the Americans went in over the beaches and to the north they attacked at Mehdia, anxious to secure the only concrete landing strip in the country so that Allied fighters could stream in from Gibraltar and the nearby naval carriers. In the center they landed at Fedala, only 15 miles from the main target at Casablanca. The southern assault was at Safi, 150 miles south. Patton paced nervously in his cabin onboard the *Augusta*, anxious to join his troops as soon as he could. The French had let rip with every gun they had as soon as the Americans approached the beach, signaling that this would be a real fight.

As Patton prepared to clamber aboard a landing craft later that morning, the *Augusta* was hit by the opening salvo from the Vichy French Navy, which had sortied in a brave death ride against the overwhelming force of the U.S. Navy. Patton was more frustrated than frightened, but since he was unable to intervene, he merely sat back and watched a naval battle from the front row.

When he did eventually get ashore, he was not happy with what he found, even though the combat troops had cleared the beach and were already advancing towards Casablanca. Heavy equipment was still at sea, supplies were disorganized and a competent counterattack would likely find the Americans off-balance. True to form, he strode along the beach, barking instructions, literally lending a hand when required, instilling order and hustle. Immediately, he contacted the navy and browbeat them into bringing their ships closer in so that the offloading process could be speeded along.

The fighting in Morocco, as well as the fighting to the north in Algeria, did not persist. Patton's rapidly maneuvering and highly trained units plunged inland at all three landing points. The city of Casablanca was surrounded and a dawn assault prepared. Told that the French had stopped firing, Patton refused to cancel the attack until they formally acknowledged a ceasefire. The following morning he met the French commanders. The situation was politically difficult, because Patton's instructions were to disarm the French should they show any resistance, which they had, but he also needed these same people to maintain order and governance so that he could set up training and logistics facilities in support of the strategic advance to the north and east. He did not want to use his corps as a governing body or police presence in a French colony while the other Allies dealt with the Desert Fox.

Conducting the entire meeting in fluent French, Patton deftly put forward a compromise of his own devising. The French would retain their weapons, but for a time they would remain confined to barracks. National sensitivities were protected, and he cracked open the champagne with his new allies. Though he has long been easily caricatured as a bull in a china shop, this episode underlined Patton's sensitive political skills, as well as the value of his Francophile sympathies.

British and American troops in Algeria encountered similarly short-lived opposition, and within a week the French were governing their colonies, leaving the Allies to concentrate on the thrust into Tunisia, where two Axis armies awaited them. But for the time being at least, Patton's fighting was done. While his rival General Mark Clark was given his third star, much to his chagrin, Patton was left with rear area duties, and his 1st Armored division was switched to the Tunisian front. The Americans in that sector, organized as II Corps led by Fredenhall, were operating under British command, something Patton resented and which would fuel future tensions. Their baptism against German opposition would not be long in coming.

General Lloyd Fredenhall

Meanwhile, Patton organized the reception and training of new formations and acted as the host of the Casablanca conference for Allied leaders in January 1944. These duties were likely tiresome to him, but he still handled them well and again exhibited sophisticated diplomatic skills in building a rapport with the Arab leaders in Morocco. He was feted as a conquering hero, something which perhaps sweetened the pill of not being where the real fighting was now taking place. Restless, he nonetheless visited the front on the pretext of a fact-finding mission. He was not impressed with morale or discipline, and noted that the soldiers had not seen a general for a month.

Fredenhall's corps and the U.S. Army as a whole received a mighty wakeup call in mid-February 1943 when Rommel gave them a severe mauling at Kasserine Pass. Germany's supreme exponent of fast armored action, with better tanks and highly seasoned infantry, proved more than a match for Fredenhall, but fortunately for the Allies he did not have sufficient numbers to break through. After nearly two weeks of bitter fighting, Rommel pulled back to his fortified line opposite the British Eighth Army. Nevertheless, Kasserine was a profound shock for the Americans, who had been soundly beaten in their first encounter with the Germans and their Desert Fox.

Rommel

For Patton this was frustrating, and it vindicated the views he had formed privately during his whistle-stop tour of the front. Luckily Eisenhower had reached a similar conclusion. 1942 started much like the previous 25 years for Ike, who was consigned to a staff job conducting military planning far away from the battlefield. Eisenhower shuffled through a handful of administrative jobs in that year, including serving on the General Staff in Washington, where he was tasked with creating war plans to topple the Axis in the Pacific and Europe. Later, he was made Deputy Chief in charge of Pacific Defenses under the Chief of War Plans Division, and then he became Chief of the War Plans Division himself.

It would fall on George Marshall to pull Eisenhower out of the staff jobs. After Eisenhower was made Assistant Chief of Staff and put in charge of the new Operations Division (which replaced the War Plans Division), he was once again a subordinate of Chief of Staff General Marshall, who had already taken notice of Eisenhower just recently and now did so again. In May 1942, Eisenhower traveled to London to assess Major General James E. Chaney, who at the time was the commanding general in the European Theater of Operations. When Eisenhower returned to the U.S. a month later and reported back negatively about Chaney, it caught the attention of the military brass, who already knew Eisenhower had a strong reputation for assessing military talent. Thus, that same month, Eisenhower was sent back to London to replace

Chaney himself, becoming Commanding General of the European Theater of Operations. Though he retained his title as Commanding General in the European Theater, Eisenhower was also chosen to head the American forces in the North African as Supreme Commander Allied Force of the North African Theater of Operations.

As a result, it was Eisenhower who was in position to make the command decisions in North Africa in 1943, and it was fortuitous for the man who had earned Ike's respect over 15 years earlier. On March 4th Patton was given command of the shaken II Corps, flying north to Algiers the following day. Astonishingly, Fredenhall was promoted and received a new posting back in the U.S., but Patton was more than happy with the new nature of things. In a letter to Eisenhower in late 1942, he had written, "Of all the many talks I had in Washington, none gave me such pleasure as that with you. There were two reasons for this. In the first place, you are about my oldest friend. In the second place, your self-assurance and to me, at least, demonstrated ability, give me a great feeling of confidence about the future ... and I have the utmost confidence that through your efforts we will eventually beat the hell out of those bastards — 'You name them; I'll shoot them!'" To that, Ike replied, "I don't have the slightest trouble naming the hellions I'd like to have you shoot; my problem is to figure out some way of getting you to the place you can do it."

Patton's task that March was daunting indeed. Alexander, the British commander, planned a major offensive in ten days' time, with Patton's corps to advance north and protect the Allied left flank. This left him less than two weeks to rebuild their shattered morale. Training and motivation were at the heart of Patton's leadership, arguably his greatest talent, and back in 1918 he had been awarded a medal for his work in forging America's first armored combat units. In Georgia only two years earlier he had built the 2nd Armored Division from scratch, following the sudden conversion of the Army to the armored concept. Now he brought all of that experience to bear. The tools were familiar: showmanship, attention to detail, supreme self-confidence and firm discipline. By the time the offensive kicked off in mid-March, they were a different organization altogether. For his efforts, Patton was promoted to Lieutenant General, his third star.

The fighting was not easy, and Patton resented his subordinate position. Alexander issued careful instructions which made it clear that his was a screening role - he was not to swing eastwards into the Axis flank, as he advocated. It is easy to criticize Alexander for this in light of Patton's subsequent achievements, but at the time he did not know Patton well and he had also seen the performance of the same Corps at Kasserine only weeks earlier. His was an understandably cautious approach.

General Harold Alexander

Patton's divisions performed admirably at Gafsa and Maknassy in what became known as the battle of El Guettar, but he was not entirely satisfied himself and had spent much of the battle chivvying from the front, on one occasion driving into a minefield with his command column in an effort to inspire what he saw as a tardy advance. It was workmanlike, if sedate. This time the units held together and beat off a serious counterattack by two Axis armored divisions, but what they did not do, largely due to Alexander's caution, is cut off any significant Italian or German formations. The battle is also remembered for one of Patton's more famous outbursts. Critical of the lack of close air support from the British, whom he blamed for the death of an aide in a German airstrike, he attended a meeting with senior RAF commanders. When the Luftwaffe bombed the meeting he felt his point had been made, claiming that he would send a medal to each of the "sons of bitches who flew those planes".

The campaign ended in May with over 230,000 Italian and German troops captured by the Allies. Often neglected by historians, this represented a defeat of Stalingrad proportions for the Axis. At the same time, it demonstrated some of the issues of joint command between the British and Americans. Although the operation was ultimately successful, Eisenhower suffered fits and starts dealing with battlefield command, often miscommunicating commands and causing confusion. It was also the first time the Americans had to collaborate with General Bernard Montgomery, who had won the decisive battle on the continent at El Alamein and bristled about being the subordinate of Eisenhower, who he rightly viewed to be a far less experienced commander. Nevertheless, the Desert Fox eventually quit the theater, ceding North Africa to the Allies, and Eisenhower's star was rising, literally. After his success in North Africa, he was awarded a fourth star.

General Montgomery

With Italy and Germany both having been defeated in North Africa, the Allied troops there were now free to be used in an invasion of Europe. In addition, North Africa provided the Allies a potential staging ground for an invasion of the southern part of the continent, while an invasion force from Britain could threaten from the west. Hitler now had to worry about the Allies invading not only from Britain but also from North Africa. The German army suffered a massive blow in February 1943 at Stalingrad, where a major surrender of troops marked the beginning of the end for Hitler's armies in Russia. Still, it would take another two years for the Red Army to gradually push the Nazis west out of Russia and back toward Berlin. Stalin still desperately needed Allied action on another front.

The British and Americans debated over their next course of action, with the British favoring an invasion of Sicily over the skepticism of the Americans, who believed the operation was overly ambitious and not a direct enough strike against Hitler's Germany. Eventually the British won out by arguing that invading and controlling Sicily would give the Allies a free hand across the Mediterranean Sea, facilitating both commerce and transportation. Patton, who had saved the reputation of the US Army in Africa, would now have an army of his own. Since the invasion would be made by the 7th U.S. Army (led by Patton) and the British 8th Army (led by

Montgomery), the soldiers in the North African theater, the operation fell under the overall command of Eisenhower.

In July 1943, less than half a year after the surrender at Stalingrad, the Allies conducted what at the time was the largest amphibious invasion in history, coordinating the landing of two whole armies on Sicily over a front more than 100 miles long. The plan called for Patton's newly formed Seventh Army to put 90,000 troops ashore in the first wave and build up to 200,000 over the following weeks. The plan was again a British one, with Montgomery the main architect and his own British Eighth Army attacking towards Catania and Messina on Patton's right. Messina was the key. It controlled the narrow straits across to mainland Italy, and once controlled by the Allies it would trap any remaining Axis forces on the island. The Axis had determined to make a serious effort to hold on; for Mussolini this was Italian soil, hugely symbolic for his crumbling regime. For Hitler it was important to support his ally but also an opportunity to bleed the large Allied armies in this rugged terrain, which favored the defense.

Patton was again unhappy with his allotted role. The Seventh Army was essentially supposed to screen the British flank while they advanced northeast toward Messina, which to Patton represented reprising the same previous role at El Guettar (albeit on a larger scale). He would have preferred a separate landing on the north coast, but Montgomery had insisted on adjacent landings on the south coast for fear of being defeated in detail. Again one can understand British caution here. The U.S. Army remained inexperienced, and the Eighth Army had beaten the Axis in Africa but in so doing became well aware of their tenacity. The British were also by now desperately short of men and could not afford any costly defeats. Patton's plan may have worked, but it would have been far riskier.

Patton was in his typical form before the invasion, exhorting his men, "When we land against the enemy, don't forget to hit him and hit him hard. When we meet the enemy we will kill him. We will show him no mercy. He has killed thousands of your comrades and he must die. If you company officers in leading your men against the enemy find him shooting at you and when you get within two hundred yards of him he wishes to surrender – oh no! That bastard will die! You will kill him. Stick him between the third and fourth ribs. You will tell your men that. They must have the killer instinct. Tell them to stick him. Stick him in the liver. We will get the name of killers and killers are immortal. When word reaches him that he is being faced by a killer battalion he will fight less. We must build up that name as killers."

The amphibious landings went smoothly enough for both armies, although the supporting airborne troops were largely scattered. The Americans had the worst of it, largely due to rough weather conditions. Landing at Gela on the morning of July 10th, Patton walked straight in to a serious German counterattack against his bridgehead. Taking personal command, he directed mortar fire, strolled around in full view of the enemy and remained on the front line until the crisis was past.

From there his divisions swung inland, encountering strong resistance from crack German units such as the 15th Panzer-grenadier division. Meanwhile, the British soon stalled, squeezed into the narrow corridor between Mount Etna and the sea. Montgomery wanted to lunge left and persuaded Eisenhower to reallocate a key road to his command in order to facilitate the move, which infuriated Patton. Not only were the British failing at their own plan but now his 45th Division would have no logistical network. Boldly, he switched the division across his front and built a scratch corps to advance northwest toward Palermo, an advance that would directly contradict Montgomery's plan, which called for American forces to stick closely to the British flank. Patton passed the move off as a probe, secured General Alexander's support, and by July 22 captured Palermo after a brilliant two-pronged advance to the northern coast.

Patton was now in a position to swing right along the northern coast toward Messina while the British slowly slugged their way up the eastern coast, but now progress for the Americans was slowed as well. They encountered a series of well-prepared and skillfully defended German and Italian positions, but Patton was itching to beat Montgomery to Messina. Pestering the Navy for amphibious assets, they reluctantly released enough landing craft to move a reinforced battalion. It was small, but it would be sufficient. On August 8th and 11th, the Americans made two risky "end runs" - shuttling a battalion forward by sea and around the Axis flank. On the 11th matters escalated out of control, and the battalion came close to being annihilated before Patton's relieving heavy units could arrive. He barely got away with it, and in the process he had thoroughly discomforted Omar Bradley, who in 1943 was serving as his corps commander. Bradley had opposed the concept and his perception of Patton as unduly rash would color his attitude later in the war.

Bradley

Messina fell to Patton's troops on August 16, and forward British elements arrived in the city hours later from the south, becoming the first to congratulate the Americans on their feat of arms. The invasion of Sicily had been hard fought, and most of the major Axis formations slipped away across the straits. Notwithstanding this, the Seventh Army had suffered only 7,000 casualties - less than the cautious British - and had captured over 200,000 enemy troops. For Patton it was a personal triumph, but it would be short-lived.

On August 20, Patton received a letter from General Eisenhower informing him that his conduct with respect to two of his soldiers was unacceptable and that he must apologize. It was a humiliating blow, but it could have been much worse, since Eisenhower had been under pressure to level formal charges and prosecute Patton, which would have ended his career. Earlier in the month, on two separate occasions, he had slapped soldiers who claimed to be suffering from combat fatigue. This happened in front of other soldiers in military hospitals and in one instance a doctor had interposed himself between the patient and the general, who had threatened more violence. Patton had slapped Charles Kuhl after Kuhl explained that he was in the hospital for combat fatigue because he was more nervous than wounded, to which Patton responded, "You hear me, you gutless bastard? You're going back to the front." Kuhl described the second incident in a letter to his father: "General Patton slapped my face yesterday and kicked me in the pants and cussed me." Kuhl would later explain, "I was suffering from battle fatigue and just didn't know what to do."

The famous slapping incidents almost finished Patton, but it was Eisenhower's belief in his indispensability as an aggressive combat general, rather than any sense of friendship, that kept him in his post. Historians vary as to why Patton behaved this way. He had an old-fashioned view of combat fatigue, believing that it was merely cowardice, and he was dealing with the issue of thinning ranks and "malingering" of men who wanted to leave the front. He might also have been unable to control his mood swings, or perhaps he was simply exhausted. All of these factors may have played a role. In May 1943, Patton noted, "The publicity I have been getting, a good deal of which is untrue, and the rest of it ill considered, has done me more harm than good. The only way you get on in this profession is to have the reputation of doing what you are told as thoroughly as possible. So far I have been able to accomplish that, and I believe I have gotten quite a reputation from not kicking at peculiar assignments."

Initially the press was persuaded not to run the story but it inevitably leaked during a November radio broadcast back in the U.S. Eisenhower rode out the storm, and Patton received support from Roosevelt while he was passing through Sicily on his way back from the Tehran Conference. Patton repeatedly apologized, believing that he would pay for the mistakes with his career, and when Clark's army - including most of Patton's troops - attacked the Italian mainland, he was left with staffing duties. He traveled around the Mediterranean, not quite believing Eisenhower's assurances about his future, but this was part of an Allied ploy. The Allies knew that the Germans rated Patton highly, and thus his appearance in a series of locations would cause intelligence confusion as they theorized about the next Allied invasion. Thus, Patton visited Cairo, Malta and Algeria to sow seeds of doubt. Still, he was not happy to play decoy; he wanted a combat command.

Patton spent Christmas 1943 in Sicily enjoying the company of the Italian nobility, the culture and the food. He wrote to his son, who like his old man had flunked his first year at West Point, promising him that it was a sure sign that he too would make Lieutenant General. In London meanwhile, Eisenhower was working up his plans for the invasion of France. Though he wasn't sure of it at the time, Patton was fundamental to Ike's thinking. While Bradley would command the American invasion army, a second army would be landed weeks afterwards. That army would represent America's armored fist, and Patton would lead it. He would report, ironically, to Bradley, who would get command of the entire army group. Patton received the news on January 22, 1944 and flew straight to London.

Chapter 5: Destiny

"A man must know his destiny. If he does not recognize it, then he is lost." George S. Patton

Italy may have been out of the war, but the Germans still had a strong defensive hold over the Italian peninsula in 1943. Although the Axis' attempts to resist the Allies' invasion on Sicily were badly outmanned and outgunned, leading to an evacuation of the island within a month, the Germans maintained defenses across the mainland for the rest of the year. Nevertheless, with Allied forces now possessing a foothold in Italy, Churchill and Roosevelt began to plot an even greater invasion that would finally liberate Europe.

During the first half of 1944, the Americans and British began a massive buildup of men and resources in the United Kingdom, while Eisenhower and the military leaders devised an enormous and complex amphibious invasion of Western Europe. Though the Allies theoretically had several different staging grounds for an attack on different sides of the continent, the most obvious place for an invasion was just across the English Channel from Britain into France. And though the Allies used misinformation to deceive the Germans, Hitler's men built an extensive network of coastal fortifications throughout France to protect against just such an invasion.

Largely under the supervision of Rommel, the Germans constructed the "Atlantic Wall", across which reinforced concrete pillboxes for German defenders were built close to the beaches for infantry to use machine guns and anti-tank artillery. Large obstacles were placed along the beaches to effectively block tanks on the ground, while mines and underwater obstacles were planted to stop landing craft from getting close enough.

A pillbox

The Atlantic Wall necessitated an elaborate and complex invasion plan that would ensure the men who landed wouldn't be fish in a barrel. Thus, the Allies began drawing up an elaborate battle plan that would include naval and air bombardment, paratroopers, and even inflatable tanks that would be able to fire on fortifications from the coastline, all while landing over 150,000 men across 50 miles of French beaches. And that was just the beginning; the Allies intended to create a beachhead that could support an artificially constructed dock, after which nearly 1 million men would be ferried to France for the final push of the war.

Initially, Hitler was far more concerned with the Eastern front, and though the Atlantic Wall continued under Rommel's supervision, he ignored Western Europe to his detriment. Germany's apathy to the prospect of invasion is clear from the fact that German units were woefully underprepared for the upcoming Allied invasion. However, as Allied power grew through 1944, the Germans were forced to recognize that an invasion would be soon attempted. Under the command of Erwin Rommel, the German defenders of the French coast began serious efforts to shore up defences in the areas around Pas de Calais and Normandy. Pillbox and bunker construction accelerated rapidly, millions of mines were laid and anti-landing devices were planted on the beaches of the region.

Entering 1944, France, once a lightly defended area, used largely for the recuperation of German soldiers from the Eastern front, was now the focus of Allied and German attention, with feverish plans made for the region on both sides. Reinforcements flooded into Northern France while tacticians planned for the impending invasion and counter-attack. The speed with which Germany had reinforced and strengthened the region meant that the Allies were less than certain of the success of the invasion. Britain, weary of amphibious landings after the disastrous Expeditionary Force campaign of 1940 came perilously close complete obliteration, was more than anxious. Allied military fortunes had been, at best, mixed. Professor Newton points out Britain, together with its continental allies, had lost its foothold in Europe but had managed to bloody the nose of Germany in the Battle of Britain in the summer of 1940. The Allies had lost Crete, yet stopped the Afrika Corps at El Alamein. With its American allies, Britain had successfully invaded Italy before becoming entangled in the costly German defense of the country. Britain, as a small island nation, lacked the manpower and supplies needed to singlehandedly defeat the German military. In comparison, the United States, an industrial colossus, had ample men and materials. Like Britain, American fortunes in the European theater were mixed, ranging from the successful landings in North Africa to the debacle of Kasserine Pass.

A sense of fear and foreboding marred the weeks and months in the build up to the invasion. Churchill was aghast at Eisenhower's bombing plan to accompany the landings, which would have resulted in the deaths of between 80,000 and 150,000 French civilians. It would have been an outrageous number of civilian casualties, and more French citizens killed by Allied bombing than had lost their lives in four years of German occupation. Churchill felt it was better to continue the bombing of Germany rather than inflict terrible casualties upon their French allies in support of what may be a doomed invasion. Just months before the planned invasion of France, Allied forces had landed at Anzio, just south of Rome. Almost immediately, the Allied landing force was halted and almost driven back into the sea. Churchill himself had been a leading player in the invasion of Gallipoli in 1915, a debacle which almost cost him his career. The idea of landing on the heavily defended Normandy coast filled Churchill with fear. On one occasion, just weeks before the launch of *Overlord,* the Prime Minister was heard to say, "Why are we doing this? Why do we not land instead in a friendly territory, the territory of our oldest ally? Why do we not land in Portugal?"

Churchill was not alone. Many of the British military planners had felt a cross channel invasion "smacked of a seaborne Somme". Churchill had, however, persuaded the U.S. to give priority to the war in Europe, a position which caused many difficulties for Roosevelt. Pearl Harbor had outraged America and inflamed popular opinion against Japan, yet American attitudes towards Germany and Italy were far more ambivalent, due to the large proportion of American citizens with German or Italian heritage. However, at the somewhat bizarre Rattle Conference, described as a combination of intensive study and a 1920s themed house party, organised by Lord Louis Mountbatten, the assembled company settled upon Normandy as the invasion destination. Although further from Germany, it offered the Allies the chance to capture two major ports, Cherbourg and Le Harve.

Now based in Knutsford, Cheshire, Patton had 12 divisions to train, divided into four army corps. He employed his familiar techniques, at the same time getting to know the more aristocratic members of the local community and enjoying the latest subterfuge concerning his status. Patton's Third Army was a follow-up formation, rather than an amphibious force, but by now the German High Command was so obsessed with him that the Allies used this to their advantage. Patton was to make little effort to hide his movements, but he was to stress the secrecy of what he did at all times. The result was that the Germans conflated his activities - about which they easily learned - with the more elaborate ploy by which they were duped into believing that the main Allied assault would land at Pas de Calais, rather than Normandy. In early June, just days before D-Day, Patton played along by shouting in a room full of people to paratrooper leader Jim Gavin, "I'll see you in the Pas De Calais, Gavin!" Hours later, German units moved north away from Normandy toward the Pas De Calais. Thus the arrival of a second American army at Normandy would come as a surprise and the 15th German Army would remain around Calais expecting an assault from Patton which never came.

As Patton hammered his recruits into shape, he was restless, in part due to his envy of those who would spearhead the invasion. In April he made a political gaffe, claiming in an informal address that the Allies would "rule the world" after the war. Ike was not amused when the story made the press, and when the Anzio invasion in Italy began to unravel there was talk of Patton being sent to replace the commander there, but it came to nothing and did little to improve his mood.

In the early spring of 1944, the final stages of the planning took shape. Landings would occur at five separate beaches in divisional strength. Prior to this, Beach Reconnaissance Parties were covertly landed at the five sites on dark nights to ascertain the nature, defenses and gradients of the beaches. The day before the invasion, D-Day -1, Allied minesweepers would have to be visible to the German defenses in order to complete their duties successfully. Either due to bad weather, German withdrawals or poor patrolling, the minesweepers were not detected.

In the early hours of the morning of June 4, the decision of which day to launch the invasion was made upon the advice of meteorologists. In the days before the decision to launch, the weather approaching the Normandy beaches had been the worst for years, so bad that a landing would be all but impossible. Landings could be undertaken for just 10 days per month due to the tides and the need for a full moon to aid navigation. Delaying the landings in the early part of June would have meant that another attempt could not have been made for at least two weeks, and with well over 150,000 troops already on their ships waiting to go, that situation was not acceptable. Luckily for the Allies, chief meteorologist, Captain Stagg, with the aid of a meteorological station on the west coast of Ireland, was able to inform the assembled commanders that a brief clearing in the weather for a number of hours looked likely.

Ramsay, head of Naval affairs, informed Eisenhower that the Royal Navy would do whatever was asked of it, Montgomery, commander of the ground forces favored immediate action, while Leigh-Mallory, commander of the air-fleet was hesitant, worried that the bad weather would limit the support his air force could give to the landing troops. After a brief pause of no more than a few seconds, Eisenhower simply said "Let's go". With that, the largest invasion fleet ever assembled began its journey towards the Normandy coast. On June 5, 1944, an armada of some 7,000 ships began to cross the Channel towards the Normandy peninsula. Above it, 1,400 troop transports and 11,590 military aircraft of various types (along with 3,700 fighters) supported the landings. The following day, 175,000 soldiers would attempt to land on French beaches.

Even with that horde, to say the Allies faced a daunting task would be an understatement. On the morning of June 6, 1944, General Eisenhower was carrying a letter in his coat that apologized for the failure of the operation. Found years after D-Day, Eisenhower's letter read, *"Our landings in the Cherbourg-Havre area have failed to gain a satisfactory foothold and I have withdrawn the troops. My decision to attack at this time and place was based on the best information available. The troops, the air and the Navy did all that bravery and devotion to duty could do. If any blame or fault attaches to the attempt, it is mine alone."*

Eisenhower addressing paratroopers on June 5, 1944

Patton might not have played a decisive role on June 6, but he gave one of his most animated and legendary speeches the day before D-Day to his Third Army, a colorful and expletive-laden speech designed to inspire his men: "All of the real heroes are not storybook combat fighters, either. Every single man in this Army plays a vital role. Don't ever let up. Don't ever think that your job is unimportant. Every man has a job to do and he must do it. Every man is a vital link in the great chain…" At the same time, Patton reminded them that they had to maintain their secrecy, telling them, "Don't forget, you men don't know that I'm here. No mention of that fact is to be made in any letters. The world is not supposed to know what the hell happened to me. I'm not supposed to be commanding this Army. I'm not even supposed to be here in England. Let the first bastards to find out be the goddamned Germans."

By the end of D-Day, the Allies had managed to successfully land 170,000 men: over 75,000 on the British and Canadian beaches, 57,000 on the American beaches, and over 24,000 airborne troops. Thanks to Allied deception, the German army had failed to react to prevent the Allies from making the most of their landings. Just one division, the Hitlerjugend, would arrive the following day. Despite a fearsome and bloody day, the majority of the Allied forces had held their nerve, and most importantly, achieved their objectives. This ensured *Operation Overlord* was ultimately successful, and victory in Europe would be achieved within less than a year.

Churchill was not overstating the achievements of *Operation Overlord* when he described the plan "the greatest thing we have ever attempted". On D-Day, the greatest armada the world had ever seen had landed 170,000 soldiers on the heavily defended beaches of Normandy in just 24 hours. More remarkable was the fact that the operation was a success on every major level. Deception, tactical surprise and overwhelming force had contributed to the establishment of an adequate beachhead. Confusion and dissent had stopped the Germans massing for any great counterattack. The Atlantic Wall which Hitler had placed so much faith in had been breached, and the race to Paris was on.

Operation Overlord aimed to have the Allies reach the Seine River within 3 months of D-Day, and it's a testament to the men who fought and served on D-Day that the goal was reached early. To do so, the Allies overcame firm resistance from the Germans, atrocious weather that limited resupply for the Allies, and the difficult terrain of Normandy, which included endless hedgerows providing hidden cover. And the Allies reached their objective ahead of time despite the fact the objectives of D-Day were not entirely met; the Allies had not captured Caen, St-lo or Bayeux on the first day.

Nevertheless, the landings were clearly a resounding success. Casualties were significantly smaller than those expected by commanders, and the significance of D-Day to the morale of the Western world, much of it under German domination, cannot be underestimated. For France, Poland, Czechoslovakia, Belgium, Holland and more, who had suffered over four years of occupation, the great democracies were finally coming to their rescue. American, British, Canadian, Polish, Commonwealth, Greek, Belgian, Dutch and Norwegian soldiers, sailors, and airmen all participated in the Battle for Normandy, which saw the Allies on the banks of the Seine River just 80 days after D-Day.

Jean Gordon, the niece with whom he had become involved with 12 years earlier, arrived in London with the Red Cross. She would travel to France, and she and Patton met frequently. Rumors also circulated about other women. In July he finally got the call from Eisenhower and flew directly to Normandy on the 7th, where he met with the remaining army commanders and quickly built a rapport with Otto Weyland, commander of the XIX Tactical Air Command. This unit was to cooperate with the Third Army for the entire campaign, and the two men designed a textbook model of air-land tactical cooperation for future generations. Patton called him "the best damn general in the Air Corps."

Weyland

Patton's army was not yet operational, since most of the components were still in transit from the U.K., but when Bradley launched Operation Cobra, the decisive break-out battle in the Normandy campaign, he shrewdly gave Patton the VIII Corps to command. In his element again, Patton used the VIII Corps in a slashing attack down the Contentin peninsula, securing Avranches and hooking around what became the open German left flank. It was the move of the campaign, placing him in the perfect position for his style of warfare.

When the Third Army became operational on August 1, 1944, he had fresh troops, trained his way, poised on an open flank with the rest of France in front of him. At the same time, the 1st American Army under Hodges to his left, the Canadians and the British were all fighting attritionally, crumbling away at German positions directly ahead of them. But Patton had space and he intended to use it. He thinned his forces down, sending only one corps to grab Brittany and using his other three to plunge ahead behind the Germans. On the 8th he held a division back at Mortain, following an Ultra decrypt advising of a German counter attack. When the attack came he was ready with his parry and afterward gave much more credence to the top secret intelligence service provided by the British.

The attack at Mortain barely caused a pause in Patton's advance as his divisions raced northeast to Orleans and Chartres, sealing off the southern sector of a large pocket centered on

Falaise, which had the potential of trapping most of the Germans in Normandy. It all depended on the Canadians, advancing from the north, and on Bradley's support for a further advance by Third Army towards the British sector. Bradley dithered and the Canadians were delayed by a skilled Axis defense. The chance was lost.

Nonetheless Patton was proving the validity of all he had learned since World War I. He had a fast armor-based force, open tank country ahead, and a retreating and thinning enemy. He knew now was the time to capitalize, and he reached Rheims, then Chalons, the banks of the Meuse. In 30 days his army had advanced some 300 miles, and Patton believed this was a prime opportunity to win the war against Germany. The impressive concrete and steel West Wall defenses were as yet un-garrisoned. As he had been at Avranches only a month earlier, he was ideally poised to race on behind enemy lines - this time into the heart of Germany.

What stopped him was logistics. He had run ahead of the ability of the Allied High Command to supply his army, and more to the point, Eisenhower determined that Montgomery's army should have priority. Patton was furious; even though the delay was for a few days only, it was enough for the Germans to regroup. When the Third Army attacked again they ran into organized resistance, early autumn rain and mud. The ancient fortress of Metz alone took six weeks to subdue. Whether Patton was right about this missed opportunity remains one of World War II's great what ifs.

As a result, Hodge's army broke into Germany first on September 1. On the 17th, Montgomery's disastrous airborne offensive into Holland kicked off and for a further month, Patton was again starved of supplies. Eisenhower accepted the British case of the importance of seizing the huge port of Antwerp as well as the German rocket sites in Holland. Patton would not move again until early November.

The Third Army's November offensive involved 10 divisions and a lot of mud. Progress was slow but consistent, and Patton put on a brave face, cheered perhaps by the arrival of Jean Gordon and her colleagues near to his headquarters. Beatrice had heard about these activities and sent him a series of plaintive letters, to which he responded with denial.

By late November Patton was beginning to suspect the possibility of a large-scale German counterattack to the north of Third Army's sector. He had a hunch, no more, but it was strengthened by Bradley's decision to use that area to rest the battered VIII corps and to introduce green units fresh from the U.S. It was a seen as a safe backwater, which was why in Patton's view it was dangerous. He noted that much in his diary, and mindful that Third Army would likely be sucked into any such battle, he had his planners study and map the road network to the north.

Sure enough, the last major German offensive of the war began on 16th December 1944 in blizzard conditions. As Patton had suspected, the Germans attacked in the Ardennes, punching through the thinly held sector directly to the north of Third Army. They had assembled a powerful force, equipped with some of their best armor, and their ambition was to hook north and retake Antwerp. On the 17th Patton ordered Millikin's III Corps to prepare to switch axis and move 50 miles north. He met Bradley on the 18th, who endorsed the plan, and they took it to Eisenhower and the British on the 19th at a meeting in Verdun.

By now the situation for the small American garrison at Bastogne was desperate, but it still sat on a vital road nexus which was imperative for a continued Axis advance. Bastogne was at the center of a large incursion into Allied territory which gave the battle its name - the Bulge. While Patton was keen to severe the bulge at its base, he was ordered to aim instead for the trapped troops at Bastogne. When Ike asked him how long it would take to relieve the 101st Airborne at Bastogne, Patton told him, "As soon as you're through with me." Patton had in fact already devised operations for his Army that he believed could have three of his divisions attacking the Germans in two days (December 21), which astounded the unbelieving Eisenhower. Eisenhower told him, "Don't be fatuous, George. If you try to go that early you won't have all three divisions ready and you'll go piecemeal." Eisenhower insisted that he play it safe by delaying any counterattack until the 22nd, after which Patton walked over to a telephone and contacted his command center with the order, "Play ball."

In an astonishing feat of planning, logistics and discipline, Patton's army redirected 133,000 vehicles, 62,000 tons of supplies, and the vehicles and men covered a combined distance of 1.5 million miles. To his superiors' amazement, Patton was poised to reach Bastogne and attack the bulge on December 22, and the day before he told Bradley, "Brad, this time the Kraut's stuck his head in the meatgrinder, and I've got hold of the handle." The following day, Millikin's corps punctured the German positions despite stubborn resistance and truly appalling weather, and Patton's Army had reached Bastogne within four days. With a second corps now swinging up towards the southern base of the bulge and British troops securing its northern shoulder, the offensive was effectively ended. As ever, Patton had led from the front, urging his men onwards, leaping out of his jeep in the snow to help shove a stranded lorry, and deliberately exposing himself to fire. He was simply unstoppable, and for once even he used superlatives to describe the action at Bastogne, calling it "the most brilliant operation we have thus far performed, and it is in my opinion the outstanding achievement of the war. This is my biggest battle."

For some time afterwards, the momentum of Third Army's advance slowed as it again changed axis and regrouped. Patton took a rare break by spending three days in Paris, where he was treated like royalty. The war against Germany had an inevitable momentum now, as the Russians approached from the east and the Allies' western armies crept forward in careful alignment. Ike visited Patton late in March 1945, and they stayed up late together drinking. Despite the differences of opinion, they remained old friends and could enjoy each other's company.

The Third Army crossed the Rhine into Germany on March 22, and Patton ceremonially urinated into the river for the cameras. Though he remained a showman, he was increasingly despondent over fear of a Europe dominated by Stalin's Soviet Union, and he believed that he should be allowed to race for Berlin, a wish that went ignored by his more political superiors. In late March he launched a battalion sized battle group towards a Prisoner of War camp at Hammelburg in a vain attempt to rescue his brother in law, a romantic but foolhardy expedition that got his men all but annihilated and opened Patton up to criticism. Nevertheless, his troops were the first to liberate a Nazi death camp, first at Ohrdruf Nord and again at Buchenwald, and the sights sickened and depressed Patton further. He encouraged as many of his troops as possible to visit the camps in order to understand what the Nazi regime had done. Patton himself illegally smuggled out an original copy of Germany's 1935 Nuremberg laws, the anti-Semitic codes put into place by the Nazi regime, and eventually donated it to the library in his hometown of San Marino.

Towards the very end of the European campaign, his army moved south, through Bavaria and he was ordered to send a corps ahead to capture Pilsen in what was Czechoslovakia. His suggestion that he continue to Prague, already threatened by the Russians, was turned down for political reasons. As the surrender finally came on May 9, he felt disillusioned rather than elated. He had applied for a role in the Pacific but been turned down by Douglas MacArthur, for whom a second big ego alongside his own would have been unthinkable. And on top of it all, Jean Gordon had fallen for another man, which is likely to have hurt him more than he would have admitted.

Chapter 6: Patton's Final Months

"It is foolish and wrong to mourn the men who died. Rather we should thank God that such men lived." – George S. Patton

Patton flew to Paris in late May, then London and Cheshire, where he met up with old friends. After that he traveled home to the U.S., touring a number of states and making surprisingly emotional speeches wherever he went. He broke down in tears at an amputees' hospital, and again in Denver. He was desperately tired, and his behavior was becoming increasingly erratic.

Before returning to Germany he somberly told his son and daughters that he would die shortly, and that they would never see him again. The words of a sick man, or perhaps something more? Patton had always had a belief in premonitions, reincarnation, and destiny.

The respite had done him some good, but he found it hard to muster a great deal of enthusiasm for the minutiae and politics of the military occupation of Bavaria. In September he rashly compared the Nazis with the Democratic and Republican parties during a press conference, then compounded the error a few days later when he was supposed to be making amends. He made a series of racist remarks about the Russians and the Jews. As Martin Blumenson astutely put it, "Fatigue, not only physical but mental, robbed him of equilibrium." He felt he had no future.

In October Patton was moved from the Third Army and given a job heading a unit which was working on the history and lessons from the war. Though saddened to be leaving his old team, he welcomed the change, which would be less contentious, less stressful and would jive with his passion for academic analysis and military history. The dyslexic boy had come a long way.

Life started to get better for Patton, who now seemingly had the time and ability to enjoy all that the area offered. He traveled around Europe and was feted wherever he went. He went shooting, he ate well, and he was once again good company. Christmas approached and he would travel home to be with the family in Massachusetts.

On December 9, 1945, the day before he was to fly back to the U.S., Patton was a passenger in a car being driven out with a friend for a pheasant shoot when his staff car was involved in a low speed collision, rear-ending a truck in front of it at about 30 miles per hour. Everyone in the vehicle emerged unscathed except for Patton, who had not seen the accident coming and had not braced for impact. His forehead had struck a piece of metal between the front and back seats, and he had gashed his head badly. But more importantly he could not move; he had broken his neck.

Hospitalized in Heidelburg and placed in traction, Patton was told that he would never walk again or ride a horse, but Patton seemed to realize the more serious nature of his situation, noting, "This is a hell of a way to die." Beatrice flew over, and he maintained a stoic cheerfulness throughout his final battle. But 12 days later, on December 21, 1945, as his wife had left the bedside to eat, he passed away. He had just turned 60.

Chapter 7: Patton's Legacy

"He was tough. War is tough. Leaders have to be tough. He drove his army hard, yes, and he made many enemies among colleagues and subordinates, but he also produced results. He was indeed arrogant, but sometimes a good leader has to be larger than life. … But the fact is: again typically, Patton's admirers are no more specific in their praise than are his disparagers in their criticism." - Alan Axelrod, *Patton On Leadership* (1999)

Patton's two daughters both led happy married lives, and his son reached the rank of Major General in the United States Army. His wife Beatrice continued to be active until she died suddenly while out riding in 1953. Jean Gordon took her own life just two weeks after learning of the death of her uncle.

Patton's grave is in the U.S. military cemetery in Luxembourg, a reflection of the fact that war dead are not reinterred and relocated back home. His body lies beneath a simple headstone alongside many of the men from his Third Army, and thousands visit the site every year to celebrate and remember one of America's greatest generals.

Patton had no shortage of flaws. He was an egotist, illiberal, racist at times and possessed a percussive temper. But Patton was nonetheless a driven man with astonishing martial skills. The primary architect of America's armored corps, he was an unparalleled battlefield exponent of mid-20th century mobile warfare. Lidell-Hart and Fuller wrote better theory, Guderian and Rommel were talented, but none came close to Patton's actual achievement on the battlefield. What made it possible was study and hard work. Obviously, this included his intimate knowledge of military history and the deep thought he gave to the development of the tank, but Patton himself understood success was mostly about the men themselves. Patton was the consummate leader - colorful, motivating, courageous, and loved by his men – and he was the first to admit this was the source of the army's strength, noting, "Wars may be fought with weapons, but they are won by men. It is the spirit of the men who follow and of the man who leads that gains the victory."

Patton has also been misjudged, far too often. For all of his challenging opinions, he never disobeyed an order and always did as instructed to the best of his ability. In fact, it was he who insisted, "Never tell people how to do things. Tell them what to do, and they will surprise you with their ingenuity." Far from being a loose cannon, Patton proved to be politically shrewd, as exemplified during the delicate negotiations with the French in Morocco and in his modern use of "networking" to promote his position throughout his career. Patton was well aware of his reputation, especially for being profane, but he believed it to be essential and at one point noted to his nephew, "When I want my men to remember something important, to really make it stick, I give it to them double dirty. It may not sound nice to some bunch of little old ladies at an afternoon tea party, but it helps my soldiers to remember. You can't run an army without profanity; and it has to be eloquent profanity. An army without profanity couldn't fight its way out of a piss-soaked paper bag...As for the types of comments I make, sometimes I just, By God, get carried away with my own eloquence."

He did have his inner doubts and prejudices, and he suffered from wild mood swings which impaired his performance. Towards the very end of his life in particular, his outbursts were surely evidence - ironically - of combat fatigue. But as an historic figure, despite being contentious and disliked by some; he was one of the best combat commanders the world has ever known.

Speech to the Third Army on June 5, 1944

"Be seated.

Men, this stuff that some sources sling around about America wanting out of this war, not wanting to fight, is a crock of bulls***. Americans love to fight, traditionally. All real Americans love the sting and clash of battle.

You are here today for three reasons. First, because you are here to defend your homes and your loved ones. Second, you are here for your own self respect, because you would not want to be anywhere else. Third, you are here because you are real men and all real men like to fight.

When you, here, everyone of you, were kids, you all admired the champion marble player, the fastest runner, the toughest boxer, the big league ball players, and the All-American football players. Americans love a winner. Americans will not tolerate a loser.

Americans despise cowards.

Americans play to win all of the time. I wouldn't give a hoot in hell for a man who lost and laughed. That's why Americans have never lost nor will ever lose a war; for the very idea of losing is hateful to an American.

You are not all going to die. Only two percent of you right here today would die in a major battle. Death must not be feared. Death, in time, comes to all men. Yes, every man is scared in his first battle. If he says he's not, he's a liar. Some men are cowards but they fight the same as the brave men or they get the hell slammed out of them watching men fight who are just as scared as they are.

The real hero is the man who fights even though he is scared. Some men get over their fright in a minute under fire. For some, it takes an hour. For some, it takes days. But a real man will never let his fear of death overpower his honor, his sense of duty to his country, and his innate manhood. Battle is the most magnificent competition in which a human being can indulge. It brings out all that is best and it removes all that is base. Americans pride themselves on being He Men and they are He Men.

Remember that the enemy is just as frightened as you are, and probably more so. They are not supermen.

All through your Army careers, you men have bitched about what you call "chicken-s*** drilling." That, like everything else in this Army, has a definite purpose. That purpose is alertness. Alertness must be bred into every soldier. I don't give a f*** for a man who's not always on his toes. You men are veterans or you wouldn't be here. You are ready for what's to come. A man must be alert at all times if he expects to stay alive. If you're not alert, sometime, a German son-of-an-ass***-b**** is going to sneak up behind you and beat you to death with a sock full of s***!

There are four-hundred neatly marked graves somewhere in Sicily, all because one man went to sleep on the job. But they are German graves, because we caught the bastard asleep before they did.

An Army is a team. It lives, sleeps, eats, and fights as a team.

This individual heroic stuff is pure horse s***. The bilious bastards who write that kind of stuff for the Saturday Evening Post don't know any more about real fighting under fire than they know about f***ing!" "We have the finest food, the finest equipment, the best spirit, and the best men in the world. Why, by God, I actually pity those poor sons-of-bitches we're going up against. By God, I do.

My men don't surrender, and I don't want to hear of any soldier under my command being captured unless he has been hit. Even if you are hit, you can still fight back That's not just bulls*** either. The kind of man that I want in my command is just like the lieutenant in Libya, who, with a Luger against his chest, jerked off his helmet, swept the gun aside with one hand, and busted the hell out of the Kraut with his helmet. Then he jumped on the gun and went out and killed another German before they knew what the hell was coming off. And, all of that time, this man had a bullet through a lung. There was a real man!

All of the real heroes are not storybook combat fighters, either. Every single man in this Army plays a vital role. Don't ever let up. Don't ever think that your job is unimportant. Every man has a job to do and he must do it. Every man is a vital link in the great chain.

What if every truck driver suddenly decided that he didn't like the whine of those shells overhead, turned yellow, and jumped headlong into a ditch? The cowardly bastard could say, "Hell, they won't miss me, just one man in thousands." But, what if every man thought that way? Where in the hell would we be now? What would our country, our loved ones, our homes, even the world, be like?

No, Goddamnit, Americans don't think like that. Every man does his job. Every man serves the whole. Every department, every unit, is important in the vast scheme of this war.

The ordnance men are needed to supply the guns and machinery of war to keep us rolling. The Quartermaster is needed to bring up food and clothes because where we are going there isn't a hell of a lot to steal. Every last man on K.P. has a job to do, even the one who heats our water to keep us from getting the "G.I. S***s."

Each man must not think only of himself, but also of his buddy fighting beside him. We don't want yellow cowards in this Army. They should be killed off like rats. If not, they will go home after this war and breed more cowards. The brave men will breed more brave men. Kill off the Goddamned cowards and we will have a nation of brave men.

One of the bravest men that I ever saw was a fellow on top of a telegraph pole in the midst of a furious fire fight in Tunisia. I stopped and asked what the hell he was doing up there at a time like that. He answered, "Fixing the wire, Sir." I asked, "Isn't that a little unhealthy right about now?" He answered, "Yes Sir, but the Goddamned wire has to be fixed." I asked, "Don't those planes strafing the road bother you?" And he answered, "No, Sir, but you sure as hell do!" Now, there was a real man. A real soldier. There was a man who devoted all he had to his duty, no matter how seemingly insignificant his duty might appear at the time, no matter how great the odds.

And you should have seen those trucks on the rode to Tunisia. Those drivers were magnificent. All day and all night they rolled over those son-of-a-b****ing roads, never stopping, never faltering from their course, with shells bursting all around them all of the time. We got through on good old American guts. Many of those men drove for over forty consecutive hours. These men weren't combat men, but they were soldiers with a job to do. They did it, and in one hell of a way they did it. They were part of a team. Without team effort, without them, the fight would have been lost. All of the links in the chain pulled together and the chain became unbreakable.

Don't forget, you men don't know that I'm here. No mention of that fact is to be made in any letters. The world is not supposed to know what the hell happened to me. I'm not supposed to be commanding this Army. I'm not even supposed to be here in England. Let the first bastards to find out be the Goddamned Germans. Some day I want to see them raise up on their piss-soaked hind legs and howl, "Jesus Christ, it's the Goddamned Third Army again and that son-of-a-f***ing-b**** Patton."

We want to get the hell over there. The quicker we clean up this Goddamned mess, the quicker we can take a little jaunt against the purple-pissing Japs and clean out their nest, too — before the Goddamned Marines get all of the credit.

Sure, we want to go home. We want this war over with. The quickest way to get it over with is to go get the bastards who started it. The quicker they are whipped, the quicker we can go home. The shortest way home is through Berlin and Tokyo. And when we get to Berlin I am personally going to shoot that paper hanging son-of-a-b**** Hitler. Just like I'd shoot a snake!

When a man is lying in a shell hole, if he just stays there all day, a German will get to him eventually. The hell with that idea. The hell with taking it. My men don't dig foxholes. I don't want them to. Foxholes only slow up an offensive. Keep moving. And don't give the enemy time to dig one either. We'll win this war, but we'll win it only by fighting and by showing the Germans that we've got more guts than they have; or ever will have.

We're not going to just shoot the sons-of-b****es, we're going to rip out their living

Goddamned guts and use them to grease the treads of our tanks. We're going to murder those lousy Hun c*** suckers by the bushel-f***ing-basket. War is a bloody, killing business. You've got to spill their blood, or they will spill yours. Rip them up the belly. Shoot them in the guts. When shells are hitting all around you and you wipe the dirt off your face and realize that instead of dirt it's the blood and guts of what once was your best friend beside you, you'll know what to do!

I don't want to get any messages saying, "I am holding my position." We are not holding a Goddamned thing. Let the Germans do that. We are advancing constantly and we are not interested in holding onto anything, except the enemy's b***s. We are going to twist his b***s and kick the living s*** out of him all of the time.

Our basic plan of operation is to advance and to keep on advancing regardless of whether we have to go over, under, or through the enemy. We are going to go through him like crap through a goose; like s*** through a tin horn!

From time to time there will be some complaints that we are pushing our people too hard. I don't give a good Goddamn about such complaints. I believe in the old and sound rule that an ounce of sweat will save a gallon of blood. The harder we push, the more Germans we will kill. The more Germans we kill, the fewer of our men will be killed. Pushing means fewer casualties. I want you all to remember that.

There is one great thing that you men will all be able to say after this war is over and you are home once again. You may be thankful that twenty years from now when you are sitting by the fireplace with your grandson on your knee and he asks you what you did in the great World War II, you won't have to cough, shift him to the other knee and say, "Well, your Granddaddy shoveled s*** in Louisiana." No, Sir. You can look him straight in the eye and say, "Son, your Granddaddy rode with the Great Third Army and a Son-of-a-Goddamned-B**** named Georgie Patton!"

That is all."

Patton's 1918 Poem "Through a Glass, Darkly"

Through the travail of the ages,
Midst the pomp and toil of war,
I have fought and strove and perished
Countless times upon this star.

In the form of many people
In all panoplies of time
Have I seen the luring vision
Of the Victory Maid, sublime.

I have battled for fresh mammoth,
I have warred for pastures new,
I have listed to the whispers
When the race trek instinct grew.

I have known the call to battle
In each changeless changing shape
From the high souled voice of conscience
To the beastly lust for rape.

I have sinned and I have suffered,
Played the hero and the knave;
Fought for belly, shame, or country,
And for each have found a grave.

I cannot name my battles
For the visions are not clear,
Yet, I see the twisted faces
And I feel the rending spear.

Perhaps I stabbed our Savior
In His sacred helpless side.
Yet, I've called His name in blessing
When after times I died.

In the dimness of the shadows
Where we hairy heathens warred,
I can taste in thought the lifeblood;
We used teeth before the sword.

While in later clearer vision
I can sense the coppery sweat,
Feel the pikes grow wet and slippery
When our Phalanx, Cyrus met.

Hear the rattle of the harness
Where the Persian darts bounced clear,
See their chariots wheel in panic
From the Hoplite's leveled spear.

See the goal grow monthly longer,
Reaching for the walls of Tyre.
Hear the crash of tons of granite,
Smell the quenchless eastern fire.

Still more clearly as a Roman,
Can I see the Legion close,
As our third rank moved in forward
And the short sword found our foes.

Once again I feel the anguish
Of that blistering treeless plain
When the Parthian showered death bolts,
And our discipline was in vain.

I remember all the suffering
Of those arrows in my neck.
Yet, I stabbed a grinning savage
As I died upon my back.

Once again I smell the heat sparks
When my Flemish plate gave way
And the lance ripped through my entrails
As on Crecy's field I lay.

In the windless, blinding stillness
Of the glittering tropic sea
I can see the bubbles rising
Where we set the captives free.

Midst the spume of half a tempest
I have heard the bulwarks go
When the crashing, point blank round shot
Sent destruction to our foe.

I have fought with gun and cutlass
On the red and slippery deck
With all Hell aflame within me
And a rope around my neck.

And still later as a General
Have I galloped with Murat
When we laughed at death and numbers
Trusting in the Emperor's Star.

Till at last our star faded,
And we shouted to our doom
Where the sunken road of Ohein
Closed us in it's quivering gloom.

So but now with Tanks a'clatter
Have I waddled on the foe
Belching death at twenty paces,
By the star shell's ghastly glow.

So as through a glass, and darkly
The age long strife I see
Where I fought in many guises,
Many names, but always me.

And I see not in my blindness
What the objects were I wrought,
But as God rules o'er our bickerings
It was through His will I fought.

So forever in the future,
Shall I battle as of yore,
Dying to be born a fighter,
But to die again, once more.

Bibliography

Axelrod, A. and Clark, W. (2006) Patton: A Biography

Blumenson, M. (1986) Patton the Man Behind the Legend, 1885-1945

Bradley, O. (1951) A Soldier's Story

Churchill, W. (1951) The Second World War: Closing the Ring

D'Este, C. (1996) A Genius for War: A life of General George S. Patton

Eisenhower, D. (1948) Crusade in Europe

Farago, L. (1964 - e-book edition) Patton: Ordeal and Triumph

Farago, L. (1981) The Last Days of Patton

Hogg, I. (1988) Patton

Kadari, Y. (2011) Patton

Mellor, W. (1946) Patton, Fighting Man

Semmes, H. (1955) Portrait of Patton

Stallings, L. (1963) Doughboys

Stone, N. (2008) World War One: A Short History

Made in the USA
Lexington, KY
23 April 2019